THE ECONOMY AND SOCIETY OF POMPEII

DUTCH MONOGRAPHS ON ANCIENT HISTORY
AND ARCHAEOLOGY

EDITORS

P.W. DE NEEVE – H.W. PLEKET

VOLUME IV

WILLEM JONGMAN

THE ECONOMY AND SOCIETY OF POMPEII

THE ECONOMY AND SOCIETY OF POMPEII

BY

WILLEM JONGMAN

J.C. GIEBEN, PUBLISHER
AMSTERDAM 1988

 / ISBN 90 70265 24 9 / Printed in The Netherlands

TO THE MEMORY OF MOSES FINLEY

CONTENTS

LIST OF TABLES

LIST OF FIGURES

LIST OF PLATES

PREFACE

My intellectual and personal debts are many; I cannot hope to repay them. Scholarship is a social activity rather than the lonely existence of popular imagination. Much of this book was written in admiration for and disagreement with the work of friends and colleagues. Some of this can be traced in my references, but much cannot.

Sir Moses Finley has forcefully insisted on the importance of asking the right questions. Without his questions (and questioning) this book could not have existed. I cherish the memories of our discussions when, within minutes after the first cup of coffee, he would have moved just enough pieces of my puzzles to evoke patterns which had not been there before. The sadness about his death, however, is not just for the loss of a great teacher and scholar. The generous hospitality he and Mary extended to scholars from all over the world was part of the special experience of being an ancient historian in Cambridge. Their death was the death of two friends.

Professor H.W. Pleket was the *promotor* of this book as a doctoral dissertation at Leiden University. For many years he has with admirable alteration of patience and insistence, supervised and inspired my research. He was the first to teach me that some questions matter more than others, and he taught me many of the means to answer them. He also took his role as *advocatus diaboli* very seriously. I hope our wrestling matches will not be over for a long time, even if they sometimes hurt.

Professor Keith Hopkins has at various times 'sorted me out' in his characteristic fashion. I think the book is much the better for it. As external examiner he went well beyond the normal call of duty. The other members of the examining jury, professors W.P. Blockmans, W. Eizenga, P.H. Schrijvers and H.S. Versnel, read the manuscript with great care, and I am grateful for their comments. Part or all of the book was read in earlier drafts by professor Michael Crawford, professor J.A. Crook, Peter Garnsey and Roger Ling. Each of them saved me from some errors, and each of them disagrees with some that remains.

Over the years I have learned a lot from friends and colleagues. I cannot hope to thank them all. An exception should be made for my friends Paul Halstead and Philip Lomas. Our joint years as research fellows at King's College Cambridge taught me much, and made us good friends.

The most important financial support for my research has come from my successive employers, King's College Cambridge and the Erasmus University in Rotterdam. The Netherlands Organization for the Advancement of Research (N.W.O.) acted as intermediary for a grant from the Italian research council (C.N.R.) to do my field work in Italy.

I should like to express my appreciation to the Italian archaeological authorities for the permission to work in Pompeii and publish my photographs. Their courteous hospitality has been invaluable. Without the assiduous assistance of the staff of many libraries my work would have been much harder. I am grateful to Frau Liselotte Eschebach for her generous permission to reproduce some maps from her late husband's book on Pompeii, and to Mrs. Sylvia Willink and the Boymans van Beuningen Museum in Rotterdam to reproduce Carel Willink's painting 'Pompeii' on the cover of my book.

At various points in my research I have received important practical help. I wish to acknowledge my debts to: Todd Whitelaw, who wrote the computer program to rank Iucundus' witnesses; Glynis Jones who helped me with computing; Tineke Huijssen who did much of the original typing and later taught me the small print of word processing; Eric de Jager who drew the figures; and my brother Pieter Jan Jongman who jointly wrote Appendix IV with me, and helped turn it into respectable mathematics. Professor J.A. Crook kindly made some improvements to my English style.

CHAPTER ONE

QUESTIONS AND RULES

The ambiguity of development

Why did the Roman Empire fall? Ever since the Renaissance western man has wondered and been amazed. For a man like Petrarca Roman society had in many respects been superior to his own - so how could it have disappeared? The wonder has remained for many centuries, only to fade in our modern industrialized world. *We* can no longer be overawed by the display of Roman engineering skills in public works, nor do we find Roman deployment of state power at all remarkable. Our own recently acquired skills no doubt surpass anything the world has ever seen, but this should be no reason to ignore the many differences between societies unlike our own, or to implant a simple unilinear and teleological scheme on human history before industrial society.

Petrarca's admiration (and that of his successors) may be a good starting point, but for us such admiration has many seductive pitfalls. The admirer wants to be close to the object of his admiration, and relishes the thought of unmediated access. How can this aim be reached more easily than by a transformation of the object into a mirror image of the admirer and his world?

The temptation is obvious to anyone who has ever observed tourists' reactions to a classical site. The immediate contact with material remains of Roman society imparts the illusion that their meaning is unproblematic. The visitor to Pompeii is invariably impressed by the wealth and the splendour of the private houses he is shown. And quite rightly so. But to conclude that the Roman standard of living was high would be fallacious. The splendour goes with vast social inequality.[1]

The temptation to equate the Roman past as much as possible with our own world (or with what we would like our world to be) has been strong. It has produced much apologetic writing, but little history. Yet it poses the question how it is possible for us to understand a society so different from our own. Empathy is no good guide; trying to think we are Romans only serves to show the impossibility of it. But how can we understand Roman society with rules of thought developed in a world so different from that distant past?

Empathy and intuition may not be good guides, but the example about Pompeian housing standards also shows the advantage (or at least the difference) of the modern perspective. This critical perspective is something we would not want to be without, even though our concern with inequality would probably have escaped all Romans, for whom wealth and inequality were quite unproblematic, and not normally worth commenting upon. The critical distance is a device of considerable power; its success depends on the scholar's critical evaluation of his own society, and on his readers' willingness to follow him in this double discourse. Each generation rewrites its history, a process that - usually - owes little to the availability of new data or the 'definitive solution' of tricky problems of scholarship: 'no new weapon is lethal; and none of the battles is finally decisive.'[2]

And yet historiography cannot and should not be the endless succession of each generation's own story telling. We tell our own story, but we also try to demonstrate that other stories are untrue, because they are logically inconsistent, or because the ancient evidence does not warrant them. It may be that

[1]Below, p. 187 ff, 255 ff.

[2]Hopkins (1983c) ix.

'documents themselves ask no questions', but 'they sometimes provide answers.'[1]

Ancient historians have a proud tradition to uphold, a tradition of meticulous care with their few remaining sources. However, they have also, perhaps because of their dedication to what is left, been less than sensitive to its defects, and ignored the large crevice between their propositions and their data. Often they have fallen into the trap of what may be termed the 'positivist fallacy', which assumes that the remaining evidence is a true and unproblematic reflection of past reality, and that we need not worry about the evidence that did not survive, and even less about the evidence that never was.[2] Aggravating the problems even more is that for much of the literary evidence we should ask the skeptical question: 'Evidence for what?' Many literary authors cannot possibly have really known whether what they wrote was factually correct, and many clearly did not care (or insufficiently to restrain them from publication). An elementary distinction such as that between primary and secondary sources was never made. So what can we do with these 'sources'? No one put the problem better than Finley when he wrote: 'I cannot imagine that, even as a slip, a Renaissance historian would compile a list of primary sources made up of John Addington Symonds, Burckhard and Chabod. I suspect that [it] reflects, no doubt unconsciously, the widespread sentiment that anything written in Greek or Latin is somehow privileged, exempt from normal canons of evaluation.'[3] And he adds: ...'It is in the end not very surprising that university students of history, with some knowledge of the sources for, say, Tudor England or Louis XIV's France, find ancient history a "funny kind of history".'[4] Skepticism about

[1]Finley (1985b) 46.

[2]Clarke (1973) 16 puts it succinctly by distinguishing these steps in archaeological interpretation: '(1) The range of hominid activity patterns and social and environmental processes which once existed, over a specified time and area. (2) The sample and traces of these (1) that were deposited at the time. (3) The sample of that sample (2) which survived to be recorded. (4) The sample of that sample (3) which was recovered by excavation or collection.'

[3]Finley (1985b) 10.

[4]Finley (1985b) 12.

the sources leads him to write elsewhere: 'In the end, I believe that the history of *individual* ancient towns is a *cul-de-sac*, given the limits of the available (and potential) documentation, the unalterable condition of the study of ancient history.'[1]

One of the aims of this book is to illustrate that even for a very well documented town such as Pompeii the evidence does not speak for itself, but on the other hand that progress is possible through rigorous techniques of evaluation of the data. Many of those techniques have a statistical aspect and are, therefore, not always easily intelligible to ancient historians; but they are less of a departure from 'traditional' modes of argument than their unfamiliarity suggests, for many of our arguments contain an element of implicit quantification, and are - sometimes fuzzy - cases of what can also be expressed in mathematical relations. So it is only fair not to duck the responsibility to make use of techniques, the advantage of which lies in their power to control our flights of fancy. I am aware that statistical techniques carry the stigma that they may actually generate flights of fancy, and it is only fair to admit that the danger exists. It does so because the ancient world did not create the sort of social statistics that we take for granted in our own world.[2] Surviving figures are often no more than rhetorical devices and are rarely part of neat series.[3] Pretending that the situation is different can only lead to disastrous pseudo-history.

If, therefore, analyses of secular trends in Roman price history, or of fluctuations in international trade, are beyond what we can legitimately do, does this mean that there is no room in ancient history for any statistical analysis? I do not think so. Using surviving figures is not the only possible statistical approach: at least two other serious possibilities

[1]Finley (1977) 325 = Finley (1981) 20.

[2]Finley (1985b) 27-46 is the neatest statement of this view.

[3]Although Frier (1982) is a good example of what intelligent and controlled surgery may do. Cf. below, p.267 f; 320 ff.

exist. The first of these I shall call the 'artefact approach'[1], the second I shall call the 'simulation approach'.

That the ancients did not leave us any trade statistics is no reason for us to abstain from, for example, elaborate analysis of chronological and geographic distribution patterns of amphora finds. What we do here is to count surviving units of data, and some of their properties. In other words: we are constructing statistics, rather than just using the bad surviving ones. We may do this well or badly. The quality does not, however, depend on the statistical mentality of the ancients, but on our own. *We* must worry about the quality of *our* model and how it can be falsified or validated by surviving data. And *we* must usually worry about the extent to which surviving data may be treated as a random sample to test *our* hypotheses.[2] To worry comfortably, it is better to be a decent statistician than to be blissfully unaware.

My second type consists of exercises in the simulation of the ancient past.[3] Often enough, conclusions need hardly be affected by the inaccuracy of data, but, to establish that, simulation may be required: how sensitive are our conclusions to the imperfections of the data? If the sensitivity is only small it may be legitimate to supplant defective or non-existent ancient data with our estimates, and investigate the consequences of alternative assumptions. And where ancient data are available, simulation techniques are of great help in evaluating their quality.[4] The logic of simulation is that, even when

[1]I use this term because it draws attention to the similarity with the work of archaeologists, who are becoming more and more subtle statisticians these days. It should however not be taken to imply that the approach is limited to archaeological data, if only because what archaeologists are usually counting is not so much artefacts themselves, but rather their properties. Phrases in a literary text or in inscriptions may equally be the object of this approach. To illustrate more clearly what I mean, Saller and Shaw (1984) provide a model example of the approach.

[2]Even if we know that it is not a random sample, all need not be lost. If we know the direction of the bias, we may still be able to use the data as a test. For examples of this argument: below, p. 120 ff; 238 ff.

[3]Barendregt (1984).

[4]Quality of data is not only a matter of source criticism, but is relative to the questions asked. So we may ask: how different would the data have to be for the opposite conclusion to be true?

we have little documented knowledge, the range of possibilities is still limited, and the more it can be limited, the more successful simulation may become. Man as part of an ecosystem provides a narrow limitation. We do not need ancient documents to have a fairly accurate idea of minimum calorie requirements for survival.[1] And even if mortality may vary a lot, the age-specific incidence of death follows a very narrow path.[2] Sometimes an accumulation of - plausible - assumptions multiplies the uncertainties to the extent that no conclusion is permitted[3], but at other times these uncertainties may cancel each other out and permit pertinent conclusions. Simulation may be a powerful aid when it is not prudent to remain silent in the face of a lack of directly documented information.

Data, however, even if very good, do not speak for themselves. They may give answers, but it is the historian who must ask the right questions. And he must develop theories and rules before the data can provide answers to those questions. Wrong answers to interesting questions are of no value, but right answers to unimportant questions are boring. My first task, therefore, is to sketch briefly the questions that I shall ask and try to answer, and to explain how and why they are interesting.

That Petrarca - and many after him - were impressed by Roman civilization was only too justified. The Roman empire was a state which existed for more than a thousand years. As a superpower (without much competition) it lasted for some six hundred years, if we ignore Byzantium, where the empire eked out its existence for yet another thousand years. European history cannot give us any later examples of such long-lived hegemony.

[1] I have used this approach quite frequently, as the reader will discover. Whether it is revealing obviously depends on social structure. For modern capitalist society it would tell us little more than that people were very prosperous. The concern of classical political economists with subsistence suggests that it is more relevant to a preindustrial world.

[2] Hopkins (1966) is classic.

[3] This also applies to imperfect real data.

It was a large and populous empire; the limits of the empire were the limits of civilization, the eastern borders excepted, where it sometimes met its match.[1] At its peak, the total population measured perhaps slightly more than the 54 million estimated by scholars for the time of Augustus.[2] That is large by pre-industrial standards - it is about the same as the populations around 1700 of France, Germany, the British Isles and Italy together.[3] Some - mediterranean - parts of the Empire never had a much higher population density in their entire preindustrial history.[4] Moreover, an impressively large proportion of the population were urban dwellers. Roman society was an urban society; a case-study of the best preserved Roman town may not be a bad research strategy.[5] The size of the city of ancient Rome is unmatched by any later city of pre-industrial Europe, and even apart from Rome, levels of urbanization were remarkably high, especially - though not exclusively - in Italy.[6] Roman urbanism exceeds nearly everything in later European pre-industrial history. And that is important, because urbanization is often used as an index of development.

Rome was not only a very urban society, it was also a, mostly, effectively ruled central state. When the new nation states of the later middle ages tried to establish their internal authority, they took Roman law as the perfect tool to do so. And when in the seventeenth century they tried to modernize and professionalize their armies, they studied the classical texts on the art of warfare.[7] Roman armies had 'fought well most of the time. In a straight fight they could, and they usually did, defeat superior numbers of Germans, because they were better

[1]Banditry was often not only socially but also geographically marginal to Roman civilization. For such 'bandits': Shaw (1984).

[2]Hopkins (1980) 118 ff, based on Beloch (1886) 507.

[3]Cipolla (1981) 4, table 1-1. Kriedte (1980) 12.

[4]Below, p. 71 ff;.

[5]Cf. below, p. 55 ff.

[6]For substantiation of these claims: below, p. 66 ff.

[7]Howard (1976) 56 f.

trained, better equipped, better led.'[1] But Roman armies had not been cheap: soldiers received a regular income of six to eight times subsistence, and those who survived could count on considerable retirement bounties. Their standard of living and status was well above that of the mass of the population, unlike that of their medieval and early modern counterparts.[2] The Roman army may ultimately not have been large enough, but it was considerable: at least 300,000 men in the early empire, and, perhaps, more in the later empire to face the mounting pressures.[3] Total military expenditure was considerable, and may be equated (in the early Empire) to minimum yearly subsistence for 3.5-4 million people.[4] The army, however, had not been the only major item of public expenditure. Court and bureaucracy must have cost much as well, even if precise figures largely escape us.[5] Hopkins' estimates for taxation and state expenditure suggest that these were higher than in early modern Europe

[1]Finley (1968b) 150.

[2]Hopkins (1980) 124 f. for a survey of the cost of the Roman army. Roman soldiers had the advantage over later mercenaries that they were regularly paid. Compare that to the following complaint by the Spanish captain-general in Flanders Requesens to his king in 1574 (quoted in Parker (1972) 158): 'Everything is so expensive that even if wages could be paid in full every month, [the soldiers] could not live on three times as much because even the most efficient and most frugal soldier needs just for food 10 pattards a day and his wages are 4; and the light cavalry trooper, who causes the greatest resentment here, needs almost 30 pattards daily to feed himself, his horse and his lackey, and his wage amounts to no more than 9.' And the stricture that even this only applied if wages were paid at all was only too realistic. At best they received - in the 1590's - 1.5 lb. of bread per day plus 15 florins per year (worth at best about as much as the bread) - Parker (1972) 163. See also: Corvisier (1976) 78-81.

[3]The early imperial figures are quite good: we know nearly all army units, and their size conformed more or less to regulation. The later empire witnessed a substantial increase in the number of army units, but these became smaller and less uniform in size. Does the army grow, or just our ignorance? Recent discussion in: Duncan-Jones (1978), MacMullen (1980), Whittaker (1983) 118, Carrié (1986) 457 f. Noethlichs (1985) discusses the problems of payment in cash; for that, compare Parker (1972) 158 ff. Braudel (1979) I 34 ff. provides some comparative early modern figures; most battles were fought by armies that could be counted in tens of thousands, and no more. Finley (1985a) 30 for a comparison with the armies of Louis XIV: 'the Roman empire was incapable of a comparable effort, whatever the price.' But compare the different standard of living of soldiers.

[4]Hopkins (1980) 125. Estimated annual cost of the army in the first century AD: HS 445 (+/-50) million. I take the annual minimum subsistence cost as HS 115 per head - below, p. 135; 195.

[5]Braudel (1979) I 462 ff. gives a vivid account of the problems of early modern state finances.

until the eighteenth century (even if he qualifies them as 'low').[1]

Public amenities in Roman towns were impressive. What would a Roman town be if it did not have its temples, amphitheatre, public water supply, bathhouses, paved roads, and so on? The survival of such structures is proof enough of the quality of their construction. None of this had been cheap, even if much would not have been paid directly by the state, but was given by private benefactors, either as a demonstration of their elite position, or as a claim for such a position in the future.[2]

And yet the empire declined and fell. Rising military pressure was met by an increase in the proportion of the empire's income that was spent on military matters. In a state where the mass of the population was living barely above subsistence, there were strict ceilings to the increase in military expenditure. A substantially increased military expenditure might have been financed by an improved economic performance of the empire.[3] But this did not happen. Agricultural technology changed little over the course of many centuries - as far as we can tell. And the same holds true for production in other spheres of the economy. There is no indication that the standard of living of the mass of the population improved over a long period of time, and neither is there any obvious indication of sustained

[1]Hopkins (1980) 119 ff. for a tax rate of 10% on gross product, and for extensive comparative evidence. Braudel (1979) I 474 believes that 5% was normal, and 15% about the maximum in exceptional circumstances. Cipolla (1981) 48: 'it is difficult to imagine that, apart from particular times and places, the public power ever managed to draw more than 5 to 8 percent of national income.'

[2]Duncan-Jones (1985) is the best discussion of the cost and financing of public buildings. A theatre might easily cost H.S. 600,000. At an estimated subsistence cost per head of the population of about H.S. 115 (below, p. 195) the cost of a theatre would thus be roughly equivalent to subsistence for 5000 people for one year. One metre of paved road would cost about six months subsistence for one man. Brunt (1980) for public works at Rome. Veyne (1976) is the classic study of euergetism, even though disappointing for the cities of the Empire. For that: Duncan-Jones (1982) 'passim', Andreau (1977a) and Garnsey (1971). Public works might, however, be executed with the use of convict lower class labour: Millar (1984) 132 ff. This use of convict labour may have lessened potential popular resistance against the harsh penal laws.

[3]Finley (1968b) is perhaps the most elegant and economical formulation of the problem. I admire the logic in Gunderson (1976), but deplore its cavalier attitude to the deficiencies of our sources. Neesen (1980) and Brunt (1981) for taxation.

increases in national income or *per capita* income. Of course, the data are pitiful, but even bad data should have shown *something* in the course of so many centuries. And of course, ultimately the Roman economy went into serious decline, whether it was as a cause or as a consequence of the demise of the empire in the West.

If shipping is an index of economic development (and if shipwrecks are a good index of shipping), Hopkins' famed distribution of dated shipwrecks is a striking illustration. 'The dated shipwrecks show that in the period of Roman imperial expansion and in the High Empire (200 B.C. - A.D. 200), there was more sea-borne trade in the Mediterranean than ever before, and more than there was for the next thousand years.'[1] This demonstrates that Roman society was not static, but it also demonstrates the absence of *sustained* growth. The correlation with the political vicissitudes of the Empire is striking.

Even if *per capita* income did not increase in the long run, the rising military expenditure could - perhaps - have been met if members of the elite had been more willing to sacrifice some of their prosperity for the public good. However, evasion of public duties, and in particular tax evasion, become a constant theme in the later Empire. The continuity of the state might have been beneficial to the elite, but for each of its members individually it was more attractive to be a free rider, and hope that the Empire would survive on the contributions from others.[2]

If we try to draw up a balance sheet of Roman economic performance, we find ourselves in a curious position because we somehow do not seem able to arrive at a coherent picture. Inevitably this assessment is an exercise in comparative history, and the late medieval and early modern European experience provides the yard-stick. The scale to measure development and underdevelopment is derived from those periods. The problem is that Roman performance does not seem to fit the scale. Is it better to compare Rome with, say, thirteenth century Europe,

[1] Hopkins (1980) 106.

[2] Popkin (1979) for norms and coercion as means to avoid the free rider problem in the production of social goods (such as, here, military protection).

with fifteenth century Europe, or perhaps with eighteenth century Europe?[1] The problem is that whatever period we choose for comparison, differences remain. In some respects (such as state power, urbanization, public amenities or elite standard of living) Rome scores impressively high, but in other respects (such as the welfare of the mass of the population or manufacturing technology) it scores remarkably low. Small wonder that the debate on the modernity of the ancient economy has excited so much passion. Both sides in the debate can point to some examples which appear to support their case. Forcing Roman history into the mould of later European experience - our yard-stick for modernity - seems only possible at the expense of one side of the Roman experience. Can we avoid this without returning to the historicist skepticism as to comparison and its refuge into a discourse on the peculiar and the particular; is it possible to understand the differences and discover some logic in them?

The examples I have given of Rome's economic successes had one important thing in common: they often concerned the power of the state and the welfare of its elite. Rome may have been successful in pushing a traditional economy to its limits, but proper economic growth requires more than that, as we shall see. The power of the state and elite welfare are a measure of large income inequality rather than of high *per capita* incomes, and I shall argue later that this inequality reflects a failure to cope with population pressure and maintain or increase the standard of living for the mass of the population by a transformation of production.[2]

The apparent ambiguity of Rome's position on the scale of development raises a number of interesting questions. The ancient historian's view of late medieval and later history is of course important. I have so far refrained from being more specific about that. I shall later argue that part of the problem is indeed due to misunderstandings as to the nature of later

[1]This is not a silly example. Meyer (1924b) 118-9 contains precisely such equations.
[2]Below, p. 76 f; 85 ff; 199 ff.

development and growth.[1] Comparing the Roman world with an inappropriate ideal-type of later society is bound to create problems. However, even if we make necessary corrections, some of the ambiguity will remain. Economic growth may seem a simple enough concept, but that is misleading. We should distinguish between growth of total production, and growth *per capita*. Both are important concepts, but they are not the same. Total production in the Roman Empire undoubtedly increased (even if periods of decline can also be demonstrated), but the evidence for a growth of *per capita* incomes is much more ambiguous.[2]

Ensuring that all productive resources in an economy are fully employed can often generate some growth. It will not, however, create sustained growth over long periods of time: once everybody and everything is fully employed, no further gains are possible. Further growth can only come about through changes in factor supplies (labour, capital and land), or by increasing factor productivity (output per unit of factor input).[3]

Increasing the labour supply obviously increases total production.[4] But if the supply of the other factors of production is not increased at the same time, labour productivity will decrease and, therefore, *per capita* income. Growth of total production and decline (or stagnation) of *per capita* income may thus go hand in hand. This was indeed the spectre haunting classical political economists. They realized that the supply of land was relatively fixed, and they were pessimistic about the opportunities for increased capital investment.[5] As a converse to population growth, demographic crises (such as the Black

[1]Below, p. 48 ff.

[2]Hopkins (1983c) xvi ff. argues that there was an increase in productivity, even if that did not benefit the mass of the population. He does not, however, seem to distinguish sufficiently between production and productivity, and between productivity of land or of labour, or between productivity and technology. For my views on this: below, p. 76 f; 85 ff; 147 ff; 199 ff.

[3]Lipsey a.o. (1984) ch. XXXVIII for a clear introduction.

[4]Below, p. 76 f; 85 ff; 147 ff; 199 ff. for theoretical and comparative discussion.

[5]In other words, they were assuming a fixed marginal efficiency of capital schedule. See: Lipsey a.o. (1984) 737 f.

Death) may, because of a relative scarcity of labour, lead to higher *per capita* incomes and lower total production.[1]

So how can sustained growth be achieved? If we demand that this must entail both (moderate) increases in population and increases in *per capita* income, then it is not easy. Using a lot more land (if at all possible) and capital may help for a while, but to sustain the growth rate over a longer period, the creation of new and profitable investment opportunities is necessary (to avoid the diminishing marginal productivity of both land and capital).[2] In the end, sustained modern economic growth requires increased productivity of the factors of production, and not just the application of more of them. The quality of the factors has to be increased, not only the quantity.[3] This is what distinguishes modern from traditional economic growth.[4]

Growth, therefore, is not at all an unambiguous concept. Pushing a traditional economy to its limits may raise total production (and allow for example substantial state or elite expenditure), but at the expense of the standard of living (and, sometimes, freedom) of those who have nothing to offer but their labour.[5] But could it lead to the sort of structural transformation that brought about sustained modern economic growth? Perhaps not; the transformation of the European economy occurred after the demographic stagnation and contraction of the seventeenth century (which did bring about increases in *per capita* income).[6]

Development and underdevelopment may not be just more or less of the same, but may entail differences in social struc-

[1]Incomes of labourers and land-owners always move in opposite directions in the model; below, p. 85 ff; 147 ff. Critical introductions are often most useful: Brenner (1976) 32 ff.

[2]What is required is a shifting marginal efficiency of capital schedule: Lipsey a.o. (1984) 738.

[3]Kuznets (1966b) 30 ff.

[4]Van Zanden (1985) is a neat case-study of the transition from traditional to modern economic growth in agriculture.

[5]Cf. Hopkins (1983c) xvi ff, esp. on p. xvi: 'accumulation through intensified exploitation rather than increased total production.'

[6]De Vries (1976) esp. ch. 3; Cipolla (1981) esp. ch. 10; Cf. Geertz (1963).

tures and divergent routes. We shall even see that, for some, this has far-reaching methodological consequences, in that they no longer accept that modern concepts from economic theory may legitimately be applied to underdeveloped economies. But before we concern ourselves with that, and with the character of late medieval and early-modern economic development, an introduction to the debate on the ancient economy is in order.

The ancient economy: Finley and his critics

The publication in 1973 of Sir Moses Finley's Sather lectures (*The Ancient Economy*) has been a watershed in the study of ancient society.[1] A work of seeming simplicity, it contains a complex - and at times elusive - argument that the economic and social structure of the classical world differed significantly from that of other societies, and in particular from that of medieval and early modern Europe. This is in clear contrast to earlier scholarship on the ancient economy, which had asserted that the differences that there were, were differences in mere quantity (if that was granted at all), and not in kind.[2]

Finley begins with the observation that the ancient world, though capable of great intellectual achievement, has left us without any form of economic analysis. Why should this be so? His answer is that this is because the object of such an analysis - 'an enormous conglomeration of interdependent markets' - did not exist in the ancient world.[3] The economy of antiquity is 'embedded' within the social structure, and cannot be separated from it. This entails that much economic behaviour was governed

[1]Now available in a second - revised - edition: Finley (1985a).

[2]The classic references are Meyer (1924b), Beloch (1899), and Beloch (1902), all reprinted in Finley (1979), and Rostovtzeff (1957). For surveys of the debate: Will (1954), Austin and Vidal-Naquet (1973) and Cartledge (1983).

[3]Finley (1985a) 22. These interdependent markets should allow equilibration at the margins. Mathias (1987) argues that - apart from a few exceptions such as bullion - this marginal equilibration was a very late phenomenon: it existed before 1800, but only became a source of critical influence on economic transformation after that. Andreau (1977b) 1132, 1134 f. formulates the consequence: it will not do to lump together modern industrialized society and medieval and early modern society. O'Brien (1982) for the limited importance of intercontinental trade in early modern Europe.

more by the value systems of social groups than by economic rationality.

The prevailing value system could find little attraction in commercial and manufacturing activities. 'Ancient cities in the great majority counted farmers, whether working or gentleman farmers, men whose economic interest lay chiefly and often exclusively in the land, as the core of their citizenry.'[1] As a consequence, the social elite hardly involved itself in these commercial and manufacturing activities. No bourgeoisie emerged, commerce and industry remained underdeveloped, and the Roman economy did not grow.

The fundamental distinction between antiquity and later pre-industrial Europe is most apparent in Finley's discussion of the ancient city.[2] Here the approach is strongly Weberian: how did the ancient city pay for its food, imports of slaves, metals and other necessities? His answer is that it largely paid for them out of its income from rent on agricultural land, and from empire.[3] Export of manufactures is notable for its absence. This is the sense in which the typical ancient city is best characterized by the Weberian ideal-type of the 'consumer city'. The city is dominated by an elite that derives most of its income from agricultural property outside the city walls, and spends that income on food, services, and urban manufactures. The ideal-type does not exclude the presence of manufacturing within the town, only such manufacturing is largely of local importance: it does not produce for external markets to provide income for the elite and to pay for essential non-urban products.

The contrast is with the Weberian ideal-type of the 'producer city', a city dominated by a mercantile and manufacturing elite, which derives its income from the export of manufactures, to some extent to the immediate countryside, but also to more distant markets. It is this income - rather than that from agriculture - which allows the 'producer city' to acquire the

[1]Finley (1985a) 131.

[2]Finley (1985a) ch.5 and Finley (1977).

[3]Finley (1985a) 139.

necessary products from elsewhere. If, for Finley, the 'consumer city' is the most appropriate ideal-type to characterize the ancient city and its place in society, the 'producer city' is characteristic of the expanding economies of later medieval and early modern Europe.[1] The 'producer city' is the embodiment of economic innovation and growth, allowing new values and modes of economically rational behaviour to take effect.

A central assumption in Finley's argument is, therefore, that economically rational and innovative behaviour is not universal, but historic. It is characteristic of a peculiar historical formation which saw the emergence of a commercial bourgeoisie (the embodiment of such values and behaviour). Without it, the ancient economy was doomed to stagnation. That is an assumption with a long ancestry of famous scholars such as Werner Sombart and Max Weber, and it has important methodological implications.[2] It, and the absence of a system of integrated markets, make it inappropriate in Finley's view to apply modern economic theory to the study of the ancient economy.[3]

Although no one would deny that *The Ancient Economy* was a seminal work, and has dominated debate ever since, it must also be said that much of the reaction has been critical. Efforts have concentrated mostly on supplying examples of elite involvement in trade and manufacturing, and arguing that those activities were of a larger scale than Finley had allowed for. By substituting Finley's name for that of his precursor Hasebroek, Finley's own words on an earlier round of the debate are perhaps the most economical formulation:

[1] Cf. Sombart (1916-28) I 124-179; Weber (1976) 727-814. Bruhns (1985) criticizes Finley (1977) for misrepresenting Weber. Confusion seems to reign: the status of the ideal-type of the 'consumer city' is that of an analytical tool. Retaining the ancient city as a type is a substantive decision, as is a decision whether the 'consumer city' ideal-type is an appropriate label for the ancient city (granted deviations). Weber's typology may be analytically correct, but badly applied by himself, that is no contradiction.

[2] Weber (1976) esp. 31-121 and 727-814; Sombart (1916-1928).

[3] The relationship between the two assumptions of a 'market economy' and 'economically rational behaviour' remains unclear to me.

> My feeling of depression comes rather from the friendly critics, the ones who welcomed the books as important and salutary, who said, in effect, 'The modernizers have been defeated, and high time, too. If only Hasebroek didn't exaggerate....' That word 'exaggerate' is crucial: it implies that under dispute are mere quantities, or points along a continuum; that Beloch, Eduard Meyer and the other modernizers stood too far at one end, that Hasebroek stood too far at the opposite end, and that all that was now required was to find some comfortable station between them (just where depending on the bent of the individual writer).[1]

The efforts of most critics have been directed towards demonstrating that the ancient world was not as 'primitive' as been had suggested, but was much more modern and like later pre-industrial times. The argument, however, is largely one by exception. We are treated to long series of ingeniously constructed cases, many of which, on closer inspection, show insufficient respect for the evidence, or are at best inconclusive. They *might* refer to large scale trade and prestigious traders, but only if we already knew that we could expect them because they were prevalent in the ancient world. Finley has called this the 'missing persons argument'.[2] The clearest - and most sophisticated - version of this 'missing persons' argument is that of D'Arms' comparison with the economic activities and ideology of the French nobility in the eighteenth century.[3] He notes the co-existence of an aristocratic rentier mentality and a commercial origin of their fortunes. If we had looked just at the ideology, we would not have known about the real background of the fortunes of these French aristocrats. So the question is: would the same not be true in the Roman case?

It is an argument that is not easy to refute, but that is not a virtue. Insofar as it is about the *original* source of

[1]Finley (1965b) 12.
[2]Finley (1985a) 193.
[3]D'Arms (1977).

fortunes it is not very pertinent, either. No one doubts - I hope - that fortunes could be made in trade. The question is on the one hand whether those were the very large fortunes, and on the other hand whether trade was the predominant means to further, increase, and secure such fortunes, whether it was not just 'Gelegenheitshandel'. Did successful traders remain traders?[1] And if so, could they become part of the social and political elite, or was membership of the elite conditional upon a change in the sources of one's income? No elite is completely closed, and this is certainly true of the Roman elite, which, it has recently been argued, was surprisingly open, at least with regard to the senate.[2] This, therefore, poses the question whether elite values may not have been altered by the incorporation of newcomers if they had made their fortune in manufacturing and trade. Intertwined - due to the political nature of the Roman elite - is the question whether there was any room to express alternative sets of social values and modes of behaviour politically.

It remains, however, remarkable that all critics appear to share Finley's view that the status of traders is of key importance, and that trading and manufacturing are the touchstone of economic modernity. Clearly, that is essential to the Finley model, and understandably it has received much attention. But it is surprising that even his critics have accepted this frame of reference for the debate, which reduces criticism mostly to a debate about individual instances, and obscures the question whether they were the exception or the rule. But however many instances we may collect, they are inevitably too few to prove or disprove the rule. My argument will partly be along a different line: I shall argue that the importance of trade and traders as agents of economic rationalism and modernization may be questioned, both theoretically and from a comparative historical perspective; some of the historical debate may, therefore, have been ill-directed.

[1] Cf. below, p. 262 f. for an early modern comparison.

[2] Hopkins (1983) ch. 2 and 3.

If critics may have been wasting some of their energy, Finley himself was not entirely clear about the causal relationship between economic development and the social status of those in trading and manufacturing. Were these people socially unimportant because trade and manufacturing were of only limited importance, or were trade and manufacturing hampered in their development by the low status of the people involved? Finley appears to hold the view that it is because of the low status of those involved in trade and manufacturing that those activities did not attain great importance in the ancient economy.[1] The idea seems to be that because of this factor of status, the vast wealth of the elite was not available as investment capital,[2] and so the innovative values and modes of behaviour characteristic of such activities did not permeate the rest of society. But this begs the question why the elite would not involve itself. Of course, there was trade in the ancient world, and of course there was manufacturing. Their aggregate importance cannot be neglected, even though they have often been exaggerated. Assuming for the moment that the elite was indeed hardly involved, two explanations would seem possible. Were those activities insufficiently rewarding to get involved with, or did (profitable) involvement run counter to elite values and carry an unacceptable social stigma? Did a contradiction exist between desires for enrichment and elite social ideology?

Finley is characteristically down-to-earth about the acquisitive attitude of the elite. A desire for profit was at the root of,

[1]That, at least, is my reading of Finley, which I hope to document in the following pages. Hopkins (1983c) xi ff. interprets the 'new orthodoxy' the other way around: 'Just as the volume of trade was small, so the status of traders was generally low.' And about craftsmen: 'Their generally low status reflected their low total output.' As a historical proposition I find this indeed far preferable, but I do not think it accurately reflects Finley's views. If it is an indicator rather than a factor, status should not have been so central to his polemic.

[2]Finley (1985a) 53 ff, 142 f; cf. Andreau (1977b) and Andreau (1979), while waiting for the publication of his thèse d'état on banking. Capital needs in preindustrial manufacturing were, however, quite limited - Cipolla (1981) 96 ff, also below, p. 155 ff. Many have in recent years pleaded for indirect ('invisible') elite involvement: below, p. 177 ff.

for example, both slavery and imperialism.[1] So lack of elite involvement in trade and manufacturing is seen as hampering economic development and the emergence of economically rational behaviour, and yet the elite is supposed to be sufficiently greedy not miss a chance of quick enrichment. But were all sources of income equally acceptable in the prevailing ideology of status?

> The issue is one of choice. Given that no man, not even Robinson Crusoe, is absolutely free, how free was a Greek or Roman to choose among a range of possible 'employments', whether of his energies or his goods? More precisely, perhaps, how much weight was attached to what we should call economic factors in the choice, maximization of income, for example, or market calculations? Still more precisely, how free was a rich Greek or Roman, since obviously fishmongers, craftsmen and performers in low music-halls were rigidly restricted and could think of leisure and independence only as Utopian?[2]

This is a question, not an answer. But is it a rhetorical question? The question is repeated in a discussion of the social context of Cicero's famous passage about the respectability of various sources of income in the *De Officiis* (1.150-1): '... it must be decided whether or not the new freedom of enrichment was total, even for the nobility, or whether, by law or convention, men were still being pressed towards certain sources of wealth according to status.'[3] But this time we get an answer:[4]

> The answer is that ... the citizen-élite were not prepared, *in sufficient numbers*, to carry on those branches of the economy without which neither they nor their communities

[1]Finley (1980) 91 f; Finley (1978a); Finley (1985b) ch.5.

[2]Finley (1985a) 43.

[3]Finley (1985a) 52. Below, p. 261 f., for a discussion of the Cicero passage.

[4]Finley (1985a) 60.

> could live at the level to which they were accustomed. The élite possessed the resources and the political power, they could also command a large personnel. They lacked the will; that is to say, they were inhibited, as a group (whatever the responses of a minority), by over-riding values.

Finley's reconciliation of the desire for wealth and the desire for status is elegantly simple: 'In short, the strong drive to acquire wealth was not translated into a drive to create capital; stated differently, the prevailing mentality was acquisitive, but not productive.'[1] The justification for this answer is in a preceding and penetrating discussion of the absence of actual elite involvement in those branches of the economy. It contains many salutary observations about actual behaviour, but that is not enough to explain the behaviour. In the end, Finley's procedure is to reconstruct the predominant value-system of a status group from its actual behaviour ('taking Cicero as our guide'), and then use this 'mentality' to explain the behaviour.[2]

Even more puzzling than the critics' belief in Finley's authority on late medieval and early modern history is that they have - almost without exception - also accepted Finley's argument that modern economic theory is an inappropriate tool for the analysis of the ancient economy.[3] This is puzzling in its inconsistency, since insistence on a bigger role for markets and trading would remove the obstacles for a use of modern economic theory. I am not aware of any additional arguments, so I can only explain the neglect of economics by invoking the humanistic tradition of the subject and its practitioners.

[1]Finley(1985a) 144.

[2]And, methodologically, that is not very satisfactory. What do we mean to say when we use this fashionable word 'mentality'? How can it be anything other than behaviour, and, if that is so, how can it cause behaviour? It seems as if the myth of the 'Ghost in the Machine' has not yet been laid to rest: Ryle (1949). An alternative explanation for observed behaviour may be to drop the assumption of an identity between individual and social returns on economic activities - cf. North and Thomas (1973). Slavery, for example, may be profitable to the individual slave-owner, but perhaps not conducive to growth.

[3]Hopkins (1980) is - implicitly - the nearest thing to a methodological rejection. For critique, below, p. 187 ff.

Economics, anthropology, and the ancient economy
In the following pages I shall argue that the neglect of modern economic theory is mistaken, and that it can indeed be profitably used. My argument will, however, not be based upon the claim that specific historical conditions prevailed that warrant its use, but rather on the claim that economic theory can still operate in the absense of such conditions. My plea for economics should, therefore, not be read as a substantive statement about ancient society, but as an argument about how we might investigate it. If convincing, this argument will provide ancient historians with a rich body of theories and methods. It will also show that we no longer need to search for the presence or absence of economic rationality in the objects of our investigation (the search for the historical emergence of *homo oeconomicus*), but can redefine economic rationality as a strategy of the researcher, rather than as a property of his object.

Finley's objection to the use of modern economic theory was not something out of the blue; it stands in a long tradition of scholarship, going back more than a century, though its direct ancestry is in the substantivist economic anthropology of Karl Polanyi and his school.[1] Karl Polanyi and his followers claim that it is not legitimate to use modern - mostly microeconomic - theory for anything other than modern market economies.[2] This polemic runs, therefore, in many respects parallel to that on the ancient economy.[3] Introducing the anthropological perspective has a double advantage for the ancient historian. It allows a fuller appreciation of the background and importance of Finley's contributions, and an escape from the sometimes excessive empiricism characteristic of the debate among ancient historians. Ignoring the conceptual sophistication of the debate among economic anthropologists has not been to the benefit of the study of ancient history.

[1]See especially Polanyi a.o. (1957).

[2]Polanyi (1944) shows the undercurrent of his political dislike for market economies. Cf. Cook (1966).

[3]The similarity is not surprising: Finley was closely involved in the Columbia project that resulted in Polanyi a.o. (1957), even though he ultimately refused to contribute a paper himself (which was later published as Finley (1970)).

The debate among anthropologists - commonly referred to as the formalist-substantivist debate - may have reached something of a stalemate in recent years, but that is no reason for ancient historians not to catch up.[1] The starting point for all discussion is Polanyi's distinction between a substantive and a formal meaning of the word 'economic':

> The substantive meaning of economic derives from man's dependence for his living upon nature and his fellows. It refers to the interchange with his natural and social environment, in so far as this results in supplying him with means of material want satisfaction.
> The formal meaning of economic derives from the logical character of the means-ends relationship, as apparent in such words as 'economical' or 'economizing'. It refers to a definite situation of choice, namely, that between the different uses of means induced by an insufficiency of those means. If we call the rules governing choice of means the logic of rational action, then we may denote this variant of logic, with an improvised term, as formal economics.[2]

He then continues to argue that only the substantive meaning is of universal relevance - for all societies, past and present. The rules of choice as expressed in formal economics, however,

[1]The problems are complex, and bibliography is enormous. I cannot possibly provide more than titles which I have personally found enlightening, plus some of the classics and works of reference for the debate. Polanyi a.o. (1957) is the basic substantivist text. Leclair and Schneider (1968) provides a good survey of points of view, with a preference for the formalist side of the debate. See also: Firth (1967). Other milestones in the debate are: Polanyi (1944); Dalton (1971); Bohannan and Dalton (1962); Godelier (1971); Sahlins (1972); Clammer (1978) for some more recent - Marxist - contributions. The series 'Research in Economic Anthropology', originally edited by George Dalton, contains many relevant articles. Schneider (1974) is a pertinent formalist contribution. Melitz (1970) criticizes the substantivist view of money, from an economist's point of view. Van der Pas (1973) provides extensive bibliography. Malinowski (1922) and Herskovits (1940) are, so to speak, the anthropological prehistory of the debate, whereas Congdon (1976) discusses Polanyi's early Hungarian background. The best introduction to the ancient history link is in: Humphreys (1969), reprinted in: Humphreys (1978) 31-75.

[2]Polanyi (1957) 243.

only apply if the economy has a system of price-making markets, such as the western world has known in the recent past. Other economies did not - or do not - have such markets, and consequently modern formal economic analysis is of misleading value. The relationship between the substantive and the formal meaning of the word 'economic' is contingent. As alternatives to market exchange he then suggests two other 'forms of integration', which need not be exclusive, but may exist side by side with the other forms.[1] The first of these he calls reciprocity ('movements between correlative points of symmetrical groupings'), best exemplified here by Finley's work on the role of gift exchange in Homeric society.[2] The second he calls redistributive (designating 'appropriational movements toward a center and out of it again').[3] The ancient historian's prime example would be Mycenean palace economies,[4] but the grain supply of the city of Rome might perhaps also be claimed.[5] Polanyi acknowledges that trade is possible in societies where the market is of only peripheral importance (market-less trade), but this fact has consequences for the status of traders:

> Archaic society in general knows, as a rule, no other figure of a trader than that which belongs either to the top or to the bottom rung of the social ladder. The first is connected with rulership and government, as required by the political and military conditions of trading, the other depends for his livelihood on the course labor of carrying. This fact is of great importance for the organization of trade in ancient times. There can be no middle-class trader, at least among the citizenry.[6]

[1]Polanyi (1957) 250 ff.

[2]Polanyi (1957) 250; Finley (1978b); Finley (1955), reprinted in Finley (1981) 233-245.

[3]Polanyi (1957) 250.

[4]Inevitably, the reference is to Finley (1957-8) and Finley (1957), both reprinted in Finley (1981) 199-232.

[5]For Finley's views: Finley (1985a) 198 ff. For a formalist analysis of 'market interference': Jongman and Dekker (1988).

[6]Polanyi (1957) 259.

Reasons for trading are originally very specific, for example because there is an urgent and concrete need for a specific import, and they are unrelated to other simultaneous needs. 'Trading ventures are, for this reason, a discontinuous affair.'[1] Exchange may take place in markets; it is, however, not co-terminous with the market. Exchange *at set rates* occurs in both reciprocal and redistributive systems of integration.

If price-making markets are the stuff that economics is about, money is both measure of value, unit of account, medium of exchange, and standard of deferred payment on these markets. So, inevitably, the question arises as to money's function in economies other than modern market economies. There is, after all, no doubt that money goes back much longer than the supposed emergence of the market economy. Polanyi's solution is that whereas modern money would unite all of these functions (all-purpose money), in the primitive economy money is special-purpose money. Each kind of money is restricted to a specific range of transactions.[2]

As a summary of the substantivist position we may say that it emphasizes the link between 'economic' and the provision of material needs, stresses that the market is a fairly recent and certainly not universal institution, and claims that as a result modern formal economic analysis is of no use in case of primitive economies, since it would operate outside the limits of its constituent assumptions. However, I shall argue that Polanyi fatally distorts the assumptions and pretensions of modern economic theory. But before that, a further excursion into intellectual history is in order.

For a period in the late nineteenth century, economics was dominated by a fierce debate (the 'Methodenstreit') that shows an uncanny resemblance to the later formalist-substantivist debate in economic anthropology. Again, the issue was the extent to which the rules of economic theory are of universal

[1]Polanyi (1957) 261. The similarity with Sombart's 'Gelegenheitshandel' is obvious: Sombart (1916-28) I 115 f, 279 f, 302, 611, II 95 f, 165.

[2]Polanyi (1957) 264 ff.

relevance.[1] From the mid-nineteenth century a school of economic thinking (the 'historical school', with economists such as Roscher, Knies, Hildebrand, Schmoller, and, in a way, Karl Bücher, Werner Sombart and Max Weber) developed in Germany arguing that the predominant classical - liberal and English- economic thinking of the day was not of universal relevance. The historical school had its roots in the political activism to abolish intra-German custom barriers and raise external tariffs.[2] Free international trade, it was argued, was detrimental to the interests of the infant German industry. This argument for the protection of an infant industry is no major theoretical break with classical theory, but it did create an awareness of the more problematic sides of the claims of economics for universal validity.

Those doubts soon turned into an interest in the institutional aspects of the economy, and in particular into an interest in economic history. It was strongly emphasized that the economy could not be studied in isolation, and that it was imperative to pay attention to the social, legal and political context.[3] From here, the step to an historical interest was only a small one. History provided the setting for the uniqueness of the German situation, and it also provided many instances of economic institutions that were at odds with the market, or showed the market as an emerging historical phenomenon. Interest turned to such institutions as medieval guilds, or the role of the state in the economy. The two strands, emphasis on the specific and attention to the level and organization of exchange, come together in theories about the stages of economic development, with concepts such as *Hauswirtschaft*, *Stadtwirtschaft* and *Volkswirtschaft*.[4] The similarity to Polanyi's 'forms of integra-

[1]Authoritative introductions can be found in Roll (1973) ch. 7 and 8; Schumpeter (1954) 807 ff. and 843 ff; Blaug (1985) esp. ch. 8; For the - older - historical school: Eisermann (1956).

[2]For the role of Friedrich List in this: Roll (1973) 227 ff.

[3]Schumpeter (1954) 423 f. for the parallel developments in the legal science (von Savigny).

[4]Bücher (1919) I esp. 83 ff.

tion' is unmistakable, even though his forms may be contemporaneous and not represent a chronological sequence.

German nationalism was no doubt an important factor in the emergence of history as the source of alternatives to the market economy. But equally, triumphant Rankean historicism was available as the suitable kind of history to look to, for it too stressed the singularity of periods, and the impropriety of modern concepts, and it too advocated the primacy of induction over deduction.[1]

The choice between induction and deduction obtained the centre stage in the ensuing polemic with the Austrian school of economists, who were developing the marginal utility analysis (which was to remain the foundation of modern economics until the addition of Keynesian macro-economics). Central in this type of economics is the maximization principle.[2] It analyses the optimum allocation of scarce resources to obtain the greatest possible value to the maximand, be it profit, leisure or bland 'utility'.[3] If means are scarce, and ends unlimited, maximization involves such allocation of scarce means that any other combination results in a lower value of the maximand. Each of the alternative uses to which means are put is characterized by diminishing marginal returns: if the choice is between leisure and salary, starving in complete leisure is not attractive, but neither is working for 24 hours a day. The first hour of leisure gives more pleasure than the last hour of leisure, just as the first unit of money gives more pleasure than the last. The marginal utility (the pleasure from the last added unit) of both leisure and money income diminishes (i.e. the more one gets of them). The optimum combination is that where the choice is indifferent between one more unit of leisure (and a

[1]Iggers (1968) gives a classic account of German historiography, with enough nuances to permit me here to limit myself to some rather rough generalizations.

[2]More extensive discussion than I can give here can be found in good introductory economics textbooks, such as Lipsey a.o. (1984) or Stonier and Hague (1972).

[3]This economics assumes the universality of maximization behaviour and does not pronounce on the rationality of one maximand over another. That does not remove the importance of historical differences between societies as to the preferred end to maximize. However, an economist would say that it is not his task to explain that, but the sociologist's or psychologist's.

correspondingly lower salary) or one unit more of salary (with correspondingly less leisure).[1] The reasoning is deductive, and the theory claims universal validity.

Polanyi would be right to reject the use of modern economic theory if it, indeed, necessarily made unduly modernizing assumptions about economies other than those of our own times. Yet, I shall argue, no such assumptions need to be made. Polanyi's description of modern economic science is a caricature, and modern economists have abandoned the assumptions that he posits as necessary parts of their theories.[2]

We shall, first of all, distinguish between two uses of the word 'economic'. The first of these concerns the aim or intention of 'economic' behaviour, the second concerns the means of such behaviour. I shall argue firstly that economics cannot and does not distinguish between ends which are economically rational and ends which are not. Secondly I shall argue that economic behaviour hardly presupposes any of the calculating introspection that Polanyi ascribes to it. Thirdly I shall argue that economics does not presuppose specific institutions such as markets or money for it to apply.

Polanyi equated 'economic' with material want satisfaction. But does economics really concern itself with all behaviour aimed at the satisfaction of material wants, and with nothing else? No doubt the provision of some material wants is covered in economic theory[3], but it is equally true that the provision of some other material wants (air and water are the classic examples) remains completely outside the realm of economics:

[1]Opportunity cost is the economist's term for this tactic of expressing more of one thing in terms of less of the other. The classic - and dense - formulation of utility maximization is Gossen (1889) 12: 'Der Mensch, dem die Wahl zwischen mehren Genüssen frei steht, dessen Zeit aber nicht ausreicht, alle vollaus sich zu bereiten, muss, wie verschieden auch die absolute Grösse der einzelnen Genüsse sein mag, um die Summe seines Genusses zum Grössten zu bringen, bevor er auch nur den grössten sich vollaus bereitet, sie alle theilweise bereiten, und zwar in einem solchen Verhältniss, dass die Grösse eines jeden Genusses in dem Augenblick, in welchem seine Bereitung abgebrochen wird, bei allen noch die gleiche bleibt.'

[2]For what is to follow I rely on the classic statement: Robbins (1937). This is elaborated at great length in Hennipman (1945).

[3]But it has been argued - Fischer (1906) esp. ch. X - that in the final analysis all utility from material goods is immaterial.

when the supply of means to satisfy these material wants is unlimited - when there is no scarcity - economics has nothing sensible to say.[1] If you can have your cake *and* eat it you do not need an economist. Conversely, economics may have a lot to say about the allocation of scarce resources to achieve immaterial ends. Life is short, and constitutes the most precious (because finite) commodity man has available to satisfy his wants. One cannot at the same time attend the ballet and go to the cinema. An important commodity for a subsistence peasant is his own time. He may allocate this between - various forms of - leisure, preparation of the soil, improved drainage or irrigation, he may add to his storage facilities, or tend his animals. All the time he is trading-off one possible allocation of a scarce resource - time - against another to maximize his utility. Some of this utility would be that of leisure, some of it would be security, and some of it would be various forms of, for example, food. Restricting the economic to the material is not very sensible, and is at variance with the realities of economic discourse.

A consequence of abandoning the equation of 'economic' with 'material' is that we can no longer use it to make a distinction between economically rational and economically irrational ends. No longer can we legitimately brand behaviour as economically irrational if it reduces the satisfaction of material wants.[2] It all depends whether other wants are satisfied instead. A second consequence is that we can no longer view the economy as a sector of society (relating to the provision of material wants).[3] Economic behaviour is an aspect of all behaviour (as long as there is scarcity), rather than a peculiar sphere of behaviour (to the exclusion of other spheres of behaviour).

[1]When air or water are scarce, economics does have something to say.

[2]Which are often enough defined in a very restrictive sense as well, ignoring, for example, the need to ensure that their satisfaction is secure in the face of various risks. Popkin (1979) is a classic demonstration here of the ability of economic analysis to penetrate behind what may seem 'irrational' social traditions and customs. Jongman and Dekker (1988) for an economic analysis of risk avoiding strategies (in the preindustrial urban food-supply).

[3]The reader may wonder why I chose to give my book its present title. I have preferred to abstain from programmatic polemic in the title, and choose a title that is informative in its conventionalism.

We may distinguish economic behaviour, but we cannot separate it. In modern theory, utility is a subjective concept. Profit or money are not valuable in themselves.

If we cannot define economically rational behaviour by its ends, how far can we define it by its deployment of means? Is there a particular economically rational way of going about achieving ends which is perhaps not universal? No doubt the past was not the same as the present; we do things differently. What is at stake is whether the same logic applies. It has, for example, been argued that ancient accounting practices were so deficient that they made profit maximizing behaviour impossible.[1] For Polanyi (as for Weber and Sombart before him) rationality in this sense was an exclusive characteristic of modern economies, and a crucial assumption behind the deployment of formal economic analysis. Here, *homo oeconomicus* is not so much that peculiar man who wants more and more material goods, but the perhaps even weirder creature who constantly evaluates his economic choices in the light of all alternative options.

Original marginal utility analysis assumed that utility could indeed be measured, and the proponents saw nothing problematic in their introspective assumptions about economic behaviour. Attempts at empirical validation soon showed up problems, however.[2] The need for *cardinal* measurement of utility was overcome in the so-called indifference curve analysis.[3] This still makes introspective assumptions about economic behaviour, but they are less heroic. Indifference curve analysis assumes

[1]Macve (1985) is the best recent discussion. He argues - 'inter alia' - that ancient historians have been too demanding: modern practice would often not have been of great help either. Depreciation inevitably involves rules of thumb, and expectations of future income are indeed just that. What indeed is the value of farm buildings that cannot be sold-off without the farm itself? Conversely, does one need accounts to make sound business decisions? Macve argues (p. 257) that for calculations of business income and capital the famed double-entry book-keeping (absent in antiquity) is neither necessary nor sufficient. If Graeco-Roman society was unable to carry out certain economic activities which are a feature of modern societies, this was not because of inadequate accounting technology (p. 260).

[2]Blaug (1985) 328 ff.

[3]Discussed at length in any introductory economics textbook. E.g. Stonier and Hague (1972) 52-86; Lipsey a.o. (1984) 153-168. The technique had a long period of gestation, but Hicks and Allen (1934) put it on the map. Also: Hicks (1946).

that an individual can rank his preferences consistently, and that he can indicate 'indifference' between two alternatives at a given time. Indifference curves show the various combinations of two goods yielding the same total satisfaction. The optimum is that combination which can be realized at the lowest cost.[1] Even though this is a theory that no longer assumes cardinal measurement of utility, it still remains a big step removed from reality, because only one 'indifferent' combination can actually be documented. This one combination is then 'explained' by the assumption of an introspective 'curve' (and constraints from reality).

So indifference curve analysis makes problematic assumptions, or, more precisely, assumptions which cannot be tested for their realism (even though they can be tested for their effectiveness). But does that justify Polanyi's assertion that such theories can only be applied to modern capitalist societies? It is not clear to me why these assumptions would be more problematic in the case of one society than another. Methodologically they are, in principle, always problematic. There is no more reason to assume that modern man walks around with indifference curves in his head than that ancient Romans did so. So does it matter that indifference curve analysis makes unrealistic assumptions?

The demand that a theory should provide a perfect and complete relation to reality is a very stringent one, and perhaps unnecessarily strict. The world is complex, and understanding can be facilitated by simplification; a theory that only gives approximate predictions about reality may still be more valuable than nothing at all. A theory that presumes economic subjects to maximize their satisfaction/utility is probably better than a theory that presupposes that they minimize their utility. And a theory that presupposes that people make up their minds all the time is probably better than one which assumes that they act the way they do because they never make up their minds. The judgment here is a practical one (how large is the mismatch between predicted and actual behaviour?), and only in that

[1] Where the price-consumption or budget line (straight, under full competition) is tangential to the indifference curve.

sense may Polanyi's criticism be pertinent, though even then I can see no reason to privilege modern man.

In any case, the untestable and perhaps untenable assumptions of indifference curve analysis have been embarrassing to economists. And at least as annoying, and of greater practical importance, was the impossibility of relating indifference curves to data on actual behaviour: the lack of operational consequence left econometricians out in the cold. The emergence, in the last few decades, of an alternative type of analysis, 'revealed preference', killed these two birds with one stone. Revealed preference analysis 'does not require any more of the consumer than that he is able to go out and spend the money he has available.'[1] The assumption about rational action is reduced to 'transitivity': an individual must not prefer *A* over *B* in one situation, and then choose *B* over *A* in another. His choices must be consistent. This economic analysis abandons all introspective assumptions, and is satisfied with observed behaviour.

Economic rationality (whether of ends or of means) was not, however, Polanyi's only concern. He also argued that economics, for it to apply, required the presence of specific institutions, without which economic theory would be irrelevant. The first is the institution of modern money. Only modern money, integrating all monetary functions in one medium, could play the central role in the price-mechanism; the 'special-purpose money' of primitive society was unable to integrate markets. But is modern money indeed all-purpose money? Melitz has argued in a long attack on substantivist views about money that economic theory does not require this kind of 'modern money', and that modern money is also 'special-purpose money'.[2] If 'all-purpose money' does not exist in the modern world either, we may of course conclude that modern economic theory does not apply to the modern world, but it is perhaps wiser to stop worrying about 'special purpose money'.[3]

[1]Stonier and Hague (1972) 52. The technique was first presented in Hicks (1956).

[2]Melitz (1970).

[3]Though not, of course, about money's role in the economy. For that, Crawford (1970) remains classic.

Polanyi's second institutional requirement is that of the market. For him the market is only one of the possible 'forms of integration', and if it is absent - or of only minor importance - formal economic analysis is useless.[1] Polanyi is right that the market is an important concept in economic analysis, and that, historically, concrete markets and division of labour have not always been very important. But he is wrong to be believe that concrete markets are central to economic analysis. The market, in economic theory, is only an analytical construct to understand the relationship between supply and demand. It does not presuppose that supply and demand are exercised by different persons, even if that is often so in modern economies.[2] A subsistence peasant needs to allocate his own time between various competing uses. Leisure is obviously one of these, as is work (but not as a purpose in itself). The peasant may decide to spend his time to work the soil just enough to have a decent harvest in the near future, or to also make improvements from which he will only later reap the benefits. He may decide to enhance his security by building more storage space for food, or to spend his time tending some animals and thus improve his diet. He may make his own tools, or he may go to the (concrete) market in town, and sell a lamb and buy some tools. All the time he is trading-off one possible allocation of a scarce resource - time - against another to maximize his utility. In other words, an abstract market for time can be conceived. The existence of possibilities to sell labour time to others, or buy it from them, would of course make a difference, but not the difference marking the limit of where formal economics may be applied. In fact, economics is the best tool for understanding the difference that such trading opportunities make.

We may, therefore, reject Polanyi's equation of formal economic analysis with assumptions about 'economic rationality' (which would or would not be appropriate depending on the

[1]Above, p. 37 ff.

[2]Applying modern economic theory to the distant past therefore does require historical sensitivity. It can only be applied in its bare analytical form, stripped of all modern institutional connotations, if we want to avoid justified criticism of anachronism. Hicks (1969) is a good example of the difficulty, for even the best modern economists, to take this striptease to its bare end.

type of society) and specific institutions. It should by now, however, also be obvious why the choice to apply modern economic theory implies in itself no substantive statement about the ancient economy. It still remains important to investigate how far consumer preferences are shaped by concerns for status, or how a preference for status (as a utility to be maximized) may put constraints on efforts at profit maximization. And it still remains important to investigate the extent of self-sufficiency or division of labour, and how interregional and 'international' trade play their part in this.

The comparative historical perspective

The debate on economic theory is not, however, the only theoretical issue with which we shall have to be concerned in our analysis of the ancient economy. The second issue concerns the - usually fairly implicit - comparison made with late medieval and early modern Europe. Here again, Finley's critics have, on the whole, accepted the terms of the debate as they were set by him.[1] They have accepted the view that Europe's later economic development rested on the growth of urban manufacture and trade, controlled by an innovative and entrepreneurial bourgeoisie, the embodiment of the new acquisitive values and of the economically rational conduct to satisfy these ends. For Finley, as we have seen, this is in clear contrast to the ancient city, which had only catered for the consumer interest of the land-owning elite resident in the town. As long as his critics adhere to the view that a commercial bourgeoisie is the touchstone for development, their criticism of Finley implies a claim for such development in antiquity. Whether they are right or not as to the scale of trade and the status of traders is a matter of empirical investigation, but their claim

[1]Notable exceptions are Andreau (1977b), Carandini (1979) and especially Pleket (1984). Andreau (p. 1136 ff.) surprisingly accuses Finley of a neo-classical mode of economic argument. I fail to find any justification for that in Finley's work, other than that the economics that he rejects for antiquity (and would seem-implicitly - to accept for modern economies) is indeed 'neo-classical'. Note also Andreau's objection against a binary opposition between 'antiquity' and 'the modern world'. Indeed, medieval and early modern society remains in a curious limbo state in Finley's work. Pleket's contribution here is to emphasize that ancient historians have been too 'modernistic' as to later preindustrial history.

implies that they think that he was right about the nature and causes of later development and growth. If it can be shown that those had nothing, or little, to do with a commercial bourgeoisie (and all that that implies), then we may wonder what the debate is all about (and think of better explanations for Rome's development or stagnation).

The city as engine of economic improvement is well formulated in the theories about the rise of capitalism of eighteenth century political economists.[1] Adam Smith writes: 'It is thus that through the greater part of Europe the commerce and manufactures of cities, instead of being the effect, have been the cause and occasion of the improvement and cultivation of the country.'[2] The separation of town and country allowed the expansion of the market and increased division of labour. And, not surprisingly, these were seen as the causes of development.

A similar effect is attributed by Henri Pirenne to the emerging medieval cities.[3] 'La formation des agglomérations urbaines ébranla tout de suite l'organisation économique des campagnes.'[4] From now on it became attractive to produce a surplus, because this could be sold to the urban market, where in turn the attractive urban manufactures could be bought to make life more pleasant. And the cities not only provided the motive to increase production, but also a new type of liberty, independent from feudal constraints, which allowed the emergence of an essentially lay culture. The commercialization of the countryside resulted in the liberation of the peasantry from feudal servitude. For Pirenne urbanism was the cause of the emergence of a free and prosperous society, a process already well under way by the end of the eleventh century.[5]

The protection from a hostile feudal world which the towns

[1] Merrington (1976) 170.

[2] Smith (1976) III, iv, 18 / p. 422.

[3] Pirenne (1927) esp. ch. VIII.

[4] Pirenne (1927) 187.

[5] Pirenne (1927) 188.

afforded to the new milieu of trade and traders is emphasized by Postan:[1]

> [The towns] were non-feudal islands in the feudal seas; places in which merchants could not only live in each other's vicinity and defend themselves collectively but also places which enjoyed or were capable of developing systems of local government and principles of law and status exempting them from the sway of the feudal regime. If so, the story of how and why the towns arose and proliferated should be told not only in economic but also in political and social terms.

Seclusion and protection of the trade which had developed at an earlier stage are the key, in Postan's view. We may note that for him the rise of towns is, therefore, as much a consequence as a cause of the emergence of trade.[2] This problem of the prime mover is manifest in the so-called Dobb-Sweezy debate.[3] Was the transformation of the feudal mode of production internal to it, or did it have an external origin, merchant capital, which was harboured within the protection of city walls? Urbanism and capitalism, therefore, share a long history. So long that we may wonder, with Rodney Hilton, what is the point of such concepts:[4]

> Pirenne's definition [of capitalism] referred to the activities of European merchants in the 12th and 13th centuries. Such definitions face the history teacher and student with the puzzling phenomenon of 'the rise of the middle classes' (associated of course with the growth of trade), which seems to start so early, to go on for so long, and to be the explanation of so many historical movements and events. For although the urban middle class of medieval

[1] Postan (1975) 239.

[2] Cf. Brenner (1976) 42 ff.

[3] Hilton (ed.) (1976) contains the most important contributions.

[4] Hilton (1976) 145 f. Similarly: Mathias (1987) 2 f.

> Europe is said to have begun its notorious career as early as the 10th century, the teacher is faced with the problem of explaining why it was not until the 17th and 18th centuries that this class became the dominant force in society. Why did it take more than 700 years to reach this position if during the whole period it was 'rising'?

One answer could be that early modern cities were no longer as central as their medieval counter-parts.[1] Another could be that they had never been the engines for growth: 'Nothing reveals better the limits of this municipal economy than its decline and involution in the context of the growing world market and the establishment of territorial state sovereignty from the 16th century.'[2] In either case, the rise of the industrial city is a major discontinuity.[3] What is at stake, however, is no less than the credibility of the town as a generic social object.[4] No doubt the town is contemporaneous to many of the social and economic developments with which it is being associated. And no doubt urbanization and commercialization are correlated (though perhaps less perfectly than some would wish - most of Europe's towns were sleepy, small provincial towns, rather than hectic centres of commercial expansion). But does the 'townness' of these towns cause and explain the other developments?[5]

Finley's work on the ancient city has the virtue that for antiquity it abandons, in practice, the notion of the town as a generic social object, or slight reductions in generality such as Sjoberg's 'preindustrial city'.[6] It may seem that Finley's insistence on the ancient city as a type of its own, distinct from

[1]Braudel (1966) I 300.

[2]Merrington (1976) 183.

[3]Which seems to be at variance with current historical thinking: de Vries (1984) 8; Kriedte a.o. (1977).

[4]Abrams (1978) esp. 14.

[5]Cf. de Vries (1984) ch. 1, who pleads for a history of urbanization, rather than urban history: 'cities possess more dimensions than those usually emphasized in studies of individual towns'(p. 9). He emphasizes the system of cities.

[6]Finley (1977); Sjoberg (1960).

the oriental and the medieval town, is hardly an improvement.[1] The elements in his definition of it as a type do not, however, stress the 'townness' and separateness of the ancient city, but present it as a specific enactment of ancient social relations. 'The Graeco-Roman world ... was a world *of* cities (italics W.J.).[2] ...' The city does not exist in isolation: it is an integral part of a larger social structure, in the Graeco-Roman world a pivotal institution.'[3] This stress on integration is what makes Finley's ancient city type a success.[4]

A problem emerges, however, in the implicit comparison with later urbanism and its relation with growth and development. How and why did these occur? By making urbanism the pivot of a comparison we all too easily reify later cities into an engine of development; but why should 'townness' have become a reality and a force for change when it had not been before? Or how can we explain the emergence of this specific type of town (with the potential to bring about such change) which had not existed before?[5] Later medieval or early-modern towns, too, were an integral part of their societies, and cannot *per se* be the explanation of social change.

The virtues of urbanism may seem obvious enough. Division of labour between town and country, specialized craft manufacture, international trade and finance, a more open social system and more tolerance to new ideas, these are all signs for the good. And though the correlation is usually (though not invariably) obvious enough, causality is more problematic. Does more trade improve the economy, or, conversely, is increasing trade a consequence (or manifestation) of a growing economy?[6] What is so special about trade that it is always better to have

[1] Abrams (1978) 15.

[2] Finley (1977) 305 = Finley (1981) 3.

[3] Finley (1977) 327 = Finley (1981) 22.

[4] Cf. Abrams (1978) 26 on Sjoberg (1960).

[5] Cf. Abrams (1978) 26 f.

[6] Cf. Mathias (1987) on the rise of the international economy. Prior to the mid-nineteenth century it does not seem to have been a force in its own right for transformation; it mostly reflected the changes in the economy. O'Brien (1982) strongly questions the presumed importance of intercontinental trade for early modern Europe's development.

more of it, and why is it then that people do not trade more than they do?

We may assume that when and where trade and division of labour occurred, they were advantageous. That is not at stake. But should we also assume that it would have been more advantageous if there had been more of them, *ceteris paribus*? Division of labour (especially if spatial) and trade also have their costs. Transport costs were high in pre-industrial societies.[1] And prevailing pre-industrial production technology was often not such that the economies of very large scale production could be substantial.[2] An increase in geographical division of labour may be a sign that transport costs had become lower, or that the benefits from specialization had increased (or, more likely, in the real world, that both costs had been reduced and benefits improved). Without lower transport costs or more possibilities for economies of scale, further division of labour would probably have been inefficient. Who are we to know so well that the costs from the 'friction of distance' and the greater hassle from division of labour would be offset by economies of scale? Would it not be better to assume that the amount of trade and division of labour reflect an optimum *given prevailing conditions*?

If we accept this argument, it follows that urbanization can no longer be seen as an engine for growth unless and insofar as it alters the conditions for trade and division of labour (or is related to such changes). It is quite conceivable that we may find forms of urbanization which did not have this effect.[3] And it is also quite conceivable that insofar as conditions for trade and division of labour were indeed improving, that was due not to urbanization but to improvements in transport and manufacturing technology which had nothing, or little, to do with urbanization itself.

[1] Below, p. 78 f; 140 f; Braudel (1979) I 365-377; Duncan-Jones (1982) 366 ff.

[2] A proper argument would be somewhat more complex. Cf. Lloyd and Dicken (1977) and Caves and Jones (1981).

[3] Hopkins (1983c) xiii: 'Finley's intention here, I think, was that we should not automatically assume that the high level of Graeco-Roman urbanization was an index of its high economic development, just because urbanization was an index of economic development in post-mediaeval Europe.'

Specialization between town and country is, however, not solely a matter of the urban economy. It also presupposes specialization of the rural economy. Here again, such specialization may bring benefits, but it also entails costs. The production of cash crops may bring high returns, but often entails an increased risk of starvation in bad years.[1] The broad range of products grown by the subsistence farmer not only provides a hedge against crop failure, but may also employ available manpower more efficiently since it avoids the huge seasonal peaks in labour requirements which are inherent in most single crop strategies. That is especially important when labour is provided by the farmer's family, for such labour has a near zero economic cost because it cannot realistically be discarded.[2] Not only might it be perfectly rational for a peasant not to specialize in market crops, but we must also realize - as we have been reminded again in recent years - that it need not be the *peasant's* best interest which was decisive.[3] The power to decide may have lain with big landlords, and for them squeezing dependent subsistence peasants harder may have been more attractive than increased commercialization. The growth of the market for agricultural products has in some cases even been an important contributing factor to a refeudalization of rural relations of production.[4]

Absence of towns may be a good indicator for lack of growth potential; their presence, however, should not be seen to necessarily imply a stimulus for growth. As we shall see, the ancient city is a case in point here. Although some later urbanism coincides with commercial expansion, we need not interpret that expansion as a consequence of the 'townness' of those towns: enough towns existed which were in no way strongly linked with the commercial expansion. The commercial

[1] Cf. Jongman and Dekker (1988).

[2] This is changed of course when alternative uses for such labour become available, as is the case in proto-industrialization. Chayanov (1966) is the classic analysis of peasant behaviour. For proto-industrialization, see e.g. Kriedte a.o. (1977).

[3] Brenner (1976) and the subsequent discussion in the pages of 'Past and Present' are a case in point.

[4] Brenner (1976) 47 ff; Wallerstein (1974) 90 ff; Lis and Soly (1979) 158 f.

towns are a reflection and a symptom of a changing economy, rather than a direct cause. If for Finley the stagnation of the ancient economy is, perhaps, ultimately due to the strangulation of the ancient city by social relations concerning agricultural property and labour, there is a parallel in the more recent discussions on early modern growth: here too the emphasis of explanations (though now of growth, rather than of stagnation) is shifting away from the city *per se*, and towards changes in the relations between towns *and country*, and in particular towards changes in rural social relations of production.[1] Urbanization has become the stage, rather than the stage machine.

Why Pompeii?

Town-country relations, then, are crucial for the debate on the ancient economy and for an understanding of ancient social structure. For nearly all ancient cities the evidence is so pitiful, however, that it would not be very sensible to take an individual city as the object of research. On the whole, thematic studies with data from a large number of cities are the best research strategy. But their disadvantage is that for practical reasons they inevitably have to neglect the interrelationship between the different aspects of the social and economic structure of ancient cities. Precisely this interrelation became so important in scholarly polemic, and it can only be studied in the context of an individual city.

Apart from exceptional cities such as Athens or Rome, one city stands out as a potential candidate for such research: Pompeii. Buried under the thick layers of volcanic ashes from Vesuvius' eruption in 79 A.D., it gives the ancient historian the nearest thing to a time-capsule. Even if a sample of one can, of course, never be representative, we could have fared worse in this respect. Pompeii is an Italian site of the first century A.D., and in that sense it represents Roman urbanism at its most impressive: this is the area where and the period when we would expect it to be most highly developed. With its 8000-12000 inhabitants (within the walls) it was probably bigger than

[1] de Vries (1974); Brenner (1976); Merrington (1976); Kriedte (1980).

most Roman towns - but it was no metropolis. The Pompeian territory is very fertile, and population density was well above the Italian average. In studying Pompeii we study Roman urbanism under a magnifying glass. That may be an advantage or a disadvantage, depending on the argument.[1] I hope to show that it is an advantage: 'even at its most developed, the Roman city was no producer city.'

This is not to say, however, that there are no problems with the Pompeian time-capsule. The unique top layer of the site provides abundant data for the most recent history of the town. The lower layers, however, are not at all privileged compared to other sites. This, and a justified hesitation to damage the surface layer for excavation of lower levels, have had the effect that, compared to other sites, there is an enormous wealth of information for one period, and little for the period before (or, naturally, for the period after 79 A.D.). The consequence is that, unfortunately, Pompeii is unsuitable for dynamic analysis: it is a necessarily static cross-section at more or less one moment in time (albeit an important moment).

But the chronological concentration of the data is not the only sense in which Pompeian data are unique. The specific conditions of conservation have preserved whole types of data for us which have not (or hardly) survived at other sites. The archive of writing tablets that will figure so prominently in chapter six is near unique, and is certainly far larger and more homogeneous than anything from elsewhere.[2] This is also true for the electoral posters analysed in chapter seven, and in a different way for the extent of surviving housing. Other data, however, are conspicuous by their absence. Inscriptions on stone, in particular public ones, are few in number. Though many villa sites have survived, their interpretation is hampered by the impossibility of normal field surveys: the layer of ash is too thick to yield much. The unique composition of the evidence

[1] Biased data need not matter, provided we know the direction of the bias. A small later provincial town (perhaps more representative for the average ancient city than Pompeii) would be an even less likely candidate as a producer city. Cf. below, p. 65 ff; 106 ff; 108 ff; 243.

[2] I shall not discuss the recent Agro Murecine tablets. Their relationship to Pompeii is tenuous, and they are a far less homogeneous series.

poses methodological problems: we cannot rely much on our experience from other sites to interpret the data. All too easily we may make the mistake of using the same data both to formulate our hypotheses and to validate them. I have tried to employ two strategies to combat the problem. Firstly, I have always looked with one eye to the world outside Pompeii, and preferred that as a source of hypotheses and a potential control. Secondly, I have preferred to concentrate on larger sets of more or less serial data. That should constrain and control speculation at least to some extent.

A prospect of the argument

I have already commented briefly on the importance of the relationship between population and production. In *chapter two* I elaborate on this point, in part with further theoretical analysis. In good economic fashion I begin with an analysis of demand and supply in Roman Italy. I argue that food plays a major role in both, and that at prevailing high levels of population density, producing enough food required a major effort. Such intensive agriculture requires large labour inputs, and inevitably labour productivity will be low. This was all the more so since the lack of good pasture-land militated heavily against a large-scale use of working animals. In that sense the history of mediterranean agriculture is different from that in more northern areas.

The problems and possibilities of increasing agricultural output to feed growing numbers of people have long been a field of economic reflection. In recent years the work of Ester Boserup has drawn attention to the possibilities of more frequent cropping to achieve a higher productivity of the land; but the other side of the coin is that under traditional conditions that requires a disproportionate increase in labour input, with low labour productivity (and, therefore, a declining standard of living) as a result. Elaborating on this analysis, Jan de Vries has argued that specialization between town and country may alleviate this. Whereas under traditional conditions population pressure is responsible for the fragmentation of holdings and increased dependence of impoverished peasants upon big landowners, specialization may avert these evils. Then the peasantry may remain relatively strong and independent, and the urban elite can be a commercial and manufacturing elite, rather than one of landowners resident in towns. What happened in Roman Italy?

Chapter three takes the argument into Pompeii, and is focussed in particular on its agriculture. The traditional view of Pompeian agriculture emphasizes the production for external markets of cash crops such as wine and olive oil. I argue that it is mistaken. It ignores the prominence of cereal agriculture in literary sources about Campania, and is naive in its implicit conviction that the surviving archaeological evidence for villa agriculture can be extrapolated to parts of the territory for which no such evidence exists. I argue that where traces of villa agriculture are absent, there were no villas in antiquity. Instead, I posit small (and probably more or less dependent) peasants concentrating on cereal agriculture.

I then offer three efforts at validation of my hypothesis. The first of these is that it appears no coincidence that the villas are where they are: their location coincides with what one would predict from location theory. The second validation comes in the form of an effort to calculate aggregate supply of and demand for food in the town and its territory. The traditional view of Pompeian agriculture never bothered about the origin of the grain that was needed to feed the population, nor did it ever consider whether the quantity of wine likely to have been produced was large enough to leave a major surplus for export. My tentative calculations indicate that the traditional view is improbable: the wine surplus would be non-existent and a large area would be necessary to grow enough cereals. The third effort at validation consists of a comparison with early-modern Campania. It is reassuring (even if no proof) to note that, in that period too, the area was devoted to cereal agriculture. This comparison with later times permits a more detailed analysis of the logic of the very intensive agriculture in the area. Population density was so high (and roughly equal to that in antiquity) that production per hectare had to be very high as well. The result was that labour productivity was low: the standard of living of the working population was appalling. A higher labour productivity would have been possible if working animals had replaced some of the human labour. Inevitably population density would have been lower, however: the food requirements of the animals would not have permitted the high prevailing population density.

Chapter four then shifts focus to the urban economy: can we find evidence for major manufacturing directed towards external markets? And, can we find evidence that the urban elite was substantially involved in this manufacturing and in the trade in its products, and that it was, therefore, not just a group of landowners resident in town? Rather than run the gamut of all craft production in the town, I have chosen to concentrate on the one branch of industry that constitutes a decisive test: the textile industry. If medieval and early-modern cities develop a substantial exporting manufacturing industry (often enough they do not) it almost invariably concerns textiles, and Moeller has recently argued that this was the case in Pompeii.[1]

He is, however, wrong. Of course there were textile workshops, but there is nothing to suggest that their scale exceeded the requirements of the local market. Neither is there any evidence to validate his view that the Pompeian fullers fulfilled a coordinating entrepreneurial role for the entire industry, or that the elite were directly involved. Pompeian industry was not heavily concentrated on one particular industry (textiles), but was very differentiated. This suggests production for a sophisticated local demand, rather than for export.

Elite income and expenditure seem important for an understanding of the ancient city. To understand better how important, we leave, in *chapter five*, the confines of Pompeii. After a brief critical review of Hopkins' 'Taxes and Trade' model for the economy of Roman towns, I propose a tentative model to relate elite income and expenditure and its place in the Italian economy of the early Empire. Already a very conservative estimate of elite income and its purchasing power demonstrates

[1] Moeller (1976).

that it would be enough to keep the economy of Italian towns fully occupied. The coincidence between the number of people that could be fed on estimated elite consumer spending and the actual number of urban residents in Italy is remarkable. Conversely - assuming an agricultural origin for elite income - the number of people necessary in agriculture to produce this income amounts to nearly the entire rural population of Italy. Although this model - deliberately and perhaps unjustifiably- ignores the additional income from imperialism, it still is a novel corroboration of the 'consumer city' thesis and its emphasis on the social relations between town and country.

The second half of the chapter then returns to the question of the nature of Roman economic development and its potential for further growth. I conclude that the economic specialization between town and country was of only limited importance. Urbanism in itself was not enough for commercialization. The Pompeian economy is a good example of a traditional economy driven very hard. Treading water at this level could provide many impressive examples of urbanism and sophistication, even if the benefits accrued mostly to a small elite. It was a situation, however, in which the road to further growth was blocked precisely by the mechanisms which had allowed it to get where it got.

If, so far, the emphasis has been on the economic aspects of Pompeian society, it will be different in the last two chapters. At various points I have argued (and will do so at greater length in the chapters which are to follow) that social inequality and subordination are important if we want to understand the nature of ancient economic performance. The argument about the relative scarcity of factors of production should be reflected in an inequality between people: some only have their labour to offer, and should, therefore, not expect a high standard of living (given low labour productivity). The really scarce factor was land. Therefore, ownership of land marks the 'haves' from the 'have nots'. I suggest that nearly all Pompeian land was probably controlled by the elite. That, unfortunately, is about as far as we can take speculation about rural social relations in Pompeii. The urban evidence (which fortunately also refers to rural Pompeii at times) allows far more possibilities. The central question which will concern us is whether or not a social group with some of the characteristics of a bourgeoisie emerged. Did social mobility change the nature of the elite, or was it only renewal without structural change? The second question concerns the ideological cohesion of society. Was the elite able to impose acceptance of prevailing inequality, and how could that be so? We shall, in other words, be concerned not only with social structure as a reflection of economic inequalities, but also with the social potential for structural transformation of economic relations.

The dimensions of social inequality take the central stage in *chapter six*. Using L. Caecilius Iucundus' famed archive of writing tablets, I reconstruct a hierarchy of prestige positions which is, I suggest, representative of Pompeian society. I then investigate the basis of prestige. I argue that even if wealth is a necessary condition for prestige, it is demonstrably not sufficient. Traditional requirements such as free birth and office-holding must be fulfilled before wealth can be transformed into prestige. Getting rich quickly (as may be possible in trade) is not enough. Anticipatory socialization towards elite values and modes of behaviour (such as landownership) is necessary-as is patience. Social risers (such as wealthy freedmen) have to transform themselves in order to be accepted. Social mobility does not transform social structure, but only renews the elite. No bourgeoisie could emerge.

Chapter seven then takes these problems into the area of power and obligation. The wealth of Pompeian electoral propaganda has suggested to some that political participation was substantial, and could lead to a transformation of the political elite and its behaviour. I shall argue, however, that Pompeii was not a bourgeois democracy. The language of the electoral propaganda suggests relations of patronage rather than opposition between social groups. How was the elite able to control the votes of the mass of the population at elections? I shall argue that voting procedure suggests that voting was governed by localized patronage networks. The landowning elite's ability to control was strong, and the electorate obliged. But how about social risers: could they obtain election? And more particularly, could social mobility seriously alter the values and behaviour of the elite so as to make it more amenable to the sort of economically innovative behaviour characteristic of the later bourgeoisie? I shall argue not. The elite's power of control over aspiring candidates was strong, and support was conditional upon socialization. The need to conform was strong, and social mobility could, therefore, not be a challenge for transformation. The elite was renewed rather than transformed by the incorporation of newcomers.

PART ONE

ECONOMY

CHAPTER TWO

INTRODUCING THE PROBLEM

Population: the mouths to feed

In order to assess the performance of the Roman economy, we should first obtain a rough idea of the task that the ancients had to face. The anti-modernizing broom which has swept clean the study of the ancient economy in recent years has done a lot of good. That the ancients were not very modern in solving their economic problems should however not lead us to belittle the task which stood before them, a task which we can summarize as that of feeding an inordinately large population. I write feeding, because food represented by far the largest proportion of production and consumption. For antiquity, proper figures are largely lacking, but it has been estimated that in fifteenth to eighteenth century Europe, food represented close to 80% of the private expenditure of the mass of the population.[1] On the supply side agriculture enjoys a similar prominence. Around 1750 some 75% of the total labour force was employed in agriculture in France, Sweden or the Republic of Venice, while in England this proportion was still about 65%. To quote Cipolla: 'On this basis it does not seem absurd to maintain that in the centuries preceding 1700, in every European society, the percentage of the population actively employed in agriculture varied, as a rule, between 65 and 90 percent, reaching minima

[1]Cipolla (1981) table 1-7, p. 30. Compare table 1-8, on p. 35, to see the impact of income inequality.

of 55 to 65 percent only in exceptional cases. The reason for this concentration lay in the low productivity of agriculture.'[1] And even in cities large sections of the population were engaged in agriculture and the distribution of food.[2] For the ancient world we have Hopkins' estimate that 32% of the Italian population in 28 B.C. would be in urban occupations, 'very high for a pre-industrial state'.[3] Excluding Rome the urban figure reaches down to almost 20%. Providing subsistence for large numbers of people was the core problem of the ancient economy.

For an assessment of aggregate demand it is not enough to know that much of this demand would be for food. To assess the scope of the problem we also need some idea of the size of the population of Roman Italy and of its distribution. To place this in a proper context we shall subsequently make comparisons with population figures for early-modern Italy and other countries. We shall see that early-imperial Italy had a very high population density: the task of feeding these people was gigantic. Subsequently I shall turn to the supply side of the problem: how was all this produced?

Present-day consensus on the population of Roman Italy is all derived from Beloch's contention that known Roman census figures are a reliable guide to a reconstruction of the total population.[4] Much higher estimates than Beloch's all assume that the census is only a very partial registration. Quarreling over the sources is pointless here: the higher estimates are simply implausible in the light of Italy's later population history.

Beloch estimates the population of Roman Italy - including Cisalpine Gaul - at the end of the first century B.C. at 3.5 million free persons and perhaps 2 million slaves; slaves who had to be fed, but who also constituted a considerable part of

[1] Cipolla (1981) table 2-6, p. 75.

[2] For the six, mainly Italian, cities mentioned in Cipolla (1981) table 2-7, p. 77, on average more than a fifth.

[3] Hopkins (1978a) 69h. It should be pointed out that his urban/rural split indicates the kind of job, not the location. Comparative early modern data on urbanization in de Vries (1984) 38 f, 71 ff. and Cipolla (1981) 75. The ancient figures suggest a higher level of urbanization than in early modern Europe.

[4] Beloch (1886).

the work-force.[1] Brunt accepts Beloch's basic reasoning but decides that some under-registration of the free population must have taken place, and therefore increases this figure to 4.5 million.[2] The number of slaves remains problematic, Brunt decides to choose 3 million instead of Beloch's 2 million.[3] Latest arrival on the scene is Hopkins, who opts for a free population of 4 million, that is between the two best available guesses, and a slave population of 2 million, following Beloch.[4]

If we turn Hopkins' figures into figures for population density we obtain a figure of 24 per sq. km.[5] This includes the arguably very exceptional concentration of perhaps almost 1 million inhabitants in the capital.[6] Excluding Rome, population density was 20 persons per sq. km. If we accept Beloch's guess that at the time not more than 40% of Italian land was used for agriculture - not unlikely as it was still only 55% in Beloch's own time - then this allowed almost 2.5 hectares per person on the land.[7]

In Beloch's view the population of Italy rises in the relatively peaceful first century A.D. to perhaps 7 million in the middle of that century as compared to his estimate of 5.5 million in 28 B.C.[8] Adding the same increase to Hopkins' and Brunt's late Republican figures, we obtain 7.5 million and 9 million inhabitants for early Imperial Italy.

Exact data on the distribution of the population within Roman Italy are lacking. Some systematic approximation can be obtained from the density of urbanization and the amount of

[1]Beloch (1886), 436. Excluding Sicily: 0.6 million inhabitants on 26000 sq. kms.

[2]Brunt (1971) 124.

[3]Brunt (1971) 124.

[4]Hopkins (1978a) 7 n.13, 8 n.14, 68(f).

[5]Land-surface of Italy at the time: 250,000 sq.kms, see Beloch (1886) 390.

[6]For the population of Rome, see now Hopkins (1978) 96 ff.

[7]Land surface: 250,000 sq. km. At 40% agricultural use we have 100,000 sq. km. agricultural land. Rural population estimated at 80% of Hopkins' 5 million outside Rome. Therefore, 4 million rustics use 100,000 sq. km. of land, leaving them about 2.5 hectares per head. Hopkins (1978a) 7 n.13; Beloch (1886) 417, 439; Brunt (1971) 126.

[8]Still excluding Sicily. Beloch (1886) 437.

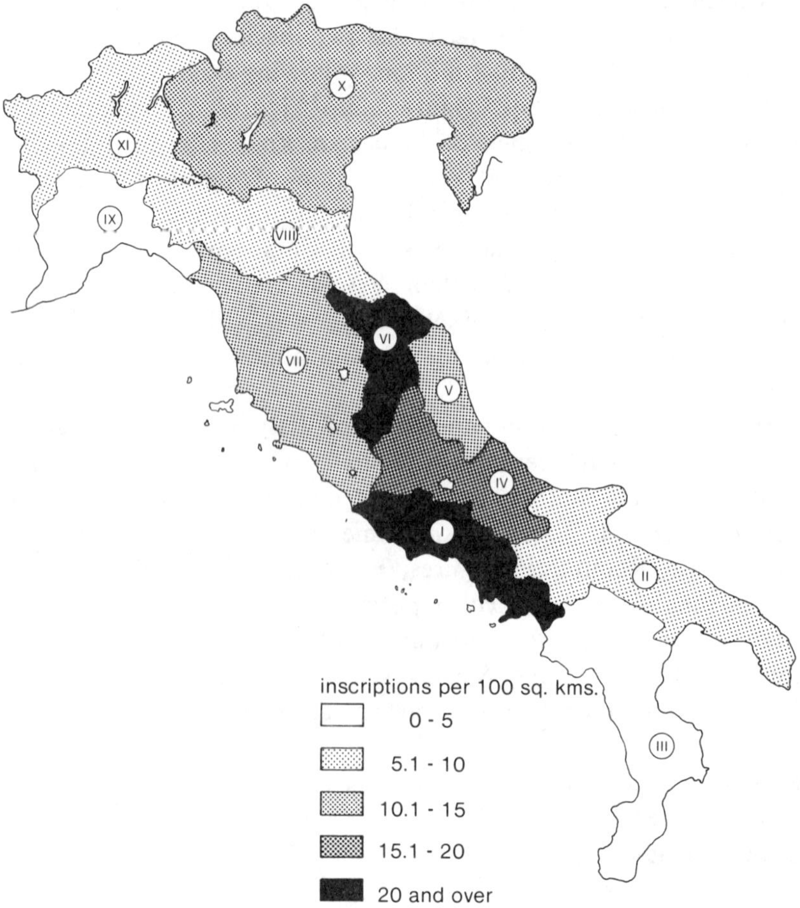

Figure I: Epigraphic density

source: Duncan-Jones (1982) 337 ff; Thomsen (1947)

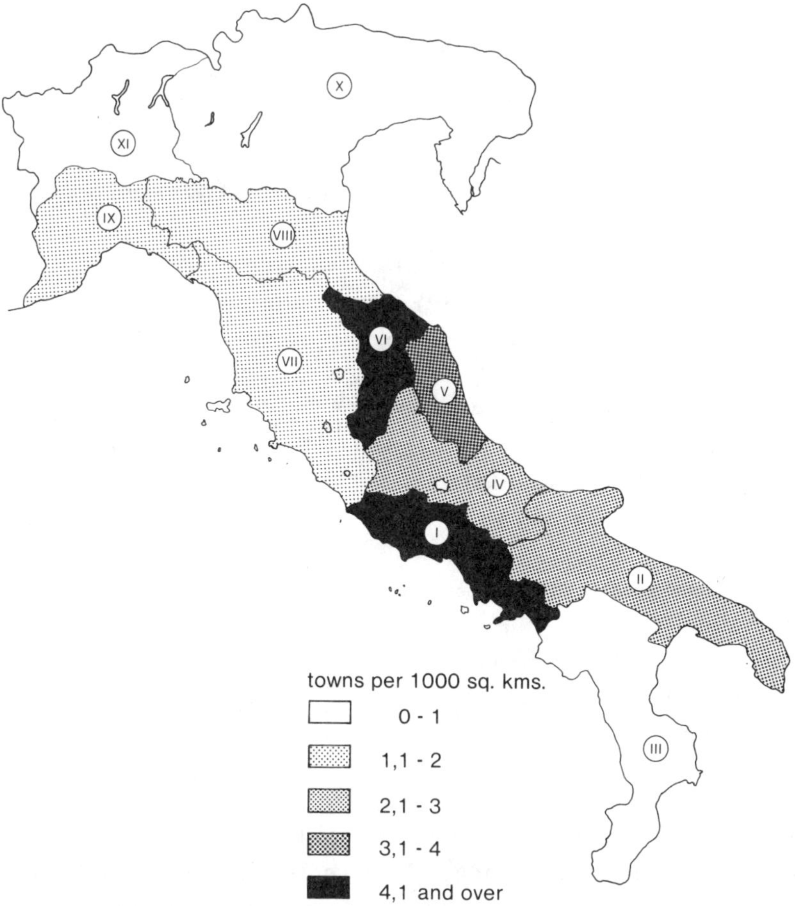

Figure II: Density of towns

source: Duncan-Jones (1982) 337 ff; Thomsen (1947)

surviving inscriptions for the different regions of Italy (Table I; Figures I and II).

Table I: Urbanization and epigraphic density
Source: Duncan-Jones (1982) 337 ff.[1]

Regio		Inscriptions per 100 sq.kms.	Towns per 1000 sq.kms.
I	(Latium, Campania, Picenti district)	55.0	5.5
II	(Apulia, Calabria, Hirpini district)	10.0	3.0
III	(Lucania, Ager Bruttius)	2.0	0.9
IV	(Region inhabited by Samnites, Frentani, Marrucini, Marsi, Paeligni, Aequiculi, Vestini, Sabini)	16.1	2.4
V	(Picenum, Praetuttii district)	14.6	3.5
VI	(Umbria, Ager Gallicus)	28.3	4.9
VII	(Etruria)	14.9	1.6
VIII	(Gallia Cispadana)	7.8	1.3
IX	(Liguria)	3.6	1.2
X	(Venetia, Istria, Cenomani district)	11.5	0.5
XI	(Gallia Transpadana)	6.7	0.4

The preponderance of central Italy is obvious. The four regions I, IV, V and VI are among the five regions with the highest epigraphical density and among the five with the highest density of towns. Latium and Campania are top of the league. Beloch estimated that in 220 B.C. Campania had a population of 140,000 (and thus a density of 140 per sq. km.).[2] He estimated that around the same time Latium, Campania and the Apennine areas

[1]Rome and Ostia have been excluded from these figures. Also graffiti and the like have been excluded. For the regions of Italy: Thomsen (1947).

[2]Beloch (1886) 420.

between Ariminum and Venusia had a *free* population of 1.75 million on 60,000 sq. kms. (density 29 per sq. km.).[1] Lower densities were estimated by him for regions II and III: 11-13 free inhabitants per sq. km.[2] Augustan figures for Sicily are 600,000 inhabitants (including slaves) on 26,000 sq. kms, resulting in a density of 23 per sq. km.[3] The northern regions VIII, IX, X and XI were but thinly populated. By Augustus' time their total population had risen to at most 1.5 million on an area of 116,400 sq. kms, or at most 13 per sq. km.[4]

Obviously this is only a mixed bag of observations, but the pattern seems reasonably clear, and runs parallel to the distribution figures for towns and inscriptions, though these latter two series appear to show the demographic differences in an exaggerated form. It may perhaps be added that the figure for central Italy does not, as a result of its early date, take sufficient account of the later importance of the capital.

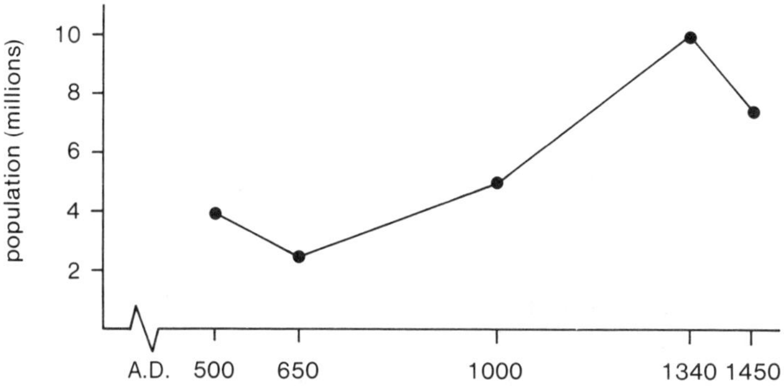

Figure III: Italian population (A.D. 500-1450) Russell (1972) 36

To put these figures into a meaningful historical and geographical perspective is not so easy. For a very long time after the

[1]Beloch (1886) 426.

[2]Hannibalic age. 50-600,000 free; surface 45,000 sq. km. Beloch (1886) 426. Beloch, p. 391, disagrees with the higher surface figure as used by Nissen (1883-1902) II p. 3 and Duncan-Jones (1982) 339.

[3]Beloch (1886) 301, 262.

[4]Beloch (1886) 436, 391.

early Principate the data leave a lot more to be desired. Very tentative estimates by Russell for the Italian population are shown in Figure III.

Around 1500 Beloch estimates a total of 10 million, or perhaps more.[1] For the period thereafter, based on fairly precise data, he gives the figures in Table II.

Table II: The early modern population of Italy
Source: Beloch (1937-61) III 352.

	1550	1600	1650
N.Italy	4,746,000	5,412,000	4,255,000
peninsula	5,592,000	6,235,000	5,588,000
islands	1,253,000	1,625,000	1,701,000
total	11,591,000	13,272,000	11,543,000

It should be observed that, compared to the Roman era, total population is higher.[2] The big increase has been in the north, an increase which is responsible for nearly all differences with antiquity.[3] The densest part of Italy around 1600 was the Lombard plain. Densities around 100 persons per sq. km. were not unknown here.[4] The area had not been particularly densely populated in antiquity. In the south the area around Naples still stands out, but less markedly. The Terra di Lavoro had an average density - excluding the city of Naples - of 54 per sq. km. around 1600, with peaks of 160 per sq. km. in the plains

[1] Beloch (1937-61) III 349.

[2] The difference depends of course on the set of Roman estimates that we choose. Brunt's early Empire estimate would be quite close: 9-10 million (including Sicily).

[3] Pounds (1973) 277 for agricultural expansion in northern Italy from about 1100.

[4] Beloch (1937-61) III 378 ff.

around Vesuvius.[1] To the extent that the early modern Italian population is larger than that of antiquity, this is not the result of further large increases in high density areas, but of the spread of the high density pattern into northern Italy.

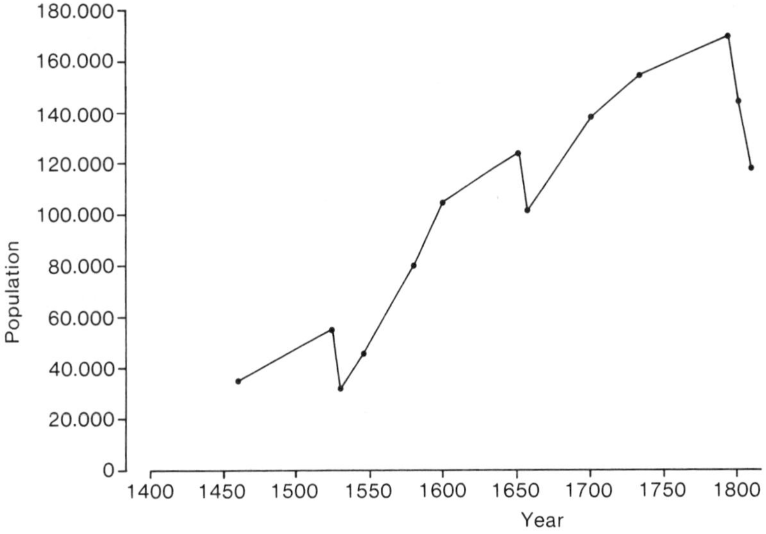

Figure IV: The population of the city of Rome
(source: Beloch (1937-61) III 21)

Markedly different from ancient times is the size of the city of Rome. Various estimates put it close to the one million mark in the early Empire, and even for the fourth century a similar figure has been proposed.[2] For the period thereafter Hodges and Whitehouse write: 'It is not unreasonable, therefore, to guess that the population of Rome was 400,000 ±25 percent in 452. In 523-7, Cassiodorus implied that it was considerably smaller, and between the sixth and the ninth centuries the

[1]Beloch (1937-61) III 378 ff; Beloch (1937-61) I 235.
[2]Mazzarino (1951) 230-8.

population was whittled down to a few tens of thousands.'[1] After Rome's decline it takes until 1601 to surpass the 100,000 (Figure IV).[2]

To understand this, we should realize that the medieval and early modern European economy has never in any country been able to support a metropolis like Imperial Rome.[3] For a comparative historical perspective on the size of cities, we may reproduce here some of the recent estimates of the American economic historian Jan de Vries (Table III).

Table III: A comparison with later European times
(source: de Vries (1984) 70)

population size	c.1300	c.1500	c.1700
1 million and over	-	-	-
100,000-999,000	4	4	11
40,000- 99,000	15	14	32
20,000- 39,000	33	37	64
10,000- 19,000	73	99	117

The changes in Rome's population figures are intimately bound up with its political vicissitudes. The exceptionally high figures are only comprehensible by reference to Roman state power.[4]

A different perspective is offered by a geographical comparison. Beloch estimates that on the death of Augustus Italy

[1]Hodges and Whitehouse (1983) 51.

[2]Beloch (1937-61) II 21. For sixteenth century Rome: Delumeau (1957-59).

[3]Paris reaches 500,000 inhabitants around 1700, London 600,000 at about the same time. For these and other figures, see Cipolla (1981) Table A-1, p. 302 ff. For London see also Wrigley (1978a).

[4]Jongman and Dekker (1988) elaborates on this from a comparative perspective.

(excluding the islands) had a density of 24 persons per sq. km.[1] He thinks that Gallia Narbonensis had a population density of 15 persons per sq. km. at that time, Spain had 10 per sq. km, Tres Galliae 6.3 per sq. km, and the Danube area 4.7 per sq. km.

For the sixth century A.D. some admittedly hazardous population density estimates have been made, suggesting densities of 5.5 per sq. km. in Gaul, 2 per sq. km. in England and 2.2 per sq. km. in Germany.[2] And on the eve of the Black Death these northern countries have still not yet overtaken Italy, although they have shown marked increases. France had perhaps a density of 32 persons per sq. km, England of 29, and Germany had possibly around 16 persons to the sq. km.[3]

A comparison of high population densities around 1600 would give the following figures: Italy 44 per sq. km, Low Countries 40, France 34, Germany 28, Iberian peninsula 17, Poland and Prussia 14. China around that time had a density of hardly above 20.[4]

However dubious some of the data presented above may be, the general picture that emerges is clear enough. Demographically late Republican and early Imperial Italy were something special, and would remain so for a long time.[5] Similar population densities from later times also tend to come from Italy, and other lands along the northern shores of the Mediterranean, accompanied by a similarly high degree of urbanization.

Yet, it would be unjustified to see the later medieval rise in the Italian population as just a revival of the ancient world. The distribution pattern has changed fundamentally. In the first place the enormous size of the city of Rome is of course specific to antiquity. But secondly, the medieval and renaissance

[1]Beloch (1886) 507.

[2]Duby (1973) 21.

[3]Russell (1958) 119, 118, 112.

[4]Braudel (1979) I 39 ff.

[5]It should be pointed out that what has been portrayed here as specifically Italian, also applies, though to a somewhat lesser extent, to the other areas along the northern shores of the Mediterranean. For figures see Russell (1972) 36, 39.

growth is most marked in northern Italy, an area that was but thinly populated in antiquity.

What we should retain for our discussions is that the task of feeding these people was historically enormous, and roughly on a par with the situation in many early modern countries - in some cases even larger. How did the Romans cope? The large population made labour abundant; was it also responsible for a low standard of living for the mass of the population? The very high population density of Campania makes the region an attractive place to find out.

Production: agricultural

Production does not happen from nothing; it needs labour, capital and natural resources (or 'land', as economists say). In combination these 'factors of production' enable the entrepreneur to produce his goods or services. He must decide on the best (that is, cheapest) combination of factors to produce what he wants. To express the relation between input of factors and output, economists use the concept of the 'production function'.[1] A very simple production function may state how much labour, capital and land are necessary to produce a given quantity of a specific crop, and that, if a farmer wants to double the production of that crop, he needs to double the input of labour, capital and land. Often enough, however, it is not feasible to increase the input of all factors to the same extent. What happens if no extra land is available? The production function may, in that case, suggest that three times more labour and capital are necessary to double production.

Production may contract or expand because the input of one or more factors has altered. In the real world the supply of at least one of the factors is usually more or less fixed. Contraction and expansion, therefore, usually involve changes in the proportion between the factors. If, in an agricultural community, the population has doubled over a period, this will not be so for the land: each peasant only has half the amount of land a peasant used to have. Two things follow from this: (1) total

[1]Stonier and Hague (1972) 'passim'.

production in this community will have increased (the work-force has doubled), (2) production per head of the population will be lower (each peasant now only has half the land he used to have). The production function specifies by how much total production increases, and by how much production per head decreases. On a large scale, the medieval and early modern history of Europe provides ample illustration of this: periods of population growth saw a decline in wages, whereas periods of demographic contraction witnessed rising wages.[1] It is important, however, to distinguish these opposite oscillations in total output and output per head from proper growth, where both total output and output per head obtain a higher level.[2]

Inevitably, the data are lacking for a detailed reconstruction of Roman production functions, and for an accurate measurement of the relative scarcity of factors of production. All I can hope to do is give an impressionistic sketch of the contours of such a production function, and hazard some hypotheses about the relative scarcity of factors, about the possibilities of more capital-intensive production, or the possibilities of innovation (through specialization).[3] Did the high population densities coincide with labour-intensive production and a low standard of living for the mass of the population, or is the high population density a sign of heavy demand for labour and rising prosperity?

Much has been written on Roman agriculture, and I cannot hope to add significantly to existing knowledge.[4] I only want to make two related points here. The first concerns the staple diet of the mass of the population. This consisted to a large extent of cereals, and I shall argue that that is no coincidence, but is appropriate to the prevailing level of population density.

[1]Below, p. 151 f.

[2]Either because much more of a third factor - capital - is used, or because innovation changes the relation between input and output.

[3]These issues are inevitably tightly interwoven with social structure. In part they are a result of social inequality, in part they generate inequality.

[4]White (1970a) is the best survey; sometimes it is unfortunately too apologistic, and should be read in conjunction with Brunt (1972). White (1970b) provides extensive bibliography. Delano Smith (1979) is an interesting contribution by a geographer.

The second point concerns the kind of agricultural technology that was typically used in Roman Italy. I shall argue that the dominant system (dry-farming in a two field system) is not only consistent with levels of population density, but - more importantly - that it is a technique which clearly differentiates Mediterranean Europe from northern Europe. I shall later argue that this is important for the possibilities for (and the limits to) growth in agriculture.

The ancient evidence on the composition of the diet is not abundant. But it is unlikely that cereals would not have provided the largest part. Modern data from Greece show that they still form a substantial part of the diet.[1] The conclusion of thc recent study by Foxhall and Forbes is that the proportion was even higher in ancient times: 70-75%.[2] This is plausible because the cost of food must have been a large part of the budget of the poor.[3] And cereals are relatively cheap. 'The lower the income, the higher will be the percentage spent on "poor" items such as bread and other starchy foods.'[4] Meat may be more tasty, but its production is biologically very inefficient: it involves an extra conversion of plant material into animal meat - with considerable calorific losses. Of course, the elite would eat far more meat, but the aggregate size of elite food consumption was small: only few Romans were rich. The importance of cereals is reflected in their prominence in distributions of food to the populace of ancient cities. And famine is invariably depicted as a shortage of cereals.

These cereals were almost entirely of local production. Transport costs were so high that differences in productivity between regions are unlikely to have been larger than transport costs.[5] It has been calculated that in the sixteenth century traded grain represented about one percent of Mediterranean

[1]Foxhall and Forbes (1982) 65 ff.

[2]Foxhall and Forbes (1982) 68ff.

[3]Below, p. 131 ff., esp. 135 n.6; cf 195 n.2.

[4]Cipolla (1981) 28.

[5]For transport costs, below p. 140 f.

consumption.[1] This may have been somewhat higher in the ancient world. But even there, short-haul transport to the nearest town (for consumption there) forms the largest part of transported food.[2] Medium and long-haul is predominated by the supply of the metropolitan cities of Rome, Alexandria, Antioch and Carthage, and by irregular transport to alleviate famines.[3]

Meat formed probably only a small proportion of the diet of most people, if they could afford it at all. The most important type of meat was pork, perhaps not so surprising, because the big advantage of pigs is that they can feed on leftovers or make use of wasteland.[4] They did not, therefore, compete for valuable agricultural land. Small amounts of vegetables - esp. pulses - were also eaten.[5] They could supply a valuable amount of proteins and had the additional advantage of fixing nitrogen to the soil.[6] Other important items were olive oil and wine. Olive oil was expensive: two to three times more per calorie than wheat.[7] Cato gave his farm labourers just over half a litre per month, about 5% of their calorific intake.[8] This is obviously not representative of the entire social spectrum, but serves to illustrate that it was an expensive commodity. Using olive oil to light one's room must have been beyond the means of many poor Romans. Wine probably provided a somewhat

[1]Bairoch (1973) 476.

[2]Not, of course, of transport costs. Each ton transported over a long distance incurred far larger transport costs. Long and medium haul transport, therefore, formed a large proportion of transport activity. In Hopkins (1983b) 93 short-haul represents 70%, medium-haul 19%, and long-haul 11% of tons transported. If- and this is no more than a calculation example - medium haul is five times more expensive than short-haul, and long-haul is ten times more expensive, distribution of transport costs is as follows: short-haul 26%, medium-haul 35%, and long-haul 39%.

[3]Hopkins (1983b) 93; Garnsey (1983a), Garnsey(1983b) and Rickman (1980) are recent accounts of Rome's grain supply; See also: Jongman and Dekker (1988). Pleket (1985) criticizes some of Hopkins' estimates.

[4]White (1970a) 316 ff; Delano Smith (1979) 219 ff.

[5]Frayn (1979) 57 ff. for wild plants. Wild (1970a) 189 ff. for legumes.

[6]White (1970a) 190 f.

[7]Calculated from the Pompeian prices tabulated in Étienne (1977) 209 and calorific contributions as quoted in Foxhall and Forbes (1982) 90.

[8]Cato, 'de Agr.' 58.

larger proportion of the diet. Cato's rations provide 350-500 calories per day, or some 10-15% of daily needs.[1]

The medieval historian Georges Duby is explicit when he contrasts Roman and Germanic eating habits.[2] In the Roman model, the other food only accompanies the bread, is called 'companagium'. Meat and dairy products form only a small part of the diet, and the drink is wine. The Germanic people on the other hand would eat far more meat, dairy products, garden vegetables, fish and gathered fruit. And of course they would drink beer instead of wine. The production requirements for these two different types of diet are substantially different. The 'Germanic pattern' needs a lot more space for the production of a given number of calories than the Roman pattern. The Germanic diet is more varied, contains more proteins, and - as it uses a broader spectrum of production possibilities - is inherently more stable and resistant to famine danger. But the drawback is that it would not support the numbers that had to be fed in Roman Italy.

This brings us to techniques of agricultural production. Comparative evidence suggests that at the prevailing population densities in Roman Italy we should expect a system of short-fallow.[3] This squares well with received opinion. Considerable attention has of course been given to possible exceptions, especially of the more intensive kind.[4] And it is now also being argued that we should allow for much more variation.[5] That may be true - indeed I shall argue that Campania was one of these exceptions.[6] But it still leaves us with the question what

[1]Cato, 'de Agr.' 56-58, see also below, p. 131 ff; Foxhall and Forbes (1982) 58 for calorie content of wine.

[2]Duby (1973) 26 ff.

[3]Boserup (1981) 19 f.

[4]White (1970a) 110 ff. provides a survey, to be read with Brunt (1972). White is perhaps too generous as to crop rotation, and too easily slips from knowledge and existence of a technique to prevalence.

[5]Garnsey (1985) 66 shows a justified skepticism as to the assumption that half of Attica's cereal land would be fallow at any one time. Halstead (1987) is the most explicit statement of this view so far. I should like to thank Paul Halstead for showing it to me before publication.

[6]Below, p. 100 ff; 147 ff.

was most typical. The traditional view is that this is the two field dry farming system with fallowing in alternate years. One of the virtues of this view is that it provides plausible results if we calculate its consequences. We can estimate the number of people in Italy that could be fed under this system. For the traditional view to be plausible, this estimate should be roughly equal to the independent estimates for the Italian population under the early Empire. This is indeed the case: both figures are around 8 million.[1] Such calculations are very rough, and we run the risk of only putting numbers to our prejudices. They constitute no facts, but they are comforting.

Of all the cereals known, only two were of importance in the ancient world: wheat and barley.[2] Of these, barley was in some ways the more suitable for Mediterranean conditions, and is receiving increasing attention. It needed less rainfall than wheat (an important advantage in many parts of the Mediterranean), and it was less demanding as to soil fertility.[3] Production per hectare would be larger than that of wheat, but this seems mostly to have been offset by a larger proportion of inedible material.[4] This makes barley into the self-sufficient peasant's preferred crop. It is less sensitive to the devastating effect of that crucial variable in Mediterranean agriculture: drought.[5] That it is heavier and bulkier to transport, makes little difference to the peasant. This difference between wheat and barley equally makes wheat into the preferred crop when famines can only be alleviated by long-distance transport.[6]

[1]Assumptions: 100,000 sq. km. agricultural land, i.e. 40% of Italian land surface - above, p. 67 - of which 80% used for cereals, with half the land in fallow. A net production per ha. of 400 kg. wheat equivalent, and a cereal need of 200 kg. wheat equivalent per person. The outcome of the sum is 8 million. For justification of the assumptions, below p. 135 f. For population, above p. 65 ff.

[2]For this survey I rely on Rickman (1980) 3 ff. Spurr (1983) adds millet. Its main virtue is that it is spring sown, and can therefore be sown after a harvest failure. It has a high yield ratio, thus necessitating only a small stock of emergency seed, which also keeps better than that of other cereals.

[3]Garnsey (1985) esp. 66.

[4]Foxhall and Forbes (1982) 42 ff. for calorie content.

[5]For an excellent survey of climate and its relation to vegetation in the Mediterranean: Le Houerou (1977) 214-233.

[6]Nice examples in Rathbone (1983).

Apart from such logic from the dismal science, another important factor comes into play. Cereals need to be prepared into food for consumption. Either in the form of porridge, or in the form of - preferably leavened - bread. By the time of the late Republic bread had become the preferred form of food, and was consumed by large portions of the population. Barley is unsuitable for this, and so are the hulled varieties of wheat. Bread required a high gluten content, and wheats that could easily be freed from the husk. *Triticum durum* and *triticum turgidum*, both from the Emmer group of wheats, gained prominence for this reason. A variety of the Spelt group however - *triticum vulgare* - came to be the most favoured wheat; it alone made the fine white bread that was the real favourite. In Imperial times this had become the predominant autumn-sown crop in areas such as Etruria and Campania.[1] That this cultural preference for bread could be honoured is no doubt a measure of rising prosperity. It is less certain that it should be seen as a genuine improvement of productive performance. One might after all say that Romans could only indulge in their preference for (fine) bread once they had assured for themselves that they could squeeze subject people when the need arose.

The overriding problem of cereal agriculture in Mediterranean lands is lack of water, especially in the precarious periods in the autumn, just after sowing, and in the spring, just before harvesting. The seasonal shifts from dry to humid and back may be fairly predictable, but not quite, and even in an average year no water could be wasted.[2] Thus, one of the functions of fallowing was to conserve in the soil the humidity of two years of rainfall for the crop of one year. Therefore no heavy ploughing (such as was later practised in northern Europe) was feasible.[3] That might have improved fertility, but it would have opened up the soil too much, exposing it to wind and sunshine, and thus wasting valuable water. Therefore, the soil is worked only lightly, and not more than surface deep. On the fallow land

[1]Still following Rickman (1980) 3 ff. in these matters.

[2]White (1970a) 173.

[3]For heavy ploughing in the north: Pounds (1974) 194 ff.

weeds are prevented from seeding; they should not be allowed to diminish the humidity of the soil.[1]

Low levels of rainfall not only endangered the growth of cereals, but were also at the root of that other problem of mediterranean agriculture: a shortage of working animals. The summer drought scorched lowland pasture - if that was available at all. Sheep and goats would, therefore, spend that period on the lusher mountain pastures. In northern Italy this was also possible in the case of horses and cattle, but not so in the South.[2] The natural pasture for a plough team was often not available.

Fodder crops, of course, provide alternative means to feed working animals.[3] A range of such crops are available, but with serious limitations. The problem is that they compete with man for scarce agricultural land.[4] This may not be a problem for the aristocratic land owner who need not entertain any worries about feeding his family. The discussion - for a well-heeled public - of fodder crops in the agricultural writers of antiquity should be seen in this context. But even there the competing claims of human consumption are apparent.[5] No wonder oxen remained prized possessions. 'Nothing illustrates more forcibly the limitations imposed by nature on the Italian cattle farmer than the list of foods given by the authorities as suitable or possible when normal supplies ran out.'[6] In book VI, Columella begins his discussion of farm animals with the ox, the most important of farm animals, 'to be ranked above all other cattle', and 'man's most hard-working associate in agriculture' (Columella *R.R.* VI preface 7).[7] In the eighteenth century, in the Kingdom of Naples, the cost per day of a pair of oxen was

[1] White (1970a) 113; Slicher van Bath (1960) 67 ff.

[2] White (1970a) 200. The ecology of the Po valley places it outside what I here call 'Mediterranean agriculture'.

[3] White (1970a) 202 f.

[4] Jongman (1988).

[5] White (1970a) 203 f.

[6] White (1970a) 283 f.

[7] With thanks to Professor Hopkins, who pointed this out to me.

about ten times higher than that of a day labourer.[1] Clark and Haswell equally provide interesting documentation to the effect that at low levels of income (and, therefore, low marginal productivity of labour) it would often be cheaper to use human labour than animal power.[2]

The climatological limits to production are serious, and this of course invites a comparison with other areas. The area that I choose is northern France. The first reason is the availability of relatively abundant data for a long period of time. The second reason is that this region was one of the earliest to adopt more productive techniques such as the three-field system.[3] For the Carolingian era we possess a number of calculated yield-ratios.[4] They are not at all impressive, and are typically in the 1:2.5 - 1:3 range, and in some years the yield was smaller than the amount sown. This is lower than what most of us would expect for Roman Italy, even admitting all our ignorance. This same area of northern France would however be involved in substantial expansion a few centuries later.

In the twelfth century we can see the hesitant emergence of the so called three-field system. This normally involved sowing a winter grain in the first year (wheat or rye), a summer grain in the next year (barley or oats), followed by one year of fallowing. This obviously had the advantage of a higher production; it was often the consequence of population pressure. In order to plough more frequently, these summer grains were important, because they provided fodder for horses.[5] The slower oxen had not been so specific in their demands for food. More frequent ploughing has been shown to be closely correlated to increases in yields.[6]

[1]Delille (1977b) 130.

[2]Clark and Haswell (1967) 53 ff, esp.62 ff. Below, p. 85 ff; 147 ff; 199 ff. for discussions of productivity.

[3]Pounds (1973) 277 and Pounds (1974) 190 ff. for the complexities of and variations within the three-field system.

[4]Slicher van Bath (1960) 75 ff; Slicher van Bath (1963a) and Slicher van Bath (1963b) give the fullest account.

[5]Slicher van Bath (1960) 67 ff.

[6]Duby (1973) 217-22.

What we see is that these changes are closely interconnected. Increasing production demands more ploughing, and thus preferably horses. These horses need a summer grain. And this provides an important clue: the summer grain that the horses need could not easily be grown in Italy, owing to the summer heat. And heavy ploughing would have let the soil's humidity evaporate. The benefits were, therefore, less and the costs higher. The three-field system has never penetrated southern Europe, but has remained a feature of temperate Europe only.[1]

Population and production, a theoretical approach

Theoretically, the analysis of the relationship between demographic development and production has a long history. And in some respects we can say that no solution is possible to the questions that are being asked. The problem is that we are employing two variables which are each both cause and effect. Therefore two different approaches are possible: either we consider population development an independent variable (and production as dependent), or we treat the development of production as an independent variable (with demography as the dependent variable). This latter approach is the best known and found good expression in the work of Malthus.[2]

The 'passion between the sexes' is responsible for Malthus' rabbit paradigm of human society. He assumes a very high natural growth rate of the population, held in check by the limited possibilities of increasing production. Malthus would prefer moral restraint to limit the birth rate, but he has little faith in the lower classes. The alternatives of abortion and contraception are sins in the view of this clergyman. If the two methods of reducing the birth rate (morality and sin) fail, it is up to the death rate to act as limiting mechanism. Production possibilities constrain the size of the population, which has a tendency to increase until wages have dropped to subsistence level, thus making it easy for the death rate to act as limiting mechanism.

[1] Slicher van Bath (1960) 68 f.

[2] Malthus (1976).

Malthus is not only pessimistic about the standard of living, but also about the possibilities of increasing agricultural output. He assumes that the best land has been brought under cultivation first; successive increases in agricultural production take the form of bringing more and more 'marginal' land under cultivation. But this new land is less fertile than the existing land: the productivity of the marginal units of land declines.

This Malthusian analysis has been useful for historians trying to explain certain periods of *crises de subsistence*. However, it has its limitations. It does not, for example, offer much help if we try to understand how societies have sometimes managed to maintain a state of equilibrium within the carrying capacity of their land for long periods. Population does not always grow to the limits of production possibilities, but may remain well below that. A second, and for us more important, limitation is that if this analysis may be useful in understanding the constraints on population growth and the concomitant disasters, it is, because it takes production possibilities as given, less adequate to explain the long term trend in human history of successfully coping with increases in population.

In recent years an alternative type of analysis has gained ground, especially among prehistorians and development economists, that proposed by Ester Boserup.[1] She turns the problem upside down by treating demographic development as the independent variable. She describes how, in the course of human history, societies have successfully adapted to population pressure by intensifying their systems of food procurement. Essential in her description is the observation that the frequency of cropping increases with increases in population density. In her analysis there is no room for 'unused' land. Instead, she makes a distinction between crop land and fallow land. For her, fallow land is not unused land, but production land that is temporarily in the part of the production cycle devoted to regeneration of fertility. As the population grows, more land is used as crop land, and consequently alternative means of maintaining soil fertility have to be found; these tend to be labour-intensive. In

[1]First presented in Boserup (1965), later developed in Boserup (1970) and Boserup (1981). Recent discussion in Grigg (1983) 37-43.

addition, shorter fallowing also involves more work to prepare the land for sowing. Slash and burn agriculture requires far less work than removing the grasses and weeds of short-fallow land.

We can therefore summarize her analysis as a description of a process of intensification, accompanied by decreasing marginal returns to the other factors of production, capital and most of all labour. Thus, the course of history is seen as the depressing road from Sahlins' 'original affluent society' to the long hours of the peasant working in the ricefields.[1] Production per hectare can be increased, but only at the expense of a disproportionate rise in the use of the production factor of labour.

For the poor historian it is all very well to encounter such formidable model building, but it might occur to him that he cannot find any faults in either of the two models, at least not *a priori*. And some well-chosen examples may not convince him either: each school seems capable of showing some excellent empirical work to back up its case. We need to establish some rules to find out under what circumstances the outcome of the peasant's or farmer's conscious or unconscious decision-making will more accord with the Malthusian view, and when it will be more like that predicted by Ester Boserup. Common ground for both approaches is the need to cope with a rising population and consequent increases in food prices. Malthus' solution is essentially to use more land, and that of Ester Boserup is to use more of the other factors of production - most of all labour. Rephrased in this fashion it is a classic problem for the economist, for which the Ricardian theory of ground rent is an appropriate analytical tool.[2]

The question he faced - and solved - is a simple one: why does rent exist? Why do farmers have to pay landowners in order to use this gift of nature, and why do they have to pay the sums that they have to pay? Obviously, if there is still unused land available, landlords will not be in a position to

[1]Sahlins (1968).

[2]Ricardo (1951). A very clear modern exposition to which I owe a lot is Stonier and Hague (1972) 309 ff. The reader is asked to consult this work for a more rigorous exposition than is appropriate here.

demand any rent from a farmer. Any such demand would be met by the farmer's departure. The situation changes, however, once all usable land has been brought under cultivation. If, under these circumstances, a farmer wants more land, he will have to entice landlords to make more land available to him rather than to another farmer: he has to pay rent. Even though farmers now compete with each other for land, and have to pay rent, this does not increase the total supply of land. Landlords remain mortals and cannot supply more land, even if they want to.[1] The effect of a rising population is that it will induce farmers - through rising food prices - to increase their production. Ricardo's analysis of rent allows us to follow the logic of the farmer's choice making behaviour.

We may distinguish two principal ways in which the individual farmer can expand his production. The first of these is to use more land. He will continue to do this until the cost of the marginal unit of land equals the marginal revenue from cultivating that last unit of land (the extensive margin). If rents are high he will stop expanding earlier than if rents are low.

But there is also a second way to expand production, because wheat grows not by land alone; it requires the use of other factors of production: capital and above all, labour. Let us ignore capital for the moment and assume that it comes with labour in direct proportion. With these factors too the farmer will expand with more and more doses of labour (plus capital) per hectare until the revenue produced by the marginal dose equals the cost of this last dose (the intensive margin).

Characteristic of both margins is that they are brought about by diminishing marginal revenue productivity.[2] The first dose of labour (or land, or capital) is more productive than the

[1]In the economist's jargon: land is in completely inelastic supply. Formally rent is nowadays defined as the reward for any factor of production, not just land, where price elasticity of supply is zero.

[2]If we relax the assumption of perfect competition in factor markets, equilibrium is possible without diminishing marginal returns.

last.[1] The steeper the decline of marginal revenue productivity, the sooner the extensive or intensive margin is reached.

Obviously adjustment does not take place at only one margin. The farmer has to ensure that the last currency unit spent on land produces as much revenue as the last currency unit spent on labour. This equation does not, however, predict the actual quantity of land or labour. The optimum in one situation can involve actual quantities of factors of production which are radically different from the optimum under other conditions: sometimes it makes more sense to expand by using mostly more labour, sometimes by using more land. Factor proportions are thus dependent on the cost and productivity of factors of production.[2] When the farmer wants to expand, factor proportions will only remain the same if marginal returns to factors diminish at an equal rate. If that is not the case, factor proportions will change. If the marginal returns to land diminish more quickly than those to labour, it is obviously worthwhile to expand by mostly using more labour, and vice versa. This means that the limits to expansion are mostly set by the decline in marginal returns to the factor with the least decline of such returns. If there is little point in expanding by using more land, the limit to expansion is set where it makes no point to use more labour.

The supply of land, necessary for expansion, has, however, a peculiar characteristic: once all land is being used it is completely inelastic. Further demand from farmers intent on increasing production only pushes up the rents; the available quantity of land cannot be increased. On the other hand, if there is still some unused land, no rent can be demanded (not even for the cultivated land). If marginal returns to land diminish over the entire range, it follows that population pressure will first result in expansion at the extensive margin, until all land is being used - but with a low intensity. Further

[1] Clark and Haswell (1967) 92 ff. provide some neat empirical examples of decreasing marginal labour productivity in agriculture.

[2] Population pressure is expressed in these models by a rise in the price of agricultural products: the marginal revenue productivity curves are shifted upwards, inviting expansion of production.

growth is then only possible through intensification.[1] The Malthusian riposte would be to point out that not all land has been created equal. The best land will be used first; subsequent population growth will encourage cultivation of more 'marginal' land, leading to problems of soil exhaustion and famine. But such sudden changeover from total disuse to intensive cultivation of cereals is relatively rare. More normal is that such marginal land would have been used before, but far less intensively. Wooded land for example is excellent for hunting and some gathering, and a few pigs could also be kept.

It would appear that expansion at the extensive margin had ceased to be a very serious option in Roman Italy long before the first century A.D. This must certainly have been the case in Campania. Beloch points out that in his own time 55% of Italian land was under cultivation, as opposed to his estimate of 40% in the late Republic.[2] Large parts of Italy would never have been suitable for cereal agriculture because they were too mountainous. The valleys and plains had already come under cultivation in very early times. The remaining land was to a large extent so much less suitable that we can almost treat it as unproductive.

By the end of the prehistoric period in Central Italy settlement had extended into marginal zones. Detailed research in the Biferno valley in Molise has shown this clearly. From then on we witness a process of intensification.[3] Barker concludes: 'In short, the evidence from the Biferno valley suggests a classic example of the Boserup model of agricultural change: the system of production was maintained as long as possible in the face of increasing land hunger, until finally the population

[1] This transition from extensive to intensive expansion constitutes the attraction of the Boserup model for prehistorians grappling with the transition from hunter-gathering to primitive agriculture. See e.g. Bender (1975) ch. I & II. Clark and Haswell (1967) 112 ff. give interesting examples of the correlation between population density and the level of rents: the higher the population density, the higher rents are. Labour productivity decreases through intensification, but the productivity of the land increases, and as a consequence rents go up as well. Cf. below, p. 147 ff.

[2] Above, p.67; 81.

[3] Barker a.o. (1978); Barker (1981) 211-19.

levels in the valley forced a change to a more productive but also more labour intensive system of agriculture!'[1] That intensification was the norm can also be derived from the predominance of short fallow systems with fallowing in alternate years.[2] Discussion should focus on the ways in which the problems of intensification were coped with.

Intensification and urbanism

Even though the previous pages have demonstrated the possibilities of increasing production per hectare, the story was not a very cheerful one. The price that had to be paid for such increases of production was that of a decline in marginal labour productivity, a decline that could affect peasants very badly in their standard of living. Of course, they could work longer hours. Comparative research has clearly shown that intensification is accompanied by longer hours. The hunter-gatherers living in the Garden of Eden needed only a few hours a day to procure their food.[3] The peasant had to face a trade-off between his preference for maintaining his subsistence income and his preference for leisure. The extent to which extra labour could be profitably used would have varied a lot. In many agricultural systems the range is only small between the minimum amount of work that is needed, and the maximum that is sensible. Extra labour input usually requires transition to an altogether different and more intensive system. The transition from the two-field to the three-field system was one such. The contemporary persistence of two-field dry-farming in southern Europe shows that such transition is ecologically not always possible.

And yet we know that the history of European agriculture has known periods and areas with growth of both production and productivity. When this is so, it is almost invariably in the

[1] Barker (1981) 214.

[2] White (1970a) ch. IV argues for even more intensive agriculture with annual and even multicropping in certain areas. His evidence is slight and his conclusions are too optimistic, but serves to indicate that the system postulated here for most of Italy is probably not an exaggeration of the intensity of cultivation.

[3] The seminal study is Lee and DeVore (1968); for surveys of the relation between intensification and duration of the average working day: Boserup (1965) 28 ff.

context of a commercialization of agriculture, and closer links with - growing - cities. What I propose here, is to present - in a very schematic way - two alternative responses to this problem of declining labour productivity which was the result of intensification. One remains within the confines of traditional society, the other points the way to growth and things to come. It is a typology developed to understand the success of early modern Dutch agriculture: if you want to know what a loser looks like, you have to know a winner first, and if we want to give marks to the Roman economy for possible 'modernity', we should have a clear and reasonably up to date ideal type of a successful modernization of agriculture.

Analysing the success of Dutch agriculture in the sixteenth and seventeenth century, the American historian Jan de Vries proposes two alternative (ideal types of) responses to the pressures of population growth: the 'peasant model' and the 'specialization model'.[1] His analysis is heavily influenced by the work of Ester Boserup. Like her, he assumes that population is the independent variable. He equally stresses the problems of a declining labour productivity. Where he goes beyond her is in his effort to understand the qualitative transformation that put an end to the trap of diminishing labour productivity. Differential response to trading opportunities is the key to his two ideal types.

In his 'peasant model' de Vries sketches a common response to population pressure. This consists of reductions in the size of peasant holdings. More people have to share the same amount of land as before, and thus plot size decreases. Fathers may have more surviving sons to leave their land to, or outsiders may avail themselves of large tracts, leaving less for the local population. In any case, the population pressure results in a *morcellement* of peasant holdings.[2] This is no fun for the

[1]de Vries (1974) 1 ff.

[2]Herlihy (1958) analyses this 'morcellement' - and efforts to cope with it - for ninth to twelfth century southern Europe. He observes an increasing 'fluidity' in the early stages (sales and exchanges of land increase in order to regain viable plots) followed by a period dominated by purchases by bigger landowners. In other words, population pressure leads to increasing social inequality. He claims that the pattern is characteristic for southern Europe.

peasants. They have to work harder to offset declining labour productivity. And that may not be enough - they might have to do additional work as day labourers to supplement their income. As population increases, the relative price of food is likely to go up. This is no advantage to the peasant: he has less chance than before to have some marketable surplus. Periodically, peasants may even become food buyers. Their declining income forces them to reduce purchases of non-food items. They have to avoid trading opportunities with the towns.

This economic process has substantial social consequences. The misery of the peasants gives good chances to wealthy people, whether noble or bourgeois, or to institutional landowners such as the church, to profit from rising grain prices. They may have kept their holdings intact, or else have bought up land from peasants who were forced to sell out (and perhaps lease back). Substantial increases in social inequality are the inevitable outcome of the 'peasant model'. Rents will have gone up, wages will have come down, and food is more expensive.

The peasant model has consequences for the opportunities for urban growth, too. The rural population's purchasing power for urban produce is only limited. They are no attractive market for an urban industry. At the same time, food supply remains problematic, thus putting severe limits to urban growth. The development of urban crafts is limited to satisfying the demand for consumer goods of the wealthy elite. The town - country relationship is one of inequality. The cities dominate the countryside by extracting rent.

In de Vries' specialization model, peasants do not split up their properties in response to population pressure. Instead, they reallocate their own labour time.[1] They spend less time on non-agricultural activities, and more time to increase agricultural production. In this way they can produce a marketable surplus. The other side of the coin is of course that they will have to buy non-agricultural goods to satisfy their demands. They become participants in a proper market economy.

[1] de Vries (1974) 7 ff; his analysis is derived from Hymer and Resnick (1969).

In the specialization model, the more labour intensive agricultural production cannot avoid the problems of declining labour productivity. But the problem may be less. The peasant is now producing in part for the market, and need therefore not necessarily limit his crop choice to what is suitable for his own subsistence. He may choose a crop with a less steeply declining marginal labour productivity. Dairy farming is such a possibility in the Netherlands, and perhaps wine growing or market gardening was one for the Italian farmer or aristocratic landowner.[1] In the second place, specialization gives more freedom to tailor crop choice to what the land is most suitable for. With a bit of luck the specializing farmer will feel less of the pinch of diminishing labour productivity. There are also possibilities for gains, emanating from the fact that specialized urban production of non-agricultural goods may result in better and/or cheaper products.

Whether this means much depends of course on the specific advantages of urban production. If that is backward too, the difference may not be great. In the second place it depends a lot on the importance of these non-agricultural goods in the farmer's life. A prettier oil lamp may be nice, but that is almost all there is to it. But a high quality iron plough could improve agricultural production. There are no ready-made answers here.

But what happens to the increased population, if peasants do not divide their holdings? The increased demand for urban goods provides a pull away from the land and to the cities. Redundant agricultural labour migrates to the cities, preventing urban wages from rising too steeply.

The relationship between town and country becomes fundamentally different from that under the 'peasant model'. No longer does the opportunity exist for members of the urban elite to get a stifling hold over the countryside. The peasantry remains sufficiently strong to ward off such overtures. Possibilities for investment and enrichment do exist, however: in urban manufacturing. The previous predatory hold over the country is replaced by one of market exchange. And peasants have got

[1] Purcell (1985) describes the possibilities, and the risks.

hold of the right end of the stick: they are sellers of more expensive agricultural goods, and buyers of cheaper manufactures.

No real-life history will conform to such schematic treatment. But that should not be our intention. What this typology should provide is a rough idea of what to look for, and the outlines of the constituent parts of such alternative responses. Much less can this typology predict what will cause a response akin to that of the 'peasant model', and what will cause one akin to the specialization model. Systems of property transfer from one generation to the next can vary widely, and are at present a subject of considerable interest among ancient historians.[1] Ecological constraints may play an important role, just as existing customs on regimes of land tenure. In the following chapters I shall try to do some of the groundwork to establish where in this spectrum of possibilities we should place the Pompeian (and if we may extrapolate, the Roman) economy.

[1]Saller (1984); Corbier (1985a).

CHAPTER THREE

AGRICULTURE

The liquid meal?

In his most recent survey of Pompeian agriculture, Robert Étienne summarizes his and others' views very neatly: 'Qu'il s'agisse dans cette Campanie du Vesuve de proprietés essentiellement viticoles, les sources littéraires et épigraphiques autant qu'archéologiques en permettent l' éclatante démonstration!'[1] A long tradition of scholarship links this wine growing in Pompeii to the large number of villas discovered in its territory.[2] A large number of these villas have been found and have captivated the minds of scholars and other people alike: sources of treasures such as the famous 'Boscoreale treasure' and of beautiful wallpaintings. But, equally, sources of more mundane information such as storage rooms for wine, wine presses and the like.

Already in the nineteenth century Michele Ruggiero heavily relied on the agricultural writers from antiquity for the interpretation of many parts of the villas from Stabiae.[3] Consequently not only was a link provided between the archeology

[1] Étienne (1982) 184. I should like to thank Professor Étienne for providing me with a copy in advance of publication.

[2] E.g. Étienne (1977) esp. 137 ff; Carrington (1931); Day (1932); Skydsgaard (1961) 10 ff. I hope I don't do injustice here: I can't claim perfect command of Danish; Lepore (1950) and Sergejenko (1953) 246 ff. are a bit more skeptical. Of more general works e.g. White (1970a) 418 ff.

[3] Ruggiero (1881) 'passim'.

of the architecture and products grown, but also with the mode of production. If slave chains were not enough, Columella was there to provide the rest of the picture. Day has formulated it thus: 'this information, though slight, where correlated with the comparatively abundant archaeological material unearthed in Pompeii and the immediate environs, suffices to give us a rather clear cut picture of agriculture in the life of this city!'[1]

Employing this methodology of combining literary with archaeological sources, Day has used the storage capacity of one of the Boscoreale villas to calculate the area used for wine growing on this villa. Topping up this figure (58 *iugera* = 14.5 ha.) with land for olive trees, subsistence food and a few other items, he arrives at a total estimate of about 100 *iugera* = 25 ha. 'Incidentally one hundred *iugera* plots for estates, where vineyards are cultivated with other products, are assumed as standard by Cato for the wealthy villa owner.'[2] Whatever may be the truth of these speculations, the sites are certainly neither peasant farmsteads, nor big ranches; and wine and to a lesser extent olive oil, are the cash crops.

No doubt this asserted predominance of a villa agriculture producing cash crops for external markets would historically be quite remarkable. It would be a very early example of what we have called the specialization model of adaptation to population growth.[3] Provided the area is not a very peculiar exception, it would contradict many cherished views of the ancient economy.

In addition it would be surprising if such an economy were without consequences for social structure. Indeed, Day claims that winegrowers are predominant among the elite, and that a

[1]Day (1932) 168.

[2]Day (1932) 180 ff. It should be noted that such calculations are fraught with difficulties. On the one hand, the storage capacity is supposed to refer to one year's production only, and on the other hand Day's productivity per hectare - following Columella - is unbelievably high. For more sane figures, see Rathbone (1981) 12, following Duncan-Jones (1982) 45 and White (1970a) 243, who does not seem to be able to make up his mind, however, on page 244. Not all villas would have been the same of course, although Day is convinced that his reference villa is only slightly above average. The bottom end of the scale would be around 50 'iugera'/12.5 ha, whereas the upper range would be 200-300 'iugera'/50-75 ha. But around half the total number of cases would be in the typical 90-100 'iugera'/22.5-25 ha. range.

[3]Above, p. 91 ff., following de Vries (1974).

large proportion - at least 50% - were freedmen.[1] I shall argue that this is conceptually problematic, and factually wrong.

My main argument against the traditional view of Pompeian agriculture will be that it completely ignores the need to feed a large local population. Campania may have been *Campania felix*, but I doubt whether the liquid meal was as popular as the tradition implies. Surprisingly, none of those who believe in a Pompeii specializing in viticulture seem to even worry about this aspect. Nobody has estimated the total food needs of town or countryside, and indicated possible sources of supply. Equally, it is all very well to say that on the supply side wine is 'important', but surely for such a claim to have any meaning, it requires a demonstration that local supply probably exceeded local consumption of wine to an appreciable extent. I shall argue that this is not the case. Equally, I hope to demonstrate that the alleged high quality of Pompeian wines finds no support in the evidence. This disposes of the other possible basis for export viticulture.

We shall commence with a survey of ancient descriptions of the area, mostly taken from literary sources. Perhaps surprisingly, these literary sources provide a strong antidote against a tradition founded on a naive positivism with regard to archaeology. In the literary accounts cereal agriculture appears predominant. No assessment of Pompeian agriculture is possible without an estimate of population numbers: subsistence requirements per head, multiplied by the number of heads, provide an estimate of minimum local consumption of food. Subsequently the often cited data on villas will be questioned. The sample character of historical and archaeological data will be emphasized, and an argument will be developed that they cannot be treated as a random sample adequately representing Pompeian agriculture in its entirety. The tricky data from *amphorae* will be used in two ways. First as possible evidence of exports from Pompeii. Unfortunately I shall have to argue that our knowledge has not progressed sufficiently to identify *amphorae* accurately as Pompeian. Secondly the epigraphy of *amphorae* (amplified by

[1] Day (1932) 177 ff. and Table E.

other data) will be scrutinized for information on producers and distributors of wine. Here too the conclusion will be skepticism.

The second part of the chapter will abandon the inductive survey of evidence. A tentative reconstruction of aggregate local supply of and demand for food will demonstrate that Pompeian self sufficiency in cereals is possible, but only if we discard the notion of major net exports of wine. But possibility is no proof. My model includes propositions about the spatial distribution of various types of land-use. My reconstruction of the spatial distribution of types of land use will be shown to be consistent with a distribution predicted by location theory. Further validation of a different kind will be provided by a comparison with the area's agriculture in the eighteenth and nineteenth century.

Geography and literary descriptions

Present-day historians have become more aware of the importance of the landscape than some of their predecessors; and also more aware of the historic nature of landscapes.[1] The all-important geological feature of the Pompeian area is of course Mt. Vesuvius: responsible for preserving Pompeii for posterity, but also the cause of some distinct features of the economic geography of the area. Though the ancients believed the volcano to be extinct, it had of course erupted before, and was therefore the source of great fertility of the land. Pompeii itself was built on the southern edge of the lava flow of a prehistoric eruption. From the town to the north (Plate VI), the land is slowly undulating, to rise at the modern village of Boscoreale, and further and further up the slopes of Mt. Vesuvius. To the west, the modern coastline is at a distance of approximately two kilometers; in antiquity Pompeii was much closer to the sea.[2] To the south and east of the town we find the large plain of the river Sarno, closed off at the southern end by the mountain range with Stabiae and Gragnano at its feet, and that

[1] An eye opener for Mediterranean research has been Vita-Finzi (1969).

[2] Immediately next to the Porta Marina some harbour equipment has been found. For a survey of the evidence: Étienne (1977) 156 f.

continues as the Sorrento peninsula. The ancient course of the river Sarno is presumed to have been more northerly than at present, not surprisingly perhaps when we realize that the thickness of the layer of volcanic ash from the eruption of 79 A.D. decreases, the further south we go.

At present the entire territory is densely populated, with tree groves to the north of the ancient city and market gardening in tiny plots in the plain to the south and east (Plates IV, V and VII).[1] I shall later argue that this is of little direct relevance for our understanding of ancient Pompeii's agriculture.[2] Early modern data will show that the modern pattern of exploitation is of no great antiquity.

The ancients could hardly find superlatives enough to describe Campania. The plain of Campania is praised by Strabo for its fertility, 'it is the most blest of all plains, and round about it lie fruitful hills' (Strabo V 4.3), and proof of this is that it produces the finest grain. Strabo also mentions Falernian wine and multicropping:

> It is reported that, in the course of one year, some of the plains are seeded twice with spelt, the third time with millet, and others still the fourth time with vegetables!

Pompeii itself is later referred to as the port for Nola, Nuceria and Acerrae (Plate VII)[3], situated as it is near the river Sarno which takes ingoing and outgoing cargoes (Strabo V 4. 8). Mount Vesuvius is mentioned as, save for its summit, settled with beautiful fields. Strabo assumes that the volcanic activity is responsible for the very fertile soils so suitable to vines. But his reference does not refer to the plain: (*tacha de kai tês eukarpias tês kuklôi tout' aition*, ...) but only to a circular area where these special conditions pertain (mountain and lower slopes).

[1] Houston (1964) 518 ff; Unger (1953).

[2] Below, p. 147 ff.

[3] I find it remarkable that this unique picture was found in precisely such a modest house (I, xiv, 6).

Pliny the Elder (*N.H.* III, 60) refers to both wine and cereals:

> Then comes the favoured country of Campania; in this valley begin those vineclad hills with their glorious wine and wassail, famous all the world over, and (as old writers have said) the scene of the severest competition between Father Liber and Ceres.

Viticulture and cereal agriculture are shown competing for scarce land. A competition in which viticulture appears to have gained the upper hand as regards the hills.

Pliny also has a number of things to say about Pompeian wine in particular. In his discussion of grapes he ranks the Aminaean as the best, the *gemella minor* variety of which is grown on Mount Vesuvius, unfortunately producing a very hard wine: *'asperrimus sapor sed vires praecipuae'* (Pliny *N.H.* XIV 22). Later on, Pompeii is mentioned again as home for a local variety - *Pompeiana* - of the *Murgentina* (Pliny *N.H.* XIV 35). Strength is again a key word in the description.[1] After his discussion of vines he turns to wines, not mentioning Pompeian wines in his four quality classes. Of the 'other' wines, the Pompeian are mentioned (*N.H.* XIV 70):

> As for the wines of Pompeii, their topmost improvement is a matter of ten years, and they gain nothing from age; also they are detected as unwholesome because of a headache which lasts till noon on the following day.

This is immediately followed by the correct and very telling conclusion that 'these instances, if I am not mistaken, go to show that it is the country and the soil that matter, not the grape...'

In his later discussion of cereals, Campania returns (Pliny *N.H.* XVIII 109-114). He describes the Campanian plain - defined in its wider sense, because 40 miles long - as eminent cereal land, attributing this to the supreme soil mechanics, allowing

[1] Pliny 'N.H.' XIV 38 also mentions a 'Pompeian' grape without further comment.

for easy drainage and good water retention in lower layers. Whereas in Strabo and Dionysius of Halicarnassus multicropping is still portrayed as exceptional within Campania[1], Pliny knows of no such caution and ascribes this fertility to the whole of Campania: 'The land is in crop all the year round, being sown once with Italian millet and twice with emmer wheat.'[2] The best part is formed by the Phlegraean fields. Some doubt is due, however, as to Pliny's optimism about crop frequency. We could read almost the same information in Strabo and Dionysius of Halicarnassus, but they both wrote about such multicropping as exceptions.

Columella mentions the *gemella/gemina minor* variety of the Aminean vine again as growing on the renowned slopes of Vesuvius and at Surrentum, yielding a comparatively harsh wine (Columella III, ii, 10). Columella equally mentions the Pompeian/ Murgentine *Horconia* vine, and equally without much praise (Columella III, ii, 27). Discussing various crops and areas, he informs us that the Apulian and Campanian fields are not lacking in rich corn crops (Columella III, viii, 4).

Varro has a few things to say about Campania, the soil is light and porous, which makes for easy ploughing (Varro *R.R.* I, xx, 4). And Campanian spelt is excellent (Varro *R.R.* I, ii, 6).

Whether all these descriptions are completely correct is not so easy to tell. Praise for areas is not only geographical description, but also literary convention, which could of course come up with some garbled descriptions of reality. But pleading against a completely skeptical approach are two facts. The first is that for many of the authors quoted above, Campania is more or less known from personal experience, not a faraway fairy-tale country. Nor is it so for most of their readers. The second argument against complete agnosticism is that the stories overlap to a considerable extent, even if not quite. They may of course have all been copied from each other or from another text, but the argument about personal knowledge of readers and

[1]Strabo V. 4. 3., above, p. 101; Dionysius of Halicarnassus I 37,2: 'where I have even seen fields cropped three times a year.'

[2]Pliny 'N.H'. XVIII, 111, cf. 100. Spurr (1983) for millet.

authors deals effectively enough with the possibility that such a source might be entirely wrong.

Persistent in the sources are references to wine growing on the slopes of Vesuvius, often mentioned at the same time as Sorrento. The latter obtains praise for its quality, but not the former. Vesuvian/Pompeian wine is quoted as hard or strong, giving a considerable headache the next day. As it is, these are characteristics of two types of wines: the rough and fairly cheap *'vin ordinaire'*, but also of some of the great wines if drunk prematurely. The reference in Pliny stating that ageing does not improve them a great deal is the key to the correct choice from these two alternatives. Pompeian wine was no Lafite Rothschild.

The references to cereals are more ambiguous. No doubt the Campanian plain was fertile and productive grain-land, in some areas even exceptionally so. Fallowing was probably unnecessary. The area between Naples and Capua was probably the most fertile part; in our days this is still the case.[1] Pliny's assertion that the entire Campanian plain bore fruit three times a year is probably an exaggeration, and may only have been true for parts of the territory of Capua (the *ager Campanus* in its restricted sense). His claim cannot be validated with reference to early modern practice.[2] And it is also unlikely: if true, Campania could have supported a population of about three times the size of its estimated population.[3] No specific reference to cereal growing near Pompeii can be found in the literary sources, but several passages deal undoubtedly with Campania as a whole, and make clear that cereals are the norm for the plain.

Both for Campania as a whole, and for Pompeii in particular, the literary sources seem to locate winegrowing on the slopes of hills and mountains. When, on the other hand, cereal agriculture is discussed it is located in the plain. Perhaps we may

[1]Unger (1953); Cicero ('de L. Agr'. I 21) calls the territory of Capua 'subsidium annoni, horreum belli', similarly II, 80.

[2]Delille (1977a); Delille (1977b).

[3]For population estimates: below, p. 108 ff. For production and consumption estimates: below, p. 131 ff.

quote one last literary source in respect of these distinctive locations. Varro (*R.R.* I. vi, 5) writes:

> Owing to these three types of configuration different crops are planted, grain being considered best adapted to the plains, vines to the hills, and forests to the mountains.

The Pompeian territory consists to a large extent of plain (Plates IV and V). For what it is worth, the literary evidence would not, therefore, appear to corroborate the standard view of Pompeian agriculture, and suggests a far greater importance for cereals instead.

Sometimes one would think that the need to find fine pictures for publications is the main reason why pictorial evidence gets included in discussions of Pompeian agriculture. Potentially such evidence could serve for two kinds of argument. The first is that Pompeian landscape painting might inform us of the visual aspect of the Pompeian landscape. The second is that by its existence, such mural decoration could tell us something about the owners of the houses.

Anyone perusing the picture catalogue in Peters' book on the subject will quickly have to come to the conclusion that the economic historian should tread very carefully, pleasant though the trip may be.[1] There is little doubt that these are idealized landscapes in which sacral-idyllic and mythological themes abound.[2] The only type of representation which could be linked up with Campanian reality is that of the *villae maritimae*, though here too we can only guess at the precise meaning of the relationship. Those villas are pleasure spots and not the stuff that a discussion of agricultural production is made of.[3] Equally, it is an unjustified procedure to treat the list of all vegetables and fruits depicted on Pompeian walls as a catalogue

[1] Peters (1963). Earlier discussions include Dawson (1944), Rostowzew (1904), Rostowzew (1911). Recently: Ling (1977).

[2] Ling (1977) 11 f, and the other literature quoted in the previous note.

[3] For a discussion of the Neapolitan Rivièra: D'Arms (1970).

of Pompeian agriculture.[1] One only has to flip through Casella's list to note the prominence of the exotic.[2] Vines, grapes and olives are a minority. Satisfaction with the bounty of consumption possibilities for the Roman elite is the key to an understanding of these paintings. These delicacies may not have been available very frequently, or perhaps at all, in which case representation replaces the real thing; and even to the extent that the paintings refer to real consumption, local production does not necessarily follow.

The link between pictorial representation and agricultural production is at best tenuous and indirect. The wallpaintings are therefore inadmissable as evidence of, for example, villa ownership (as they have been used by Day).[3]

Little information on the boundaries of the territory of ancient Pompeii has survived. We shall therefore have to make a rather arbitrary decision in this respect. But before doing that, it must be clear what is the object of the exercise. Political boundaries are of no great concern to us. If, to give an extreme example, the town's political power ended at its city walls, the surrounding countryside would obviously still be of great economic importance. The estimation of the extent of Pompeii's economic territory is important because it may allow us to calculate its carrying capacity, and therefore pronounce on its ability to support its own population.

Physical geography suggests some self-evident boundaries. To the west of the town the sea provides a natural limit, and it is fair enough to treat Vesuvius as the northern boundary of the Pompeian territory. To the east, the boundaries with Nuceria and Nola pose more problems, as there are no natural features to suggest how far Pompeian economic territory extended into this plain. The solution adopted here is to divide the territories

[1] Jashemski (1979) 80 ff. is far too optimistic.

[2] Casella (1950)

[3] Day (1932) 206 Table E. For a good critique: Andreau (1974) 226 ff.

at half distance between Pompeii and these towns.[1] Perhaps more uneasy is the southern limit. Both Beloch and Nissen exclude the entire plain south of the river Sarno from the Pompeian territory.[2] This may be correct politically (it is, however, quite uncertain), but economically it makes little sense. It is an area in the immediate vicinity of Pompeii, and at a sometimes considerable distance from other large settlements such as Nuceria. Discussions of Pompeian agriculture have invariably included the remains from this area, even including those of the villas at Stabiae.[3] Including the area of the Stabian villas, however, probably goes too far. These villas are located in the immediate vicinity of Stabiae, which was after all a small settlement itself.[4] The most prudent middle course is probably to allow Stabiae a modest territory of its own, and treat the remainder of the plain between Pompeii and Stabiae as part of the economic territory of Pompeii. Thus, the total Pompeian territory can be estimated at about 200 sq. km. (=20,000 hectares or 80,000 *iugera*).

This estimate for the economic territory of Pompeii is about twice as much as the two available estimates for the political territory. Nissen opts for at most 110 sq. km, and more likely approaching 80 sq. km, while Beloch's estimate is about 100 sq. km.[5] One test for the likelihood that my estimate for the size of the Pompeian territory (200 sq. km.) is correct, is to see

[1]Justification for this procedure may be found in the context of central place theory in economic geography. Starting point here is the assumption of the so called isotropic plain: a landscape that is identical in all respects in all directions. The theory supposes that centres of similar magnitude are spaced more or less equally in the landscape, thereby producing hexagonal territories. Overlaying such a grid is a grid of larger dimensions for the larger centres, each of which caters for the needs of the smaller centres. Lloyd and Dicken (1977) ch. 2 and Chisholm (1979) esp. ch. 1 provide convenient introductions to the theory. De Neeve (1984) is an application to Italian agriculture. The territory between Pompeii, Nuceria and Nola is sufficiently homogeneous, and the sizes of the towns are sufficiently similar - Beloch (1890) 460 - to warrant my adoption of the procedure.

[2]Nissen (1877) 375; Beloch (1890) 18, 456 f, map I.

[3]Below, p. 112 f. for bibliography.

[4]Di Capua (1938-39) 109 f. argues that from 89 B.C. Stabiae belonged to Nuceria. Whatever its precise political position, Stabiae was not part of the Pompeian territory, and socially and economically it seems a more or less separate entity. Reynolds and Fabricotti (1972) for some recent Stabian material.

[5]Nissen (1877) 375; Beloch (1890) 18, 456 f.

how compatible it is with demographic estimates. The literary descriptions have given us a first idea of what would be growing on this land. Time now to populate it with some people, necessary as a labour force, but also as potential consumers of production.

Population

Estimating population density remains a hazardous operation, but if we want to speculate at all about the nature of the relationship between population pressure and production possibilities, we need to establish orders of magnitude. I shall attempt to stay as closely as possible to Beloch's reconstruction of the Italian population of the time, but some deviations from him will be inevitable.[1] For Campania as a whole Beloch estimates a population density figure of 180 people per sq. km in the early imperial period.[2] This makes the area into the most densely populated part of Italy - Rome and its immediate environs excepted. This high population density estimate is corroborated by comparison of the level of urbanization for various parts of Italy. In Campania we find one town per 130 sq. km, whereas for the whole of Italy we find one town per 600 sq. km.,[3] a pattern which is also reflected in an exaggerated form in the epigraphic density of various parts of Italy: in Campania this is some twenty times higher than in Italy as a whole.[4]

For the urban population of Pompeii Beloch originally followed Nissen's estimate of 20,000.[5] Later he scaled down the figure to 15,000.[6] The problem is that very drastic assumptions are required to make these estimates of urban dwellers compatible with their proponents' estimates for the size of the Pom-

[1]Beloch (1886) is the fundamental study. Beloch (1890) 454 ff. applies its principles to Campania, superseding earlier discussion in the first edition, Berlin, 1879. For an epilogue: Beloch (1903). Recent research such as Brunt (1971) or Hopkins (1978a) 68 f. has vindicated or accepted Beloch's figures in general terms.

[2]Beloch (1890) 457.

[3]Beloch (1890) 454. Cf. Duncan-Jones (1982) 339.

[4]Beloch (1890) 455, Duncan-Jones (1982) 337 ff. For epigraphic density as an indicator, see above, p. 67 ff.

[5]Beloch (1890) 459; Nissen (1877) 379.

[6]Beloch (1898) 274.

peian territory or with Beloch's estimates for average Campanian population density. If Beloch's average Campanian population density holds true for Pompeii, its territory (as defined by him: 100 sq. km.) would have been inhabited - town and countryside together - by about 18,000 people (100 x 180 = 18,000), i.e. about the same as his two estimates for the urban population alone (20,000 and 15,000 respectively). In practical terms it implies that the entire (or near entire) population consisted of urban dwellers. And indeed, for Campania as a whole Beloch assumes that 300,000 of its 400,000 inhabitants lived in towns.[1] Campania may have been highly urbanized, but such a high level of urbanization is unmatched anywhere in preindustrial history - it is quite simply wildly improbable.[2] One way in which one might try to save the assumption of an extremely high level of urbanization is to assume that the agricultural workforce lived in the town. For Pompeii one could refer to the '*agricolae*' in an electoral *programma* (CIL IV 490). In the slave quarters of the Casa del Menandro many agricultural implements, *amphorae* and a farm-cart were found.[3] Though these two examples may indicate some urban residence, in general terms the opposite position, as argued by Garnsey, is to be preferred.[4]

For Nissen the figures were not nearly so incompatible, because he assumed much higher population levels.[5] But modern research has decidedly rejected such high estimates.[6] A variation of this argument would be to assume that Beloch's Campanian average is indeed correct, but that Pompeii had a population density well above this average. Nobody has used this argument, and quite rightly not: there is no ancient or early modern evidence to suggest that Pompeii had a much higher population

[1]Beloch (1890) 457.

[2]de Vries (1984) 38 f, 71 ff. provides excellent discussion of the comparative data. Above, p. 65 ff.

[3]Ling (1983) 55.

[4]Garnsey (1979a); equally Duncan-Jones (1982) 260.

[5]Nissen (1883-1902) vol.2 99-130, esp. 122. His estimate is 16 million for Augustan Italy.

[6]Above, p. 66 ff.

density than the rest of Campania. We may therefore conclude that the estimates of 15,000 or 20,000 urban dwellers are incompatible with an estimated economic territory for Pompeii of about 100 sq. km. They either presuppose an improbable level of urbanization, or an improbably high level of population density.

The only acceptable procedure in this hazardous guessing game is to use estimates for the different variables which are supported as much as possible by ancient sources. These estimates should not be demonstrably improbable in the light of evidence from later historical periods, and - perhaps most important of all - they should be compatible with one another. We do not need to have much confidence in each of the individual guesses, but together they must make sense.

My own estimate that Pompeii's economic territory measured some 200 sq. km. certainly reduces the compatibility problems, but does not remove them altogether. At a population density of 180 per sq. km, 15,000 or 20,000 urban dwellers would still constitute about half the joint population of town and country (200 x 180 = 36,000), which is still improbably high.

It would not be prudent to change Beloch's estimate for the average Campanian population density. That figure can be inferred from the sources, and it is compatible with early modern figures.[1] The estimate for Pompeii's urban population is very uncertain, however. The figure of 20,000 as proposed by Nissen was never more than a rough guess, based on observations of numbers of rooms and houses.[2] Beloch originally adopted this estimate, but later he scaled it down to 15,000.[3] Yet the methodology remains problematic. Duncan-Jones has clearly demonstrated that urban population densities may vary considerably, and that arguments from archaeology alone are dangerous.[4] The second criticism of the figures of 15,000 and

[1]Beloch (1890) 455; above, p. 70 ff.

[2]Nissen (1877) 374 ff.

[3]Beloch (1898) 273 f.

[4]Duncan-Jones (1982) 259 ff. The dangers are evident in Beloch's extrapolation from 20,000 urban dwellers in Pompeii to 300,000 in all of Campania. Beloch did this by assuming that his high urban density for Pompeii prevailed in other cities

20,000 is that they assume that the area within the walls was entirely built up with houses. We now know that a large proportion of the eastern side of the town consisted of, for example, gardens, and was but thinly populated. This is taken into account by Eschebach's more recent estimate, and has resulted in a reduction to 8,000 - 12,000.[1]

The third criticism is that we do not really know how cramped people were prepared to live. This argument is used in the most recent estimate, that of Russell.[2] He reduces the estimated urban population even further, down to 7,000 - 7,500, on the grounds that urban population density is unlikely to have been higher than in medieval towns, with their two or three story houses. This may be true, but the logic is problematic. The structures of these societies are quite different, particularly with respect to what the lower strata of society may have had to endure. Social inequality in the Roman world is likely to have been substantially greater.[3] Many Pompeian poor will not have had their own households, but lived (whether slave or free) in houses of the city's magnates.[4] Russell's second argument extrapolates from the number of 'adult' males known from Pompeian epigraphy. Undoubtedly Pompeian evidence is very good, but it would be too optimistic to assume that it is perfect.

Estimating Pompeian population remains a hazardous game. Applying Beloch's average Campanian population density of 180 persons per sq. km. to Pompeii and its territory is probably least problematic.[5] Estimating the number of urban dwellers remains difficult. The higher estimates imply densities on a par with that of the city of Rome, which is improbable if only because we now know that quite considerable parts of Pompeii were only thinly populated. These high estimates also presuppose

as well. The end result of the calculation is improbable. Beloch (1890) 457.

[1] Eschebach (1970) 66 f. In Eschebach (1975) this is further reduced to 8,000 to 10,000.

[2] Russell (1977), reprinted in Russell (1985) 1-8 (reviewed in Hopkins (forthcoming)).

[3] See e.g. Duncan-Jones (1982) 4 f.; below, p. 187 ff.

[4] This also occurred in medieval Italy, however: Heers (1974) 156.

[5] And this will be the most crucial assumption in some calculations that are to follow.

an improbably high level of urbanization. The final test of all estimation, however, remains that of compatibility. Taken together, it must all make sense. If Pompeii's economic territory measured 200 sq. km, with an average of 180 per sq. km, its total population would be 36,000. Eschebach's estimate for the urban population (8,000-12,000) means that 25-33% of the population would be urban dwellers. This is plausible, but high.[1]

The archaeology of the villas

The traditional view about Pompeian agriculture has been dominated by the many excavations of villas in its territory. On these villas cash crops such as wine and olive oil seem to be predominant. I shall argue that in a number of cases these alleged villa sites can by no stretch of imagination be called villas. If some sites obviously fit accepted conceptions of villas (and their mode of production), it does not follow that each and every piece of excavated debris is part of a proper villa. My second line of argument will concentrate on the distribution pattern of the sites. They are heavily concentrated in certain parts of the Pompeian territory, and almost absent elsewhere. This non-random spacing will become even more evident once we have removed the imaginary villas from the dossier. In subsequent parts of this chapter I shall argue that these concentrations of discovered sites represent an ancient reality, and I shall try to explain the pattern.

The vast majority of the evidence used consists of excavations from around the turn of the century. We may expect this to change within the next ten years, because the Pompeian countryside has now been given proper emphasis in excavation programs. It is never very satisfactory when one has to argue from the results of old excavations, and in the Pompeian case it would often be more appropriate to treat them as treasure hunts. They were executed by private landowners, and the finds/spoils were shared by the landowner and the government. Both parties concerned were primarily interested in treasure, and therefore scant attention was given to the agricultural

[1]Above, p. 66 ff; de Vries (1984) for comparative early modern data.

parts. The 'academic observer' at many of these operations was Matteo Della Corte, who alledgedly lost a large part of his notes, and had to publish a lot from memory. Publications are usually extremely slim; even the location of many villas is far less secure than the texts of the publications suggest, and most excavated villas were filled in later.[1] The entire context of the discovery of the villas makes it more than likely that the available documentation contains a very biased sample of information. Common sense would predict a preponderance of larger and wealthier structures, but a more sophisticated analysis of the nature of the distorted relation between the reality of the past and surviving remains will have to redress the balance. This will result in a considerable reduction of the importance given to villa agriculture.

But before we embark on such speculation about *terra incognita*, it would be well to describe the available evidence in a few words. Distribution pattern and the size and character of sites will be the main focus.[2]

The numbers of the villas (Figure V) are those allocated by Rostovtzeff.[3] For the numbers above 36 two numbering systems are available, Day and Carrington: both will be given.[4] As the distribution pattern is crucial to the argument, the exposition will be ordered geographically.

Villas 33 and 34, in the middle of the Sarno plain (Plate IV), are proper villas, beyond doubt. Villa 33 had a number of rooms in fourth style painting; this part of the villa was linked to the rustic remainder of the villa by a corridor. It also

[1]Local enthusiasts have been very active in recent years, doing a job no foreigner could possibly have hoped to do. For results see Casale and Bianco (1979). I am very grateful for having been given an early manuscript with the results of their efforts up to then.

[2]I deliberately abstain from any precise definition of 'villa'. If anywhere, precise definition should come after, and not before the empirical research. For a recent conceptual discussion: Leveau (1983a).

[3]Rostovtzeff (1957) 552 f. The map draws its data from the maps in Carrington (1931) and Casale and Bianco (1979). Unfortunately the two do not always concur. I am not convinced that the additions in the latter necessarily refer exclusively to villas. Their concentration, however, in the Boscoreale area does not undermine my argument.

[4]Day (1932) 202 f; Carrington (1931) 110.

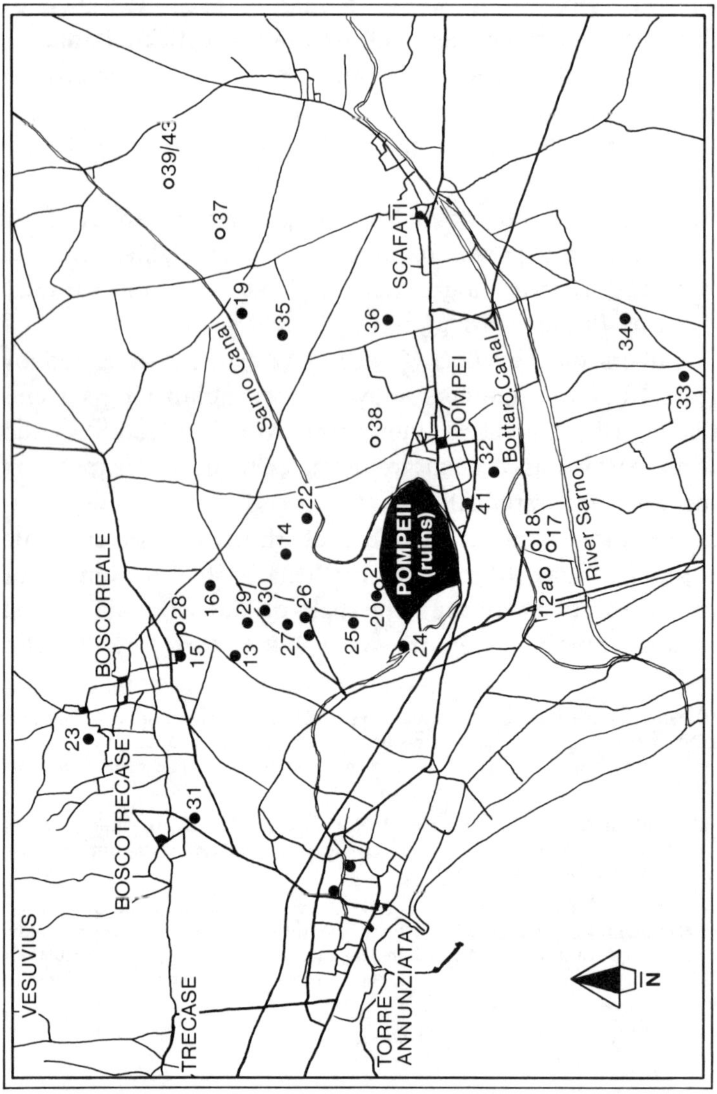

Figure V: The distribution of alleged Pompeian villas (numbers as in text)

contained a bath. The productive activity can be gauged from a large *cella vinaria*, a *torcularium*, and 34 *dolia*. A large number of wooden poles were also found: props for vines. Villa 34 was a very big affair and probably a real slave estate, with a considerable *cella vinaria* and *torcularium*. It also included an *ergastulum*, with instruments for locking/chaining the slaves at night clearly present. There was also a stable, with skeletons of horses and cattle. In addition to this there was a kitchen area, and a bronze vessel large enough to have suggested that this was a cheese factory; I suppose size is as much in the eyes of the beholder as beauty, but the measurements are: diameter: 1.06 m. and height 0.32 m.[1] Here, as in many other Pompeian villa reports, we find a number of references to *amphorae*, but no description at all. It is therefore impossible to say whether these had anything to do with production or with consumption.

Villas 17 and 18, located between the present mouth of the river Sarno and what was probably the mouth of that river in antiquity, were probably not villas at all. Neither of the two are referred to by the report as villas and the scant information available gives no indication that we do indeed have a villa here. Nearby, in Contrada Moregine, Day (Day 37 = Rostovtzeff 12A) mentions another villa. The original report contains little detail, but enough to reject the villa identification, and perhaps warrants the hypothesis of a port suburb.

Also near the town are a few other villas or possible villas. Villa Carrington 38 is in all honesty not more than a few small remains, not nearly enough to deserve the label 'villa'.[2] Villa 32 is probably a real villa, although of unknown size. It had *dolia*, a *cella vinaria* and a rustic *atrium*. Villa Day 41 is a fairly large building. It was located near the modern village of Pompeii, but as the description of the location depends on the local situation and names of many years ago, a more precise indication of the location is waiting for an enthusiast.

[1] 'Notizie degli Scavi di Antichità.' 1923, p. 277; Rostovtzeff (1957) 565.

[2] 'Notizie degli Scavi di Antichità.' 1928 p. 375 D.

If we turn our attention to the plain east of the town (Plate V) we find a few more villas, including some proper ones. Villa Carrington 39/Day 43 is no more than a few remains of something rustic.[1] Villa Carrington 37 would appear not to be a villa at all, the slim report speaks of 'un edificio di campagna affatto rustico, pochi ambienti.' The villas 19 and 35 should both be considered real villas. Villa 19 is large, contains a *torcularium* and *dolia*, and on the consumption side two rooms with wallpaintings and a number of luxury finds. Villa 35 is fairly large and included a *cella vinaria* and *dolia.* A number of fourth style wallpaintings were discovered. Less luxurious in its excavated parts, villa 36 contained a stable, a few *dolia*, and a bath. Whether we should include villa Day 42 is somewhat doubtful. The remains are not sufficient to classify it as a certain villa, and geographically this building at Domicella is already situated on the hills to the east of the plain.

If we try to summarize our observations about 'villas' outside the main concentration area north of the town, it would appear that they are of even less importance than one might have thought. Seven of them had to be dropped because there is no indication that we are in fact dealing with a proper villa. The remaining villas do not show the luxurious splendour of owner's quarters that we observe in a number of villas in the 'Boscoreale complex'. Although the remaining numbers are small, they appear not to be randomly spaced, but seem to stretch out along a line more or less parallel to the present course of the river Sarno, but about one kilometre further north, i.e. more or less along the supposed course of the river in antiquity. It is tempting to think that this is no coincidence.

Turning now towards the area north of the town (Plate VI) we get into real villa country. Villa 24 is the famous Villa of the Mysteries. A splendid building, of which only a part of the agricultural side has been excavated. But all the paraphernalia for a wine growing estate are there (Plate VIII). Villa 26 is a medium sized building without any luxurious amenities. But it had an olive press, a barn with straw, and a room with poles

[1]'Notizie degli Scavi di Antichità.' 1928 p. 375 ff. XVIII.

of chestnut wood. Also three large *dolia* were found. The most central room, with a good view of staircase and entrances, was also the only one with stucco on the walls. Presumably it was the *vilicus'* room.

Villa 20 is in fact more suburban. No traces of agricultural activities were encountered, though arguments from silence are of course dangerous with the type of archaeology available. Villa 21 is too badly reported to decide whether this was an equally suburban type, or also contained an agricultural part.

Villa 25 was clearly devoted to wine production. We find a *torcularium*, a graffito referring to 1300 poles/stakes, three large *dolia*, a *cella vinaria* and agricultural implements. Although not exhibiting fantastic splendour, it produced a number of luxury items, some simple wallpainting, a marble table, a *triclinium*, and a private bath including a mosaic floor. Next to the villa was a family tomb, with the bust of a man and a woman. Inside was a *columbarium*, with two places in the top row, and 32 in the bottom row.

Villa 27 is large and residential. It had for example wall-paintings in second and fourth style and a bathroom. It was located on the western slope of a hill, and shows no signs of agricultural use. But as it has no oven either, Della Corte presumes that there may have been an adjacent more utilitarian building, which would not seem unlikely.

Villa 13 is large and has a residential part with second style wallpaintings, bathrooms, mosaics etc. On the agricultural side there was a *cella vinaria*, or *olearia* - as always it is hard to tell the difference - and small agricultural implements for these crops.

Villa 14 is pretty large, has a *cella vinaria*, *torcularium*, some *dolia*, but also a granary. It included domestic quarters with wallpaintings.

In villa 22 'agricultural implements' were found.[1] Two rooms had wallpaintings in first and second style, and the villa had a bath. All in all it is a fairly rustic building.

Villa 30 has only been excavated in part, but enough has come

[1] I follow Casale and Bianco (1979) for its location.

to light to get some impression. It had a *torcularium*. A number of third style wallpaintings were found, which have been discussed recently.[1] In addition to this, amenities included mosaic floors and a bathroom. The villa has been dated to about A.D. 40-45.

Villa 29 contained some beautiful wallpaintings, a mosaic floor, a bath and a water supply. On the productive side it contained a *torcularium* and a *cella vinaria* with *dolia*. Part of the building could only be entered from outside and might have been used as dormitories for slaves.

Villa 16 is the most famous of all villas in this area, and known as the villa of P. Fannius Synistor.[2] Sumptuous, with famous - and still partially extant - wallpaintings.[3] Agricultural production was not a favourite research subject for the excavators, but facilities for pressing olives and grapes are known. The rustic quarters were shut off from the rest of the building.

Villa 28 is a borderline case for classification. It is not very large, there are no luxuries such as sumptuous wallpaintings. There are indications that it may have served in part as a country inn. It also had a large stable. Yet it did not lack links with wine production, as it had a small *torcularium*.

Villa 15 is badly known. The excavated part is very rustic, and contains a *torcularium*. Yet it is not impossible that there may be more luxurious but unexcavated parts.

Villa 31 is a large building of which only a part has been excavated. The excavated parts contain a rustic *atrium* and a luxurious residential part. The villa was an imperial estate, originally owned by Agrippa Postumus, and was managed in the last years by Ti. Claudius Eutychus Caesaris L(ibertus).[4] The excavated parts contain no *cella vinaria* or *torcularium*, but wine was almost certainly produced. Graffiti referring to stakes (CIL IV 3887, 6888) were found. An instrument for chaining

[1]Bastet (1976).

[2]Barnabei (1901).

[3]Recently studied again in Andreae (1975).

[4]Rostovtzeff (1957) 553, n. 26, below, p. 129 f.

slaves similar to that found in villa 34 was found in a cell of the rustic *atrium*.

Only a part of villa 23 has been brought to light, including a *torcularium* and a room with first style wallpaintings.

Villa Day 39 (absent from Carrington's list) has only been excavated in part.[1] The excavated parts are very rustic, and contain two *ergastula* and a *torcularium*, with graffiti referring to grapes.

Villa Day 40 consists of nothing more than a find of three *dolia*.[2]

In recent times three more villas have come to light in the area north and north west of Pompeii. Most spectacular perhaps has been the so called villa of Oplontis, south of the Torre Annunziata station of the Circumvesuviana railway.[3] A splendid building surrounded by lovely gardens, it furnishes a good deal of information on the living conditions of a Roman grandee. Unfortunately the excavations have not yet provided us with information on agricultural production.

Nearby, a much more mundane structure has come to light, the so called 'Villa of L. Crassus Tertius'.[4] The plant material recovered from this site suggests a strong presence of viticulture. Proper publication and analysis will probably make this an important site for economic historians. Another interesting recent excavation is that of another villa in the Villa Regina-Sciusciello area of Boscoreale.[5] Finds include *dolia*, a *cella vinaria*, storerooms, a *torcularium*, and small residential quarters.

For what it is worth in statistical terms, these three new villa excavations form a continuation of the already existing pattern.

If we try to summarize the finds from the area north of the town we can note that the evidence from this area is far more

[1] 'Notizie degli Scavi di Antichità.' 1929 p. 178-189.

[2] 'Notizie degli Scavi di Antichità.' 1929 p. 189 f.

[3] De Franciscis (1975); De Caro (1976); Maggi (1976a); Maggi (1978); Jashemski (1979) 289-314.

[4] Maggi (1976b); Jashemski (1979) 320-322.

[5] De Caro (1977); De Caro (1978); De Caro (1979b).

resistant to the skeptical question whether we are really dealing with a villa than the evidence from the south and east of the town. Therefore the concentration in the distribution pattern becomes even more marked.

Survey theory and distribution praxis

The distribution pattern of villa sites in the Pompeian territory has shown marked concentrations, and scrutiny of the available evidence has only served to emphasize this pattern. But how do we know that the pattern in the surviving evidence corresponds to the buried reality, and does not suffer from sampling error? The sample is large enough to make it fairly unlikely that the pattern observed is entirely due to ordinary random sampling error. But as always with historical and archaeological data, the problem is that of non-randomness errors.

In recent years archaeologists have had more and more recourse to the technique of field surveys to abate such problems.[1] Unfortunately such surveys are not available for the territory of Pompeii, and it is highly doubtful whether they could be successful in any case. The layer of volcanic ash is considerably thicker than the layer of soil accumulated on sites elsewhere, and in addition it was of course deposited in a very short period. As the layer of volcanic ash decreases in thickness the further one moves away from the volcano, we would expect to find more and more sites, the further one moves away. As we have seen, this was not the case. Looking at the distribution map we can see that the largest concentration is in the area between Pompeii and the modern village of Boscoreale.

Although of course not the result of a proper survey, the data can be likened to the results of the so called extensive surveys.[2] These collect data from a large area, with a fairly limited amount of effort per unit of surface. The alternative strategy of intensive surveys only looks at randomly sampled parts of an area, but studies those in great detail. For simple reasons of statistical theory the intensive survey is far prefer-

[1] Cherry (1983); Snodgrass (1982).

[2] For such surveys, see Cherry (1983) 390 ff, for sampling: 400 ff.

able. If the sample is not too small, and the areas to be sampled have been well chosen, the sampled data will give us enough material to make valid predictions for the areas not included in the sample. Extensive surveys equally refrain from recording all data. But with these we have far less idea of what we are missing. Because archaeological sites come in different sizes, it takes only common sense to understand that the bigger sites are noticed more easily than the smaller ones. Analysis by Cherry of survey results has shown that number of sites per sq. km. is a function of survey intensity.[1] But it is equally true that the additional sites known through extra effort are smaller. Even the most perfunctory survey will record the site of a town, but in order to find the site of a small farm, a far more intensive effort is necessary. The problem with extensive surveys is that no valid statistical method exists to extrapolate from the known to the unknown.[2] The reason is that the proportion between large and small sites is not determined by statistical theory, but by variations in the economy, and also of course by variations in the 'visibility' of the data that we want to record. What we try to understand as historians is precisely these proportions between large and small sites, functional hierarchies between them, and similar problems.

From this discussion of the methodology of field surveys we may infer that a lot is wrong with our data. Three problems demand our attention: site-size, visibility, and surveying intensity, and they are all interrelated.

Common sense indicates that larger sites are discovered more easily than smaller ones. Therefore, unless we survey intensively enough to be sure that we have discovered virtually all sites of the smallest size, we know that the size distribution from our data is incorrect because the smaller sites are under-represented. Therefore, with extensive surveys, an argument from silence about small sites is unlikely to be permitted, but is not

[1] Cherry (1983) 410.

[2] In principle the method from Appendix IV could be used by drawing extrapolations of diminishing returns per unit effort for different size classes of sites, but my hunch would be that it is a technique only useful for deciding between intensive and hyper intensive. But it would be an interesting methodological exercise to try it out on a small scale.

nearly so problematic about large sites. It is inconceivable that there were no settlements at all in the areas that are as yet blank on the map of the Pompeian territory. There must have been sites: the only question is what sort of sites. We can distinguish two possibilities. Either there was a continuation of the large villa site pattern, but with villas not yet known, or there was a different type of settlements, with far smaller sites. Because larger sites have a far bigger chance than small sites to be recorded in surveys, it is more likely that the absence of recorded sites in parts of the Pompeian territory is due to a predominance of small sites, than to under-recording of large sites.

An objection could be made that 'surveying intensity' might have differed a lot, and that therefore the distribution pattern as it is is a function of this surveying intensity, and of nothing else.[1] Of course that is a difficult area of argument, because the data as we have them are the result of very haphazard archaeological activities, motivated by expectations of financial gain. In some years the reports give the impression of something like a gold fever. Success obviously breeds success in these matters. On the other hand the plain had its modern wealthy and greedy landowners just as well, and in addition, it has been the plain more than anything else which has been the scene of building activities in more recent years.

A more promising line of argument than the above speculation is to wonder what we might expect the result of such variation in surveying intensity to be. If the surveying intensity increases we may expect a small rise in the number of large sites, and a large rise in the number of small sites. Decreasing the intensity obviously has the opposite effect. A bias as a result of variation in the surveying intensity therefore is strongest with the smaller sites, and not so important with larger sites.

Unless one were to argue that villas should be considered small sites, the pattern resulting from possible variation in surveying intensity is therefore entirely different from the

[1]Cf. above, p. 120 f., for Cherry's strictures.

Pompeian pattern as it has to be explained. It would show a roughly equal distribution of large sites, and a large number of small sites where intensity had been greatest. In fact, the proportion of small to large sites appears to be higher in the plain than in the Boscoreale area.[1] It is therefore unlikely that the pattern in the data is the result of variations in surveying intensity.

The last important variable is that of 'visibility'. Not in this case the amount of bushes and the like, but the thickness of the layer of volcanic ash. This layer is obviously thinner the further one moves away from Mt. Vesuvius, and should therefore have resulted in a better recovery rate for sites further away from the volcano. The opposite therefore of the observed pattern.

One last remark about the distribution within the Boscoreale area still has to be made, although more an exhortation to further research than anything else. In quite a few cases reports mention nearby roads, and it does not seem unlikely to assume that the precise locations of the villas are dictated by a road network emanating from the city gates. This will have to remain speculation for the time being, but would appear to be well worth investigating in future.[2]

A general conclusion about the distribution of archaeological sites in the Pompeian territory remains hazardous, given the poor quality of our data. A high density of villas with agricultural activities concentrating on the production of market crops such as wine and perhaps olive oil can be observed in the hills north of the town, between the town and Vesuvius. A secondary concentration appears to stretch along the probable ancient course of the river Sarno, although reservations are needed here. But the areas thus indicated represent only a small part of the Pompeian territory. It has been argued above that the near absence of villa finds elsewhere is likely to represent a near absence of villas in those areas at the time.

[1] See the differential resistance of the two areas to the skeptical question: are these the remains of a real villa? Above p. 113 ff.

[2] For roads: Spano (1937).

Amphorae and wine growing

The third set of data concerning Pompeian agriculture is that of the *amphorae*. Containers of such cash crops as wine or olive oil, their survival in large numbers has frequently given rise to imaginative pictures of lively interregional trade. Entering the minefield of amphora studies is a dangerous thing for the uninitiated, but it is unavoidable.[1] Large numbers of *amphorae* were found in Pompeii, but the recording of the finds leaves a lot to be desired. For most *amphorae* we do not know any longer where they were found, and equally, in most cases it is no longer possible to link the inscriptions on them as published in CIL IV with the extant *amphorae* in the store rooms.[2] In addition, the classification scheme for amphora forms as employed in CIL IV leaves a lot to be desired.[3] Within the context of the present study our aims and ambitions are limited to the question to what extent they furnish evidence for a wine production on such a scale that a significant proportion would be exported to areas outside the Pompeian territory.

Although interesting in many respects, we can therefore leave aside the *amphorae* emanating from elsewhere. For us only Pompeian *amphorae* are important, whether found in Pompeii or elsewhere. To a large extent this means *amphorae* of the type Dressel 2-4. This was a fairly common type of amphora, not only produced in Pompeii, but also in Spain, Greece, and elsewhere in Italy.[4] We need not go into all the details here of the recent sophisticated research that has gone into these typological studies. Suffice it to say that it is beginning to be possible to distinguish the various centres of production.

From our point of view it is important to measure the possible flows of Pompeian *amphorae* into centres of consump-

[1]Schuring (1984) for a good introduction.

[2]Cf. Panella and Fano (1977) 134, 156; Panella (1974-5).

[3]Ibid.

[4]Panella and Fano (1977); Panella (1981); Tchernia (1971) 44; Tchernia and Zevi (1972); van der Werff (1986) 107-8 points to the possibility that a small proportion contained products other than wine.

tion such as Rome. For the Flavian era 'Pompeian' *amphorae* represent some 30% of all Dressel 2-4 fragments in the excavations of the *Terme del Nuotatore* at Ostia.[1] The late Augustan deposit at La Longarina, Ostia, provides similar proportions (Table IV).[2]

Table IV: Wine amphorae *at La Longarina, Ostia*
(Source: Hesnard (1980) 149)

Origin	N	%
Southern Campania	50	27.6
Rest of Italy	61	33.8
Spain	58	32.0
Greece	12	6.6
Total	181	100.0

If this is taken to mean wine export from the territory of Pompeii, it can easily be seen as undermining the argument that I have developed until now, that wine exports are unlikely to have made up an important part of the Pompeian economy. Yet we must read the archaeological reports very carefully. What is usually referred to as 'Pompeian amphorae', is only intended as a shorthand for Dressel 2-4 of the type best known from Pompeii. Luckily a very sophisticated piece of research has been done on Dressel 2-4 from Pompeii by Panella and Fano.[3] Using inductive statistical techniques they have subdiv-

[1]Panella (1981) 76.

[2]Hesnard (1980). Detailed tabulation of data on p. 149, discussion on p. 142 ff.

[3]Panella and Fano (1977). Earlier research in Ostia - Tchernia and Zevi (1972)- showed not inconsiderable quantities of Dressel 2-4 amphorae with a clay type which they call 'L. Eumachi' after the -'Pompeian'- amphora stamp found on some of them. The resemblance between this 'L. Eumachi' clay type (photographs

ided Dressel 2 - 4 *amphorae* from Pompeii into different groups; and using more old fashioned techniques of visual identification they have done similar things with the clay. Most frequent are their shapes 3 and 4, usually with clay types A and F. Taken together they represent 72% of the number of *amphorae* studied, and, more importantly, this is the group with the likely local origin. Yet we must be very careful here. How local is local?

In the absence of kiln finds, the epigraphy of the *amphorae* is our only help, indicating a zone from Sorrento to Mt. Vesuvius.[1] In other words, we are still talking about an area much larger than the Pompeian territory, only referred to as Pompeian for the sake of convenience, because Pompeii is where most of these *amphorae* have been found. Unfortunately the number of inscriptions on these *amphorae* is too small for a decent statistical analysis - a discussion of individual cases is our only option.[2] Shape 3 represents 57% of all amphoras studied, and the epigraphic references would seem to point to Surrentum as its origin. One amphora stamp (CIL X 8049, 6a-b) and two *dipinti* (CIL IV 5514; CIL IV 2556) mention a Surrentine origin. The only intelligible personal names are those of a Iucundus (CIL X 8049, 6 a-b) and a Clodius Clemens (CIL IV 5588), a name not included in Castrén's prosopography of Pompeii.[3] On the *amphorae* of shape 4 (15% of amphorae) we encounter '*surrentinum metellianum*' twice (CIL IV 10312, 9315) and once vesuvian wine (CIL IV 2558). The '*clodianum*' (inv. n. 500) might refer to a '*surrentinum clodianum*' known from Rome (CIL XV 4592 - Dressel 3).

What conclusions can we derive from this detailed research? Obviously even the most painstaking recent work has not been

on p. 38/39 of their article) and Panella and Fano (1977) 146, clay types A and F, is striking. A complication for such an equation is the remark by Tchernia and Zevi (1972) 51 that the majority of the amphorae which they have seen in Pompeii and Herculaneum are of a clay type which is different from their 'L. Eumachii' type. Perhaps the majority of what they happened to see in Pompeii was non-local ware. Cf. Panella and Fano (1977) 134 n. 5.

[1]Panella and Fano (1977) esp. 151, 153, 159.

[2]For the complete dossier: Panella and Fano (1977) 157 ff.

[3]Castrén (1975); CIL IV 2557, probably of shape 3, mentions 'vesuvinum vinum'. The problem is that the drawing by Schoene and the inscription need not refer to the same amphora. See Panella and Fano (1977) 158 f.

able to narrow sufficiently the origin of the type of amphora most likely to represent local production. This is so even if *amphorae* are often (presumably for convenience' sake) referred to as Pompeian.[1] Yet, we must acknowledge that the region of origin is much larger and includes Surrentum. In the, admittedly few, epigraphic indications of origin, Surrentum predominates, even on *amphorae* found in Pompeii.

A similar conclusion might be drawn from the fact that even the *amphorae* of the clay type called *'L. Eumachii'* by Tchernia and Zevi, and which one might think to be Pompeian, can still be found in second century levels in Ostia.[2] Unsatisfactory is that although the links between the clay type *'L. Eumachi'* from Ostia and the clay type A from the 'group 3' *amphorae* from Pompeii are close, the distribution pattern might be different. Panella and Fano posit a limited distribution outside southern Campania for their 'group 3'.[3]

In my discussion of the literary evidence for Pompeian agriculture I have argued that Pompeian wine does not get high marks for good quality. These same sources also contain references to Surrentine wine, with a much more favourable tone.[4] On the basis of present evidence the best conclusion about this type of Dressel 2-4 *amphorae* is therefore that they largely represent Surrentine wine production, and not Pompeian. If therefore they turn up in large numbers in Rome, they do not prove Pompeian wine exports. At the same time we must admit that our knowledge is limited, and more research is necessary before we can have any confidence in this hypothesis. Useful would be a very detailed analysis of shapes and clay of indubitably Pompeian and Surrentine *amphorae*, from new excavations

[1]E.g. in Panella's analysis of amphorae from the Terme del Nuotatore at Ostia - Panella (1981) p. 76 - 30% or more of the Dressel 2-4 amphorae are called 'Pompeiane'. The inverted commas are hers, to be fair.

[2]Tchernia and Zevi (1972).

[3]Panella and Fano (1977) 151. Their hesitation should, however, be acknowledged.

[4]Above, p. 103. Tchernia (1986) 176 f. also acknowledges that the wines of Sorrento and Pompeii may vary a lot in quality, but would still seem to overestimate the quality of the Pompeian (i.e. Vesuvian) variety. Of course, quality is not the only thing that matters: Tchernia (1986) 187 and Purcell (1985) 17 ff. are concerned with quantity, rather than quality.

of production and not consumption contexts, in order to find out whether they can be distinguished from each other, although at such short distances we must remain aware that we are only studying the container, and not the wine.

Wine growers and villa owners

In his article on agriculture in the life of Pompeii, John Day includes a not inconsiderable number of names of Pompeian wine producers, and such data are obviously of great importance for a precise reconstruction of the social position of villa owners.[1] Day concludes that they 'were members of the most wealthy and most prominent families at Pompeii. In fact, they represent the governing aristocracy of the city.'[2] Secondly, he notes a very high incidence of freedmen among his wine-growers: at least 50%.[3] When we take his two points together we have the disturbing result that we either have to assume that he means that freedmen could belong to the *ordo*, or that his definition of aristocracy is very wide indeed. Apart from such conceptual ambiguity, it is obviously important if more than half the wine-growers are freedmen. If in antiquity freedmen were the nearest thing to later enterprising bourgeois, it would be important if we find them in a sector that would in some people's view be the backbone of the economy: the export of wine. But I shall argue that most identifications of wine-growers and villa owners in Pompeii are purely fictional.

The first series of identifications is that of Della Corte's list of villa owners.[4] Not infrequently these identifications are very dubious.[5] In one villa (13) the seals of three men were found, whom we may assume to have been freedmen: L. Brittius Eros, L. Caecilius Aphrodisius and Ti. Claudius Amphio.[6] Choosing one

[1]Day (1932) 204 ff.

[2]Day (1932) 177 f. For aristocracy he refers to Gordon (1927). The unsatisfactory nature of that article will be discussed below, p. 282 f.

[3]Day (1932) 178.

[4]Della Corte (1965) 411 ff.

[5]Cf. below, p. 220; 238 ff; 354 ff.

[6]Della Corte (1965) p. 433. 'Notizie degli Scavi di Antichità.' 1895 p. 210 f. Cf. Andreau (1974) 31 ff, 225.

of them as the owner, or all three as joint owners, would be gratuitous. Della Corte's hypothesis that L. Caecilius Iucundus, the banker and auctioneer from Pompeii, was the owner, is not based on any facts.[1]

In villa 16, a seal was found reading L. HER. FLO, developed by Della Corte as L. Herius Florus, and by Castrén, tentatively, as L. Herennuleius Florius.[2] With such uncertainty about the name itself, it would seem better to refrain from any further reaching speculation. The villa is often referred to as belonging to P. Fannius Synistor, because a liquid measure with his name in the genitive was found in the villa.[3]

Villa 19 has produced the seal of a Cn. Domitius Auctus.[4]

In villa 20 a seal was found which belonged to T. Siminius Stephanus.[5] But no traces of agricultural activities were found in conjunction with this suburban building.[6]

In villa 23 the seal of L. Arellius Successus was found.[7]

In villa 27 a seal was found reading THALLI ASEL(LI) PRO, developed by Della Corte as *'procuratoris'*, and by Castrén as Proculi.[8] It is a large luxurious building, but no traces of agricultural use have been found.[9]

Villa 29 may have been owned by N. Popidius Florus. He has left two votive inscriptions with his name in the building.[10]

Villa 31 was an imperial estate, originally owned by Agrippa Postumus; the manager in its last years was Ti. Claudius

[1]Della Corte (1965) p. 434; Andreau (1974) 31 ff.

[2]Della Corte (1965) p. 430, 467; Castrén (1975) 'ad nom.'

[3]Della Corte (1965) p. 431. To assume that he was the owner would be even more rash.

[4]Della Corte (1965) p. 447, 467; 'Notizie degli Scavi di Antichità.' 1899 p. 395.

[5]Della Corte (1965) p. 448, 469.

[6]Above, p. 117.

[7]Della Corte (1965) p. 450, 465.

[8]Della Corte (1965) p. 449, 465. Castrén (1975) 'ad nom.'

[9]Cf. above p. 117.

[10]'Notizie degli Scavi di Antichità.' 1921 p. 445. N. POPIDIVS/ FLORVS/ I.O.M.// and N. POPIDIVS/ FLORVS/ VEN. LIB. HERC.// .

Eutychus Caesaris L(ibertus). Two of his seals were found in a cupboard of the villa.[1]

Villa Day 39 has returned a seal belonging to M. Livius Marcellus.[2]

On one of the three *dolia* forming the sum total of the supposed villa 40, a stamp was found reading BARNIV EROTIS.[3] Della Corte's view that the Eros would be L. Eumachius Eros is surely stretching the evidence too far.[4] Day's presumption that this man was the owner of the villa is improbable: such stamps appear to indicate who owned the kiln, and not who was the end user of the *dolium*.[5]

In a perfunctory exploration of some remains in Scafati, another seal was found, belonging to N. Popidius Narcissus.[6]

The conclusions that can be drawn from these observations are minimal. Often we do not know whether the person identified is the owner or a procurator.[7] On top of this, we lack additional information for most persons: they remain but names.

Day's 'list of families' represented among the wine producers is devoid of any meaning, because as Andreau has also remarked, our research should be levelled at individuals or families, but not at *gentes*.[8] It is unfortunately a common methodological mistake; it is meaningless not to differentiate between prestigious senators or decurions of a *gens*, and minor branches, or freedmen.

Potentially more important is Day's list of names of wine producers who were members of Pompeian families.[9] The basis of this list is mostly the painted inscriptions on *amphorae* found in Pompeii. As we have seen, although our knowledge

[1]Rostovtzeff (1957) 553, n. 26. Wrongly Della Corte (1965) p. 414 ff. Cf. above, p. 118 f.

[2]Della Corte (1965) p. 437, 468; 'Notizie degli Scavi di Antichità.' 1929 p. 186.

[3]'Notizie degli Scavi di Antichità.' 1929 p. 189.

[4]'Notizie degli Scavi di Antichità.' 1929 p. 190.

[5]Day (1932) 203; Paterson (1982) 154-6.

[6]Della Corte (1965) p. 447, 469.

[7]Andreau (1974) 224.

[8]Day (1932) 205 f; Andreau (1974) 225.

[9]Day (1932) 206 ff.

about *amphorae* has grown considerably, our awareness of the gaps in our knowledge has grown even faster. Many *amphorae* may be imports from elsewhere, with an obviously devastating effect on Day's list. Secondly, the fact that 'names' may only be available in the form of initials should make us more cautious. Both because the development of the name may be dubious, and because we remain ignorant of the case-ending of the name. To aggravate the situation, the peculiarities of the Latin language do not always allow us to distinguish between ablative, dative and genitive. Neither is the meaning of the cases as unambiguous as we would like: a dative for example might mean a producer, an intermediary or a consumer.[1]

Consequently we have to discard Day's list of Pompeian wine-growers. The net result of all this skepticism is that we no longer possess information on the identity and social position of Pompeian wine-growers and villa owners. We may expect them to belong to the wealthier and perhaps also more respectable strata of Pompeian society, but we cannot demonstrate it.

Aggregate supply and demand

Until now no macro-economic analysis of Pompeian agriculture has been given in the literature. Yet this is precisely what is necessary for a proper argument. We shall have to make an estimate of total agricultural production - and its constituent parts - and compare that with estimates of consumption. In this way we can discover whether major surpluses or shortages may have given rise to substantial interregional trade in agricultural products. Obviously the figures imply no properly documented knowledge, but they are an exercise in the specification of hypotheses: speculative quantification, as it has been dubbed by Peter Garnsey.[2] They serve to establish orders of magnitude and to distinguish the possible from the highly improbable.

The boundaries chosen earlier for the economic territory of Pompeii were Mount Vesuvius to the north, the sea to the

[1] For elaborate argument the reader is referred to Andreau (1974) 223 ff, which it would be superfluous to repeat here.

[2] Garnsey (1979b).

west, to the south the territory of the Stabian villas has been excluded, and in the plain to the east of the town the half-distance rule was used to mark off Pompeian territory from that of Nola and Nuceria.[1] The total area thus defined can be estimated at about 200 sq. km, or 20,000 hectares, or 80,000 *iugera.*

Our first target is the area of villa agriculture, to the north of the town, and the stretch to the east. The area of the first can be estimated at about 1500 hectares, that of the latter as perhaps 1000 hectares. Let us assume secondly that of this total of 2500 hectares, about 1500 hectares was planted with vines, and the rest with olive and perhaps fruit trees and cereals to keep the slave workforce alive.[2] Next we need a productivity figure. Let us follow modern authority and assume 20 hectoliters of wine per hectare, the minimum yield for Columella, and of the same order of magnitude as suggested by comparative evidence from Italy.[3] Total wine production of this area would, under the specified assumptions, amount to 30,000 hectoliters. A very conservative population estimate for Pompeii - town and country - would be 30,000, the always conservative Beloch thought higher population densities than this were not inconceivable: for the early empire he assumes a population density of 180 per sq. km. in Campania.[4] Local supply would be enough for local demand at a consumption figure of 100 litres per head of the population. This figure is identical to what seems to be a normal average consumption in early modern Europe, and is therefore comforting.[5] Cato gave his slaves

[1]Above, p. 106 f.

[2]Cf. Duncan-Jones (1982) 37 ff.

[3]Duncan-Jones (1982) 40, 45; Rathbone (1981) 12 f. Purcell (1985) 13 adheres to the old tradition of faith in Columella's claim for a yield of about 60 hectoliters per hectare. I am afraid I find this faith in the authority of literary texts from antiquity no more than special pleading. Of course, wide variation is possible, but to assume that such concentration at one end of the extremes of possibility is also probable, demands more. Early modern Italian figures in Aymard (1973) 479. Interannual variation is strong, the highest figure quoted for a good year is 40 hectoliters in Regalsemi.

[4]Beloch (1890) 457; cf. above, p. 70; 72.

[5]In Hopkins (1978a) 3 a figure of 100 litres is calculated for mid eighteenth century Madrid. Braudel (1979) I 202 quotes 100-120 litres for mid sixteenth

more, 180 - 260 litres, but that was not an average intended to include children.[1] Suggesting with Purcell that all Romans drank as much as adult males may conjure up images of bibulous Romans, but is mistaken.[2]

We shall ignore the recent discoveries by W. Jashemski of vegetable gardens and vineyards within the city walls.[3] They are an important reminder that we should not conceive of town and country as completely separate spheres - if such reminder were necessary. But they are too small to affect estimates of aggregate supply.

These quantitative speculations present a prima facie case against large scale exports of wine. They do not by their very nature exclude the possibility that part of local production was exported and that part of local consumption was imported. What they do is to show that what from the archaeological point of view constitutes a large number of villas, is not enough for the economic historian to believe that their production exceeded what was necessary for local consumption. The literary evidence and that from the *amphorae* did not point conclusively to substantial exports, either.

The land discussed until now has only an area of about one eighth of our assumed Pompeian territory. What happened in the rest? Also near the town we may expect some horticultural activities, analogous to those in a number of town gardens. Fruit and vegetables have to be brought fresh to the market, a trip that would have been necessary quite frequently. A location near the town would therefore be advantageous.[4] As it is also highly labour intensive with sharp seasonal peaks, easy access to casual labour from the town would be important as well.

century Valladolid, and 120 litres for Paris on the eve of the Revolution.

[1]Cato 56-58; cf. Duncan-Jones (1982) 146.

[2]Purcell (1985) 13, 15, n. 71 and n. 74. If the adult half of the population drinks 200 litres per head, and the children drink nothing, we obtain an average of about 100 litres for the entire population. If the average Pompeian indeed drank Cato's rations there would be even less scope for Pompeian wine export: Pompeii would probably have been a substantial net importer.

[3]Jashemski (1979).

[4]White (1970a) 246 ff.

Productivity of the land is hard to guess, as so much depends on specific crops chosen, but would be quite high.

Let us assume for lack of a better guess that the area allocated to horticulture near the town (and occasional plots elsewhere of course) is similar to that allocated to the villa estates, i.e. 2500 hectares. If that is so, three quarters of the Pompeian territory is still left, a large and fertile plain of 15,000 hectares. The literary sources inform us that this was cereal land, and the archaeology informs us of the absence of villa agriculture. These two different types of data match because it is commonly believed that the typical unit of exploitation in cereal agriculture was small.

I am aware that Frederiksen has argued for the presence in Campania of large cereal-growing estates worked by gangs of slaves.[1] But his argument rests on a fallacious analogy with Sicily. Both Sicily and Campania were important for the Roman grain supply. In Sicily he observes the presence of big slave-owners producing grain with gangs of slaves. In Campania he obviously also observes rich landowners and cereal production; he concludes that the two belong together.[2] But this conclusion does not follow. Employment of slaves must be viewed in the context of the availability of alternative forms of labour. Exploiting slaves is not the only way in which a large landowner may become rich. Squeezing tenant farmers is an obvious alternative. Campania's seven or eight times higher population density (than Sicily) is bound to have had some importance for the availability of alternative forms of more or less dependent labour.[3]

Continuing our numbers game, we must make a few more awkward choices. Probably we can safely ignore fallowing in this fertile area, and assume annual cropping. The references to multicropping in the literary sources refer to exceptional areas,

[1]Frederiksen (1981) 274 ff.

[2]The presence of slaves as such is no argument either; what is needed is a demonstration that they are employed in cereal agriculture.

[3]For population density, above, p. 70; 108 ff; I agree that peasant landowners are unlikely, below, p. 143 ff.

and Pompeii is unlikely to have been one of those.[1] Comparative evidence also suggests that at this level of population-density annual cropping is to be expected, although for us this can only serve as a circular argument.[2] Yields are perhaps less problematic than they might seem to be. Late medieval and early modern comparative evidence would suggest that we should probably expect the net return per hectare to be in the order of magnitude of 400-600 kg. per hectare.[3] Columella's calculations imply a net product of about 400 kg. per hectare.[4]

If we therefore assume that the net product (gross product minus seeds for next year) equals 500 kg. per hectare,[5] this area could produce 7500 metric tons of cereals, in an average year of course (15,000 ha. x 500 kg. = 7500 tons). That could feed 37,500 persons on the assumption of an average cereal consumption of 200 kg. per head per year.[6]

This carrying-capacity figure under the assumptions as specified above is remarkably close to the population estimate that we can derive from Beloch: 36,000.[7] The two figures have been obtained independently from each other, it makes sense that they should be in the same order of magnitude, and the fact that they are so similar inspires confidence in both of them. The uncertainty about the assumptions is such that the

[1]Above, p. 100 ff.

[2]Boserup (1981) 15 ff.

[3]Braudel (1979) Vol. I 96 ff; Fourquin in: Léon (1977) I 200 f.

[4]Duncan-Jones (1982) 370 f.

[5]Earlier, p. 81;, I have assumed 400 kg. net product as an average for Italy. I do not think Pompeii was average: the land was very fertile. I am not particularly interested in yield ratios here. High yield ratios may result from fertile land, but also from sparse sowing (and thus using more land less productively). Increasing the sowing rate is, 'ceteris paribus', bound to decrease the yield ratio, but increase production per hectare. In any case, my calculations only require information on net product.

[6]For consumption estimates: Clark and Haswell (1967) 1 ff; Hopkins (1978a) 56 (total calorie needs 250 kg. wheat equivalent). For estimates of proportion of cereals: Garnsey (1983a) 118 and Foxhall and Forbes (1982) 68ff. I ignore the potential contribution from fishing, following Gallant (1985).

[7]Density: 180 persons per sq. km. Above, p. 108 ff. The calculation is not particularly sensitive as to my assumption about the size of the territory. Varying the size of the territory not only varies production, but also consumption. The only real effect is on the presupposed level of urbanization.

slight surplus that results has no meaning. Forced to speculate, one might be inclined to increase it somewhat. The yield per hectare is a fairly average figure. In the early modern figures we can observe quite marked differences in output between regions with different soils.[1] The population figure on the other hand may be somewhat on the high side. It has been derived from an average for Campania as a whole, which includes the very fertile *ager Campanus* near Capua. In conclusion we can say that it is possible that Pompeii would export some of her grain, and this would presumably be to Rome.

But this small surplus that results from our tentative calculations is quite misleading: it refers to average years. Recent research has drawn attention to the dangers of the simplifying assumption of 'average production'.[2] It has become evident that the reality of ancient cereal farming consisted of major variations around the mean. Though obviously a cause of great hardship, this variability could also generate substantial profits. Pompeii and the rest of Campania were in a particularly favourable location to profit from the vagaries of climatic instability. Puteoli was the main port for the long-distance supply of the city of Rome. It therefore had easy access to this enormous market.[3]

The second advantage of its location was that it was sufficiently far away from the two main sources of supply, North Africa and Egypt. Its weather conditions would therefore often be at variance with those across the Mediterranean. A bad harvest in Campania could coincide with a normal, or even good, harvest in the grain-supplying provinces. Additional grain would have been available in Puteoli at a fairly reasonable price. The opposite could also occur: a normal or good harvest in Campania, coinciding with shortages in Rome due to a bad harvest in the provinces.

[1] Figures in Aymard (1973) 483 ff. are higher but may refer particularly to more productive districts. Doing away with fallowing we should probably not also posit a very high yield each year. A higher yield than I have assumed would increase the number of years in which there would be a surplus for export to Rome.

[2] E.g. Garnsey and Whittaker (1983); Halstead and O'Shea (1988).

[3] Frederiksen (1980-1); Fischer (1986) fails to take sufficient account of Campania's own agricultural potential.

But the two markets, Rome and Campania, are of quite different sizes. Campanians buying grain in Puteoli to make up for local shortfalls would not have driven up the price very much. Safeguarding against famine was relatively cheap and easy. A glut in Campania would not drive the prices down by very much, either: the Roman market could absorb a lot. If a Campanian glut coincided with a shortage in Rome, fortunes could be made. Every grain speculator must dream of escaping his fate, that he always has a lot for sale when prices are low, and only little when prices are high; for some Pompeians such dreams would have come true.[1] And the inevitable wrath of angry consumers would be at Rome, and not in his own town.[2]

The net effect of the easy access to external sources of grain supply would be more stable food prices. As fluctuating food prices are a serious impediment to high levels of urbanization, we may here have a part of the explanation for the dense pattern of urban settlement in this part of Roman Italy.

Deduction as an alternative tactic: location theory

So far the argument has largely been inductive. We have looked at the available evidence, tried to evaluate its meaning and build a coherent picture with it. But evidence is never good enough, and pure induction is of course an illusion. An alternative, more deductive approach would try to start from some first principles, and make a prediction about reality. If the hypothesis survives the testing against the data, we have succeeded, always for the time being of course.

Much of our evidence is spatial, and any hypothesis would have to include propositions about the most suitable locations for certain kinds of economic activities and why such locations would be less suitable for other activities. In other words, location may be seen as the expression of competition between alternative uses of land. Besides scarcity rent, economists

[1] At the price of not being able to profit from a local bad harvest, of course.

[2] I here assume that transport costs between Campania and Rome, and above all a measure of political restraint, would prevent unacceptable price rises in Campania. Evidence is lacking for the area, for a general argument for market control, see Jongman and Dekker (1988).

distinguish differential rent, which has its origin in the scarcity of land of a particular quality. Apart from obvious differences between lands, such as fertility, location also constitutes such a difference, because all land cannot be in the same place. In the end, rent is determined by what consumers will be prepared to pay for the products of the land. If production takes place for the market, transport costs to the market erode the scarcity rent that a location could otherwise command. We can say that the advantages of a specific location find their expression in a location rent. This is graphically represented in Figure VI.

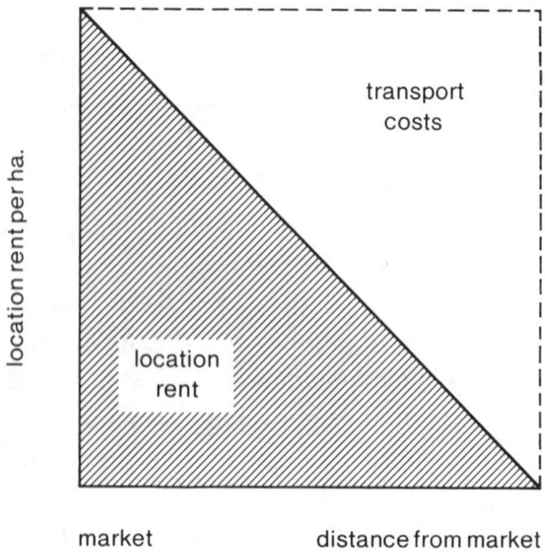

Figure VI: Location rent and distance from the market
(after: Lloyd and Dicken (1977) 36)

The slope of the curve is obviously product-specific, and we should therefore draw separate curves for all different crops or combinations of crops (Figure VII).
From the market until a distance X_1 from the market, product

'A' can support a higher location rent.[1] Thereafter it is product 'B' that supports the higher location rent. In the competition for the use of land between products 'A' and 'B' it is therefore product 'A' that wins in the zone between the market and distance X_1 from the market, and product 'B' that wins in the zone between X_1 and X_2, the extensive margin.

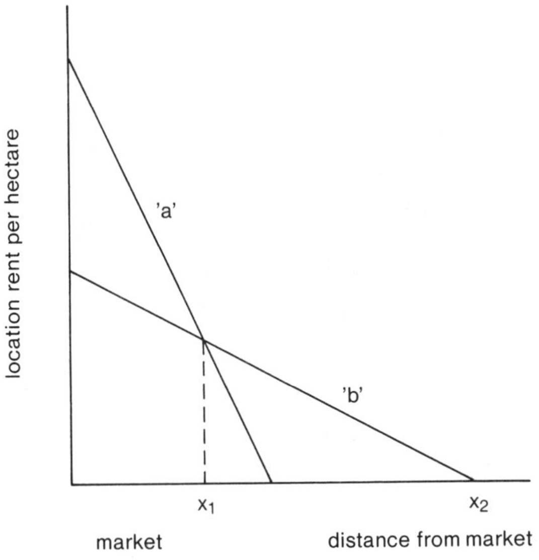

Figure VII: Location rent curves for different crops
(after: Lloyd and Dicken (1977)

But 'product A' and 'product B' still need some flesh on their bones. In our case we are mostly concerned with cereals on the one hand and the viticulture dominated group of products from villa agriculture on the other. Which one is 'A' and which one is 'B'? The curves drawn in Figure VII are linear. The intercept

[1]The curves can be seen as bid-rent curves, the rent a farmer would be prepared to pay to the owner of the land. Alonso (1960).

depends on profitability at the market, eroded by transport costs, the slope.

The ancient agricultural writers agree that viticulture is more profitable than cereal agriculture.[1] Recent research has put a not inconsiderable number of question marks to this. Duncan-Jones has shown that Columella's bookkeeping was inadequate to prove his own point.[2] That is relevant in the general debate on economic rationality, and it also invalidates the actual figures from Columella.[3] Those should, in any case, never have been taken as an accurate representation of an average reality (whatever be the meaning of such an average in a real world with sharp fluctuations around the mean). As profits are only a small proportion of turnover - six per cent seems a popular figure that gets tossed around - a small relative change in costs or benefits has a much larger effect on profits. Six per cent higher costs produce a 100 per cent disappearance of profit in our example. Any mistake we make is being amplified fifteen or twenty-fold.[4] In this case it is therefore unwise to engage in the numbers game. But even if Columella's calculations may not have been up to scratch, it is not likely that the reality was the very opposite of what he was saying. In so far as his opinion appears to have beeen shared by large numbers of wealthy Romans, he must have been right.

We are on considerably safer ground with transport costs. Here conventional wisdom will have to be revised. Conventional wisdom refers to A.H.M. Jones' calculations on transportation with figures from Diocletian's price edict.[5] The logic of the

[1]Duncan-Jones (1982) 34 ff.

[2]Duncan-Jones (1982) 39 ff.

[3]Macve (1985) is now the best statement on ancient accountancy and its relevance for the ancient economy. Above, p. 44.

[4]Even for modern historians with ample data, this is a serious problem. See for example the uncertainty surrounding the profitability calculations for slavery in the American South by Fogel and Engermann (1974).

[5]Jones (1974b) 37. In recent years this calculation has come under a certain amount of criticism because of the dubious quality of the information from the Price Edict: Duncan-Jones (1982) 366 ff; Hopkins (1978b) 46 f; Hopkins (1982) is the most skeptical account of the value of the price edict. The actual figures given by Jones now have to be revised in any case, if we accept - and I think we should - that the 'modius castrensis' equals 1 1/2 'modius italicus':

Jones argument is to calculate transport costs as a percentage of value, and Jones concludes that only goods with a high 'intrinsic' value could bear the costs of transport over long distances. Now, firstly, it is not price that matters, but profit. But secondly, and this is more important, in case of agricultural products the yield per unit of land is also important, and that was ignored by Jones. It is obvious that if an area produces a very heavy and bulky yield, the profits at the market are far more quickly being eroded by transport costs than if an area produces a flyweight crop.

If we assume for the sake of simplicity that transport costs are a linear function of weight and distance, we can perform the necessary calculations. Employing the same yield-figures for viticulture and cereal agriculture as employed for our carrying-capacity calculations (2000 kg. wine per hectare, 500 kg. cereals per hectare) it is obvious that the location rent curve for wine slopes downward far more steeply than for cereals.[1] One hectare of a vineyard implies four times more transport costs than a hectare planted with cereals. Therefore wine, starting from a higher level of profitability at the market than grain, falls off far more rapidly than grain. Wine can therefore be equated with our original product 'A' and grain with 'B'.[2] This identification is reinforced considerably by the fact that a larger proportion of the wine yield will in fact be brought onto the

Duncan-Jones (1976). Jones thought that the 'modius castrensis' was equal to the 'modius italicus'. Consequently, the price differential is even more marked now: the price of wheat doubles after about 200 miles of transport over land (the figure of 225 miles in Hopkins (1982) 83 must be a calculation error).

[1]The mathematical formula is : $LR = Y (m-c) - Ytd$.
LR = location rent per unit of land; Y = yield (quantity produced) per unit of land; m = market price per unit of product; c = production cost per unit of product; t = transport rate per unit of distance; d = distance of the unit of land from the market. Lloyd and Dicken (1977) 35.

[2]Uncertainty as to the precise level of profitability prohibits the calculation of x_1. De Neeve (1984) employs the theory to suggest that for the whole of Italy such a zoning may be postulated, with the city of Rome as the centre. No doubt there is some truth in this, but we must be careful. The theory presupposes a fairly high level of market integration, which may not have obtained over such large distances, given high transport costs. Moreover, subsistence agriculturalists may have evaded such market forces.

market than of the cereal yield. The latter has a bigger auto consumption component.[1]

Transplanting this analysis on to the Pompeian territory, the simple prediction of viticulture near the town and cereals at greater distance is largely borne out by the ancient evidence discussed previously. As the town is also a harbour, the unknown forces of external markets coincide with the local market. The stretch of supposed viticulture east of the town along the ancient course of the river Sarno was not predicted because we simplified transport costs, assuming them to be equal in all directions. In this case the cheaper river transport produced a location rent curve sloping downward less steeply for transport in that direction.[2] For a part of our viticulture area, north of the town, a second type of argument should be added: that of the special suitability of the land. It is the most fertile land of the territory, and it is also more hilly, a property considered very important. Varro (*R.R.* I. vi 5) writes: 'Owing to these three types of configuration different crops are planted, grain being considered best adapted to the plains, vines to the hills, and forests to the mountains.'

Villa density in this area is higher than in the stretch east of the town, along the ancient course of the river Sarno. The numbers involved are too small for us to be confident about the statistics, but perhaps it could be maintained that the double locational attraction of the area north of the town - proximity to the market and special suitability of the physical geography - is responsible for this extra high density.

Viticulture may be more suitable to this area, and the proximity of the market is also important. But it is not only an area of predominant viticulture, but also of the predominance of the villa system, in other words, of the source of wealth most characteristic of the Roman elite. Many of these villas had luxurious residential parts. In the discussion of the identity of owners of the villas I had to reject the identifications of

[1]Not of course because of the inherent logic of the location analysis but because in the contemporary social context peasants would try to avoid becoming dependent on a fluctuating market for their physical survival.

[2]For an analysis of such heterogeneity, see Lloyd and Dicken (1977) ch. 5.

ownership proffered by Della Corte and similar work by Day. Consequently there is not now any evidence to support the view that many villa-owners or wine-growers were freedmen.[1] These villas are the icing on the cake, and a high incidence of freedmen among their owners would have implied a high degree of recognizable freedman penetration in the Pompeian elite, leaving aside here a definition of that elite. But direct evidence for the status of the owners was minimal. We need not reject the view, however, that the villa owners would be at the top of Pompeian society.

An interesting parallel with locational implications comes from the city of Urso in Spain. Its colonial charter includes residence requirements for magistrates and members of the *ordo*.[2] They are required to live within one mile from the city. Of course no one knows whether the same applied to Pompeii, but it may have been the case. And if it was not, it is not unreasonable to think that the *lex Ursonensis* tries to legislate and formulate an already present pattern. In any case, we can observe that a circle with a one mile radius around the town includes almost all *villae*.

For the Pompeian plain we have postulated a pattern of small farms with cereals as their predominant crop. But this leaves wide open the question of the ownership of the land. Evidence is completely lacking, and speculation is our only resort. That the farmers in this area would be the owners of their land is unlikely. The first thing arguing against it is the high value of this land: it is very fertile and located sufficiently close to the pivot of the Roman grain supply in the first century, Puteoli. Surpluses are therefore probably larger and more easily marketable. It is hard to imagine that such land could have remained the property of the peasants themselves. To quote Garnsey: 'The leadership of the Roman state was always in the hands of a restricted aristocracy which controlled most of the land and showed a consistent reluctance to allow

[1] Above, p. 128 ff.

[2] ILS 6087.

their social inferiors to farm above subsistence level.'[1] My second argument relies on an impression of the inequality of wealth in Pompeii. But before we turn to that, a discussion of the effects of the settlement of Sullan colonists in 80 B.C. demands our attention.[2]

We know that veterans were settled, though we do not know how many. Lepore estimated them as between 4000 and 5000, on the assumption that Pompeii would have received its appropriate share of the 47,000 settled in the whole of Campania.[3] We can leave aside for the moment the vexed problem of the possible discontinuity in the political elite resulting from this colonization. What were the consequences for the agrarian structure? Gabba argues that they were negligible, and uses the Pompeian evidence as the main argument for his general thesis of the limited importance of the settlement of veterans for the patterns of landholding.[4] Gabba relies heavily on Day's research: 'the year 80 B.C. did not introduce a break in continuity in the system of *villae rusticae* - enterprises conducted on a planned basis, of about 100 *iugera*.'[5] If villa agriculture was dominant before and after the settlement, this may mean one of two things: either the veterans were given large (villa-type) plots, or they did not keep their (mostly small) plots for any length of time. The first solution is of course too ridiculous to entertain seriously, and we have seen above that the villa/viticulture area was not very large anyway.

On the other hand it is of course not at all inconceivable that a number of veterans did not remain owners of their plots.[6] Officers may have kept their - bigger - plots, but soldiers may not have had an appetite for agricultural work, or may have been unsuccessful and forced to sell out.

[1]Garnsey (1980b) 37.

[2]Cic. 'Pro Sulla' 60 ff; Gabba (1976) 44 ff; Brunt (1971) 294 ff; Castrén (1975) 49-55, 92; Andreau (1980).

[3]Lepore (1950) 150 ff.

[4]Gabba (1976) 44 ff.

[5]Gabba (1976) 44 f.

[6]Cf. Brunt (1971) 309 ff; Gabba (1976); Andreau (1980).

But if ownership might have passed into the hands of a small number of magnates, it still does not follow that the only way to work that land would have been as large slave estates. Smallholding veterans could have sold their land and leased it back, as seems to have happened in Arezzo and Fiesole.[1] The real flaw in Gabba's argument is his reliance on the view that the villa type of exploitation was the dominant mode in the last two centuries of Pompeii's existence. If that is incorrect, as I have argued, his entire argument falls to pieces. Of course that does not mean that Gabba may not be right that the impact of colonization was only very short lived. It only means that his argument for it (the continuity of a villa system) is wrong. But neither can we say that the establishment of the colony was the cause of the establishment of a system of small scale arable farming, because evidence for the existence of large scale farming *before* the settlement of the veterans is almost non-existent.[2]

None of this is intended to deny the great importance of the settlement, it is merely trying to change focus. Evidence for a major shift in the patterns of exploitation is negligible, but the fact that large numbers of larger and smaller landowners must have been expropriated to make room for the veterans cannot have failed to affect the position of many individuals. The expropriated peasant must have been hardest hit, but his voice cannot be heard in the evidence. Significant sections of the elite did not escape unscathed either (as has been amply documented by Castrén), even though some families - or more correctly, family names - made a comeback after a while.[3] Interesting is the possibility of tracts of city owned land, as suggested by Castrén and Andreau.[4] These may have been leased on very favourable conditions, with considerable security of tenure for the leaseholder, attractive enough to make these

[1]Andreau (1980) 196.

[2]Andreau (1980) 194.

[3]Andreau (1980).

[4]Castrén 1975) 53, 140; Andreau (1980) 188 ff.

lands a prerogative for the political elite, and excluding the old presullan aristocracy for at least a period.[1]

The second argument for the view that most of the cereal land farmed in small plots was owned by the elite relates to the inequality of wealth in Pompeii. If the cereal farmers owned their land that would imply a relatively equal distribution of wealth, which, however, was not so. In the town we can count about 500 to 600 luxurious townhouses of the *atrium* type. It seems unlikely that the lifestyle of those families could have been supported by the joint income from at most about 100 villas and from urban manufacturing and commerce.[2] It seems more likely that rents from cereal farming constituted an important part of the income of these 500 to 600 'families', supplemented by income from villas and urban economic activities. If all small-scale cereal farming was done by tenant farmers for 500 landowners resident in town, the latter would have owned an average of about 30 hectares of cereal land. Ownership of a wine villa would perhaps be the distinction that separated the more wealthy members of the elite from the less wealthy ones.[3] It is tempting to consider the correlation of the probable number of members of the *ordo*, 100, with the likely maximum of the number of villas, about 100, as more than mere coincidence. In chapter five I shall develop more fully this argument about inequality of wealth and ownership of agricultural land.

[1]Andreau (1980) 189 against Castrén. The fundus Audianus of this type quoted in L. Caecilius Iucundus' wax tablet archive (CIL IV, suppl. I, t. 138, 139, 140) must have been something more than a peasant's plot, as the annual rent was HS 6000. On the assumption of an annual rent of 6%, the capital value would have been HS 100,000, equal to the probable census for decurions, below p. 193. As it could e.g. be mortgaged it probably counted towards such a census. The similar occupation of 'ager publicus' counted towards the senatorial census - Cic. 'ad Fam.', 13, 5, 2. Cf. Andreau (1980) 195.

[2]For trade in agricultural products, see the present chapter, for urban manufacturing and trade see chapter IV.

[3]Leveau's insistence - Leveau (1983a) - that the system of villa agriculture represents romanised society, in contrast to native society, is obviously inapplicable in the Pompeian case. The explanatory power of his hypothesis is therefore less strong, even if it may apply in for example north Africa.

A comparison with early modern Campania

If, to borrow a beautiful phrase from Ramsay Macmullen, 'analogies, to be sure, prove nothing, but they comfort conjecture', we may perhaps seek such comfort, after the many conjectures we have had to make.[1] I shall therefore now expand the analysis to include some comparative material. A comparative approach may help in finding a few missing pieces of the puzzle. This is the first way comparative material is often used, and it is quite legitimate. But at the same time one should be very careful here. Employing data from later periods to fill in gaps is only justified if we may legitimately assume that there are no major differences between the two periods. Often it is exactly this that we do not know. We may expect least problems when dealing with variables of a more or less biological nature. Human food requirements, climate, the productivity and requirements of plant and animal life, may all have changed over time, but often less than many other variables. And making educated guesses as to the direction and size of these changes is not beyond our capacity, provided we do not trust our results up to the last decimal point.

The range of possible variation may be small for some variables, but that is obviously not the case for all of them. One only has to look at yield figures for modern crops to see that vast improvements have been possible. And this creates a methodological problem. The historian will often find that he is most interested in precisely those variables that have shown the biggest changes over the last one or two centuries. These are the key variables in the process of modernization. The stalemate is no less if one is interested in stagnation, because the same variables remain the core of one's concern.

Because of this high potential for variation of precisely the variables that matter, historians and archaeologists of pre-industrial societies should perhaps be more sparing in their use of some modern statistical data. The first attempts at modern social statistics often roughly coincide with the transformation of a society into a modern society: the emergence of

[1]MacMullen (1974) 14.

modern statistical registration is part of the modernization process. With some luck the earliest of those statistics may give us an idea of what the undiluted preindustrial past would have looked like, but rarely can we be sure. If we want to avoid this problem, we should turn to other historical data, from medieval and early modern times; and for many areas around the northern shores of the Mediterranean these exist, often in large quantity, and of good quality.

Of course, society in those periods should not simply be equated with that of antiquity, but at least we shall not have to worry about the recent major transformations. Similarity and dissimilarity between ancient and early-modern societies is a productive field for comparative research on growth and stagnation in the preindustrial context, while introducing the modern data is only relevant for an analysis of modernization.

A second use of the comparative method is more analytical, and often employs the differences rather than the similarities between periods. It may enable us to understand the nature and logic of the mechanisms at work, either because such mechanisms can be better documented from other periods, or because we can compare the impact of differences in certain variables on the rest of the societies concerned. This method is known in economic theory as 'comparative statics'. The more variables we can keep unchanged, the better we can disentangle the workings of the ones that do change.

The historian of ancient Campania can call himself lucky since the publication of a number of studies on early modern Campania by the French historian Gérard Delille.[1] Their central theme - especially in his *Agricoltura e demografia nel regno di Napoli nei secoli XVIII e XIX* - is an analysis of the close correlation between agricultural regime (crops and property relations) and demographic structure. The key element in the demographic analysis is the mortality pattern. Mortality is seen as the barometer of economic (mis)achievement. An analysis of labour productivity is the link between the demographic and

[1] Delille (1973); Delille (1977a); Delille (1977b) and recently Delille (1985).

the agricultural system - between wants (simplified as survival), and the means to satisfy them (food production).

In order to perceive relations between agricultural and demographic regimes, Delille compares districts that were different from each other as to the predominant crop. And here we have our first pleasant surprise: in the eighteenth and nineteenth century the 'Pompeian' plain was predominantly an area of cereal agriculture.[1] Viticulture and olive trees are found on the hill slopes. In short, the distribution pattern of predominant crop types closely resembles the pattern which I have postulated for antiquity. And most importantly, the predominance of cereal agriculture - so difficult to prove for antiquity - finds it later counterpart, which is a comfort for my conjecture. This zoning is reflected in mortality patterns. The plains with their cereal agriculture show very high levels of mortality: figures (1814) hover around 30 per 1000, with a peak of 38.69 in Scafati (i.e. Pompeii). Areas in the hills have considerably lower levels of mortality: 20-25 is the typical range.[2] In the hills, birth-rates are correspondingly lower. So, not only do crops follow some relatively simple geographical criteria (hills and plain, a classification also used by Varro *R.R.* I.vi, 5) but we witness a coincidence with variations in mortality - the most interesting measure of welfare. Differential levels of prosperity are also evident in patterns of land ownership. The viticultural areas are predominantly owned by smallholding private farmers, whereas in the cereal lands a substantial 'feudal' and ecclesiastical landownership is observed, accompanied by many day-labourers.[3]

The mechanisms at work in these regions with such different agricultural regimes can be brought to light if we look at some other demographic indicators. In areas with predominantly cereal agriculture, women marry considerably earlier than in the lands of the vine. In the latter areas the proportion of married women is considerably lower. Not only do these women marry later,

[1]Delille (1977a) 15.

[2]Delille (1977a) 7.

[3]Delille (1977a) 23. More elaborate discussion in Delille (1985), unfortunately at a much greater distance from the economic analysis.

but many never marry at all.[1] Corresponding distinctions can be seen when we observe the age structure in the two types of regions.[2] The age pyramid in the cereal agriculture areas has a much wider base (and correspondingly narrower middle and top) than the viticultural areas' age pyramid. Life in the cereal lands has a more hectic pace. Many are born, and if they survive infancy, they marry quickly - only to die young. Human reproductive capacity is heavily taxed to cope with the mortal effects of a low standard of living.

A very interesting and distinctive feature is that of the sex ratios in the two types of region.[3] The cereal lands show a marked surplus of males in the crucial 18-30 year age group, as compared to viticultural regions, an imbalance due to migration, and responsible for the vast difference in female age at marriage. A scarcity of women of marriageable age improves their chances considerably, and they marry a lot younger.

To sum up. The two types of region not only have different agricultural regimes, but they are also markedly different in demographic structure. The cereal lands have a considerably higher mortality, due to a lower standard of living, and it is compensated by a higher birth-rate and by immigration of males. Related are an abundance of males in the 18-30 year age group and consequent early marriages for women (making possible the high birth-rate). In terms of an economic historical analysis this means that Delille may have brought to light some correlations between types of crop, standard of living, and demand for labour.

In economic analysis this is the problem of labour productivity. What is the contribution to production made by additional units of labour? As wages are supposed to be equal to this last additional contribution to production (marginal productivity), we may - if wages are low (or mortality high)- presume that marginal productivity is low. In my earlier discussion of the intensification of agricultural production I have shown, following

[1]Delille (1977a) 39 ff.

[2]Delille (1977a) 49 ff.

[3]Delille (1977a) 57 ff.

Ester Boserup, that declining marginal productivity of labour may be the undesired side-effect of such intensification.[1] Delille does not quote Boserup, but the analysis is similar.

It is important that we realize the difference between production and productivity. Productivity refers to the contribution of one production factor (such as land or labour) to total production. We can therefore speak of the productivity of land or labour. Thus, labour productivity expresses the relation between the amount of labour used and the resulting production (and assumes the other factors are kept constant). Similarly, productivity of land expresses the contribution of land when the other factors (labour and capital) are kept constant. The distinction between production and productivity is important, because it is easily conceivable that production (or productivity of land) may increase and labour productivity decrease at the same time. To illustrate this, we must return for a moment to the Ricardian analysis of the expansion of agricultural production at the intensive margin.[2] In that case production was increased by employing more labour on the same plot of land. Unfortunately such an increase of production required a disproportionately larger labour input. A doubling of production might require trebling the labour input. Per kg. of agricultural product, more labour is necessary: labour productivity has declined. Yet production (per hectare) has increased.

In any discussion of economic growth this distinction between production and productivity is important. Modern economic growth is characterized by the simultaneous increase of production and labour productivity. The growth of national income outstrips population growth, and per capita income increases. In the preindustrial context that was not usually the case. Periods of increasing population and production witnessed a decline of labour productivity (and therefore incomes). Per capita incomes would be relatively high in periods of lower population and

[1]Above, p. 85 ff.

[2]Above, p. 88 ff.

production.[1] There is nothing wrong in saying that the ancient world, like medieval Europe before the Black Death, witnessed substantial economic growth, because of observed increases in population and total production.[2] But if that is so, it is not unlikely that it also implied declining labour productivity, and therefore a low standard of living for the mass of the population. To avoid implying an increase of the *per capita* income, the term 'economic expansion' perhaps characterizes such development better than the term 'growth'.

Delille's analysis of labour productivity is a chilling tale. At first sight, labour productivity in cereal agriculture might not look too depressing. Performing the calculations on the basis of production per number of days worked, he calculates that the labour of one man may feed about 13 people.[3] The picture changes dramatically, however, if we take into account the very uneven spread over the year.[4] If we calculate from requirements at peak periods, the results deteriorate dramatically: one man's labour only suffices for about 3 people - not enough for the average peasant family of 4-5 people. Mitigation of the problem is only possible through alternative employment inside or outside agriculture, or reduction of manpower requirements in the peak season. Neither of these two seem easy to accomplish.

Such blank figures require differentiation, however. Labour productivity is higher with other crops such as wine.[5] But most interesting is further differentiation to account for plot size and use of oxen. By definition, labour productivity will increase if other factors such as land or capital are used in larger quantities. Using more land or oxen with the same amount of labour obviously increases the productivity of that labour. But

[1]The problem is complex. Distinctions ought to be made between the urban and the rural sector; and per capita income is not the only thing that matters: income inequality also varies. The inquisitive ancient historian is referred to Cipolla (1981) part II for a first introduction.

[2]Above, p. 66 ff. for population.

[3]Delille (1977a) 120 f.

[4]Delille (1977a) 118 provides an informative table on the distribution of the workload over the year (for olive oil, wine, and grain).

[5]Delille (1977a) 126.

using more land is not so easy. Soon enough, available manpower will be exhausted.[1] But if, instead of hoe and manpower, plough and oxen are used, considerable increases in productivity are possible, the plot that can be worked by a peasant family increases about threefold.[2] Of course the plough and ox cost something too, yet this peasant's lot is much better. The problem is to find the fodder for the ox. Southern Italy is not a meadow, like many parts of northern Europe. At the end of the last century, it was estimated that an ox would need about 10-12 hectares of southern Italian pasture, which is three to five times more than in northern Europe. 'Small properties could not feed large animals, and working the land with the hoe, the peasant could not cultivate a plot larger than one that was barely sufficient for his survival.'[3] Thus, southern Italy had very few cattle: in 1866 there were only 14 oxen per 100 inhabitants in the province of Salerno.[4] The contrast with northern Europe is dramatic. Lack of possibilities to increase labour productivity in cereal agriculture has locked Mediterranean Europe into an almost permanent state of underdevelopment. Marc Bloch made this bifurcated development a central theme in his famous *Les caractères originaux de l'histoire rurale française*.[5]

The catch of the situation is that oxen compete with people for scarce resources. For the peasant who faces the choice between using his own labour and that of his family, and becoming more productive by making part of that human labour redundant and using oxen, the choice is obvious.[6] A higher labour productivity and standard of living would have been possible, but only at the expense of less production per hectare.

[1] Delille (1977a) 128.

[2] White (1967) 36 ff. for hoes in Roman agriculture. Also: Frayn (1979) 142 f.

[3] Delille (1977a) 135.

[4] Delille (1977a) 134; Delille (1977b) 133 n. 16; the north-western European figures are of a different order of magnitude. Already in the later middle ages we find sometimes considerable numbers of horses (more expensive than oxen): Slicher van Bath (1960) 200 f.

[5] Bloch (1931); Lamprecht (1878) for a forerunner.

[6] Chayanov (1966) is the classic analysis.

And in that case the prevailing high population densities could not be sustained. The elder Pliny seems perfectly aware of the logic when he writes (*N.H.* 18, 37-38): *'bene colere necessarium est, optime damnosum, praeterquam subole sua colono aut pascendis alioqui colente'*, 'it is essential to cultivate well, but to cultivate exceptionally well is disastrous, except if a tenant is farming with the help of his family or those whom he has in any case to support.'[1] Nineteenth century technology was still unable to break through the ceiling imposed by rapidly declining marginal labour productivity. Specialization on cash crops with a higher labour productivity was only possible after American grain had come to dominate a world market for cheap grain, and thus guarantee the availability of the staple food.

The comparative exercise has been useful. Apart from providing a later example of the predominance of cereal agriculture, it has shown the nature of the development problem. Between the traditional poles of debate on the ancient economy (primitivism and modernism) we discover the contours of a more complex reality, a reality in which production has been brought to a historically high level, by and large not through a transformation of the production function, but through the mobilization and application of more and more labour to the same amount of land. Production may therefore be high (and make possible many impressive features of Roman society), but productivity has dropped to low levels. The standard of living for the mass of the population must have been low. Land is the scarce resource, and therefore land ownership marks off the 'haves' from the 'have nots'. In chapter five I shall return to landownership and social inequality.

[1]Frayn (1984) 115 f.

CHAPTER FOUR

URBAN MANUFACTURING, THE TEXTILE INDUSTRY

Why textiles?

Remarkably enough, little attention has in recent years been paid to the Roman textile industry.[1] If we can rely on early modern parallels, textiles were a not unimportant part of the consumer budget. For the mass of the population food would obviously be by far the largest part of their expenditure, often taking up some three quarters of the budget. But of the remainder, almost all would be spent on clothing and housing (including heating and lighting), in roughly equal parts.[2] The well-to-do and rich would of course spend a smaller proportion on food (even while over-eating) and more on - luxury - clothing.[3] This prominence of textiles is reflected in the occupational distribution of urban populations. For six selected early modern cities, the textile industry's share of the working population was on average some 35% (Table V).

[1] I propose to return to the textile industry in the Roman empire at a later date. Proper discussion would go well beyond the scope of this book. The standard account is Jones (1974c) 350-64. Recently Frayn (1984) and especially Morel (1978) have begun to question some traditional beliefs. As an exercise in methodology Bücher (1922b) 40-49 remains unsurpassed.

[2] Cipolla (1981) 30.

[3] Cipolla (1981) 34 f.

The textile industry was the core of manufacturing in so far as production was for external markets. If one believes that the economic modernization of Europe was rooted in the gradual emergence of a market system linking 'producer' cities, then the textile industry should occupy the prime place in any debate about the extent of similar developments in antiquity.

Table V: Early modern occupational distributions
(source: Cipolla (1981) 77)

	Verona 1409	Como 1439	Frankfurt 1440	Monza 1541	Florence 1552	Venice 1660
food[1]	23	21	21	39	13	17
textiles	37	30	30	25	41	43
building	2	4	8	1	6	4
metalwork	5	8	8	10	7	5
leather	10	7	4	-	7	7
others	23	30	29	25	26	24

Obviously a considerable part of the productive activities of later cities was directed towards catering for local needs. Thus, the building trade and the urban food industry were very important, apart from services. In that sense these cities were little different from the ancient ones. But those are activities that by their nature do not lend themselves easily to export. If one wants to argue that ancient cities were indeed typically producer cities, the local industries are of little interest.

Some other industries which have been pet subjects of ancient historians and especially archaeologists are equally of

[1]This includes both distribution and agriculture.

only minor importance in the present debate. I am here referring to the traditional obsession with ceramics and the like. Some excellent work has indeed been done in recent years, often serving as a cautionary tale against simplistic modernism.[1] But all the water in the sea will not wash away the simple fact that such items have never been a substantial part of production or consumption. Nobody has claimed trade in pots and pans as a major contributing factor in the economic development of Europe after the fall of the Roman Empire!

The textile industry itself has only been touched on in a more indirect fashion in recent research. Morel, in what is by all accounts an exemplary analysis of literary sources, has demonstrated that the famed Tarentine woollen industry is a scholarly fiction.[2] Sources referring to the good quality of Tarentine wool have - incorrectly - been taken to refer to textile manufacturing. Frayn's book on sheep rearing equally emphasizes raw wool, and trade in it, rather than textiles.[3] The importance of raw wool has also been emphasized by Pleket, who employs it as an argument to support his thesis of indirect elite involvement.[4] Flocks would often be owned by the elite, of course, and this gave them a powerful control over the raw material. Financially, the cost of the raw material was a very important part of the cost of textiles, which again pleads for elite involvement, although perhaps at arm's length.

Enough reason to pay some attention to the textile industry. And an urgent need in the case of Pompeii in particular after the publication of Walter O. Moeller's book on the Pompeian wool trade.[5] That book is uncompromisingly modernistic in its approach, and represents one of the most vociferous attacks on Finley's work. Its main conclusions can be summarized as follows:

[1]E.g. Harris (1980); also various contributions in D'Arms and Kopf (1980), Garnsey a.o. (1983) and Garnsey and Whittaker (1983).

[2]Morel (1978).

[3]Frayn (1984).

[4]Pleket (1984) 22 ff.

[5]Moeller (1976).

1. Production was on a sufficiently large scale to supply an external market. Textiles were a major Pompeian industry.
2. The organization of production and distribution was rationally conceived and executed. There are signs of a division of labour, male weavers, and in Moeller's opinion therefore factory production of cloth. The entrepreneurial structure was not dissimilar to that of medieval guilds, and in this system the fullers execute an integrating and controlling entrepreneurial function.
3. All social classes were involved, and this includes direct involvement of the municipal aristocracy. The wool craftsmen had serious political activities, aimed at exercising some control over the government of Pompeii in order to advance the industry's interests.

One might say that in Moeller's view Pompeii was a true Weberian 'producer city'. In this chapter I propose to demonstrate that none of Moeller's conclusions are warranted by the Pompeian evidence. The first step in my argument will be an analysis of potential local supplies of raw material. I shall argue that no indication exists that local supplies of wool were of such quantity and quality that they could have fostered an export industry in textiles. I shall then analyse the archaeological remains of workshops and argue that there is little to justify the belief that production took place on a large scale.

Moeller's conclusion that the fullers played a coordinating entrepreneurial role for the entire industry would have been very important, if true. I shall demonstrate that there is not a shred of evidence for such an equation with later times. Related views on the direct involvement of the urban aristocracy will also come under attack. The interpretation of the so-called Building of Eumachia as the guild-hall of the fullers will be criticized.

I shall conclude that Pompeian industry shows few, if any, characteristics appropriate to the 'producer' city. No one (export) industry dominates. Instead we see a welter of small scale crafts catering for the consumer demand of a local elite. In this sector of the Pompeian economy, the 'consumer city' ideal type corresponds best with reality.

The supply of raw material

The origin of the raw wool for the allegedly important Pompeian woollen industry is not at all clear in the works of the proponents of the thesis that Pompeii was a textile exporting centre. Moeller writes that wool came from Apulia, and also from local sources.[1] For Apulia he refers to Rostovtzeff, Tenney Frank and a passage in Varro.[2] But Rostovtzeff, while believing that it is very possible that Apulian wool came to Pompeii, adduces no evidence at all; Frank believes that 'to assume with M. Rostovtzeff that Pompeii was the woollen market for Apulia is to mistake the scale of Pompeian production'; and the Varro passage is about transhumance between Apulia and Reate - north west of Rome - and therefore irrelevant.

For local production we have Seneca (*Nat. Quaest.*, VI, 27), who informs us that during the earthquake six hundred sheep perished *'in Pompeiana regione'*. That the sheep were kept for their wool is not mentioned by the text. Moeller assumes that it 'is certain that thousands of the animals were pastured in the aforementioned Mons Lactarius range to the south and in the mountains to the west.'[3] These 'mountains to the west' keep coming up in the literature, but it must be pointed out that to the west of the city we find the sea.[4] The evidence for sheep on Mons Lactarius is derived from its name, but if correct, it proves the presence of sheep kept for milk, rather than for wool production.[5] Although it is clear from the sources that the area produced milk of very good quality to which medical properties were ascribed, the sources are equally clear in not referring to sheep, but to cows.[6]

[1] Moeller (1976) 74.

[2] Rostovtzeff (1957) 579 n. 200; Frank (1962) 260 n. 32; Varro, 'R.R.' II, 2,9, and not II 2,10. Gabba and Pasquinucci (1979) includes no references to production of raw wool in the Pompeian territory.

[3] Moeller (1976) 74.

[4] In the same vein: Frank (1962) 260; Frank (1933-40) V, 166.

[5] Hug (1925); Herzog-Hauser (1932).

[6] Cassiodorus, 'Variae' XI, 10 'vaccarum turba'. Symmachus, 'Epistulae' VI xvii 'armentali lacte'; Galen, Vol. x ed. C.G. Kühn, p. 365: 'Ta de zôa boes men eisin en tôi kata Tabias, kai esti toutou tou zôou pachu to gala, kathaper to tôn onôn lepton.'

In conclusion we may say that the evidence from antiquity is limited. Though we hear, perhaps not surprisingly, about the odd sheep, that is totally inadequate if we want to know how large the supply of raw wool was. It is important to add here that Campania is nowhere mentioned in literary sources praising the quality of the wool of various districts.

The limited nature of the archaeological data available to reconstruct the Pompeian agrarian economy forces us to resort to speculation. We can only hope that by limiting the range within which speculation may take place, we can supply interesting and testable hypotheses for future archaeological work.

Once again we will try to speculate about aggregate supply and demand, this time of raw wool in Pompeii and its territory. Ancient and modern authors alike praise the fertility of Campania. This fertility was due to the volcanic character of the soil, and made possible a high population density for the area.[1] In such a fertile and rather humid area a very large number of sheep could in principle be fed by growing fodder crops, or even by well maintained pasture land. Yet that is unlikely because in that way the area could not have maintained its dense population. In addition, pasture land does not correspond to what we read in the literary sources.[2] We may try to reconstruct a theoretical maximum of sheep in the area, even if that is improbably large. We shall see that such a figure would still be too low to argue a major textile industry based on local sources of raw wool.

Summers would have to be spent on the more humid mountain pastures, quite easily available to the east and the south of the Sarno plain. But how much winter pasture would be available? The problem here is that of competition with cereal agriculture: the winter is the main growing season in Mediterranean agriculture. In the previous chapter I have argued that in Pompeii cereal cropping would probably be annual.[3] If that is true, there would be no possibility of feeding the sheep in winter.

[1]For a discussion of population figures, see above, p. 108 ff.

[2]Above, p. 100 ff.

[3]Above, p. 100 ff; 134 f.

Sheep could only be kept if the extent of cereal agriculture were reduced. But it would have had to be a very drastic reduction, because sheep raising is an extensive activity. A reduction of the arable by, for example, a third would bring local cereal production almost certainly well below local subsistence needs, and yet these 5000 hectares would have allowed not more than about 14,000 sheep to be kept.[1] Wool productivity of sheep varies considerably, but to indicate the possible order of magnitude, the estimated average productivity of breeds other than Merino or Crossbred in 1954-1955 was 1.13 kg per head greasy, 0.56 kg clean.[2]

It should be emphasized that these figures do not represent an estimate of the likely local production, but of the likely maximum. With figures of this order of magnitude it appears unlikely that the local supply of raw wool would have stimulated textile production for an external market. But all this should not surprise us in any way. Sheep and people compete to a large extent for the same resources. A high proportion of sheep *per capita* necessarily entails a low population density. And indeed, the famed sheep-raising areas of ancient Italy - Apulia and certain areas in and around the Po Valley - were sparsely populated. A corollary of this is that major textile producing towns would either have to be located in thinly populated - and probably not very urbanized parts, or else rely on imported raw wool.[3]

Scale: spinning and weaving

A different approach to the problem of assessing the quantitative importance of Pompeian textile manufacturing is to analyse the archaeological remains of textile manufacturing plants on the site. Unfortunately, it is a path full of uncertainty.

Moeller writes 'at a very minimum, therefore, there are about seven hundred and ten persons engaged in cloth production,

[1] Le Houerou (1977) 263. Good grasslands, managed and rationally used, sub humid zone. Using fallow land for grazing gives even lower figures: Le Houerou (1977) 259.

[2] Carter and Charlet (1956), table 3.

[3] I propose to return to these matters in future. See above, p. 155.

and I suspect that the actual number was closer to one thousand or even more. In a city whose population was something between fifty (an obvious misprint - at p. 67 it is 15,000) and twenty thousand this total represents a large portion of the community's productive energy.'[1] Though not wanting to deny that this a not insignificant number, some comparison with the medieval world will do no harm. At Ghent, the proportion of male workers in wool amounted to at least 60 per cent of the craftsmen of the work force in the middle of the fourteenth century, in Brugge it was about 25 per cent in 1338-1340, and around the same time in Florence it was about 33 per cent.[2] These figures represent both somewhat higher proportions and especially far larger numbers (total populations: Ghent 64,000, Brugge 40,000 and Florence 90,000) than the figures that are supposed to represent the Pompeian situation.

But let us now investigate Moeller's figures in more detail. He assigns numbers of workers to workshops, altogether 237 fullers, dyers and felters. He is not able to base an estimate of the number of wool combers, weavers and spinners on archaeological data, but he assumes that they must have been at least twice as numerous as the others.

Although this is perhaps not unreasonable, it is nevertheless a quantitatively very important factor. If a considerable part of these processes was done in the countryside, or in the private urban households, then it will not really do to include these in the category 'urban crafts'. Of these, spinning was perhaps the most labour-intensive, a reason why in later times it was most prone to take place in rural districts, outside the control of urban crafts, and often done by women.[3] In the Roman world,

[1]Moeller (1976) 81.

[2]Lis and Soly (1979) 10. Professor Lis informed me that the craftsmen work force itself was between a fifth and a quarter of the total population. See also: Prevenier (1975). My lower estimate for the urban population of Pompeii - above p. 108 ff. - might appear to strengthen Moeller's case - if this estimate of 700-1000 wool workers is right.

[3]Carus-Wilson (1952) 379, 387, 395 f; Kriedte a.o. (1977).

spinning, unlike weaving, seems on the whole to have been a household operation.[1] No *collegia* of spinners are known to us.[2]

The evidence adduced by Moeller for spinning and weaving in Pompeian workshops is in fact only slight. Moeller writes that in many Pompeian houses loom-weights were found.[3] One might interpret this as indicating a very dispersed production, taking place in many individual households, and perhaps largely for private consumption. But an answer can only be given by a proper analysis of the distribution pattern. Some fifty loom-weights were found in I, x, 8 (Plate XV).[4] But this is no compelling reason to think of 'large scale spinning and weaving.'[5] That number of loom-weights is not evidently in excess of the number required for one warp-weighted loom for domestic use, and validates at most the existence of small scale craft-weaving.[6] We know a number of what are presumably slaves from the house. But there is no justification for believing that they were in fact engaged in spinning or weaving. The only person with a 'textile reference' is the '*Successus textor*' - but the inscription comes from the nearby *caupona* at I x, 3.[7]

In V iii, 10 a graffito recording 29 pounds of wool was found (CIL IV 6714). But there is no further reference at all to craft production of textiles or spinning. The house VI xiii, 6 takes a prominent place: 'evidently dedicated to large scale spinning and weaving', with allegedly seven male weavers and eleven female spinners.[8] Unfortunately we know nothing more about the men than their names, their sexual appetite, and

[1]Jones (1974c) 351.

[2]Jones (1974c) 360.

[3]Moeller (1976) 56.

[4]'Notizie degli Scavi di Antichità.' 1934 p. 317.

[5]Moeller (1976) 39.

[6]On the technology: Wild (1970) 61 ff; Hoffmann (1964) esp. 297 ff.

[7]CIL IV 8259; Moeller (1976) 39 assigns it to I, x, 5, incorrectly. Della Corte (1965) p. 301.

[8]Moeller (1976) 40.

their love of gladiatorial games. The female slaves are indeed spinning their *pensa* of weft and/or warp.[1]

House VII iv, 5, 7 is an interesting case. Three graffiti indicate the *locus* of three men.[2] In one case the line *'ERATI LOCUS'* is preceded by *'TEXE'* in much smaller letters.[3] So presumably Eratus was a weaver. The next step by Moeller and Zangemeister, the CIL editor of these inscriptions, is that the other two men must also have been weavers. From here Moeller proceeds to invent one foreman, three to five wool combers, three assistants for the weavers and nine spinners,[4] and he concludes that we are dealing with a small factory.[5]

In House IX vii, 20 an inscription recording eighteen pounds or weights of wool is all that we get to know.[6] In IX xii, 1 - 5 a graffito records the price of a tunic with a date, and another one records that weaving was begun at a specified date.[7] It must be clear that this kind of data could just as well refer to consumption and buying as to production and sale. For the scale of the possible production we depend on Della Corte's judgment that the premises were very suitable for the purpose, and on a Mercury holding a *marsuppium* in his right hand.[8]

Adding it all up we have references to at most four weavers, and eleven female spinners; on two occasions a certain amount of wool was written down on a wall, a tunic once changed ownership and some weaving was begun somewhere at a specified date. And this is supposed to prove that 'the number of persons engaged as *textores* in the city was large.'[9] Moeller's hypothesis that spinning and weaving took place on a large scale and in

[1] CIL IV 1507.

[2] CIL IV 1569-1572.

[3] CIL IV 1570, 1571. The lettering leaves some doubt of course as to whether they really belong together.

[4] Moeller (1976) 78.

[5] Moeller (1976) 40.

[6] CIL IV 5363.

[7] CIL IV 9108, 9109.

[8] Della Corte (1965) p. 321.

[9] Moeller (1976) 78.

the context of a craft organization is not borne out by the evidence. The next step must be to investigate those establishments about which he feels more secure - those for dyeing, feltmaking, and fulling.

Scale: dyeing, feltmaking and fulling

We shall first discuss the somewhat separate category of felt-making workshops, four in total. In the case of two of them, only the façade has been uncovered.[1] Both are identified with felt-making by *programmata* with *quactiliari* as supporters.[2] As these establishments, which are so near to each other, have not been excavated, we cannot in fact be certain that we are not dealing with a case where supporters had a recommendation painted on a neighbouring building.[3] In any case, one of the two was not solely devoted to felt-making (Plate XX). It appears that wool was also combed here, and that clothing was being sold.[4] Whether the Verecundus associated with this shop was the same person as the M. Vecilius Verecundus, *vestiarius*, known from House V ii, 16, is uncertain, but not impossible.[5]

Two other 'felt-making' shops (I xii, 4 and IX iii, 16) have been excavated but have not yielded any epigraphical data about their function. Each is characterized by a furnace in the middle of the room. The one in IX iii, 16 has not been preserved, and could therefore have been any kind of furnace for any purpose. The furnace in I xii, 4 has been excavated, but was in a broken down condition when it came to light (Plate XIX).[6] The photograph of the furnace taken before restoration would not seem to make the conclusion inevitable that it was used for felt-making. The room appears to be a bit cramped,

[1] IX vii, 1 and IX vii, 5-7.

[2] CIL IV 7809, 7838.

[3] If that were the case, we would not have two feltshops, but only one.

[4] Moeller (1976) 54.

[5] CIL IV 3130. See Della Corte (1965) p. 280.

[6] Moeller (1971) 188 f. Plate 46, Fig. 3 shows the original state of the furnace, whereas Plate 46, fig. 4 shows that the drawing on p. 188 places the furnace - incorrectly - too much in the centre of the room. See also my Plate XIX.

especially on the eastern side, and it is not too farfetched to suggest the alternative of a furnace for preparing food.

Of dyehouses, six are known from Pompeii. They present us with a problem that we will also encounter with the fullers. Dyeing could take place after the cleaning of the raw wool, that is as part of the production process of new cloth, or as the redyeing of faded cloth. Probably the word *infectores* was used for those engaged in the former, and *offectores* for those doing the latter.[1] Moeller believes that he can distinguish archaeologically between establishments for these two purposes. He argues that the shop IX iii, 1-2, housing *offectores* known from CIL IV 864 on the house, is archaeologically different as it lacks soaking-vats and the cauldrons are not of equal depth.[2] Other dyehouses have cauldrons of equal depth and soaking-vats. On IX vii, 2 an inscription with *infectores* was found. But this shop has only been partially excavated, and it is therefore impossible to know if it shares all the characteristics of the supposed workshop for dyeing new wool (Plate XVI).

Making an estimate of the total production of these six workshops with a total of 32 furnaces and cauldrons is not easy, but if they only served the needs of the population of Pompeii and its territory, there would have been about one furnace with a cauldron for every 1,000 inhabitants. This would not appear to leave much scope for a large export industry. Although the total number of fifty-three dyers that Moeller arrives at is perhaps somewhat inflated, it is probably not so by a very wide margin: a fairly full use of the available capital goods does not seem too unlikely.[3]

The first uncertainty with fulling is that the *fullones* of antiquity were from our point of view doing two different things

[1]Festus 112.6; p. 99 ed. Lindsey: 'Infectores, qui alienum colorem in lanam coiciunt. Offectores, qui proprio colori novum officiunt.' See Moeller (1973a) 368f.

[2]Moeller (1973a) 368 f.

[3]Moeller (1976) 81.

(Plate X).[1] On the one hand they were finishing newly woven cloth, but on the other hand they were also doing what we might call laundry work. Moeller also includes the initial cleaning of the raw wool among the activities of the members of the *collegium fullonum*, an important prop for his thesis that the fullers were the entrepreneurs of the trade. The evidence he adduces for this is weak, as I shall argue later.[2] He believes that he can identify one specific type of Pompeian workshop as being used for wool washing, and calls them *'officinae lanifricariae'*.[3] They are characterized by masonry tables with one or more built-in lead pans above furnaces, and one or more small vats (Plates XI and XII). Moeller rightly stresses that they form an archaeological type, and are clearly different from the Pompeian *fullonicae*.[4] But their function is considerably less clear: fulleries, dyehouses or laundries have all been suggested.[5]

Moeller's solution is principally based on an analysis of VII xii, 17 (Plates XI and XII), 'called an *officina lanifricaria* from the admonition *lanifricari dormis* found in a programma that decorated the wall of no. 15'.[6] Unfortunately the word *lanifricarius* is a *hapax*, but worse is the fact that the graffito does not come from the alleged *officina lanifricaria* at VI xii, 17, but from the *caupona* at number 15. It could therefore easily refer to a customer of the inn. The other possible indication of wool related activity is a series of notations on the

[1]Blümner (1912) 170 ff. remains the best discussion of techniques and terminology. Frayn (1984) 148 ff. for a more recent discussion.

[2]Moeller (1976) 75; below, p. 170 ff.

[3]Elsewhere, however, the core of his argument is that these workers were called 'fullones' - below, p. 170 ff. It may not be of great importance as an argument, but it would appear that both in Greek and in Latin separate words were used for those who did the initial washing ('erioplutai' and 'lanilutores') and those who did the fulling ('knapheis' or 'pluneis' and 'fullones' or 'lavatores'), see Blümner (1912) 106 ff. and 170 ff, cf. Frayn (1984) 148 ff. The distinction may, however, be artificial, for in both groups reality and terminology contain references to washing.

[4]Moeller (1966) 493-6.

[5]Ibid.

[6]Moeller (1976) 33.

wall.[1] They include in line 11 the word LAIVI, presumably lavi, I washed. But what had been washed? The graffito includes a column with seven times the abbreviations PL and another with P's and numbers. Fiorelli thought that the letters PL stood for *panni lanae*, cloth of wool, while Moeller suggests that they are an abbreviation for *pondo lanae*, or *pondera lanae*.[2]

The solution is a different one. The letters P.L. followed by numbers are also found on a number of *amphorae*, and can therefore not have anything to do with wool. Andreau has studied them and shown that the abbreviation stands for '*pondo librarum*'.[3] This also implies that the P's with numbers cannot be standing for *pensa* but only for *pondo*. That eliminates all indications that this shop had anything to do with wool. The other - archaeological - indications produced by Moeller cannot stand on their own.

Most of the other supposed *officinae lanifricariae* only inform us that they belong to the same type of establishment, but not to its function, apart perhaps from I iv, 26 (Plate XIV). This small shop contains 'the remains of a soaking vat and a furnace.'[4] The workshop was owned or run by Dionysius, a freedman of L. Popidius Secundus.[5] Dionysius calls himself a *fullo*, which is used by Moeller to conclude that the *lanifricarii* were part of a very large *collegium fullonum*.[6] The identification of this shop as *officina lanifricaria* is, however, rather optimistic since all that remains is some debris,[7] so it is unjustified to include it in the category of *officinae lanifricariae*.

This analysis of the alleged *officinae lanifricariae* has unfortunately not left us with a great deal of insight into their

[1] CIL IV 816.

[2] Fiorelli (1875) 285; Moeller (1976) 34.

[3] Andreau (1974) 260 ff.

[4] Moeller (1976) 31. It should be noted, however, that M. does not include I iv, 26 - crucial to his argument - in the list of 'officinae lanifricariae' in Moeller (1966).

[5] CIL IV 1041, 1045, 2966, 2674.

[6] Moeller (1976) 75. Cf. above, p. 158, below, p. 170 ff.

[7] Fiorelli (1875) 68 wrote more than a century ago: 'Bottega nel cui fondo stanno gli avanzi di un focolare o vasca, che non bene se distingue; a sin. una grande cella rustica, a dr. la latrina.'

real function. All we know is that they form a group of archaeologically similar workshops of unknown function, and that the name given to them by Moeller is misleading.

A counterexample of an archaeologically similar workshop - though not mentioned by Moeller - but which is hard to reconcile with a wool-washing function, is VII xiii, 21 (Plate XIII). This shop also contains a masonry table, a hearth with pan, and a vat. But it is part of one building with VII xiii, 20, and has an open connection with that room. Eschebach calls the whole complex a 'Thermopolium und Caupona mit 4 Terrakottaurnen und Herd; Wohnung im Obergeschoss' though Kleberg considers it very difficult to decide whether 21 is a part of the taberna. The two front rooms are interconnected by a door.[1] And obviously the equipment present could have been very suitable for the preparation of food.

Frayn has argued, with good reason, that it is in fact likely that the greasy raw wool was normally washed on or near the farm.[2] In Diocletian's Price Edict prices of wool are normally for washed wool. And this makes sense: as much as half the weight of the raw wool might consist of grease and dirt. Transport costs would be less for clean wool.

Turning now to the 'real' *fullonicae* we end up with the problem that we have no way of telling what proportion of the production-capacity was used for fulling new cloth *de tela* and what for laundering *ab usu*. Moeller's argument that the bigger ones would serve for the fulling of new cloth is only a guess.[3]

Moeller's estimate for the labour force employed in these fulleries appears to be on the high side. The first assumption that he has to make is that all capital equipment is being used to the full. A worker using different pieces of capital equipment along the process, and leaving the ones not necessary for that part of the process idle, changes the figures dramatically.

For the three largest establishments (I vi, 7; VI viii, 20-22; VI xiv, 21-22 - Plates XVII and XVIII) Moeller arrives at a

[1] Eschebach (1970) 143; Kleberg (1957) 42, 133 n. 34; Fiorelli (1875) 299.

[2] Frayn (1984) 142 ff.

[3] E.g. Moeller (1976) 43.

figure of nineteen workers each. The middle sized VI xvi, 3-4 is assigned thirteen as a minimum, and the small ones five.[1]

Personal inspection on the site gave the impression that these figures were rather inflated, but replacing such an interpretation by an argument is probably impossible. The three largest fulleries are all in former private houses, apparently changed over to industrial purposes subsequent to the earthquake of A.D. 62.[2] Whether this dating is correct or not, the fact remains that the size of the houses is not necessarily a function of the space needs of the fulleries. Though big, the houses could have been the only space easily available.

If my criticism of Moeller's extreme modernism and his careless use of the evidence has been severe, that should not lead us to believe that there was no textile production in Pompeii at all. Romans did not walk around naked, and aggregate demand for textiles must have been substantial. That is not at stake in the debate: what is at stake is whether this demand was met by small scale local production or by the specialized production of a number of Weberian 'producer cities'. It is my contention that Pompeii was not such a 'producer city'.[3]

The fullers as entrepreneurs?

Moeller and Frank assert not only that the Pompeian wool trade was on a not insignificant scale, but also that it had a coordinated entrepreneurial structure, that some of the entrepreneurs obtained high social status and that they were a not insignificant group.[4]

Moeller asserts that the fullers were the entrepreneurs of the trade.[5] That would be in distinct contrast to medieval times, when, if any craftsmen were successful at all and became

[1]Moeller (1976) 81.

[2]Maiuri (1942) 165 f, 173.

[3]I also believe that the number of such 'textile towns' elsewhere in the Roman world has been vastly overestimated, but I shall have to leave my arguments to support this for a later occasion.

[4]Frank (1933-40) V 202, 253 ff, 262.

[5]Moeller (1976) 75.

entrepreneurs, it was the weavers, not the fullers.[1] Frayn has recently argued for what must be a vindication of this parallel with later times. She emphasizes the importance of trade in raw wool, and proposes the traders in raw wool as the entrepreneurs: 'The *lanarii* as *negotiatores*, or the wool-merchants if *lanarii* is adjectival here, bought wool or yarn of better quality from the countryside, sometimes a considerable distance away if it was not available locally. They completed the processing of it until it could be sent to the fullers as garments or by the piece for finishing.'[2]

Moeller's first argument for the thesis that the fullers were the entrepreneurs is that the *lanilutores*, the wool-scourers, form part of the *collegium fullonum*. 'As the fullers were the first and the last in the chain of processors, it was only natural for them to have regulated, through their association, the flow of wool to assure a profitable outcome. The fullers were the entrepreneurs of the Pompeian wool trade'.[3] But if both groups are in the same collegium, is it therefore 'highly probable that in many cases the wool-scourers and finishers were either the same persons or had long standing familiar relations?'[4] None of the names of persons identified by Moeller or Della Corte provide any support for the thesis, although this argument cannot, of course, disprove their case. More important is that ultimately the inclusion of the *lanilutores* in a large *collegium fullonum* depends on the belief that the *Dionysius fullo* was in fact a wool-washer/scourer.[5] And we have observed above that there is no archaeological support for that belief (Plate XIV).[6]

Another argument against the view that the fullers were the entrepreneurs organizing the trade concerns their corporate activities. Because even if they did have a corporate identity, that does not necessarily imply that it bore any resemblance to

[1]Lis and Soly (1979) 11.

[2]Frayn (1984) 153.

[3]Moeller (1976) 75.

[4]Moeller (1976) 75.

[5]CIL IV 1041, 1045, 2966, 2974.

[6]Above, p. 168.

medieval guilds. The touchstone would be the existence of efforts to fix prices, quantity and quality of production, plus a limitation on entry into the craft. Modern consensus seems to be that ancient *collegia* were social rather than economic organizations.[1] The little that we know of the Pompeian fullers' corporate activities refers exclusively to the social side. In the fullery of Primus a wall painting can still be seen, although now very faded, depicting scenes from collegiate life (Plate XVIII). It is divided into two parts, one about a festival for their patron deity Minerva, and one depicting a trial scene.[2] In other words, both refer to their internal social life. For the involvement of fullers in other parts of the production process, such as spinning or weaving, or the supply of raw wool, we have no evidence whatsoever.

Social status and political involvement

Various authors have believed Pompeii to supply the evidence that wealthy business men like fullers obtained high social status as decurions, and did not mind continuing to be seen as business men.[3] The first person who is alleged to be both a magistrate and a fuller is L. Veranius Hypsaeus. He was undoubtedly an important man, twice *duovir* and once a *quinquennalis* candidate.[4] But that he was 'a master fuller' as Moeller calls him, is considerably less certain.[5] Hypsaeus is supposed to have been

[1]The classic analysis of the 'collegia' of antiquity is Waltzing (1895-1900). A recent addition to the bibliography is Ausbüttel (1982). For medieval guilds also Mickwitz (1936). One should never say never, however. Lewis (1983) 144 quotes 'collegia' as dealing with the economic interests of their members, by setting prices. The examples given in Graeber (1983) 16 n.55 (CIL XIV 4144 and CIL V 4341) would suggest a defending of interests (e.g. 'immunitas'), rather than a fostering of them, and should therefore not be seen as a deviation from the traditional role of 'collegia' and their patrons, for which see 'inter alia' Clemente (1972).

[2]Moeller (1976) 86 ff.

[3]E.g. Frank (1933-40) V 253 ff, 262; Moeller (1976) 'passim'; Della Corte (1965) p. 15 ff, p. 58. Gordon (1927) 170; Wiseman (1971) 91.

[4]Castrén (1975) 'ad nom'.

[5]Moeller (1976) 91. Moeller's assertion that Hypsaeus belonged to the 'conservative party' seems even more insecure. For this see also Moeller (1973b) 517 ff. For the problem of the riot of A.D. 59 see: Moeller (1970b) 84 ff. Further references and discussion, below, p. 300 ff.

the owner of the big fullery VI viii, 20-21,2, but this depends first of all on a restoration of CIL IV 193, where *vicini* are supporting ...SAEVM QVINQ / D.R.P. The restoration Hypsaeum is not impossible because in the same street there are several other programmata in which he is supported, although Castrén does not include this CIL IV 193 in his references about L. Veranius Hypsaeus.[1] More serious than these reservations about the text, we may add that the address identifications based on *vicini* as supporters are very shaky. *Vicini* do not always paint their electoral recommendations solely on the houses of the candidates.[2] In chapter seven I shall argue that *vicini* should not be read as 'neighbours' but as members of the *collegium* for the *lares compitales* of the *vicus*, the ward.[3] It is therefore not at all certain that Hypsaeus was the owner of the fullery.

Moeller also connects Hypsaeus to the textile trade via a different route. The well known banker and auctioneer L. Caecilius Iucundus rented a fullery from the city in the year A.D. 58 for H.S. 1,652 a year. Moeller remarks that 'it may be of some significance that Hypsaeus was *duumvir* in the year of these transactions'.[4] But, as Andreau remarks, A.D. 58/59 is in fact the third year of the lease, not the year in which the lease was taken up. That must have been, given the fact that it was the *quinquennalis* who was responsible, in 55/56, for a period from 1 July 56 until 1 July 61. In 58 Hypsaeus was only responsible for making sure that the rent was paid.[5]

That Iucundus rented a fullery from the town does not necessarily link him closely to the wool interests, as 'd'autres tablettes concernent une propriété, et une autre la taxe du marché.'[6] Moeller writes that Iucundus rents city owned pasture-land, but what he rents is in fact the tax on this land, *'vectigal publicum pasquorum'*. Similarly, the possibility should not be

[1]Castrén (1975) 'ad nom'.

[2]See e.g. the case of Ti. Claudius Verus, Della Corte (1965) n. 215. For a discussion of 'vicini', below, p. 289 ff; esp. 304.

[3]Below, p. 289 ff., esp. 304.

[4]Moeller (1976) 95.

[5]Andreau (1974) 282 f.

[6]Ibid.

excluded that what is meant by *fullonica* was not a fullery, but a tax on fulleries or fulling.[1]

'A second boss fuller who was active in Pompeian politics was Marcus Vesonius Primus, also an aristocrat.'[2] This man had already been introduced by Tenney Frank, but unfortunately his very existence is probably a scholarly fiction.[3] All problems result from the confusion of a Vesonius Primus with a magistrate M. Vesonius. Vesonius Primus was indeed probably a fuller. On the house VI xiv, 20 we have Vesonius Primus as supporter (CIL IV 3471) and in an inscription on a marble herm: *Primo. N. Anteros. arcar.* (CIL X 865). Although we cannot be absolutely sure that in this latter case it is the same person - as Castrén points out - it still seems probable. On the fullery VI xiv, 21/22 (Plates XVII and XVIII) we find *'Vesonius Primus'* as a supporter (CIL IV 3477) and *'Primus fullo'* (CIL IV 3478). A minor complication is that in the fullery a seal was found reading Ti. Babini Alexan.[4] We could of course interpret this as the name of a foreman. Other inscriptions show possible traces of the name Primus.[5]

There can be no doubt that one Vesonius belonged to the magisterial group: M. Vesonius Marcellus, *duovir* in A.D. 33/34.[6] He was probably also a *quinquennalis* candidate.[7] On the tannery I, 5, 2 we find a M. Vesonius as supporter - Della Corte identifies him enthusiastically, but not necessarily correctly, as the

[1]Moeller (1976) 95; Andreau (1974) 67 ff, 282; CIL IV 3340 CXLV- CXLVII; Frank (1933-40) V, 202.

[2]Moeller (1976) 92.

[3]Frank (1933-40) V, 253 ff, 262.

[4]Seal n. 11 in the list of Della Corte (1965), p. 465.

[5]CIL IV 3480, 3481. A warning against too ready generalizations is offered by CIL IV 3482, where 'Primus cum suis' supports Cn. Helvius, the same candidate as is supported by Vesonius Primus in 3477. Mau thinks that the Primus in 3482 is our Vesonius Primus, but the house where we find the notice - VI xiv, 34 - is listed in Eschebach (1970) 133 as 'Bäckerei, stillgelegt, mit Wohnung, Backofen und Mühlen.' As Primus is one of the most common Pompeian 'cognomina', it is very possible that the Primus associated with this bakery is another person than our Vesonius Primus.

[6]CIL X 901,903; CIL IV 273, 830, 3448, and possibly also 7147 and 9876c, and in Iucundus' tablet 143 (CIL IV 3340 CXLIII).

[7]CIL IV 7283, 9876c.

owner.[1] The next hypothesis is that we are here dealing with M. Vesonius Primus - although there is no reason at all for choosing the cognomen Primus.[2] Then T. Frank writes as if 'M' Vesonius Primus belonged to the local aristocracy, though he does not give any further evidence.[3] Perhaps he was misled by some inscriptions with Vesonius or M. Vesonius as candidate, but it is of course much more likely that those refer to M. Vesonius Marcellus.[4]

That these examples of (M.) Vesonius do not refer to a M. Vesonius Primus is further corroborated by Iucundus' tablet 31. Here, a Vesonius Primus signs as fifth witness, an indication that his social status was not high, as one would perhaps already have expected from someone with such a humble *cognomen*.[5] In addition, the abbreviation of the *praenomen* here makes Zangemeister - the CIL editor of the tablets - remark: *'potest et P esse et (ut Petra legit) T'*. But certainly not M. We may therefore conclude that there is no evidence whatsoever to make us believe that Vesonius Primus was M. Vesonius Primus, a decurion of Pompeii.

That Moeller tries to save the case by using the argument that another Vesonius - M. Vesonius Marcellus - had been *duumvir*, 'indicating that scions of the Vesonii could aspire to high office', implies apparent ignorance of the existence of freedmen, and the point is not that some Vesonii could reach high office, but that some could not.[6]

As this has eliminated the last of the possible fullers in the *ordo*, we can move to other political links and actions of the fullers and the other textile craftsmen. That fullers or others supported individual candidates for office, as can be seen on

[1] CIL IV 4012; Della Corte (1965) n. 564.

[2] Della Corte (1965) n. 564, referring to Fiorelli (1875) 452 as origin of this hypothesis. But Fiorelli does not add a 'cognomen.'

[3] Frank (1933-40) V, 255, 262.

[4] CIL IV 4012, 3528, 7283, 9876c.

[5] Cf. Castrén (1975) 264; Andreau (1974) 177-299; Kajanto (1965) 'ad nom'. Below, p. 241 ff.

[6] Moeller (1976) 92. Vesonius Primus' 'cognomen' and his low ranking as witness make him into a probable freedman.

several occasions in Pompeii, does not in itself mean that they made concerted efforts 'to influence Pompeian affairs by controlling the government'.[1]

Formulating it in such a way creates a picture of Pompeian politics as an arena where different economic interest groups with perhaps different political ideologies fight for political power to further their interests. In chapter seven I shall attempt to investigate the flavour of Pompeian 'politics'. Here we will confine ourselves to an investigation of the 'political' activity of the textile craftsmen. Dionysius the fuller supports his patron L. Popidius Secundus, a perfectly proper thing to do for any freedman, and Dionysius does not give any other reason than that he is Popidius' freedman.[2] Interesting is CIL IV 3529, where *'Mustius fullo'* supports M. Pupius Rufus for the duovirate. He also mentions that he has done the painting of the programma *'unicus sine reliquis sodalibus'*. These *sodales* could certainly be the *sodales* of a *collegium* of the fullers. It is hard to decide whether this means that the other fullers supported a different candidate, or that he was more zealous than the others in supporting the same one.[3]

The vocabulary used by Mustius to praise his candidate - *Dignum Rei Publicae* - is characteristic of the language of Pompeian political support. Its proximity to the world of patronage will be discussed in chapter seven.[4] Incidentally, Moeller leaves this phrase *'Dignum Rei Publicae'* out of his transcription and translation.[5] The words *dignum rei publicae* are also used by the feltmakers when they support a Herennius and a Suettius.[6] Vesonius Primus calls a candidate *utilem r(ei) p(ublicae)* and another candidate *d(ignum) r(ei) p(ublicae)*.[7] In the rest of the electoral support by textile craftsmen, no

[1]Moeller (1976) 94.

[2]CIL IV 1041, 2966, and perhaps 2974.

[3]Cf. Moeller (1976) 93 f.

[4]Below, p. 284 ff., esp. 286 f.

[5]Moeller (1976) 93 f.

[6]CIL IV 7809.

[7]CIL IV 3471, 3477.

further reasons are given at all. But nowhere do we find any indication that the supporters expected some specific economic policy.

Possible indirect elite involvement in craft production and trade has been a favorite hypothesis of more 'modernistic' scholars.[1] The argument is that even though we cannot see the precise links between the many freedmen and their patrons, it is to be expected that their activities are mostly a continuation of what they did before manumission, and that the involvement of their *patroni* was probably hardly less than before.

The predominance of freedmen in the funerary epigraphy of craftsmen is indeed very striking.[2] In fact, the proportion of freedmen is so high (well over half) that scholars should have realized that these figures cannot be taken to represent the composition of the craftsman population. Libertine status was only reached after many years in slavery, and libertine prominence in funerary epigraphy is therefore an indicator of frequency of manumission, but it disguises the prominence of slaves amongst the work force. Many urban slaves died as freedmen, and it is only at the moment of their death that they leave a record for posterity.[3]

But if the craft work-force was predominantly servile, we are still ignorant about the identity and social position of their masters. Neither do we know if crafts were the main source of income for these masters. Conceptually there is also a lot of confusion. On the one hand it could be argued that involvement in crafts and trade by the land-owning aristocracy supports a more 'modernistic' interpretation, but a counter-argument could be that such involvement (which would inevitably be a sideline to agricultural pursuits) obviated the need for a specialized social group of commercial entrepreneurs.[4] Aristocratic

[1] D'Arms (1977) and D'Arms (1981); Pleket (1984).

[2] Garnsey (1980b) 44; Treggiari (1980) 55.

[3] The funerary epigraphy, therefore, informs us about the flow of those who leave the work force - through death - rather than about the composition of the stock. If the composition of the stock is analysed, as in the case of the potters of Arezzo, the proportion of freedmen is far lower - Garnsey (1980b) 44.

[4] Cf. Pleket (1984); Leveau (1983b) 280.

involvement in trade might thus have precluded the emergence of an innovative bourgeoisie with its counter-values of economic rationalism.

The case for the independence of freedmen has been argued by Garnsey.[1] He argues that we have exaggerated the ties between freedmen and their former masters. In quite a few cases slaves would have been manumitted only upon the death of their masters, in which case they would would have been independent for all practical purposes. That may be true, even though the possibility of such manumission does not automatically imply that it was frequent. But could these independent freedmen have functioned as a bourgeoisie? Freedman status is transient, in the sense that it need not be inherited by the next generation. The absence of large numbers of *ingenui* in the epigraphy of traders and craftsmen suggests that the sons of these freedmen either did not remain in those economic activities, or that their fathers' manumission had come too late for them to be freeborn. Either way, we are not talking about a permanent class. And even as a transient class we may wonder whether they could serve as our bourgeoisie. Independent they were, but precisely for that reason also less affluent, we may assume. The great possibilities for enrichment would be for freedmen who could operate with the financial backing of their patrons.

With regard to the Pompeian textile industry we can confidently say that the epigraphic record shows no instances of more or less indirect elite involvement. Perhaps it is the nature of the evidence which precludes our knowledge of such involvement, but perhaps there was none. If the epigraphic evidence is inconclusive - and it has been stretched too far - the archaeological evidence from the town's buildings has not been used sufficiently. Even a very brief visit is enough to reveal that a large proportion of the workshops are integral parts of the aristocratic houses. The street fronts were presumably sufficiently valuable to convert many front rooms into shops. This need not mean more than an interest in commercial property,

[1] Garnsey (1981).

rather than commerce itself, but it is suggestive that one can easily give scores of examples where the shops were in open connection with the big house. It is difficult in those circumstances not to think of some elite involvement in the commercial and manufacturing activities of the shop.

Unfortunately no systematic study of this phenomenon has been undertaken, and to do so would be well beyond the scope this work.[1] I would venture the hypothesis that surviving textile workshops are less frequently parts of a rich house than other workshops. The reason, however, need not be anything other than that they may have required more space than was ordinarily available, or that these processes (it is mostly fulleries and dyehouses that have survived) were particularly smelly and unpleasant to have next door.

A guildhall?

A building that has taken a prominent place in previous accounts of the Pompeian woollen industry is the so called 'Building of Eumachia' (Plates XXII, XXIII, XXIV and XXVI). This is a prominent building on the east side of the forum and it has been assigned various functions by authors on the subject. It has been called a *fullonica*, a meeting place for members of the *collegium fullonum*, a cloth market, or recently, by Moeller, a guildhall of the fullers and a 'cloth exchange where goods in large quantities were sold at auction.'[2]

The building takes its name from an inscription above the entrance on the Via dell' Abbondanza and in a fragmentary form from the front.[3] The text informs us that Eumachia L.f., a

[1]Maiuri (1942) touches on these issues, but is of doubtful statistical value because it is not based on a randomly drawn sample. The discussions of commercial property in Eschebach (1975) and Raper (1977) are too uncritical of traditional interpretations of usage of space, and ignore the problems of the relations between shops and private houses.

[2]Moeller (1976) 57 ff. Analogously, Kolb (1984) 215 claims - following Lepelley (1979-81) II 405 - a 'basilica vestiaria' for Cuicul (Djemila). The inscription (ILS 5536), however, suffers from restoration in the crucial word '[basili]cam'; more caution here would do no harm. And, secondly, it is not certain which surviving building is referred to in the inscription, or what is supposed to have happened in it.

[3]CIL X 810, 811.

priestess, in her own name and that of her son M. Numistrius Fronto, *'chalcidicum cryptam porticus Concordiae Augustae Pietate sua pequnia fecit eademque dedicavit'*. And we find Eumachia again in the back of the building where a statue was erected for her by the fullers.[1] Eumachia was undoubtedly an important woman: she had a magnificent tomb outside Porta Nocera (Plate XXI), and she was *sacerdos publica*. Her husband was *duovir* in A.D. 2/3.[2] The dating problems created by the dedication need not detain us here.[3]

The evidence that links the building with the fullers is only slight. Early scholars believed that it was a fullery because vats and basins were found in the central courtyard.[4] This idea was crushed by Mau who pointed out that the vats and basins were very dissimilar to the equipment of a proper *fullonica*, and Maiuri writes that excavations have shown that they simply belonged to some masons doing restoration work.[5]

Therefore the only hard evidence for a link is the inscription on the base of the statue of Eumachia erected by the fullers (CIL X 813):

> EVMACHIAE.L.F./
> SACERD.PVBL./
> FVLLONES//

But this does not specify a connection at all. So, if there is

[1]CIL X 813.

[2]There is a problem with M. Numistrius Fronto. Moeller believes that there is only one person with that name: 'duovir' in A.D. 2/3 (CIL X 892) and the son of Eumachia mentioned in the dedication of the building of Eumachia (CIL X 810-811). See Moeller (1976) 57 ff. Castrén notes that in 'E.E.' 316 the name of M. Numistrius Fronto is not mentioned as magistrate, though it should have been. He concludes that there are two persons of this name. The father, husband of Eumachia, 'duovir' in A.D. 2/3, who probably died in office, and a son, mentioned in the later dedication of the building of Eumachia. I prefer this latter solution, though this choice is irrelevant for my argument.

[3]For a recent discussion: Moeller (1976) 59 ff; also Castrén (1975) 101, and s.v. Eumachii and Numistri. Cf. my previous footnote.

[4]Nissen (1877) 287-303.

[5]A. Mau in Overbeck (1884) 133, and his footnote 60; Mau (1892) 141 ff; Maiuri (1942) 42.

any, it is the archaeological remains of the building that will have to supply the specification.

Moeller is right to point out that it is unlikely to have been a cloth market.[1] Such structures definitely look different; for an example one could look at the Macellum in Pompeii. They consist of sometimes large numbers of booths that can be closed with shutters.[2] Although the inside corridor along three sides of the Building of Eumachia could be closed off from the central court, the openings between court and corridors are not doors. They do not open from ground level upwards, but are more akin to windows. In addition, they were not closed by sliding shutters, typical of shops, but are provided with square, and therefore luxury, swivel holes.[3] For street vending Pompeii possessed a large amount of space under the porticoes of the forum, and it had a large basilica as well.[4]

The alternative solution for a wool trade function is that of a guildhall of sorts for the fullers. In this view it provided a meeting place with office space and storage facilities on the first floor. It would also have provided a quiet place to conduct business, while the *chalcidicum* served as a wool and cloth exchange where goods in large quantities were sold at auction.'[5]

But this solution is completely speculative. The alleged auction blocks could have had a very different function. They are nothing more than stone platforms in a niche, and would have served perfectly well as bases for statues or portrait busts, or as an altar (Plate XXIV). The similarity with some structures in the eastern part of the Pompeian Macellum has already been commented upon by Andreau, although he also believes they were perhaps auction blocks (Plate XXV);[6] but that area in the Macellum is called a *'tempietto'* by Fiorelli, and

[1]Moeller (1976) 65 ff.

[2]Nabers (1968) 169. I have not been able to get my hands on de Ruyt (1983).

[3]For a discussion of locking mechanisms: Rickman (1971) esp. 32 ff.

[4]For the Pompeian basilica: Ohr (1973).

[5]Moeller (1976) 71. Partially similar: Breton (1869) 124-131, and Spano (1961) 14-16.

[6]Andreau (1974) 78f.

although his interpretation of the building as a *Curia* of the *Augustales* is wrong, he is likely to have been right about this part, as it also contained statues and images of members of the imperial family.[1]

The imperial connection is also in evidence in the case of the 'Building of Eumachia'. Apart from the dedication, the front of the building contained niches with images of Aeneas and Romulus, with fitting inscriptions (Plate XXII).[2] Fiorelli believed that the two remaining niches contained images of Caesar and Augustus.[3] A structure similar to the 'auction blocks' of the building of Eumachia can also be found along the back wall of the building of the decurions.

Storage space on the first floor is speculation, as this floor has not been preserved: only a narrow staircase remains. The locking arrangements in what Moeller believes to have been the *chalcidicum* are somewhat problematic. Moeller thinks the area could be closed when an auction was held.[4] As seen in 1978, the spacing did not correspond with the columns, which could either be the result of restorations after A.D. 62 or of inadequate modern restoration. As the adjacent entry to the forum from the Via dell' Abbondanza could also be locked, it is not immediately apparent what the meaning of these locking arrangements could have been.

The only link between the building and the fullers is the inscription already mentioned (CIL X 813: EVMACHIAE.L.F./ SACERD.PVBL./ FULLONES//). But that is no proof that the building fulfilled a special role for the fullers, only that the fullers had a reason to honour Eumachia with a statue in this building.

In the dedicatory inscriptions by Eumachia on the building she too calls herself a *sacerdos publica*.[5] One other inscription

[1]Fiorelli (1875) 265.

[2]Fiorelli (1875) 258 ff; CIL X 808, 809.

[3]Fiorelli (1875) 258 ff; Mau (1908) 111.

[4]Moeller (1976) 70; Maiuri (1942) 41.

[5]CIL X 810, 811.

mentions *sacerdotes publicae*: again, one of them is Eumachia.[1] But that does not exhaust the epigraphic harvest from this building. A certain C. Norbanus Sorex is honored by the *'mag(istri) pagi Aug(usti) felicis suburbani ex d(ecreto) d(ecurionum) loc(o) d(ato).'*[2] It is hard to believe that permission from the decurions would have been necessary if the building was a private guildhall; the 'building of Eumachia' must have been a public building. Fiorelli writes that in addition several other herms of illustrious citizens were found in the interior, but without inscription.[3] Finally, an inscription with the text *'M. Lucretius Rufus Legavit'* was found in the building.[4] This important man had been *duovir* three times, *quinquennalis*, *pontifex*, *tribunus militum a populo* and *praefectus fabrum*.[5] Castrén believes that he was a member of the group of Augustan partisans.

The painted inscriptions and the graffiti do not yield anything of relevance, other than that in an election poster on the building *aurifices universi* support C. Cuspius Pansa for the aedileship: a minor pointer that the fullers' relationship with the building was not exclusive.[6]

That the dedication to Eumachia of a statue by the fullers would show that the building was a guildhall of the fullers must be denied. The recurrent element in the epigraphy of the building is not manifestations of fullers, but public religion. The references to the imperial house and romanization are not insignificant. Castrén interprets the inscriptions figuring Aeneas and Romulus as inspired 'by models in Rome, in particular the Forum of Augustus' and also refers to the Temple of Concordia restored by Tiberius in A.D. 10. The building 'may as *Basilica*

[1] CIL X 812.

[2] CIL X 814. This inscription was also found on the temple of Isis. Cf. Castrén (1975) 'ad nom'.

[3] Fiorelli (1875) 259 f.

[4] CIL X 815.

[5] CIL X 788-789, 815, 851, 952-954; 'Notizie degli Scavi di Antichità' 1898, p. 171; Castrén (1975) 'ad nom.' and 70, 95, 97, 100, 103.

[6] CIL IV 710.

nova have served more general political or social purposes.'[1] The reason why it was the fullers who wanted to honour the public priestess Eumachia in this building is not clear: perhaps she was the patroness of the fullers, but if so, we are not told so.[2]

Conclusion and a digression

The Pompeian textile industry was quite unlike its counterparts in such later centres of growth as the communes of northern Italy or Flanders. Its scale was incomparably smaller, and there are no signs that it did any more than cater for a fairly local market. If there is a similarity with later times, it is with the numerous small towns of medieval and early modern Europe that equally catered for their own needs. The possibility even remains that those parts of the production process best known from archaeological remains (fulling and dyeing) were substantially concerned with refinishing used cloth. They may have been the ancient equivalents of modern dry-cleaning.

Moeller's case for a 'modernistic' interpretation of the social organization of production turns out to have been built on three groups of incorrect arguments.[3] The first is the view that the fullers were not only engaged in the finishing of cloth but also in the cleaning of raw wool. I hope to have shown that there is neither any evidence that such wool-cleaners were called *fullones*, nor that their supposed workshops had anything to do with wool. That relieves us of any further need to worry about the consequences for the entrepreneurial structure of such a dual presence. Secondly, although one should never exclude the possibility of indirect involvement in trade or industry by members of the urban aristocracy, there is no direct evidence from Pompeii that this was indeed the case. More importantly, there is no evidence that 'master-craftsmen' as such penetrated the elite *ordo decurionum*. Moeller's third

[1]Castrén (1975) 101.

[2]Waltzing (1895-1900) I, 432; For 'patroni': Clemente (1972).

[3]I add inverted commas to 'modernistic', because it is becoming less and less clear whether the 'modernistic' view is appropriate for medieval and early modern Europe as well. Above, p. 48 ff.

argument revolves around his interpretation of the Building of Eumachia, so prominent on the forum. But closer inspection of the evidence shows that equating the building with a medieval guildhall is unwarranted. There is no indication of commercial activities, nor of an exclusive link between the fullers and the building. Its precise function remains a mystery, but should have been public rather than private.

I have chosen to concentrate a discussion of urban production on the textile industry, because the production of textiles is, from what we know through comparative evidence, the most likely candidate for the role of stimulus for the emergence of a 'producer' city.

A different type of argument as to a possible 'modernity' of ancient craft production has been put forward by Hopkins. He gives some examples of the wide variety of crafts found in some ancient cities.[1] He counts 110 different trades in late antique Korykos, a small town in Asia Minor (Table VI).

In Pompeii he counts 85 trades.[2] Such division of labour is impressive. It serves as a salutary warning not to equate the opposite of the 'producer city' with something very primitive, approaching the 'closed household economy' stage of earlier theorists of economic development.[3] Particularly striking is the substantial number of establishments for the preparation and sale of food. Not only was baking bread obviously not a household production, but restaurants, bars and the like must also have done good business (Plate XXX).[4]

[1]Hopkins (1978b) 72 ff, employing data also discussed in Patlagean (1977) 156-70. Treggiari (1980) 61-64 quotes some 160 occupations for the city of Rome. She stresses the prevalence of luxury trades, but takes the argument no further than to say that 'it may provoke other reflections about the inclination of the richer classes to finance extravagant subdivision of labour and about the ingenuity of the poorer Romans in finding ways to earn a living.' (p. 56).

[2]Hopkins (1978b) 72.

[3]Goudineau (1983) 286 in kindred spirit: 'La notion de "ville de consommation" ne renvoie pas la société gallo-romaine au néolithique, elle n'implique pas non plus une rigoureuse autarcie.'

[4]Kleberg (1957) discusses Pompeian inns. Patlagean (1977) 164-5 emphasizes their importance in Korykos. These data give the strong impression that eating out was quite common, perhaps more common than in our own society. One could therefore say that in this respect modern north-western Europe is closer to the household economy, but it would rather suggest that the household economy

Table VI: Trades in Korykos
(source: Hopkins (1978b) 72)

food sales	15%
textiles	18%
building	5%
pottery	10%
smithying	5%
luxury trades	13%
shipping	8%
others	26%

On the other hand, the wide spread of different crafts in both Korykos and Pompeii suggests that nearly all requirements for goods and services could be met from local production. The impressive differentiation within the occupational structure is not only an index of economic sophistication, but also a sign that geographical division of labour was of limited importance.[1] In this sense the contrast with the archetypical 'producer cities' is manifest. They were centres of geographical specialization, and usually had a substantial concentration on one type of industry (mostly textiles), whether for reasons of availability of factors of production, or for the sake of economies of scale.[2] Occupational diversity is a sign of the 'consumer city', rather than of the 'producer city'.

concept is perhaps not a very useful one.

[1]Further corroborated by the cumulation - in Korykos - of more crafts in one person.

[2]Above, p. 48 ff.

CHAPTER FIVE

EPILOGUE

Elite income and expenditure: a flow model of the Italian economy?

Up to now we have concerned ourselves with a sectoral analysis of the Pompeian economy. One justification is that a large part of the debate on the ancient economy has been conducted in such terms: retaining the existing terms of reference permitted a more head-on attack on the many improbable propositions about the Pompeian economy. The second advantage was a more straightforward exposition of the evidence, which was necessary to demonstrate that many current views on the nature of the Pompeian economy are rooted in incorrect assessments of the meaning of surviving evidence.

But we should not live under the illusion that once we have lifted the veil of incorrect statements of fact all is automatically revealed. Pure induction is an illusion (as is pure deduction, of course), and besides, most of the past is irretrievably lost. What we need is a model to establish links between sectors, and make sense of otherwise incomprehensible evidence. The model must be powerful enough to integrate elements of social organization. One model which has attracted some attention in recent years is the 'taxes and trade' model developed by Hopkins.[1] Its logic is based on the observation that taxes were not levied and spent in the same measure in all parts of the Roman Empire. For a long time, the Italian economy remained largely untaxed; at the same time its position as political core of the Empire implied considerable expenditure of tax income that had been collected elsewhere. Although border provinces would not be exempt from taxation, the amount of money spent on the military would have exceeded local tax income by a pretty wide margin. Between these two regions - Italian core and provincial periphery - we find an intermediate type of region: paying sometimes substantial taxes, and hardly profiting from public expenditure.

Hopkins then contends that resulting balance-of-payment shortages in provinces such as Asia Minor or Gaul would necessarily be compensated by export trade from these provinces to areas with balance of payment surpluses (surpluses which are due to net tax expenditure). To make this possible, the high volume/low value agricultural product has to be converted into low volume/high value manufactured goods. This took place in the towns, hence the pivotal role for towns in the process of economic growth.

It seems an interesting model, relating different sectors of the economy in an explicit and apparently logical way. And even though it has been around for a while now, it has not yet come under severe attack. Traditional ancient historians have politely ignored it, others have deemed it very useful, and even Finley (his 'consumer city' ideal type was undoubtedly part of Hopkins' target) choose to reply mildly that at present he does not 'prefer' it because it overlooks 'the possibility of exploitation without any increase in productivity.'[2]

Yet it contains some problematic logic. Essential to the argument is that long term balance-of-payment deficits are impossible: they have to be compensated - so they will be.

[1]Most explicitly in Hopkins (1980), but also in Hopkins (1978a), Hopkins (1978b), Hopkins (1983c). Not unrelated is Crawford (1977).

[2]Finley (1985a) 182; Mitchell (1983) 134 ff. argues that mining of gold and silver may have been an alternative to taxation as a means of paying armies; Goudineau in Duby (1980 -) I 374 ff; Leveau (1985); Drinkwater (1983) esp. ch. 6; Corbier (1986).

Indeed, on a balance of payments total credits must equal total debits, as is the case with all standard double-entry book-keeping.[1] But this is just as meaningless as the fact that credits equal debits in the books of a company on the eve of bankruptcy. The point to remember is that the balance-of-payments consists of a number of accounts, and unlike the total account the part-accounts (such as the merchandise account, the current account, or the capital account) can indeed show surpluses and deficits: a deficit on one account may be compensated by a surplus on another.

The books must be balanced by items compensating for the tax flows, but accountancy cannot predict what form this compensation will take: a number of possibilities exist. One solution would be borrowing by the taxed and vexed provincials, a recourse well known from the late Republic. Another would be 'transfer' of assets, a euphemistic way of describing the removal of temple treasures and the acquisition of provincial estates by the Italian elite. Obviously, export of manufactured goods would be a very attractive alternative, but it depended on the ability to supply the right goods at the right price in 'foreign' markets. In reality there will have been a mixture of solutions for compensating the tax flows; the composition of the mixture cannot be predicted from first principles, and will have varied from place to place and from time to time.

Another - Keynesian - way of looking at the impact of Roman taxation in the provinces is to speculate about its effects on their macro-economic equilibrium. The payment of taxes by a province without compensating public expenditure upon that province amounts to the leaking away of purchasing power. The negative effect on 'national' (or rather: 'provincial') income is larger than the amount of the taxes, because a downward multiplier is at work. A new equilibrium will indeed obtain, but probably below full capacity. In other words, if nothing else happens, poverty and unemployment prevail. The beauty of export trade is that it prevents the downward multiplier from

[1] A good introduction to the theory can be found in Kindleberger and Lindert (1978) ch. XIV. But almost any introductory economics textbook will equally provide a serviceable account.

playing its vicious game. Provincials may have to pay taxes - nothing new to them, presumably - but if those taxes are spent in their region they are kept at work.

In short, the model usefully draws attention to the havoc that may have been created by Roman taxation, but is too simplistic and optimistic about possible reactions. Exporting manufactures is a very attractive solution, but may not necessarily have come about. Here, the deductive method cannot replace empirical observation.

In the case of Italy, the 'taxes and trade' model is also less than satisfactory for a second reason. It predicts the emergence of Italian craft production for local consumption, demand for these (and imported) products was stimulated by the flow of taxes into Italy. In terms of testing the 'taxes and trade' model against the 'consumer city' model, we therefore face a real problem as long as we are working with Italian data, namely that the two different models give nearly indistinguishable predictions about Italian craft production. The 'taxes and trade' model predicts that Italian craft production will be stimulated to meet local demand, but the 'consumer city' model equally predicts that Italian craft production will be for local Italian demand. We therefore have two alternative explanations for the same observed reality, and Italian data are unsuitable to substantiate a choice between the alternatives.

Of course, there are also differences between the predictions of the two models. One might say that the 'taxes and trade' model emphasizes the income from outside Italy, and expenditure on imports. Income from empire, however, can easily be incorporated in the 'consumer city' ideal type, in the sense that the provinces may be seen as a hinterland which is one step further removed than the immediately surrounding countryside.[1] And there is no complementary flow of goods from Italy in return for the money coming into Italy. Equally, Hopkins would never deny the importance of revenue from Italian land.[2] The major difference between the two models is in the assessment of the

[1] Cf. Finley (1978a).

[2] See e.g. Hopkins (1978a) 1-19.

impact of Italian purchasing power and that of the frontier provinces on urban manufacturing in the inner ring of provinces. Did it stimulate growth, or exploitation and possibly decay? Finding answers to those questions is well beyond the scope of this book, and would still leave us without much understanding of the underlying Italian structure.

The task before us is to devise a method to help us choose between a view of Italian urbanism - in the early Empire - as largely corresponding to the 'consumer city' ideal type, or the view that the 'producer city' ideal type would be more appropriate. But first, we must rid ourselves of a methodological fallacy: ideal types may be mutually exclusive and not leave any middle ground, but that should not be transposed to social reality. A whole spectrum of intermediate positions is conceivable, and likely. No actual city will conform entirely to an ideal type, nor is it the contention of ideal type analysis that that must be so. The corollary of this is that the appropriateness of the 'consumer city' ideal type for antiquity can never be disproved by a few counter-examples.[1] For that, many examples of ancient 'producer cities' would be necessary, and they will never materialize, if for no other reason than that our evidence is so pitiful. If the counter-examples indeed held - and often enough they do not - it would only disprove the proposition that all ancient cities conformed one hundred per cent to the 'consumer city' ideal type; and to the best of my knowledge nobody has ever made that extreme claim.

Instead, we should try to establish where on this spectrum of urban types we should locate the Italian city of the early Empire. Efforts until now have mostly started at the 'producer city' end of the spectrum.[2] Yet that is a route fraught with difficulties, as I hope my previous chapters have illustrated from the Pompeian material. Almost nothing can be documented

[1] I am afraid that Frederiksen (1975) is mostly in this vein.

[2] Not infrequently showing an innocent faith that archaeological data are straightforward and simple to use. For good and bad examples see e.g. D'Arms and Kopff (1980); Garnsey a.o. (1983); Garnsey and Whittaker (1983); Leveau (ed.) (1985); Giardina and Schiavone (1981).

comprehensively, and very little control is possible on variables in speculative quantification.

I therefore propose a different tactic: a start from the 'consumer city' end of the spectrum. How much can this ideal type account for? My conclusion will be: most, or almost all. Essential to this tactic is elite income and expenditure. I shall try to demonstrate that even if we make a low minimum estimate of the income of the Italian elite, it still represents an enormous figure, and is enough to account for all or nearly all urban services and manufacturing.[1] In the consumer city model it is elite income and expenditure which is supposed to provide the link between town and country. We shall therefore commence with an estimate of minimum elite income. That may seem impossible, but it will be seen that even the minimum estimate has such staggering implications that it is worth taking the plunge.

Wealth counted for much in the Roman world. In the next chapter we shall try to work out how much. Here we only need to know that membership of the various orders of Roman society (the senatorial, the equestrian and the decurional orders) entailed meeting the requisite census criteria. Multiplying the numbers of each order by the minimum census for membership of that order, we can produce a minimum estimate for the total wealth of the Roman elite (Table VII). When we know the capital value of elite wealth, we can estimate income. We can estimate roughly how many people would be necessary to produce this income and how many people could be employed producing the goods and services for elite consumption. I shall conclude that income inequality must have been very sharp and that the vast majority of the Italian population was probably engaged in generating elite income and producing the goods and services for elite consumption - apart from providing their own subsistence, of course.

[1]Much higher elite income therefore presupposes that not only the entire Italian urban economy was occupied catering for the consumer demand of the elite, but that other cities in the Empire had to make their contributions as well.

Table VII: Elite composition and wealth

group	number	census (H.S.)	total
senate	600[1]	1,000,000[2]	600 million
equestrians	5,000[3]	400,000[4]	2,000 million
decurions	20,000[5]	100,000[6]	2,000 million
		minimum total elite wealth:	4,600 million

We may estimate total elite wealth in Roman Italy at H.S. 4,600 million at a minimum (Table VII). I assume that all this wealth refers to Italy. This is plausible enough for decurions, and quite likely to be roughly correct for senators and equestrians. There is some scholarly disagreement as to the extent to which these latter two orders were allowed to keep property

[1]Hopkins (1983a) 147; Talbert (1984) 131 ff.

[2]I follow received opinion that the 1.2 million figure in Suetonius, 'Augustus' 41, is wrong. Talbert (1984) 10 f. Contra: Duncan-Jones (1982) 4. My only justification for deviating from such authority is a desire for methodological purity: I am constructing a minimum case.

[3]This is a hazardous guess, based on no more than Dionysius of Halicarnassus' (VI, 13, 4) count of 5000 'equites' in an Augustan 'transvectio equitum'. Nicolet (1966-74) I 121 ff. posits further subsequent increases in the number. My figure is a low minimum estimate.

[4]This figure is generally accepted. Duncan-Jones (1982) 4.

[5]Beloch (1886) 391 lists 431 Italian towns. Nissen (1883-1902) II, p. 3, and Duncan-Jones (1982) 339 give a figure of 430. I do not believe that all these had an 'ordo' of 100 members. A figure of 30 may have been the norm in smaller towns (see Duncan-Jones (1982) 283 ff. for references and discussion). The figure of 63 from Irni - Gonzáles (1986) Ch. 31 - is surprising because it is not a round number. It is also remarkable for its similarity to the results of my simulations, below, p. 317 ff, esp. 322. I assume that bigger towns are fewer than smaller ones. My estimate breaks down as follows: 100 towns with 100 decurions each, plus 330 towns with 30 decurions each.

[6]It is unclear to what extent the documented cases may be generalized. But where we have documentation, H.S. 100,000 seems to be the norm: Duncan-Jones (1982) 243.

outside Italy and whether such property would count towards the census.[1] I assume that in so far as they would indeed possess such property, it would probably not yet be very substantial by the middle of the first century, and would probably be in addition to sufficient land in Italy to satisfy the censors. Remember that mine are only minimum estimates.

It is often assumed that many exceeded the census required for membership of their *ordo* by far.[2] My calculations will show that this view is perhaps exaggerated. No doubt some will have had far more than the census requirement, but if this were to be true for a large part of the elite, we would have to assume unrealistically high levels of production.[3] The view that there were large numbers of people of sufficient wealth who choose to - or had to - remain outside the appropriate order is equally difficult to reconcile with my findings.

I have deliberately provided a minimum estimate for elite wealth, excluded the emperor's wealth, and assumed that everyone who did not belong to these orders lived at the level of bare subsistence. That is of course unrealistic. But even at this very minimum, elite wealth is staggering - it could buy a lot.

The next step in the argument is therefore to estimate the likely minimum income from this total capital of H.S. 4600 million. Six per cent would appear to be a generally accepted conservative estimate for net income from agricultural property.[4] Some scholars would of course object that trade, manufacturing or finance would offer much higher returns on investment. Perhaps, but even that would not make very much difference to my estimate of total income: these high return activities are

[1]Nicolet (1976a) 71-121, esp. 100 f, Rawson (1976) 90 ff; Hopkins (1978a) 47 f, 105; Talbert (1984) 46 protests that there is no proof of a legal ban. My guess is that the disagreement is at most about chronology.

[2]Duncan-Jones (1982) 4, 17 ff; Nicolet (1966-74) I 58 says the census was not large; Friedländer (1919-22) I, 126 f; Sherwin-White (1966) 150; Hopkins (1983a) 75 is a bit more careful.

[3]In due course we will of course have to allow for more and more provincial property. The senate's transition from Italian elite to imperial elite seems to go hand in hand with the emergence of fortunes of ever more gigantic size. For some examples: Finley (1985a) 98 ff.

[4]Duncan-Jones (1982) 33 n. 3, 132 ff.

unlikely to represent more than a minor proportion of investment. And their higher return was no doubt partly due to higher risks; the higher return contains a risk premium.[1] Six percent return on our minimum elite wealth works out at H.S. 276 million per year.

But what was the purchasing power of this sum? Can we somehow get a fix on the importance and impact of this elite purchasing power in respect of the entire Italian economy? Our knowledge of prices of goods and services is pitiful. And patterns of elite expenditure are only known in a very impressionistic fashion. But it need not matter too much. If we allow that a wheat price of H.S. 3 per *modius* is typical for our period, we may equate minimum estimated elite income with about 2.4 million subsistence rations of 250 kg. wheat each.[2] As long as incomes for the vast majority of the population were at or near subsistence, we may conclude that elite purchasing power equals the productive capacity of at least a third of the Italian population.[3] Part of those people would be domestic servants, others would be craftsmen producing consumer goods. Food consumption by the elite, for personal consumption, would

[1]Duncan-Jones (1982) 133. Veyne (1979).

[2]The sum works out as follows: 1 subsistence ration = 250 kg. wheat. At H.S. 3 per 'modius' of about 6.5 k.g. the cost of 1 subsistence ration for a year = H.S. 115. Therefore, the total minimum annual elite income of H.S. 276 million equals about 2.4 million subsistence rations. For wheat prices: Duncan-Jones (1982) 50 f; Hopkins (1980) 119. Mrozek (1978) has suggested considerably lower wheat prices in Puteoli: H.S. 1.2. I am not convinced. He compares the amount of a loan with the goods given as security for the loan. But the value of the security is of course very likely to have exceeded the amount of the loan. Secondly, the security does not only consist of specified quantities of wheat, but also of other commodities, partly in quantities which I at least am unable to reconstruct. Uncertainty at both ends of the equation therefore. But even if the figure were correct, it refers to a wholesale price, in a town where grain would presumably be fairly cheap. If one were yet to employ it in my model, it implies that elite income equals about 7.2 million subsistence rations. This may seem to strengthen my argument, but I find the result historically implausible. But we must not delude ourselves into a false sense of security. Better documentation for wheat prices is highly desirable. Foxhall and Forbes (1982) on subsistence levels leaves me puzzled by their wavering between trust in ancient and in modern data.

[3]For estimates of the Italian population, above p. 66 ff. Economists may disapprove of this reappearance of the labour theory of value. But they will admit that it gives a fair enough approximation in economies such as that of the Roman empire. Good discussion in: Blaug (1985) esp. 44 ff, 73 ff, 92 ff.

have constituted a negligeable proportion.[1] We may therefore qualify elite demand as demand for urban produce. That does not, of course, exclude the possibility that some demand was met by imports. My point is simply that elite consumer demand was enormous, and at least equal to - and in reality probably larger than - local Italian production possibilities.

If this elite demand was indeed nearly entirely for urban produce (buildings, manufacturing, services), we may use the estimate that it represents 2.4 million subsistence rations as an estimate of Italian urban population. If we compare this with other, independent, estimates of the urban population of Roman Italy, it provides us with a check on our flights of fancy.

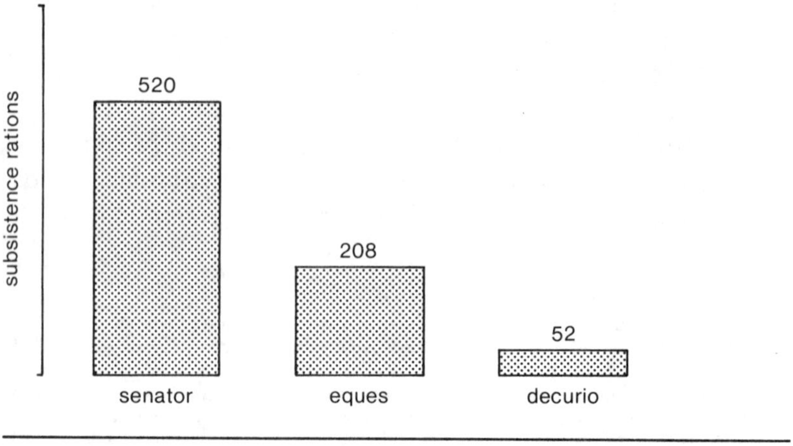

Figure VIII: Elite purchasing power of subsistence rations

The level of urbanization that it implies (2.4 million people equals 32% of an Italian population of 7.5 million) is, by a remarkable coincidence, identical to published estimates.[2] Estimated minimum elite income from Italian property appears

[1]Comparative figures could be misleading here. Many budgets from wealthy early modern families include large sums for the purchase of food - to feed the domestic servants. Cipolla (1981) 35.

[2]Hopkins (1978a) 68 f: 32% urban in 28 B.C. My estimate for total Italian population refers to the mid first century A.D., see above p. 66 ff.

to be roughly equal to estimated Italian urban production possibilities.[1]

We may now try to estimate the number of people involved in the production of this income. This boils down to a hypothesis for the typical level of rents. Proper evidence is lacking, but we need not despair. Thirty percent of gross crop is probably a high estimate.[2] If 20% of the gross yield is required as seed for next year, gross yield would be allocated as in Figure IX.

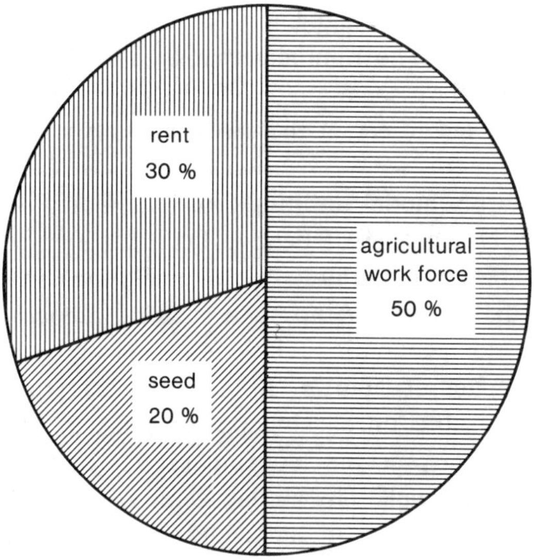

Figure IX: Hypothetical destination of gross yield

This enables us to estimate the size of the agricultural

[1]This does not exclude the possibility that part of elite income was spent on imports, and that part of urban production was exported, but this phenomenon is unlikely to have been very important, particularly with regard to services.

[2]Following Hopkins (1978a) 55f. I also adopt his other assumptions (yield ratio 5:1, a wheat price of H.S. 3 per 'modius' of 6.5 kg, and a 250 kg. wheat equivalent subsistence ration). Not because they are necessarily correct, but it seems pointless to replace one set of guesses by another, and thereby suggest that mine would be better. More important is the question: how much does it matter if they are wrong?

population engaged in generating elite income. It works out at about 4 million people.[1]

None of the figures employed in these calculations inspire a great deal of confidence, and yet the end result is curiously plausible. Almost two thirds of the Italian population is used to generate elite income, and the remaining third works as domestic slaves, craftsmen, mule drivers, builders, and so on, to satisfy elite consumer demand. Very few Italians remain outside the sphere of influence of elite property or consumption.

We may ask what we have achieved with all this speculation. Not, let us be clear about that, factual knowledge about many of the variables of the model. The numbers that I have chosen are what they are because they seem to be of the right order of magnitude. But I have tried to err in the direction that might weaken my own claims.

I have tried to insulate my model building from the world of the empire outside Italy. Not because I believe that that empire was unimportant, but because without such insulation any control on calculations disappears. Without an idea of autochthonous Italian social and economic relations, it would be difficult to assess the impact of empire. But even apart from the income out of empire, elite purchasing power was already staggering.[2] The tactic to start at the 'consumer city' end of the spectrum has worked quite well. The model seems capable of covering almost all economic activity in Italy. Unless we assume radically different levels of population and/or production, the need for supplementary explanations is not pressing.

Yet it also has some weaknesses. Apart from the limitation to Italy, I can see two areas. In the first place, it does not specify the form taken by the extraction of income from the countryside. It could mean physical transport of agricultural output from elite estates to their urban households and feeding domestic slaves directly off this. We have a modest amount of

[1]Of course, some income would have its source in the robberies of Roman imperialism, rather than Italian agriculture. But remember that I have given only minimum estimates for income.

[2]Income from empire is important enough, and I hope to return to it elsewhere-a book on Pompeii is not the right place to discuss it. My calculations here are deliberately constructed as minimum estimates.

documentation that that did indeed take place.[1] And that should of course not surprise us. Cato's maxim (*de agricultura* 2.7) that it is better to be a seller than to be a buyer, makes good sense if it is not taken to its extreme.[2] It obviously makes most sense if one's estates are located at reasonably close distance from the urban residence. Domestic slaves are obviously part of the urban household. There, some craft production could take place too, either for own consumption or for sale.[3] But many craftsmen will have bought their food in the market. Unfortunately my model is helpless in these matters.

The second weakness is that it *assumes* that all elite income is of agricultural origin. That has been a very contentious area in recent scholarly debate, and no doubt my assumption distorts reality. But I am not aware of any serious publication claiming that the majority of the Roman elite derived most of its income from sources other than agricultural property. More realistic assumptions about the sources of elite income may mitigate my claims somewhat, but cannot, I believe, lead to an opposite conclusion.

Conclusion

Roman economic performance was remarkable, and yet the empire declined and fell. Much of the work of many generations of ancient historians has uneasily tried to cope with this paradox. Whether through political and aesthetic nostalgia for a world we have lost, or through genuine bewilderment how such a complex society could be succeeded by the much simpler social formations of early medieval Europe, historians were right in thinking that there was a question to be answered. But we could not even conceive of the question if it were not that we are ourselves living in a western world which is the outcome of many centuries of growth and development. For us, this process has become the natural course of events, and steeped in a cultural tradition of unquestioning identification with many

[1] Trimalchio provides the literary hyperbole, as often (Petronius, 'Satyricon' 48. 1. 3).

[2] Finley (1985a) 36, 109 ff.

[3] Treggiari (1980).

of classical antiquity's intellectual feats, we are surprised. So we blame Germanic tribes or a loss of heart.

But decline and fall is not our theme. Instead I have tried to point to the static nature of the ancient economy. That is not to say that there was no change at all. No doubt the Roman economy of the first century A.D. had reached a higher level of performance than that of - say - the third century B.C. But the question is to what extent this increased performance was a result of change of structure, rather than just more of the same. The concomitant - and perhaps more interesting - question is to what extent late Republican and early Imperial levels of economic performance were (or could have been) the overture to growth, or were the finale of something which had reached its inherent limits. By now it will be obvious that my answer is that the Roman economy had indeed reached such limits.

No doubt this view of the Roman economy as just treading water merits - and requires - documentation and elaboration beyond the confines of first century A.D. Pompeii.[1] Yet Pompeii is a good test case. Chronologically, the abundance of Pompeian data coincides with what was perhaps the peak of Rome's power. Its location in the heartland of the Empire in a densely populated and highly urbanized area may not make it representative of the average Roman town (if a sample of one could ever be representative), but does make it near-perfect for the question at hand. In a society where so much of production and consumption is bound up with agriculture and food, labour productivity in agriculture is obviously of prime importance. It, rather than total production, is the indicator of society's ability to raise the income of the mass of the population above mere subsistence. And although total production within the territory of Pompeii must have been very substantial, it would appear that labour productivity was low. At the prevailing levels of population density, land was a scarce resource, and those owning land could expect substantial incomes. Equally, labour was a factor of production that was in abundant supply: its rewards

[1] I have derived some inspiration from Geertz (1963).

would be low. The application of more and more labour to the same land goes hand in hand with declining labour productivity.

Escape from this trap is conceivable. One way would be increased use of labour-saving capital goods. Apart from problems as to the cost and productivity of such capital goods, the more important catch is that, while improving labour productivity, these capital goods compete with human labour. Saving labour means pushing it over the edge of the cliff of survival: a labour-saving ox makes humans redundant. This may mean little to a farmer employing wage labour, but matters are different for the subsistence peasant who gives high priority to feeding his family.[1] Once he has accepted the need to feed them, he might as well use their labour. Using an ox (and 'firing' the wife) his labour productivity would be higher, but his wife would starve.

One alternative route - increased division of labour between town and country - has for many years been in the forefront of attention among preindustrial historians. The virtue of Jan de Vries' ideal types of responses to demographic pressure is that they not only specify different relations between town and country, but also go into the logic of the peasant's behaviour. His responses (and the constraints upon them) are seen as the linchpin of the potential for specialization and growth. The presence of cities in itself is not enough to generate this; sometimes peasants do better avoiding trading opportunities. This approach avoids the need to employ 'traditional mentality' as a banker of last resort to explain a lack of commercialization in the presence of cities.

Received opinion on Pompeii has it that its agriculture was mostly producing cash-crops for external markets and that its urban economy was strikingly modern and commercialized: the most extreme example is Moeller's imaginary export textile industry. If all that was true, one wonders why the Roman economy never took off. This doubt necessitated the detailed scrutiny of the evidence in my third and fourth chapter. Those chapters are not an exhaustive description of all the evidence

[1]The classic analysis is Chayanov (1966).

that may concern the Pompeian economy: scholars interested in that must do their own spade work. Instead I have tried to select certain series of data that could serve both as a test for received opinion and as building stones for an alternative reconstruction. That has left many data undiscussed; interpretations of these may have to be revised in the light of my findings, but doing so would perhaps amount to little more than a filling-in operation: I could not think of ways to make them serve as decisive tests, either because they seemed too incomplete, or because they concern what are - to me at least - secondary problems. Contrary to received opinion I have argued that the importance of cereal agriculture has been grossly underestimated. The fallacy that surviving data (here: villas producing wine) represent past reality in an unproblematic fashion has played its tricks again, even to the extent that traditional literary sources were ignored or misread when they speak of cereal agriculture. The bottom line of my own reconstruction is none other than that local agricultural production roughly equals local consumption, both in quantity and in composition. The amount of import and export must have been limited, and probably largely concerned adjustments to fluctuations in output from one year to the next. The relations between the urban elite and the peasants could not be documented from Pompeian sources. Yet it is obviously important to know whether the peasants owned (most of) their own land, or were largely tenants. To supplant intuition about social inequality and ownership of this valuable land, I have developed my 'elite income and expenditure' model. It shows the staggering social inequality in Roman society, and suggests that substantial elite ownership of agricultural land is to be expected.

But what about the urban economy? The number and variety of workshops is indeed impressive. But what was their market? Whatever the role of the urban economy, a substantial amount of goods and services produced would always be for local consumption. Critical for an argument about the commercialization of relations between town and country are only those types of manufacturing that we may reasonably expect to be part of such commercial exchange. 'Reasonable expectations' can be founded on a comparison with later periods of European history, where it is above all the textile industry that is at the sharp edge of the commercialization of manufacturing. Therefore I have singled out the textile industry for analysis, which has led to a complete rejection of Moeller's modernizing views. Units of production were not particularly large, and there are no signs that production was for anything more than local markets. The wide spread of different occupations in the town, and the lack of concentration on any one of them, appears to indicate a preponderance of production to satisfy the demand of the landowning elite resident in the town. And elite purchasing power was considerable.

The Pompeian situation therefore closely resembles de Vries' peasant model of response to demographic pressure, and I have little hesitation in using the label 'consumer city' to characterize the urban economy, provided that it is clear that this does not imply a lack of ability to feed large numbers of people and support a heavily urbanized elite with its taste for sophisticated luxury goods and services. It was a situation, however, in which the road to further growth was blocked precisely by the mechanisms which had allowed it to get where it got.

PART TWO

SOCIETY

CHAPTER SIX

THE DIMENSIONS OF SOCIAL INEQUALITY

An introduction to the questions

In the previous chapters on the Pompeian economy we have had occasion to discuss the involvement of different social groups in various economic activities. Such discussion was necessitated by the long historiographical tradition which identifies pre-industrial growth and development with the economic mentality of a specific social group, the bourgeoisie. This is the social group that is supposed to have been the bearer of the entrepreneurial skills and zeal for economic change which would have brought about the rise of early capitalism. In my first chapter I have expressed some theoretical and comparative historical doubts whether these views, with which the names of famous scholars such as Henri Pirenne and Max Weber have been connected, are correct with regard to late medieval and early modern Europe.[1] That, however, does not absolve us from the duty to investigate it for the ancient world, and that all the more so since I shall argue that, even if a bourgeoisie may no longer be accepted as an explanation for development, it remains true that in this respect important differences exist between antiquity and later preindustrial Europe.

[1]Pirenne (1927); Weber (1976) esp. II 727-814; Sombart (1916-28). Recent surveys include Cipolla (1981); Lis and Soly (1979); Brenner (1976); Lopez (1971); Hilton (ed.) (1976). Above, p. 48 ff.

In the historiography of the economy and society of the Greek and Roman world this paradigm from later European history has undoubtedly played a major role, dividing scholars into the two camps of those who see both a *bourgeoisie* and growth, and of those who see neither, the latter group with rising influence during the last two decades or so.[1]

As I have argued in my first chapter, it is indeed remarkable that both groups appear to share the important theoretical assumption about the relationship between a bourgeoisie and growth. One of the characteristics of this bourgeoisie is that it is supposed to be a social class that is the embodiment of upward social mobility through the acquisition of wealth, while commercial and manufacturing activity are seen as a very quick route to this end.

In this chapter we shall, therefore, shift the focus away from the various sectors of the economy and focus on the social stratification itself. And more particularly, we shall try to investigate how effective in the Roman world the acquisition of wealth was as a means to obtain social standing.

Two conclusions will emerge from the laborious arguments that are to follow. The first is that wealth as such did not on its own bring about social standing. Although obviously a necessary condition, a high social status could only be obtained by persons of free birth (enough on municipal level; on the senatorial level a few generations would have had to pass, of course) who had held political office. The wealthy freedmen will be shown not to reach high social standing. This may not seem an earth-shattering result, but the persevering reader will discover that the innovation is in the methodology applied.

The second conclusion that I shall argue in this chapter is of more limited scope and concerns the nature of the activities that are recorded in the documents that we will look into in detail. The empirical cornerstone of our investigations will be formed by the writing tablets that survive from the archive of

[1]For early discussions see Finley (1979). The two paradigmatic books are Rostovtzeff (1957) and Finley (1985a). Recent contributions include D'Arms (1981); D'Arms and Kopff (1980); Hopkins (1978b); Hopkins (1980); Garnsey a.o. (1983); Garnsey and Whittaker (1983).

the Pompeian auctioneer and banker L. Caecilius Iucundus, and which have been the subject of the excellent study by Jean Andreau.[1] I shall argue two related points about these documents. Firstly, they do not concern the commercial buying and selling commonly associated with Max Weber's producer city, and secondly the persons involved as witnesses are involved not because of an interest in the content of the documents, but as participants in a ritualistic expression of social inequality.

To the historian more used to traditional methodologies, this chapter may appear unnecessarily cumbersome and abstruse. The advantage of the chosen methodology is that it allows us to analyse systematically a more or less consistent set of data and to keep fairly firm controls on possible biases. What is done here in the open and very explicitly is not so different from what others do implicitly. Whether historians like it or not, most of their data have a sample character, with sometimes strong deviations from the randomness criterion through selective survival or even production of data.[2] Data are largely in the eye of the beholder, and our eyes are not Roman eyes.

This also necessitates a short exposition of the recent history of thought on social inequality in order to show the roots of the questions that we will be asking and of the methodology that has been developed.

Although obviously over-simplifying, we can distinguish two main currents in the sociological literature on the subject of inequality. On the one hand we have a European tradition in which the notion of class, however defined, plays a key role, and on the other hand an American tradition of sometimes extreme fragmentation of the concept of inequality, expressed in very neutral terms such as 'rank' or 'stratification'. Two strands can be distinguished in this 'American' tradition. The first is the observation that 'the distribution of rewards in American society appeared to follow a more or less unbroken continuum from top to bottom, so that any decision to impose cut-off points

[1] Andreau (1974). It is difficult to exaggerate the extent to which this chapter is in debt to Andreau's book.

[2] Cf. Finley (1985b) 27-46.

separating a higher class or stratum from a lower one seemed an arbitrary and pointless procedure', the second strand is the observation that someone's social position appeared to be different if looked at from different points of view.[1] A person could be low in one rank system and at the same time high in another, thereby making the construction of a coherent stratification system pointless. No doubt this 'multidimensional' approach owes intellectual debts to Max Weber, but we need also to remind ourselves that it was the same Max Weber who wrote '"property" and "lack of property" are, therefore, the basic categories of all class situations.'[2]

One problem with the multidimensional approach is that it often lacks a fixed point of anchorage and means of weighing the relative importance of dimensions. Characteristically, one or more rank systems (dimensions) are constructed, and if indeed more than one rank system is used, these systems are compared.[3] These different rank systems can subsequently be conflated into one generalized index, but the problem is how to find weighing factors for the importance of the various dimensions. Another approach to obtaining a generalized status indicator is to construct a separate prestige rating index. This is usually not easy to do in the modern research context. In small communities we may still find a sufficiently large number of people who know a reasonably large number of persons well enough to rate them on a scale, but even that involves a large amount of work. More convenient is a procedure employing a panel of judges to rate the prestige of members of the community.

In this chapter a procedure will be employed which is not dissimilar to these prestige rating procedures. The advantage is that once we have established such a rank system of prestige ratings, we can compare it with other rank systems based on income, property or whatever dimensions of social inequality may seem relevant. Instead of *assuming* that, for example,

[1]Parkin (1978) 601 f.

[2]Weber (1976) II 532.

[3]Jackson and Curtis (1968) 112 ff.

income is an important dimension, we can actually investigate whether it was felt to be important at the time.

Although it is interesting and important to know how people in the past evaluated the relative importance of the various dimensions of social inequality, the social historian can nevertheless not afford to limit his analysis to this subjective level. Quite rightly the literature on social class and social status emphasizes the need to complement this subjective concept of social stratification with an analysis of external characteristics of social strata or classes.[1]

As so often in the field of ancient history, the complexity of the problem is brought out clearly in the work of M.I. Finley. In his *The Ancient Economy* he devotes an entire chapter to the inadequacy of a Marxist class concept for an understanding of ancient social structure: 'the slave and the free wage labourer would then be members of the same class, on a mechanical interpretation, as would the richest senator and the non-working owner of a small pottery. That does not seem a very sensible way to analyse ancient society.'[2] Instead he chooses the concept of 'status', 'an admirably vague word with a considerable psychological element.'[3]

And indeed, the whole book is a strong plea for the need to consider status and economic mentality when analysing the ancient economy. But his argument that status elements are strongly interwoven with the economy can also be turned round, as he himself does in his book on politics.[4] He argues that political conflict in the ancient world cannot be separated from class conflict, not employing a strict Marxist definition, but concentrating on the conflict between rich and poor citizens.

In this chapter an effort will be made to combine the two approaches to the analysis of social inequality, the class analysis and the multidimensional approach. It seems wrong either to mechanically construct a class system with complete disregard

[1] Geiger (1962) 16-205, esp. 193 f.

[2] Finley (1985) 35-61, quote on p. 49.

[3] Finley (1983) 51.

[4] Finley (1983) 1-23.

for the many different facets of inequality and the subtle inconsistencies in people's positions, or to bury every notion of the relevance of the distinction between 'haves' and 'have nots' in an ever increasing welter of detached scholarly nuances. An urgent need exists for an investigation into the relationships between the results of these two types of analysis. How manifest can we say that class distinctions were in the Roman world? Why is it that the various dimensions of status do not overlap completely, and how do the specific forms of such what has been called 'status dissonance' relate to the structure of Roman society.[1]

An introduction to the data

The evidence that will form the basis of our analysis is of a very rare type and consists of a set of wooden writing tablets found in 1875 in a Pompeian house and forming a group of 153 documents.[2] Before proceeding with our own analysis, a short orientating description will be in order, largely derivative from Jean Andreau's important study of these documents.[3]

The documents are some kind of archive of the *argentarius coactor* L. Caecilius Iucundus, containing receipts given to Iucundus for payments made by him. The documents were witnessed by three or four persons if the redaction is a chirograph (i.e. in the first person), for example *'L. Titius scripsi me accepisse ...'*, while there are at least seven and sometimes nine or ten witnesses if the document is in the third person, e.g. *'L. Titius ... habere (or accepisse) se dixit.'*[4]

The documents relate to two different types of transactions. The first group are the sixteen documents commonly referred to as *'apochae rei publicae'*. In these documents a slave of the town acknowledges that he has received the money that was

[1]For status dissonance, see e.g. Hopkins (1965), reprinted in Finley (1974).

[2]These tablets were published in the 'Corpus Inscriptionum Latinarum' Vol. IV Suppl. I.

[3]Andreau (1974).

[4]Mommsen (1877) 103, and CIL IV suppl. I, 418. In fact the situation is a bit more complicated than as described, because of the difference between 'scriptura interior' and 'scriptura exterior'. It is the 'scriptura interior' that is decisive for the redaction. See Andreau (1974) 19.

owed by Iucundus for the farming of a tax or because Iucundus had rented a property from the town. In tablet 141, *pagina* 2, 3, lines 8 ff, we can read:

> Privatus coloniae ser(vus)/
> scripsi me accepisse ab/
> L. Caecilio Iucundo sest-/
> ertios mille sescentos./
> quinquaginta du[o] num-/
> mos ob fullonicam/
> ex reliquis anni unius.//

The last line shows that Iucundus was in arrears with the payments for the fullery. The document also included a date, and a short list of witnesses.

The second type of transaction, referred to in 137 documents, is that of the auctions organised by Iucundus. The sellers declare that Iucundus has paid them the money due from the proceeds. Unfortunately we know the name of a buyer only once. But we do get the names of sellers, the prices, and sometimes the percentage that was charged by Iucundus and the nature of the product involved in the auction. Furthermore a date and a list of witnesses. A few lines (1-5) from tablet 5 will again provide an illustration:

> HS n(ummos) 1985 quae pecunia in stipulatu(m) venit L./
> Caeci(li) Iucundi ob auctionem buxiaria(m) C. Iuli Onesimi/
> in idus Iulias primas mercede minus numeratos accepiss-/
> e dixit C. Iulius Onesimus ab M. Fabio Agathino/
> nomine L. Caecili Iucundi.//

Follows a date, and an in this case largely illegible list of at least eight witnesses.

The house in which Iucundus lived gives us an indication that he was fairly well off (Plate XXVII).[1] It is a nice *atrium*

[1]The house concerned is V, I, 26. See Andreau (1974) 25 ff. for further information. Also Dexter (1975). The most charitable comment on Dexter's discussion of Pompeian social structure as reconstructed from the wax tablets would be to say

house: the floor area measures 570-910 m^2 (depending on assumptions about property boundaries). Paintings have been found on a number of walls.[1]

Iucundus was probably dead by A.D. 79. The first tablet dates from 27, and the last one is from shortly before the earthquake of 62. It is possible that he died during this catastrophe, but we do not know. The reliefs from the *lararium* of his house and which show earthquake scenes can just as well mean that he suffered considerable financial losses. But in any case, they are not solid evidence that he made a considerable profit in the aftermath of the earthquake as has been suggested in line with Maiuri's theory about a 'take-over' of the town by commercial groups as a result of the earthquake.[2]

Iucundus' predecessor L. Caecilius Felix was probably the freedman of some L. Caecilius.[3] It does not seem unreasonable to assume that L. Caecilius Felix the *argentarius* is the same person as the L. Caecilius Felix, *Minister Augusti Mercuri Maiae* in the year A.D. 1.[4] Castrén says he is the father of Iucundus, but Andreau is rightly a bit more careful.[5] Iucundus' sons are possibly Q. Caecilius Iucundus and Sex. Caecilius Iucundus Metellus.[6] There are no tablets to suggest that either might have succeeded him as *argentarius*. Maybe one of them was in charge of rural property and the other of the urban. On an amphorette we read '*Caecilio Iucundo/ ab Sexto Metello*' (CIL IV 5788). The amphorette was found in a *taberna* that formed part of the house of Iucundus.[7]

Della Corte has suggested that Iucundus was the owner of the villa in which the famous Boscoreale treasure was found,

that it has been superceded by Andreau (1974).

[1]Andreau (1974) 25. See his footnote 3 for various assessments of the quality of these paintings.

[2]On the social effects of the earthquake Maiuri (1942), and Andreau (1973).

[3]Andreau (1974) 30 f.

[4]Ibid.

[5]Castrén (1975) 'ad nom'.; Andreau (1974) 30.

[6]Andreau (1974) 36 f.

[7]Ibid.

but the evidence is not very convincing.[1] The *gens* Caecilia in Pompeii seems to have been rather unimportant: we only know two Caecilii as candidates for elections. The other known Caecilii appear to be freedmen or descendents of these.[2] It is not easy to get an idea of the organization of Iucundus' business from the tablets. There are three slaves who pay on his behalf. It seems unlikely that the witnesses who appear most often in the tablets are dependent upon him, since this would make them less acceptable as witnesses.

Not only are many tablets rather damaged, but it is also quite obvious that the tablets that remain are only a selection. The number is rather small and the chronological distribution rather uneven. Almost all tablets about auctions are from the years A.D. 54-58, while we know from for example tablet 2 that Iucundus was already in the business in 27. Because we know that the contracts with the town were for five year periods, and since Iucundus had to pay annually, we can establish that here too we have only a selection. The preserved tablets are not solely contracts with important people, nor do they only concern large amounts. And they are not particularly recent either. Two possibilities to explain the selection remain.[3] They could either be the result of an involuntary choice (i.e. the rest were destroyed in for example the earthquake of 62), or they could represent a voluntary selection on affective grounds (e.g. tablet 1 may be a memorial to his predecessor L. Caecilius Felix, who is the *argentarius* in that tablet). Since this latter interpretation does not explain the great prominence of the years 54-58, the catastrophe theory seems the more attractive, but probably the truth is a bit of both.

In the following two paragraphs we shall initiate a discussion of the content of the transactions and of the nature of the group of persons involved in the documents.

[1] Della Corte (1965) 433-437, nos 972-984; Andreau (1974) 31 f.

[2] Della Corte (1965) 433-437, nos 972-984; Andreau (1974) 31 f.

[3] Andreau (1974) 28.

Some economic observations

In the transactions from the sixteen *'apochae rei publicae'* we can distinguish the following activities:

1. Iucundus rents the *fundus Audianus* from the town (tablets 138, 139, 140). He finds it apparently not so easy to pay the annual rent of H.S. 6000, because tablets 138 and 139 mention arrears. And indeed, it is not a minor sum: it represents about 50 subsistence rations of wheat for a year.[1] Equally, it implies a capital value of around H.S. 100,000 - the same amount as the likely census for decurions. Another peg to put this capital value into perspective would be to compare the H.S. 100,000 with the land valuations in Duncan-Jones' table for Italy: the median of this table is H.S. 80,000.[2]

2. A *fullonica* for H.S. 1652 a year (tablets 141, 142, 143 and 144). This could refer to a tax on fulleries, but it is more likely that Iucundus rented a fullery from the city.[3]

3. The farming of the *'pasqua'*, probably a sort of tax on the use of city-owned pasture land, for H.S. 2675 a year (tablets 145, 146, 147).[4]

4. The *'mercatus'*, a market tax, for H.S. 2520 a year, *'nomine M. Fabi Agathini'* (tablet 151).

The sums involved in these transactions are by no means enormous, but apparently already enough to give Iucundus some problems in the year 56/57.[5] The figure for the farming of the market tax - if reliable - may be an indicator of the limited importance of the annual turnover: if the tax rate was indeed 1%, as Andreau believes, it implies a turnover of H.S. 252,000 per annum.[6] This is about 6% of the minimum estimate for the

[1]For details on the assumptions behind these calculations: above p. 195. As this was probably very good land we are more likely to have underestimated than to have overestimated the capital value (the rule of thumb being that the better the quality of a property, the lower the rent is, as a percentage of the capital value).

[2]Cf. Andreau (1980) 188 ff; Duncan-Jones (1974) 210 ff.

[3]Andreau (1974) 69 ff.

[4]Andreau (1974) 56, 61, 67-78; Cf. Andreau (1980) 187 ff.

[5]Andreau (1974) 58 f.

[6]Andreau (1974) 82.

Net Pompeian Product which can be derived from my calculations in the previous chapters.[1]

The remaining 137 documents concern payments made by Iucundus to the sellers in the auctions organised by Iucundus. These auctions have inspired earlier authors to images of an exciting business life.[2] Andreau, fully aware of the theoretical and methodological pitfalls, tones this down, but I shall argue that he does not go far enough, perhaps disappointed that it was not the ideal way to tackle Roman finance that he thought it would be. The central problem is the extent to which the documents reflect the business activities of a commercial bourgeoisie or alternatively the dealings of a consumer elite.[3]

We do not know whether the auctions were held at regular time intervals. The tablets were drawn up several days after the auction and do not provide the date of the latter. Sometimes *argentarii* were attached to a particular regular market.[4] In Pompeii a regular market appears to have been held on Saturdays, but we are ignorant of possible auctions at these markets.[5]

I suppose that the scale of the activities of the auctioneers attached to Roman and Ostian markets must have been smaller than that of Iucundus' activities.[6] Unlike them, Iucundus is not known to be involved in retail auctioning of e.g. fish, and the amounts involved in Iucundus' auctions do not suggest such a view either (Figure X, next page).[7]

[1] Above p. 108 ff; 131 ff; 195. Net Pompeian Product equals at least the subsistence cost per head (H.S. 115, i.e. 250 kg. wheat at H.S. 3 per 'modius') multiplied by the total population (36,000). Lifting production above subsistence, only serves to lower the share of local production that was sold in the market.

[2] Frank (1918) 233 n. 2; Sergejenko (1953) 127-9; Wiseman (1971) 72; more carefully: Lepore (1950) 147.

[3] Above, p. 28 ff; 187 ff.

[4] Andreau (1974) 73 ff.

[5] CIL IV 8863. MacMullen (1970). Andreau (1976).

[6] Cf. Flach (1878) 659-661; cf. Andreau (1974) 95 n.1.

[7] Derived from the data in Andreau (1974) 88 ff. Both the precisely known figures and those figures only known approximately have been used. If these latter transgressed the chosen class limits, the median of highest and lowest possible value was used.

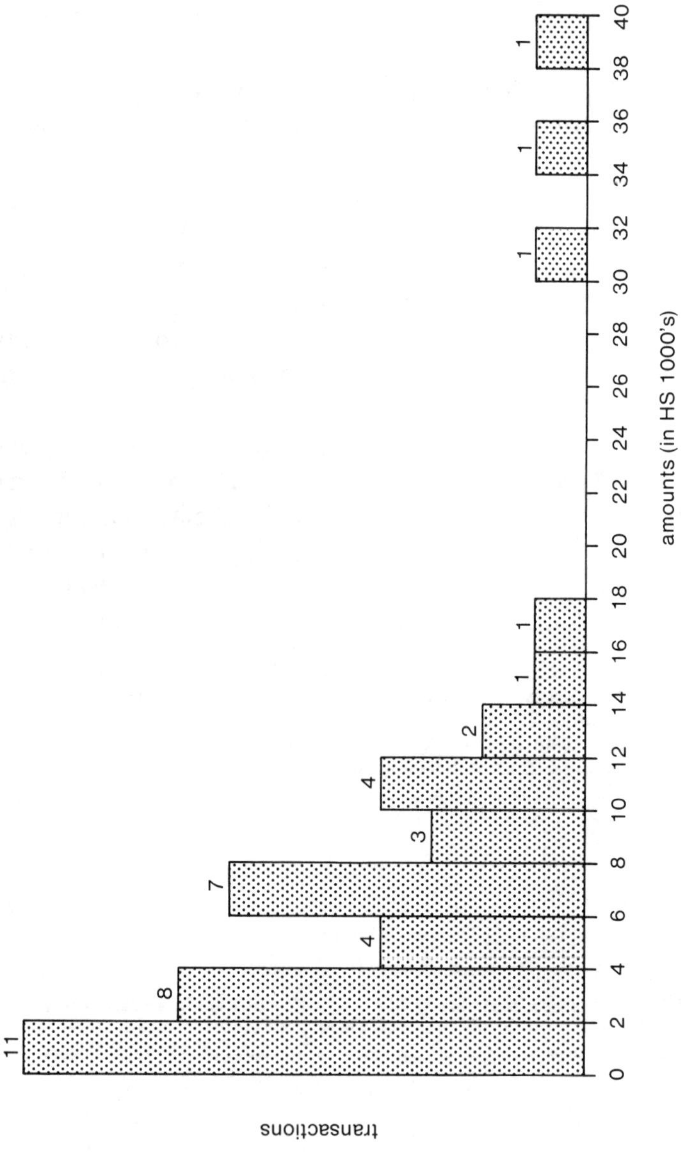

Figure X: The amounts involved in Iucundus' transactions (Andreau (1974) 88 ff.)

Of the eleven cases in the class H.S. 0-2000, only three are less than H.S. 1000, suggesting that for smaller sales one would not always go to Iucundus.

The median of the amounts involved is a figure of about H.S. 4500, which is not inconsiderable. It would perhaps buy almost 10,000 kg. of wheat (enough to feed 40 people for a year), or a few slaves, whereas in tablet 1 a mule costs H.S. 520.[1]

But how much did Iucundus himself earn from these transactions? According to Mommsen and Cicero, the general rule was 1%.[2] The two tablets that give some information suggest 2%, but this is unlikely to be the uniform rate. A remarkable feature of the figures in the tablets is that they are in no way round figures - this suggests that the deduction has already been made, contrary to what Mommsen thought. And fair enough, since the tablets are a record of what the seller actually receives. So, what percentage should we add to get round figures? Apparently not a uniform one, and sometimes quite high, like 7%. Is this not too high? Possibly not, if all sorts of other costs and taxes are included in the percentage. But quite often the trick does not work at all, and then we must assume that some costs were not charged as a percentage.[3] If Iucundus normally received 2% on an average transaction of H.S. 7650 (the arithmetic mean of the transactions from Figure X) this gives him H.S. 153 each time. Perhaps ten tablets refer to auctions in A.D. 57, and at least fifteen to 58, suggesting a minimum estimate of at least about H.S. 2000 per

[1]Andreau (1974) 93 ff. It is very unfortunate that Andreau, after warning against the dangers of converting into modern prices, nevertheless makes an effort to do so. With an ancient basket of purchased goods that is so different from the modern, no direct comparison of 'purchasing' power is possible. All we can do is compare the figure of HS 4500 with known ancient prices of obviously important goods. For some abrasive but salutary remarks on the subject of price history see e.g. Baehrel (1961) 1-20. For ancient prices see Duncan - Jones (1982). See above, p. 195 for a discussion of wheat prices.

[2]Mommsen (1877) 98 and n. 2 & 3; Andreau (1974) 81, n. 2; Cicero, 'Pro Rab. Post.' XI, 30.

[3]Andreau (1974) 81 ff.

year. This throughput equals almost twenty times minimum subsistence needs.[1]

Where the auctions were held is hard to tell. We know of *atria auctionaria* in Rome, and Andreau has suggested that a room in the north eastern corner of the Macellum in Pompeii may have served this purpose (Plate XXV), in addition to the stone structures in the front of the building of Eumachia and outside the Macellum that have been called auction blocks by Moeller (Plate XXIV).[2] But archaeologically these solutions do not inspire a great deal of confidence, as they are not based on a comparison of the Pompeian structures with other cases, where identification of function is beyond any doubt.[3]

Andreau believes that the tablets were not witnessed at Iucundus' home, but in an office elsewhere, near the forum, probably to the east of it.[4] This observation is only based on the distribution pattern of the known addresses of persons from the tablets, which shows some concentration near the eastern side of the forum. Such concentration obviously supports him in his assumption of some professional interest on the part of the witnesses: '... si la tablette de quittance est signée dans sa boutique, certains des témoins ont toutes chances d'être des clients, alors présents dans la dite boutique.' He is obviously trying here to justify his combined analysis of sellers and witnesses as a group of professionally interested persons.

For his house identifications, Andreau relies on the identifications made by Della Corte, though warning against their unreliability. A revision of these identifications - see Appendix III - produces more clearly patterned results, with a concentration in the proximity of Iucundus' house (Figure XI).[5]

Thus, the only empirical support for the hypothesis of the existence of a separate office has disappeared. Of course, it does not disprove the existence of an office. Iucundus could

[1]For an estimate of subsistence costs, above, p. 195.

[2]Andreau (1974) 77 ff; Moeller (1976) 68 ff.

[3]For some further observations on these structures: above p. 181 f.

[4]Andreau (1974) 187 ff.

[5]Below, p. 354 ff.

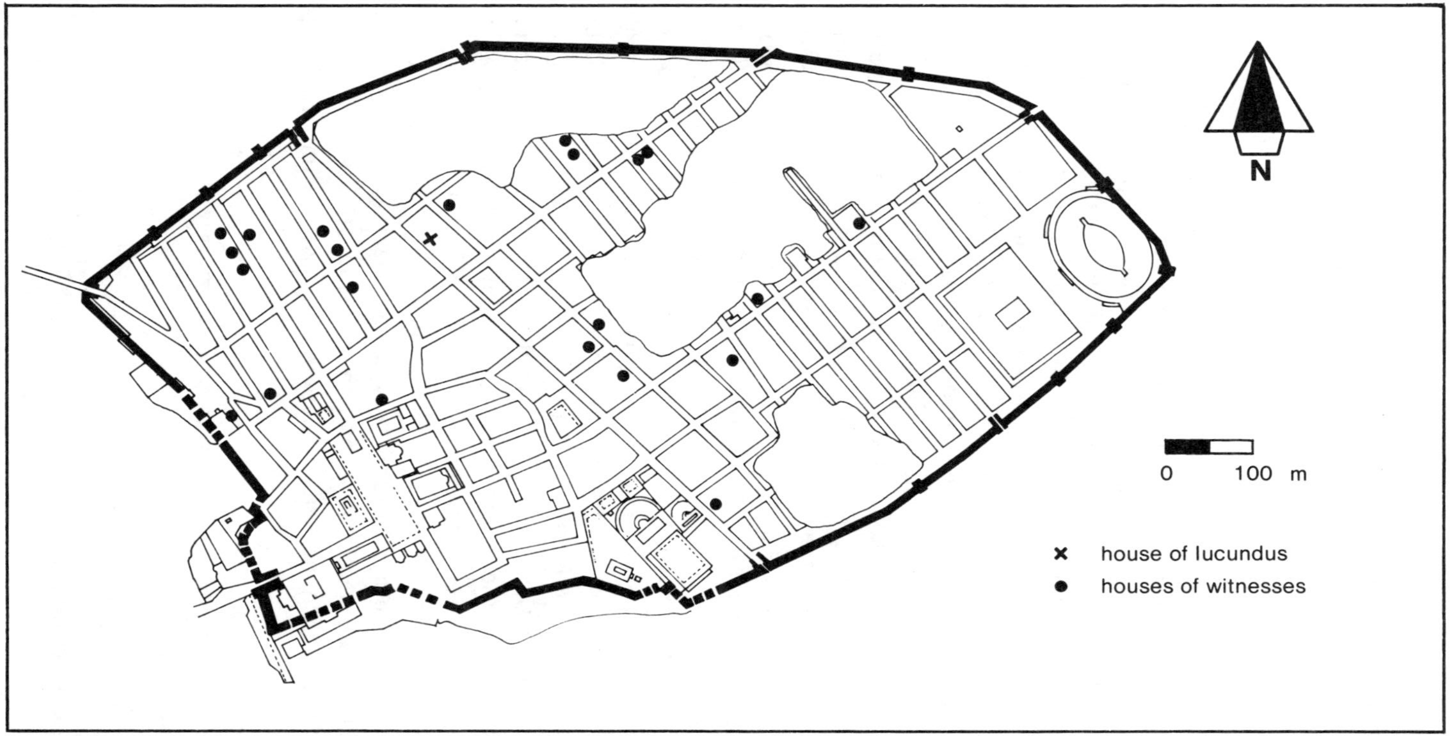

Figure XI: Houses of Iucundus' witnesses

have mainly used witnesses from his own neighbourhood, and have invited them to an office elsewhere. Though this would not appear to be the most obvious thing to do, it still means that the hypothesis of professional interest on the part of the witnesses finds no support.

The tablets also show traces of credit operations. In tablet 6 the seller leaves his money for some time in deposit with Iucundus, and subsequently draws on this credit.[1] In another tablet (t. 23) Iucundus has given credit to a seller, presumably in the expectation of the sale. Seventeen tablets show that a credit was granted to the purchaser.[2] The duration of the credit varies between 16 days and 10 or 11 months, mostly only a few months. Possibly the reason for the credit is to give the buyers the chance to await the income from their land.[3]

Unfortunately many tablets remain silent about the nature of the object sold in the auction. In part this is due to incomplete survival of the text, but even in the majority of well preserved texts, it was apparently - and perhaps significantly - not deemed necessary to mention what had been sold.[4] Of the three groups that Andreau distinguishes, occasional sales (linked with the administration of private fortunes), sales of products of the land, and those organised by merchants, objects from the first category seem to be predominant.[5] A remarkable feature of the tablets is a rather uneven distribution of the activities over the year, with a substantial peak around December, and two others for May and September.[6] For the peak in September Andreau cannot offer an explanation, but for the two others he points to the coincidence with two peak seasons in the Pompeian agricultural year, sheepshearing taking place in the spring and vinification and the making of olive oil around December. I have argued in chapter four that the importance of

[1] Andreau (1974) 96.

[2] Tablets 2, 5, 7, 11, 14, 15, 16, 19, 27, 35, 38, 46, 47, 71, 122, 125, 136.

[3] Andreau (1974) 100 f; cf. below, p. 224.

[4] Andreau (1974) 104.

[5] Andreau (1974) 74 ff, 103 ff.

[6] Andreau (1974) 109 ff, esp. 112.

the Pompeian woollen industry - and local sheepraising - have been grossly overestimated by Moeller.[1] And indeed, closer analysis reveals that only the peak around December can legitimately be considered seasonal. If we are to presuppose a seasonal pattern behind these peaks, it is not unreasonable to demand that the peak occur in more than one year and that is only the case with the December peak.[2]

Remains the problem of finding an explanation for this December peak. Is it a seasonal variation of supply that lies at its root, or of demand? None of the documents involved show any reference to the sale of agricultural produce. On the contrary, occasional sales seem to be predominant. A mule, some boxwood, and slaves are mentioned.[3] Boxwood, a very hard type of wood, would be suitable for furniture, flutes or writing tablets. The latin - *'ob auctionem buxiaria(m)'* - would also allow us to read it as 'boxwood objects', worth H.S. 1985.[4] Among the sellers we find six women, which suggests occasional sales rather than professional sales of agricultural products.[5] Tablet 6 certainly deals with an inheritance.

Summarizing Andreau's detailed discussion, we can say that occasional sales, for example as a result from the need to divide an inheritance, or sales related to the management of property (such as sales of slaves, furniture or real estate) appear to be predominant. This means that the seasonal peak around December should preferably be explained by a variation in demand. This would be the period of the highest financial liquidity on the part of wealthy landowning buyers.[6] The frequency distribution of the dates when the credits granted by

[1]Moeller (1976).

[2]For this purpose the best documented years (54-58) were inspected more closely.

[3]Tablets 1, 5 and 20.

[4]For a discussion of boxwood: Meiggs (1982) 280 ff.

[5]Andreau (1974) 114.

[6]For the limited liquidity of the rich in the ancient world, see e.g. Finley (1985) 53; Crawford (1970) 40-48; Frederiksen (1966) 128-41. Compare the observations made by Breglia (1950) 47 f. about the content of private strong boxes.

Iucundus to buyers fell due (Figure XII), supports this view (though only with a limited number of observations).[1]

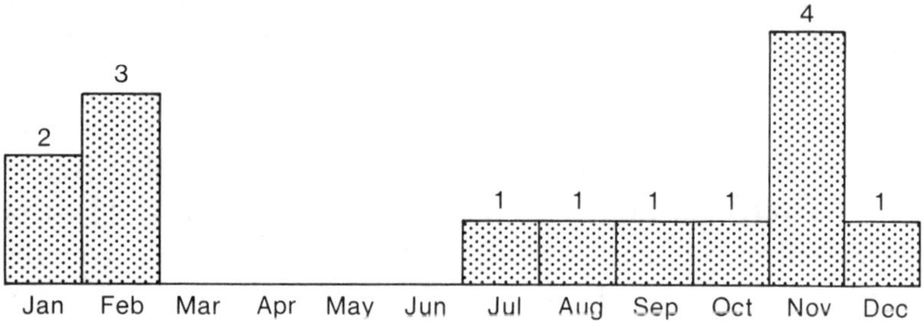

Figure XII: Frequency distribution of dates on which credits granted by Iucundus to buyers fell due
(source: Andreau (1974) 100 f.)

Concluding these remarks about the economic aspects, we may say that in all likelihood the documents do not reflect buying and selling of the commercial type prevalent in Max Weber's producer city.[2] They are not auctions of the export products of a local manufacturing industry. Nor are they auctions of raw materials to be used in manufacturing. Moeller's - in my opinion nonexistent - wool auctions, are not reflected in Iucundus' auctions.[3] What we find are Pompeians disposing of some property and probably other Pompeians buying it. The seasonal fluctuation that could be discerned was probably due to fluctuation in consumer demand, in this society dominated by agriculture.

Some social aspects

If these conclusions about the nature of the objects that were auctioned, are correct, we would naturally want to know what

[1] Andreau (1974) 100.

[2] Weber (1976) II 727-814; Finley (1981) 3-23. For some personal observations see above, p. 187 ff.

[3] Moeller (1976) 68 f, 72 ff; cf. above, p. 181 f.

interest the persons in the documents had in them. This is especially true for the witnesses: why did they bother to turn up?

One negative preliminary observation about the social composition of the group of persons who occur in Iucundus' archive has already been made: the spatial distribution of the homes of witnesses and sellers showed a concentration near the house of Iucundus, which fits less easily with an explanation of the presence of witnesses as a commercially interested group. This is an important problem because in Andreau's book on *Les affaires de monsieur Iucundus* both sellers and witnesses are used for prosopographical analysis. Andreau observes no marked social differences between sellers and witnesses, 'sans doute parce que les témoins se recrutent partiellement dans un cercle d'hommes intéressés aux *auctiones*, professionellement proches de Iucundus, - un cercle de commerçants?'[1] Indeed, the social positions of witnesses and sellers, as elucidated by an onomastic analysis, do not differ. Where sellers are also known as witnesses, these are not the most frequent witnesses. If it does not seem unlikely that both sellers and witnesses belong to the same social group and should be studied together, the question remains, whether both are 'commerçants', or neither.[2]

The documents do not supply direct information about the social status of witnesses and sellers. The bulk of the information has to be obtained by an onomastic approach. Unfortunately, the names in the documents do not include affiliation and tribe, the only unequivocal information about legal status.

On well preserved documents the names only include *praenomen*, *nomen gentilicium* and *cognomen*. The distribution of *praenomina* in the tablets does not differ markedly from that of all Pompeians (= index CIL X).[3] The tablets contain a slightly higher proportion of *gentilicia* of magistrates and more so of candidates than the CIL X index of Pompeian names.[4] The

[1]Andreau (1974) 179 f.

[2]Ibid; cf. below, p. 264 ff.

[3]Andreau (1974) 133, table 12; CIL X p. 1062 ff.

[4]Andreau (1974) 134, table 13.

difference is of course somewhat greater if we realise that the names from the Iucundus tablets have also been included in the CIL X index of Pompeian names. If significant, it is interesting to note that the names in the Iucundus tablets are somewhat closer to magisterial circles, especially for the later 'magistrates'. These 'magistrates' from later years are in fact not always actual magistrates; in many years we only know the names of candidates for office, not who were elected.[1]

The attraction of the *cognomen* is that it may give us information to decide whether we are dealing with a freeborn person or a freedman.[2] As a prelude to later, more detailed discussion, we may note a predominance of names suggesting libertine status, in the tablets, but the same holds true for the *Index nominum Pompeianorum*.[3] The score for 'Iucundus names' is even more 'libertine' than the *Index nominum Pompeianorum*, which should probably be explained by the relatively high survival rate of information on magisterial names for inclusion in the *Index nominum Pompeianorum*, rather than by the hypothesis of a real social difference. Apart from this onomastic information about individuals in the documents, one more line of inquiry has been indicated by Andreau, and it is this that will form the core of the remaining analysis.

Observing the order in which the witnesses have signed the documents, he noticed a clear pattern. Persons with high social status sign higher than persons with lower status. '[Les membres de l'*ordo* municipal] sont (sauf exception) en tête de liste, comme ils sont au sommet de la hiérarchie municipale.'[4] It is a consistent ordering, as is shown when documents are written twice. It was also apparently important to get the ranking right, proven by corrections in two tablets (81 and 89). Another indication is supplied by a comparison of the relative position of persons who are otherwise known to be of different status. An analogy is afforded by the order of precedence for the

[1] See below, p. 311 ff; Franklin (1980).

[2] A detailed discussion of methodology and results can be found in Andreau (1974) 140 ff. and below, p. 241 ff.

[3] Andreau (1974) 146 ff.

[4] Andreau (1974) 170 ff, 215 f.

witnesses of the military *diplomata*.[1] At certain periods, clear systems of seniority are operative in these documents, admittedly of a different nature from the ones postulated for the Iucundus tablets, but nevertheless they indicate that witnessing legal documents was considered an occasion suitable for the expression of social hierarchy.

Iuvenal, in *Satire* III, lines 81-82, lets Umbricius complain that foreigners sign before him, and get the better seats at banquets.[2] He continues his complaints (lines 126 ff.) by remarking that wealth had become the only thing that counts. 'A man's word is believed in exact proportion to the amount of cash which he keeps in his strong-box' (Iuvenal, *Sat.* III, l. 141-2). So, not only do we hear that precedence in signing as witness has social importance, but the complaints also suggest that, notwithstanding Iuvenal's satirical exaggeration, *nouveaux riches*, recently manumitted slaves and easterners - often enough overlapping categories - will not have been socially acceptable in the eyes of Iuvenal's readers. But a proper answer to the question whether wealthy freedmen could be respectable enough to sign before freeborn citizens will of course have to come from the detailed analysis of Iucundus' tablets. Iuvenal's direct juxtaposition of the order of signing with seating arrangements at banquets is revealing, in the sense that it underlines the awareness of discrimination and the importance of the ostentatious character of it, of the need to express inequality. In addition it invites us to turn to Petronius, that difficult guide to freedman status. At Trimalchio's dinner party the guests sit in a ranked order, and freedman status is an important criterion.[3] But the text does not allow a detailed analysis of the rules, nor does the fictional nature of the novel make it easy for us to make the step to the social reality, and more specifically, to decide of which part of the social reality it forms an adequate description.

[1] Roxan and Morris (1977). See also Roxan (1978) 104 ff.

[2] Andreau (1974) 171.

[3] Petronius, 'Sat.' 38, cf. 57, and possibly 70.

During gladiatorial shows in the Colosseum, seating was segregated by social rank. The emperor and his family obviously kept apart, but there were also separate seats for senators, *equites* or soldiers.[1] In his recent study of seating arrangements and social stratification, Kolendo observes 'le respect d'une segregation rigide entre les quatre groupes majeurs: sénateurs, chevaliers, plèbe urbaine et autres catégories - c'est-à-dire les non-citoyens, les femmes et les esclaves' in the case of the capital.[2] The *lex Ursonensis* lays down similar rules.[3] Apart from the obvious groups of privileged people such as senators and decurions, other categories in the classification are *coloni coloniae*, *incolae*, *hospites* and *adventores*. Kolendo is rightly struck by the geographical narrow-mindedness of the arrangement; the city is a microcosmos. We may add that this is an almost unavoidable counterpart of the classification system employed to rank people on a scale. It is a classification based on politico-legal criteria. The political distance between the *ordines* and the rest is reflected in the seating arrangements.

In distributions of cash to the populace, a clear social pattern can be discerned. 'The figures as a whole consistently show financial discrimination in favour of the socially powerful.'[4] Frequent categories used are: *decuriones*, *augustales* and *populus*. Sometimes women are included, at lower rates.

The expression of social inequality is apparently important, and from data such as these we get a glance at what were apparently felt to be relevant categories. And yet these data remain unsatisfactory because they do not refer to real and individual persons, but only to social categories. They project the image of a hierarchy of social groups, but they do not allow us to investigate the composition of such groups. It is like studying income inequality from the laws of a country about the tax rates for different income groups. Unless we know who earns what, such data are fairly uninteresting. It is

[1] Hopkins (1983a) 17 f.

[2] Kolendo (1981) 304.

[3] Kolendo (1981) 305-307; CIL II 5439 = ILS 6087 - for a translation see Hardy (1912) 23 ff.

[4] Duncan-Jones (1982) 141, more generally 138 ff; for detailed evidence 184 ff.

important to know that the *decuriones* are a social group above the *populus*, the fact that the *decuriones* are favoured in distributions throws an interesting light on the prevailing political mentality, but the central issue in social stratification is of course: who are these *decuriones* and others? Only through observation on the level of individual persons can we hope to discover some of the discrepancies between the various dimensions of social status.

As well as the possibility of studying social inequality on the level of real and individual persons, the second attraction of data such as the Iucundus archive is that we can study it more independently from our own modern preconceived operations. Instead of claiming to study social inequality and then only measuring wealth, income, skin colour, education, or whatever, we can start with a prestige rating made by the actual historical actors and compare that with the rankings we can conceive ourselves, based on income inequality or the rest. And instead of *assuming* that income inequality is important for an understanding of social hierarchy, we can see whether it was the inequality felt to be relevant at the time. In this way the historian should be able to make a contribution to the discussions in the social sciences about how universal certain operations are, a contribution that one might argue to be very akin to the awareness of changes in preferences that is so necessary in applying modern economic theory to past societies.[1]

Other historians have recently used similar ranking data to create a contemporary stratigraphy.[2] Edward Muir, in his study on civic ritual in Renaissance Venice, started from the internal order of official Venetian processions, and Lucassen and Trienekens used rented or bought church benches as their starting point.[3] The flaw of the church benches research is unfortunately that benches cost - sometimes a lot of - money. The authors obtain a high correlation with income, and opt for class in preference to status, but they have probably only

[1]Above p. 36 ff.

[2]Ultee (1983).

[3]Muir (1981) 183 ff; Lucassen and Trienekens (1978) 239-305.

shown a strong correlation between high income and ostentatious consumption.

For the ancient world no systematic study of the demonstration of inequality in social and civic ritual has yet been made, but the examples given above show the possibilities.

The aim of the present chapter is to make an effort to use a unique set of data to analyse social stratification in the Roman world. As always the data leave a lot to be desired and require a great deal of careful reordering and manipulation. And even then, many questions will remain unanswered. But, given the lack of studies containing anything more than impressionistic observations, however true some of them may be, it seemed worthwhile to use this unique chance of systematic analysis.

Handling the sources

That the witnesses sign the documents in a socially significant ranking order is of obvious interest to the student of social inequality. In itself, the bothering about precedence on occasions such as when these documents were drawn up would already be revealing of a great awareness of status differences, and it is underscored by the high degree of consistency of the ranking.[1] We are therefore justified in making an effort to employ these ranking data from the tablets as the equivalent of the common sociological procedure of obtaining judges' ratings of personal prestige.[2]

The problems that stand in the way of reaching a meaningful analysis of social inequality are nevertheless considerable. They can be divided into the three groups introduced below, and efforts to solve them will be made in subsequent parts of this chapter.

1. In a raw state the documents provide a large number of short ranked lists, but these are not very useful as they only place a person in relation to a few other individuals. For a

[1]Meaning that cases like 'A above B' in one document and 'B above A' in another, were quite rare. Andreau (1974) 170 f. gives a few examples. For more, see below, appendix I.

[2]Jackson and Curtis (1968) 126 f, with references. Cf. above, p. 209 f.

proper analysis we would have to find a way of ranking persons in relation, preferably to all Pompeians, but at least to as many persons in the documents as possible. The easiest solution is that adopted by Andreau and Castrén. In his prosopography of Pompeii, Castrén includes the rank number of a witness in one or more documents. With these rank numbers we would then be able to make comparisons of the social standing of persons. But this is not as easy as it may seem, because it assumes that all documents are roughly equal in their proportion of persons of high and of low social status, and have equal numbers of witnesses. And neither of those two assumptions is true. Comparing tablets 70 and 76 is revealing. In tablet 70 the first four witnesses are in all probability freeborn and of decurional status: the third and fourth witnesses, L. Albucius Iustus and M. Holconius Rufus, are known candidates for office. The fifth witness is M. Cerrinius Restitutus, an *augustalis*. This same M. Cerrinius Restitutus returns as second witness in tablet 76, only preceded by L. Laelius Trophimus, probably a freedman of L. Laelius Fuscus, a candidate for the duovirate.[1] This social dissimilarity of the tablets is reflected in the wide range of positions that some frequent witnesses occupy. L. Melissaeus Atimetus is third and eighth witness, M. Fabius Eupor occupies the range of second to seventh witness, while Cn. Helvius Apollonius, witness in seven tablets, can be found from third to ninth position.[2] Unless we take into account who signed above and below the person we are interested in, the rank number in a document is not very revealing, and possibly misleading.

2. Assuming that this problem could be solved, we would still not have gained a great deal of knowledge. Apart from the observation that ranking was important in Roman social life, we would only know that a person named X ranked higher than a person named Y. But none of us would be surprised about that. We want to know why.

To see what lies behind the prestige ranking, we need additional information about as many of the ranked persons as

[1] Castrén (1975) 'ad nom'. See also Andreau (1974) 172.

[2] Examples taken from Castrén (1975) 'ad nom.'

we can obtain. To be useful for the purpose these data would have to be of at least ordinal level themselves, meaning that it would have to be possible to rank them on a scale from high to low in relation to each other. Fortunately Pompeii is a relatively well documented society, and it has been possible to collect data on wealth, personal legal status and political office. Ideally one would like to have more, such as age, family background, source of wealth, and so on - but this has not been possible. The core of my analysis will then be formed by an effort to correlate these different indices or aspects of status.

3. The last problem that we have to tackle is to ascertain the position of our data within Pompeian society. In modern prestige ratings research it has often been difficult to create large and representative enough samples.[1] I have not been able to avoid this problem entirely with my Pompeian material. It is a sample from a larger statistical population, but not one drawn by the researcher according to the modern rules of random sampling. The sample has so to speak been drawn for us by the necessity of recording certain aspects of a social event in the past, and it has been influenced by the selection for survival of some documents, and not of others, although I have argued (above, p. 215) that this latter problem need not worry us too much.

More serious is the question to what extent it is a sample drawn from all Pompeians, or from a select group. The former is certainly not the case. For all practical purposes women and slaves are absent. But there could be more problems in store. For Della Corte a reference in one of these tablets implies that that person had commercial interests.[2] And although Andreau is as often a lot more subtle, he also treats the persons in the group as a special subgroup within Pompeian society, although ultimately not committing himself entirely.[3] In order to make generalizations about Roman - or more modestly Pompeian - social structure from these data, one would obviously have to

[1] Jackson and Curtis (1968) 127.

[2] Della Corte (1965) 'passim'.

[3] Andreau (1974) 'passim', and esp. 129.

know from what statistical population this sample was drawn, and preferably have some idea about possible biases in the sampling.

The construction of prestige rankings

If we want to construct one long ranked list of all witnesses in the documents, we have to take the relative rankings in the individual documents as our starting point. We then have 112 small groups of ranked persons, each group floating freely in relation to the other 111. Links can then be provided by those 97 individuals who occur in more than one document. The logic of this can best be explained by the small example in Figure XIII.

Tablet I	Tablet II	Combined	
a	k		k
b	l	a	l
c	m		m
d	b	b	
e	o	o	
f	p	p	
g	c	c	
		d	
		e	
		f	
		g	

Figure XIII: The construction of rankings

On the left, we see the ranking order of witnesses in two hypothetical tablets. On the right, the information from the two tablets has been combined. Witnesses A, K, L and M all occur above witness B, who in turn ranks above all remaining witnesses. The precise relation between A on the one hand, and K, L, and M on the other hand unfortunately remains ambiguous. From B all the way down to G precise ranking is possible, thanks to C who occurs in both tablets.

Obviously we run into trouble if the ranking in the tablets is not consistent because a pair of witnesses occurs in one order in one document, and in inverse order in another.

With the example above, with few documents and few witnesses, a ranking of the persons in the combined documents could easily be constructed using traditional methods, but this was obviously not possible with what turned out to be 334 witnesses in 112 documents. Only the use of a computer could make a practical reality out of a theoretical possibility to generate such a prestige ranking of the 334 witnesses.[1]

Before the data could be fed into the computer they had to be adapted and 'cleaned'. As the solution depends on witnesses occurring more than once, the spelling inconsistencies and uncertain readings posed a problem. Even the slightest differences here would make the program treat for example two occurrences of one person as two different persons. No significance should be attached to the uniform spellings that were adopted here to iron out these inconsistencies. More problematic are uncertain readings. Here we face the choice between the devil and the deep blue sea.[2] We have to decide what to do with two documents like tablet 28 and tablet 57. In tablet 28 there are the remains of some letters that may refer to the same N. Nerius Hyginus as in tablet 57. We may decide to play safe epigraphically and refuse to accept that we are dealing with the same N. Nerius Hyginus in both cases, but if this caution is mistaken because they were in reality the same person, it means we have destroyed useful information. Dangerous, because the success of the construction of one long list of ranked individuals is a function of the extent to which the same witnesses sign in more than one document. If on the other hand we feel confident that it is the same N. Nerius Hyginus, though in reality they were two different persons, this epigraphic arrogance will result in introducing incorrect ranking information, and often create nonexistent contradictions.[3] All we can do is to try to be right in as many cases as possible.

The procedure adopted was to follow the independent judgement of Castrén's prosopography as often as possible, sometimes

[1] Cf. appendix I. The program was written and executed by Todd Whitelaw of St. John's College Cambridge.

[2] Cf. the discussion of type I and type II errors in Blalock (1979) 105 ff.

[3] Cf. appendix I.

amended by Andreau or by personal judgement. As remarked above, unjustified optimism can produce unreal contradictions. Therefore it was thought advisable to bring these contradictions to light. Interestingly, eleven out of the sixteen original direct contradictions could arguably be traced to incorrect epigraphic identifications. To avoid an accusation of data massaging, these cases are discussed in appendix I.

In addition to ascertaining a uniform and correct reading of the names, some names had to be removed because we cannot be sure that their ranking followed the same rules as for the majority of the witnesses. Sellers are often ranked at the bottom qua sellers, acting magistrates at the top, *honoris causa*. Similar problems occur with Iucundus himself, or the slaves acting on his behalf. All women in the documents are sellers, and therefore had to be excluded.[1] Similarly slaves and free persons acting on behalf of others had to be excluded, because we cannot on a priori grounds decide whether their position as witnesses depended on their own social status, or on that of the persons they acted for.

It was on this data set that the program was let loose. Direct contradictions within the ranking, such as A. Messius Phronimus who ranks above N. Popidius Sodalio in tablet 28, but below him in tablet 102, were few.[2] On the other hand, transitivity was low, suggesting that no existing list such as censorial data was used to compile the rankings in the documents, but that ranking was done on a more or less ad hoc basis.[3]

Another observation that can be made is that seven out of eight persons involved in direct contradictions were ranked in the bottom half, the exception being L. Laelius Trophimus. In addition again seven - though different - out of eight are likely to have been freedmen, the one remaining being of

[1] Andreau (1974) 140.

[2] Cf. appendix I.

[3] An example of lack of transitivity could be a football league competition where the year's winning team may have lost from a middle ranking team, which may yet have been beaten by the team finishing at the bottom of that year's competition.

unknown status. None of these eight men are known to have held any office.

If we assume that a social stratification has a more or less pyramid shape, with few people at the top, and many at the bottom, it can be expected that it is easier to rank at the top than at the bottom. But perhaps it was also more necessary to be precise and consistent at the top with for example members of the *ordo*: one only has to call to mind the obsession with the minutiae of precedence witnessed by the album of Canusium.[1] It is hard to conceive that such extreme care would be necessary with the run-of-the-mill freedmen.

The computerised analysis could obviously not improve the data. Some persons' ranking was pretty narrowly determined, but for others this was not the case. So the procedure adopted was to establish highest and lowest possible rankings (see Figure XIV). For some witnesses, highest and lowest possible rank were quite close. But such precision was impossible for a number of others, for whom the highest possible rank could be in the very top of the list, and the lowest possible position right at the bottom.[2] The skeptic could of course argue that this shows the futility of the whole exercise: witness ranking does not produce prestige ratings of sufficient precision.

Methodologically there are in principle two possibilities. Either the witnesses were never ranked with much precision, or alternatively, they were ranked very precisely, but the surviving data do not allow us to perceive this very well. Cross-tabulation of the frequency with which persons occur as witnesses and ranking range gives us the answer. Seventy-seven percent of the witnesses who occur more than once can be ranked within a range narrower than half the total ranking range, whereas 89% of the witnesses who can only be ranked within a ranking range wider than half the total ranking range, are witnesses who only occur once.[3] The more frequently a person is ranked

[1] CIL IX 338. Cf. Garnsey (1974) 243 ff, and below, p. 317 ff.

[2] Cf. below, p. 237.

[3] Obviously sometimes persons occurring only once can also be ranked within a narrow range, because they happened to sign near a well defined witness or witnesses.

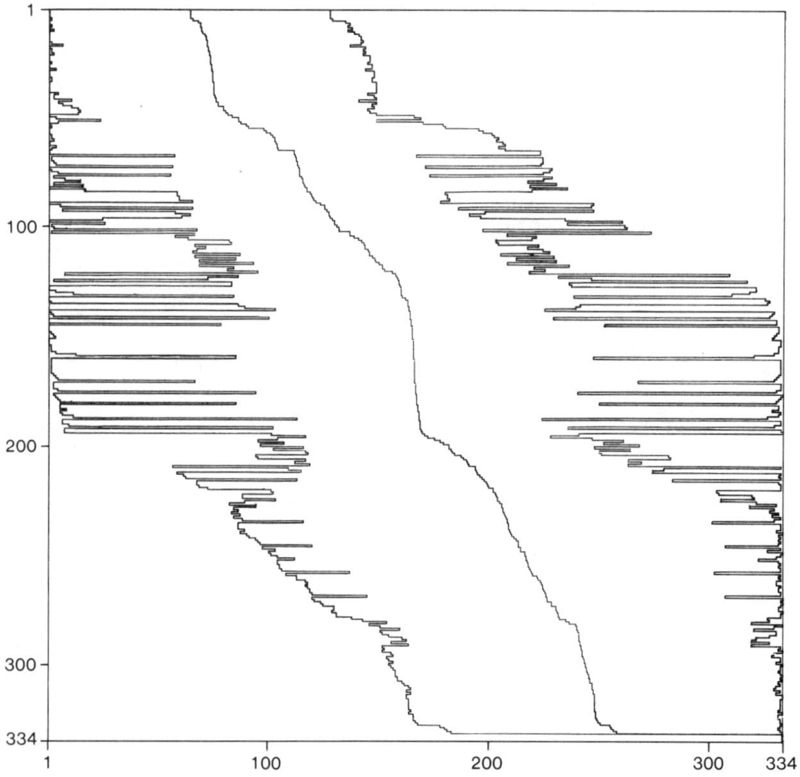

Figure XIV: Ranking range - all witnesses

as witness, the more points of reference become available, and the more precisely we can rank him. We may conclude that ranking was done very meticulously, even though incomplete record survival sometimes draws a veil. For the ultimate ranking the median of highest and lowest position was used, producing in some cases rankings of obvious irrelevance, as can clearly be seen from the thick waist of Figure XIV.

For further analysis it was thought advisable to eliminate those persons who could only be ranked within a uselessly wide range. This second set excludes all persons who could not be ranked within a range narrower than half the total ranking

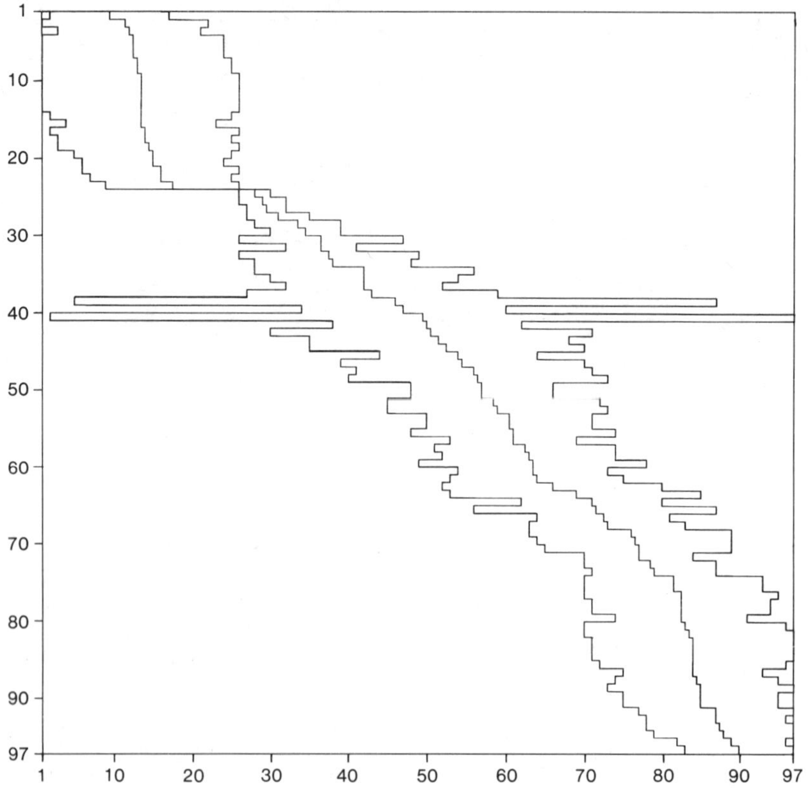

Figure XV: The witnesses who occur more than once

range. A third set can be constructed with the witnesses who occur more than once (Figure XV).

Wealth

Although Andreau was able to collect data on the economic activities of some of the witnesses, this information does not lend itself easily to a systematic and quantitative analysis. Not surprisingly no easy list with property data is available, so an indirect method had to be devised.

Pompeii is unique in that for a not inconsiderable number of its inhabitants successive generations of scholars have identified the houses in which they lived. The culmination of these efforts can be found in Matteo Della Corte's *Case ed Abitanti di Pompei.*[1] His identifications should be treated with a great deal of suspicion.[2] But at the same time these data are too attractive to discard off-hand. After all, we are not interested in the final truth in individual cases, but only in sufficient general quality of the data to make statistical observations.

Of the witnesses thirty-three have been assigned by Della Corte to specific houses. Some of these identifications had to be rejected. In Appendix II the twenty-two identifications that were retained are discussed.[3] I have next assumed that the size of the house that someone lives in is a function of that person's wealth. So the twenty-two houses involved were measured and the floor area including gardens was used as the measure of relative wealth.[4] The average size of these houses is remarkably high: 717 m^2, and nineteen out of the twenty-two houses are of the socially very respectable atrium type (Plate IX).

Although the amount of money spent on a house is not necessarily directly proportional to a person's wealth, some relationship cannot be denied. It is an expensive item in the family budget. For an expensive house a considerable amount of wealth would be necessary. And some alternative spending patterns at least presuppose an appropriate house. Domestic staff have to be housed, after all, and their employment would to some extent be a function of the size of the *domus*. The same argument also applies to works of art. Much Roman art was intended for domestic use, and requirements for wall-paintings, furniture and the like would vary with the size of the house.

[1] Della Corte (1965).

[2] Cf. Andreau (1974) 187 ff. (and of course my appendix III).

[3] The general quality of the retained information is of course confirmed by the results from the distribution map (Figure XI, p. 221).

[4] But excluding adjacent shops. Several other calculations were also performed, e.g. houses without gardens etc, in an effort to improve correlation with ranking, but to no avail. All measurements were taken from the 1:1000 map of Pompeii in Eschebach (1970), and therefore include measurement errors. These were too small to create problems for my purposes, but scholars should be warned not to use them for other, perhaps more demanding, purposes.

Some idea of what the ownership of an expensive house meant for a member of the Roman senatorial aristocracy is afforded by the debts Cicero incurred to obtain his house on the Palatine.[1] Trimalchio is not unaware of the importance of a nice house, either.[2] With this expensive house he can hope to be held in esteem. In the description, facilities for hospitality take first place: dining rooms, guest rooms, are present in ludicrously large numbers. Trimalchio relates that when 'Scaurus' came, he preferred to stay with Trimalchio and not in his own family place near the sea. With his money Trimalchio can adopt the life style of a Roman grandee, and hope to be accepted by them. It must be observed that money has to be spent to have this social significance (we will leave aside here whether Trimalchio's boast of acceptance was justified, or that as Veyne has argued, he was not even a *parvenu*, because he never arrived[3]). What is important is that spending money on his house is necessary.

In his study of the Roman conception of the family, Richard P. Saller includes a perceptive analysis of the various shades of the meaning of the Latin word *domus*.[4] The *domus* as physical building is undeniably important. Without a large house, elite public life would be impossible: 'It has perhaps not been sufficiently emphasized that in Roman society, in which wealth and social respectability were closely related, the *domus* was a central symbol of status and honor.'[5] Interlocked with this meaning was a range of other meanings. *Domus* could refer to patrimony, to the living kin group (with or without servants), or to lineage. This extension of the meaning of *domus* beyond that of the physical building is important for a proper understanding of the social meaning of wealth in Roman society. Someone living in a large and expensive house, but lacking a

[1]Frederiksen (1966) 128 n. 3, 130; Cicero, 'Fam.' 5, 6, 2. Finley (1985a) 53.

[2]Petronius, 'Sat.' 77.

[3]Veyne (1961) 213-247 esp. 213.

[4]Saller (1984b).

[5]Saller (1984b) 349.

long lineage and a large group of living kin, could still be accused of not having a proper *domus*.

Personal legal status

Of the many aspects of slavery in the Roman world, the institution of the manumission of certain slaves is beyond doubt one of the most interesting. It must be pointed out immediately that the incidence of manumission was not evenly distributed among all the different types of slaves. It was not the normal prospect of the agricultural slave, only of certain groups of urban slaves.[1] It was something which could be reckoned on by imperial slaves, and by domestic and administrative slaves in private households. The inclusion of a *puer delicatus* or of some female slaves who are manumitted for mariage to their former masters is not enough to support a case for compassionate manumission and to lose sight of the fact that the manumitted slaves were on the whole the slaves most useful to their masters.

But then manumission did not sever all ties. The duties of *liberti* are too well known to be repeated here. Many freedmen were probably just as useful to their patrons as they had been as slaves to their masters.[2] It has therefore been argued that the institution of manumission was not a mitigation of slavery, but a reinforcement.[3] It strengthened the loyalty of those slaves who could not so easily be induced by force to do their work properly. By offering advancement to individual conforming slaves, it prevented a 'class consciousness' among all slaves. The carrot for the really dangerous ones, the stick for the others.[4]

But at the same time this means that Roman society contained a not insignificant number of competent new citizens, because citizens is what Roman freedmen became on manu-

[1]Finley (1980) 74 ff; Weaver (1972); Duff (1928) e.g. 6; Hopkins (1978a) 118 ff.

[2]D'Arms (1980). For cautious dissent: Garnsey (1981) 359 ff.

[3]Hopkins (1978a) 115-171.

[4]For such distinctions made within the 'familia rustica': Martin (1974) esp. 290 ff.

mission, often with good connections with powerful men.[1] Ideal conditions for social mobility, one would say. And yet we are warned by the case of Trimalchio. Rich indeed, but as has been remarked by Veyne as quoted above, not even a *parvenu*, because he never arrived.[2] Trimalchio could not become a member of the *ordo decurionum*, the town council (which was normally closed to freedmen), let alone aspire to higher orders. The top of a freedman's public 'career' would normally have been the position of *augustalis*.[3] The company Trimalchio keeps is that of fellow freedmen, however much he tries to imitate aristocratic values. Trimalchio is only one example, and not even from real life. But the fact that he was a literary caricature drawn by a Roman senator makes him perhaps into a more reliable guide than one odd example from real life.[4] Trimalchio makes it necessary to spot the freedmen in our list of ranked individuals. If a high rank as witness can be treated as an indication that the person concerned had arrived in the social elite, did freedmen reach such elite positions, or not?

A complete Roman name includes a reference to a person's legal status. P. Cornelius L. f(ilius) Quir. Maximus would be an example of the name of a freeborn man, whereas Q. Cornelius Q.l(ibertus) Pal. Saturninus specifies that the person is a freedman. But although the tablets provide us with the *tria nomina* (P. Cornelius Maximus or Q. Cornelius Saturninus), they omit affiliation and tribe, and so we lose the only unequivocal information on legal status. That leaves us with the *cognomen*, the last of the *tria nomina*, as a status indicator. The principle behind this approach is that while upon manumission a freed

[1]For the complexity of their statuses after manumission, see Pavis D'Escurac (1981).

[2]Veyne (1961) 213 ff.

[3]Duthoy (1978) is the most complete survey of 'augustales'. Duthoy (1974) shows that some 90% of all 'augustales' were freedmen. Below, p. 258 ff; 289 ff., for a discussion of freedmen's 'pseudo' careers. Ostrow (1985) discusses Campanian 'augustales'. His case for their early prominence in the region, however, largely rests on the membership lists from Herculaneum - p. 78 ff. The problem is that there is no explicit reference at all that the many persons on these lists are in fact 'augustales', as he readily admits. Campania provides more than enough varieties of 'magistri', 'ministri', 'curiae' etc. to allow other interpretations, cf. below, p. 289 ff.

[4]For a cautious view on anecdotes in general, see Saller (1980a).

slave would normally receive his master's *praenomen* and *nomen gentilicium*, and thereby become indistinguishable from freeborn members of the family, his *cognomen* would be his former slave name. Therefore, if masters were in the habit of giving names to their slaves which were normally different from the names given as *cognomina* to their freeborn sons, this should make it possible to identify former slaves. At the same time it will be obvious that there can be no absolute certainty. Though that need not matter too much for our purposes.

In recent years much research has been done on the social significance of *cognomina*, a field in which Finnish scholars have excelled. In the case of Greek *cognomina*, Heikki Solin has argued that they do not so much indicate Greek ethnic origin, as freedman status.[1] He has to define this freedman status rather broadly however, including sons of freedmen. Although obviously some freeborn citizens would have carried Greek *cognomina*, perhaps especially in Southern Italy, I have classified all persons with Greek *cognomina* as freedmen. After all, we have no further information and any error that is introduced in this way would only weaken the correlation that we are looking for. We may assume that social ranking practice would follow the legal reality more than the onomastic consequences.

This disregard for a perfection of the data involves an important methodological principle for dealing with less than perfect data, a normal situation for almost every historian. The historian needs to be as explicit as possible about the nature of such imperfection. If the historian is arguing a strong correlation from his imperfect data, then it may well be the case that perfect data show an even higher correlation. If his data have a strong bias towards under-representation of the lower classes, and the historian finds a remarkably high number of such persons in his data, he is justified that his conclusion would only be reinforced by more perfect data. In other words, imperfect data do not matter too much as long as we can

[1] Solin (1971) 121 ff; Garnsey (1975); Duthoy (1974).

specify how our conclusions would be altered by more perfect data.

With the Latin *cognomina* the position is much less clear-cut then with the Greek *cognomina.* There is no need here to repeat in detail all the qualifications and arguments of I. Kajanto. Let me merely indicate the procedure that I have followed.[1] For each individual name Kajanto was consulted, and all names with a relatively high incidence of persons of known freedman status were classified as freedmen. This too introduces possible errors, but again, such errors can only reduce the strength of the correlation, so if the argument is for a strong correlation, it is the legitimate solution. As making decisions about these Latin *cognomina* is not so clear cut, the results of the decisions made have been included in Appendix II.

A final word of warning is due before consulting this list. In a number of cases it would have been absurd to rely on the onomastic evidence alone, because, after all, for some people we have other excellent information about their status. Therefore all persons who are known to have been members of the *ordo* - or candidates - have been automatically classified as freeborn. What was done with the *ordo*, was done in a similar way with freedmen. All persons known to have been *augustalis*, *magister* or *minister* were automatically classified as freedmen.[2]

These two categories - freeborn and freedmen - obviously do not exhaust the range of possibilities. First there is also the technical category 'unknown', meaning that in a given case it is impossible to establish whether we are dealing with a freeborn person or a freedman. Here, as in the case of establishing identity from incompletely known names, undue caution could in itself create errors. But in the end the proof of the pudding is in the eating.

The impossibility of classifying some *cognomina* with any degree of confidence might be a function of our own lack of skill, or the imperfect nature of the *cognomina* method, but it might also be the result of the existence of a real intermediate

[1]Kajanto (1965), Kajanto (1968), Garnsey (1975).

[2]Above, p. 242. For 'magistri' and 'ministri', see Bömer (1957-61) I (35) ff, (105) ff. (= p. 409 ff. and p. 479 ff. of the 'Abhandlungen' pagination).

social category, where onomastic ambiguity had the function of disguising the formal barrier between freeborn and freed.

Further categories of personal legal status include slaves and women. For correlations with the prestige rankings these have been excluded on the ground that their ranking in the documents may follow rules different from the rules applied to the other witnesses.[1]

Political office-holding

In the Roman world the importance of the holding of political office was not limited to the actual period of office-holding. Election to an office meant entry into a group, the group of those who had held the office in the past.[2] The *album* of Canusium shows that the longer ago the office was held, the higher the prestige that it offered.[3] For these social groups the term order can be used, meaning a social group where entry is defined by strict legal criteria. In Pompeii a fairly large proportion of those who held office is known. Castrén argues for about half, Duncan-Jones would place it somewhat lower.[4] On the basis of Castrén's prosopography all evidence on political office-holding has been collated.

The nature of the evidence for office-holding - electoral propaganda - makes it impossible to distinguish between successful and unsuccessful candidates. Therefore office-holding should here be understood to include unsuccessful candidacy. In the next chapter I shall argue that differences between successful and unsuccessful candidates do indeed exist.[5] If we could differentiate in our data, we would probably find even clearer results, but alas, we cannot have it.

[1]Cf. above, p. 235.

[2]Strictly speaking there is of course a censorial/quinquennalicial decision involved, but this does not affect the observation in a relevant way. See Liebenam (1900) 230 ff. also below, p. 311 ff.

[3]CIL IX 338; cf. Garnsey (1974) 243 ff; for my own discussion of the document: below, p. 317 ff.

[4]Duncan-Jones (1977) 195-198.

[5]Below, p. 312 ff; cf. Meiggs (1973) 199 ff, esp. 205.

For some, political office did not remain limited to once in a lifetime. Some aediles could later have a term in the higher duovirate. Where we know that this is the case, the person involved has been classified in the category of the highest - and therefore last - office he held in his lifetime. As a consequence, the two sets of data do not match entirely: they may represent different stages in the career of a person. A case in point is C. Gavius Rufus, third witness in tablet 89. In his recent study of electoral campaigns in Pompeii, Franklin identifies C. Gavius Rufus as candidate for the duovirate in A.D. 79.[1] He was a candidate for the aedileship in 73, or perhaps a little earlier. It is therefore highly unlikely that he was or had been a magistrate at the time he signed as witness in tablet 89, an undated document, but almost certainly not later than A.D. 62.[2] Nevertheless I have classified C. Gavius Rufus as *duovir*. A correct procedure would be to use the political office that had been reached at the time of signing as witness, but this implies that we can date all documents, and know the chronology of the political careers. Neither of these aspects of chronology are well enough known. We therefore introduce an error factor into our data, which could only be mitigated if young ex officeholders were not only ranked according to the positions they had already reached, but also according to expectations about the positions they might reach.[3] However, in so far as the error remains, the result will be a reduction of the correlation between rank and political office. In other words, correction - if possible - would only have strengthened my case.

The list of political offices was not limited to offices on the level of the *ordo*. I have also included freedman career possibilities, even though the documentation for those is much less complete. For an *augustalis* or *minister* no elections posters would be necessary, nor are the precise meanings of these

[1]Franklin (1980) 61 and 'passim'.

[2]Andreau (1974) 26 ff.

[3]Young sons of some families could have a much speedier advancement to higher post than sons of other families. See e.g. Duncan-Jones (1977) 195-198. Also note the 'praetextati' phenomenon in this respect, cf. below p. 317 ff.

functions always very clear. I have therefore sometimes grouped data together here. Thus, M. Fabius Eupor, *princeps libertinorum*, has been classified with the *augustales*, although he is not recorded as such. As the *augustales* were usually the most important freedmen, we may safely assume that a man who is called 'first of the freedmen' was in fact also an *augustalis*.

Correlating indices of status

Now that we have obtained a ranking of the witnesses in the documents, we shall have to try to correlate this ranking with the other data about wealth, personal legal status and office-holding, in order to find out what lies behind the order in which persons were ranked as witnesses. If we find a strong correlation between for example rank as witness and wealth, we may assume that wealth played an important role in determining prestige.

As I have explained, rank as witness could only be defined as a range of possible positions.[1] For P. Cornelius Erastus for example the highest possible position could be position 118, the lowest possible 229. Sometimes these two positions would be far apart through lack of information, sometimes they would be close together. If the distance between highest possible and lowest possible position is very large, we must accept that the data do not supply precise enough information. Knowing that Cn. Alfius could be ranked anywhere on or between position 1 and position 333 is not very helpful. Retaining this meaningless information could even be misleading, because for the purposes of a calculation of correlations with other variables, it is necessary to summarize the range between highest and lowest position into one point, the median of these two positions. But such a figure suggests pseudo exactitude if, as in the second case quoted, we could be wrong by more than 150 positions either way. Therefore, all rankings were excluded where the range between highest and lowest possible position was more than 166.

[1]See above, p. 233 ff.

This limitation of the permitted range improved the correlations considerably, a comforting sign.[1] If we want to increase our demands on the quality of the prestige ranking data even further, we can also restrict these to include only those witnesses who occur in more than one document. This should make the correlations stronger, but since that reduces us to using the rankings of only 97 individuals, it may sometimes create problems as to the significance when the number of cases has dropped so low.

A word for the statistically uninitiated. A large number of measures of correlations exists, the SPSS computer package has been used to calculate many of these, but only those that seemed most appropriate will be presented here. It is important not to use measures that assume a better or a worse quality than the ordinal data that we have. The measures used are Spearman's rank correlation coefficient (r_s) and Kendall's tau.[2] They vary from 0 to +1 or -1. The higher the absolute value, the stronger the correlation. A positive sign denotes a positive correlation (for example: in most traditional societies income and bodyweight are positively correlated - the rich are fat), a negative sign denotes a negative correlation (in many modern societies income and body weight are negatively correlated - the rich are slim and trim).[3]

Accompanying these correlation coefficients, an indication of the significance is given. This expresses the chance that the correlation found is not a real one, but only the result of bad

[1] Cf. above, p. 243.

[2] Those who would like to read more on these matters can be referred to almost any social sciences statistics textbook. A personal choice would include: Blalock (1979), for a thorough and authoritive treatment, or Nie a.o. (1975), i.e. the S.P.S.S. manual, for a close link with the actual computer programs most of us would use. A warning is also due. Many statistical packages prefer - or allow- calculation of correlations from cross tabulated - and therefore grouped - data. If the number of observations is relatively small, this procedure obliterates correlations.

[3] The intuitive meaning of the signs may be misleading however. Imagine the possible correlation between income and status. Intuitively this correlation is positive. Income is expressed in monetary units, the higher the number, the higher the income. Status is usually expressed on an ordinal scale: a person might belong to the highest status group - expressed as the 'first' group. The result is a negative correlation coefficient. But we could easily make the sign change. All we need to do is call the highest income group the first group. Obviously this has no substantive importance.

luck in sampling. A significance of 0.05 means that there is 5% chance that we are wrong. Conventions exist about the necessary level of significance: in the social sciences 0.01 is a stringent demand, 0.05 is perfectly respectable. As historians are more used to imperfect data, they should perhaps be prepared to take more chances, and make ad hoc decisions. In addition, the number of cases (N) is indicated. A large N has a very positive effect on the significance of correlations.[1]

Prestige and political office

To correlate prestige rating with political office-holding, the latter had to be made into ordinal data, or, in plain English, a decision had to be made which office was higher than which. The following - descending - order was used: *quinquennalis, duovir, aedilis, augustalis, minister.*[2]

For a large number of persons no information is available to show that they held office. This could either mean that they never held office, or that they did, but that we do not know of it. If we do not want to exclude these persons from our analysis, we could introduce them as a lowest category of our office-holding variable, below the *ministri*. But, if they did in fact hold office - though unknown to us - we introduce an important error, because we would misclassify a not inconsiderable number of officeholders. Any correlation between office-holding and other variables is likely to be seriously weakened by such misclassification. To avoid this, we can treat the lack of information on office-holding as a missing value, and thereby exclude these persons from calculations of correlations. In reality, both possibilities (they never held office, or they did,

[1]For a discussion of significance, and its relation to N, see e.g. Blalock (1979) 158-166, esp. 161 f. I am aware that strictly speaking significance means little without proper sampling procedures, but I follow standard practice by not worrying too much.

[2]'Pedani' have been left out, because the nature of almost all Pompeian evidence, electoral propaganda, does not allow us to perceive them. The last category ('ministri') is a bit of a mixed bag, and includes 'ministri Augusti', 'ministri Fortunae Augusti', and 'magistri' and 'ministri vici' (and 'pagi'). The 'office' category 'other offices' has been excluded, as this was only a nominal, and not an ordinal category. It only included Cn. Alleius Logus, 'omnium collegiorum benemeritus'. Cf. Castrén (1975) 116, 133.

but unknown to us) will have occurred, of course, for we know that we do not have full documentation on office-holding, but at the same time more than 300 officeholders is inconceivable.

A second reason why treating 'not known to have held office' as 'no office held' reduces the correlations with other variables, is that it is a very large group that cannot be subdivided any further. Therefore we would have an unacceptably high number of what is technically called 'tied ranks'.[1]

Using only the well ranked individuals while excluding the 'unknowns' as missing values, the following measures of correlation were obtained (N=15):

Spearman's r_s*: 0.7661 (sign. 0.001)*
Kendall's tau: 0.6302 (sign. 0.001)

Including the unknowns as lowest category, we obtain (N=128):

Spearman's r_s*: 0.2600 (sign. 0.002)*
Kendall's tau: 0.2147 (sign. 0.001)

Relaxing our demands by using all ranked individuals, while excluding the missing values, we obtain (N=27):

Spearman's r_s*: 0.3836 (sign. 0.024)*
Kendall's tau: 0.3043 (sign. 0.021)

The strongest correlations are obtained by using only the witness ranking data from those persons who occur in more than one document (N=9):

Spearman's r_s*: 0.8250 (sign. 0.003)*
Kendall's tau: 0.6901 (sign. 0.010)

In conclusion we may say that we find a strong correlation between the holding of political office and ranking as witness in the tablets. The problem that our data about office-holding would not necessarily match the precise career stage at the time of occurrence as witness, was not serious enough to weaken the correlation. The minute status differences from the *album* of Canusium are repeated in our documents dealing with a social occasion outside the realm of public affairs. The grouping together of mere candidates and actual officeholders posed no serious problems. The correlation could only be ser-

[1]For tied ranks, see Blalock (1979) 433 f.

iously weakened by bad ranking data and by treating the persons not known to have held office as not having held office.

Legal status and prestige

To correlate prestige and legal status, the nominal character of the latter had to be made ordinal. Freeborn status was defined as higher than freedman status. One real problem remains: what to do with the fairly large number of persons who could not be classified with any degree of confidence. Do they represent a real intermediate social category, consisting e.g. of freedmen who had purposely been given a slave name that would stigmatize them less upon manumission, or of free-born persons whose parents did not deem it necessary to give their sons *cognomina* that clearly marked them as freeborn. Or do they only represent the scholar's inability to squeeze more from the data? Both possibilities were investigated. If the 'unknowns' are a real intermediate social group between freeborn and freedmen, we may expect that correlations with other variables are not seriously weakened by their inclusion as an intermediate group. But if they are not, inclusion as an intermediate group means that we are giving some of them - the freeborn - a score on the legal status variable which is too low, and others - the freedmen - a score which is too high. We may expect that this would reduce correlations with other variables considerably.

Using only the well ranked individuals, while excluding the 'unknowns' as missing values, the following measures of correlation were obtained (N=99):

Spearman's r_s*: 0.6194 (sign. 0.001)*
Kendall's tau: 0.5103 (sign. 0.001)

Including the unknowns as an intermediate category between freeborn and freed, we obtain (N=129):

Spearman's r_s*: 0.4226 (sign. 0.001)*
Kendall's tau: 0.3224 (sign. 0.001)

Relaxing our demands by using all individuals ranked as witnesses, while excluding the missing values, we obtain (N=239):

Spearman's r_s*: 0.4111 (sign. 0.001)*
Kendall's tau: 0.3372 (sign. 0.001)

Because information about legal status is available for such a large number of persons, significance proves to be no problem. The strength of the correlation is markedly improved by a restrictive admission of witness ranking data.

Perhaps it should be repeated here that 'well ranked' did not demand more than that the possible range was smaller than half the total range. And already with this restriction the correlation was not a weak one. Treating the 'unknowns' as an intermediate social category weakened the correlation considerably, and the hypothesis that they might represent a socially intermediate group therefore had to be rejected. These persons should be treated as 'missing values'.

And finally a word about the onomastic method for obtaining information on legal status. The correlations obtained are a strong indicator that this method is a useful tool, although we should never forget that it is more useful for a statistical application than to obtain knowledge in an individual case. It should also be admitted that the correlation as found does not constitute real proof of the quality of the onomastic method. Because the alternative to the hypothesis that *cognomina* reflect personal legal status is not necessarily that they have no status meaning at all - they could also be dependent on another variable that has an impact on social status. It has been observed above that the variable on which the onomastics of the *cognomen* depends should preferably not be equated with the strictly legal definitions of freeborn and freed, but rather with freeborn or freedman 'environment', thereby allowing for a continuation of the 'freedman' stigma with freeborn sons of freedmen.[1]

It will be appreciated that this interesting phenomenon should preferably be analysed from other data than the present. But insofar as the proof of the pudding was in the eating, the method used did not have to be rejected. Efforts to that effect should be directed to the data collected and analysed by Kajanto and Solin.[2]

[1]See above, p. 243.

[2]Kajanto (1965); Kajanto (1968); Solin (1971).

Prestige and wealth

As noted earlier, the variable wealth had to be defined operationally as the floor area of the house, including gardens, but excluding shops. A problem for any calculation of the correlation between these two variables is the small number of observations.

Using all ranked individuals with a known house, we obtain (N=22):

Spearman's r_s*: -0.3418 (sign. 0.060)*
Kendall's tau: -0.2217 (sign. 0.075)

Improving the quality of the prestige rating information by using only the well ranked individuals, we reduce the N even further, and obtain (N=14):

Spearman's r_s*: -0.3696 (sign. 0.097)*
Kendall's tau: -0.2210 (sign. 0.136)

Even by using the best prestige rating series, that of those who occur more than once, correlations do not improve - on the contrary (N=12):

Spearman's r_s*: -0.1338 (sign. 0.339)*
Kendall's tau: -0.1086 (sign. 0.314)

Various other calculations were performed to improve the correlations, such as houses without gardens, but to no avail. We must therefore conclude that we have not been able to establish a correlation between wealth, as defined operationally here, and prestige ranking as witness.

Political office and legal status

A statistical analysis of the relationship between legal status and political office is not very illuminating. The legal position is quite clear: a freedman cannot become a member of the *ordo* (even though sometimes exceptions were made), while the non-*ordo* posts like that of *augustalis* would almost invariably be held by freedmen. So, the information on political office-holding was used to provide information about legal status.[1]

In consequence, calculating the correlation between the two implies calculating a correlation introduced by the researcher

[1]See above, p. 244.

on a priori grounds. The only justification is that it gives us a figure to use as input for further numerical analysis.

Excluding the 'unknowns' of both variables as missing values, the following results were obtained:

Spearman's r_s*: 0.7675*
Kendall's tau: 0.6955

Wealth and legal status

As I have already argued, 'unknown' legal status should be treated as a missing value. The following results were obtained (N=19):

Spearman's r_s*: -0.4716 (sign. 0.021)*
Kendall's tau: -0.3961 (sign. 0.023)

The absence of a correlation between wealth and prestige rating has obviously made us suspicious about the operational definition of the variable wealth. Absence of correlation could be real, but could also have resulted from our equation of wealth with floor area of houses, or even from incorrect identifications of occupants.

The moderate correlations between 'wealth' and 'legal status' indicate that the variable 'wealth' does indeed work, though not directly with prestige. The attraction of this is that it indicates that our indirect measurement of wealth was not so bad after all. And wealth turns out to be of some importance, although not, as we have seen, as a direct influence on prestige rating.

Wealth and political office

With this correlation we have serious significance problems because the N is so small. On historical grounds we may assume that a correlation must exist, but the present data can hardly add to knowledge.

The results are, excluding 'unknown' office as missing value (N=6):

Spearman's r_s*: -0.4629 (sign. 0.178)*
Kendall's tau: -0.3892 (sign. 0.152)

Retaining the correlation can be justified on two grounds:
1. The general historical knowledge about the relation between these two variables.[1]
2. The great similarity between the behaviour of the variables political office and legal status in relation to the other two variables (rank and wealth) and the strong correlation with each other. This would suggest that one could conceive of a new hypothetical variable 'politico legal position'. The information of the 'political office' variable can then be considered to differentiate at the top, whereas the legal status variable can be considered to discriminate further down the scale.

However, it should be stressed that the value of the correlation should not be treated as an addition to our knowledge, but only as a measure to be used in further analysis, and justified on external knowledge.

Combining the correlations: a model

After the calculation of all correlations between the variables, we can return to our original question of the determinants of social status. To bring together the information that has been obtained, an effort at visualization may be made (Figure XVI). The six correlations between the four variables can be visualized by a square with its two diagonals. The four corners represent the four variables, and each of the six lines a possible correlation, and Kendall's tau for that relation has been printed in the figure.[2] The closer the absolute value of these coefficients is to 1, the stronger the correlation. Another possibility in drawing this model is to link the variables by possible causal arrows. This cannot be done by statistical analysis, but has to be based on historical insights.

Prestige rating cannot be anything but a dependent variable in my model, since no impact of it can be conceived on the other three variables.

The reverse is true for the distinction between freedmen and freeborn citizens, since none of the other variables in the

[1] See below, ch. 7.

[2] The specific ones used are those with 'unknowns' treated as missing values, and using well ranked individuals for the variable 'prestige rating'.

model can have any impact on someone's personal legal status: a *peculium* may buy manumission, but not free birth. And free birth is necessary for membership of this *ordo*, and not the other way round.[1] The variables in the model are not, however, only dependent on other variables within the model, but also on variables outside the model. Adding an infinite number of variables would make the model a replica of the real world, but we would have lost our understanding of it. The more one can explain with the fewer variables, the better. In the present case the variables were chosen for their explanatory potential, while a further criterion was obviously the availability of data.

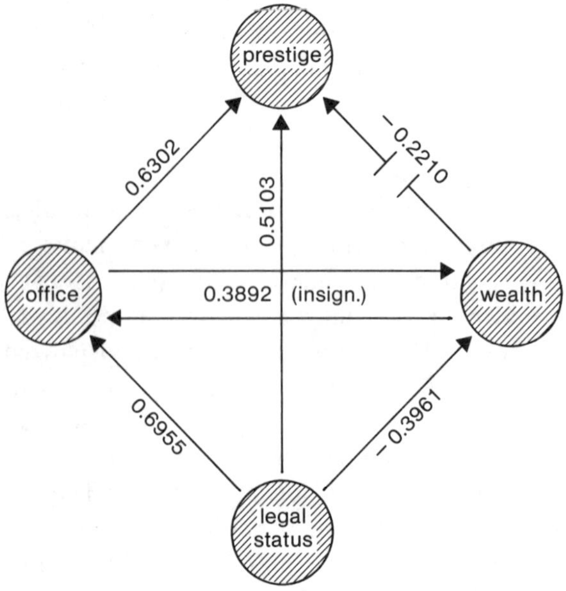

Figure XVI: Dimensions of status, a model

The weakest correlation in the whole model is that between prestige rating and wealth (the latter defined operationally as

[1] I have drawn the relationship as it is in principle. As I have indicated above, p. 244, I have in fact sometimes used information about office-holding to determine legal status. To reflect my practical operations, an arrow may, therefore, be drawn from 'office' to 'legal status'.

floor area of houses). This correlation is so weak that we may wonder whether it is not largely the result of the joint effect of political position and legal status on prestige rating and wealth. This can be analysed with the partial correlation technique, where we control a correlation for the effect of a third - and as is necessary here, a fourth - variable. The outcome of this second order partial correlation of prestige rating and wealth controlling for political office and legal status is 0.1153, showing that there is no independent correlation between prestige rating and wealth. We can therefore delete the arrow from wealth to prestige rating.

This absence of correlation between wealth and prestige is not easy to interpret. It is conceivable that my operational definition of wealth does not measure the underlying concept well enough.[1] But if this were the case, we would expect the same measurement error to have the same weakening effect on the correlations of wealth with office-holding and legal status. That wealth correlates moderately with office-holding and legal status confirms the belief that my operational definition of the variable wealth was more or less acceptable.

The absence of correlation between wealth and prestige should not lead us to the belief that wealth was of no social consequence in the Roman world. It only means that wealth was not both the necessary and sufficient condition for prestige. This was beautifully illustrated by the range of meanings of the Latin word for house, *domus* (important because I used house size as a proxy for wealth). The word *domus* could refer to the physical house, and in that sense a rich freedman could acquire a *domus*. But the word could equally refer to what was largely unavailable to such a freedman: a long lineage or a large living kin group. The manumitted slave may become rich, but manumission will hardly have raised him from his state of 'social death'.[2] This was probably most true of independent freedmen,

[1] I have argued above, p. 238 ff. that the operation was not unreasonable, but we could not be certain. For theoretical discussions of operationalism and measurement error, see Blalock (1968) and Siegel and Hodge in: Blalock and Blalock (1968) 28-59.

[2] For slavery as 'social death': Patterson (1982).

but membership of the *familia* of the *patronus* usually offered little more: subordination.[1]

The causal relationship between wealth and political office-holding is complex. On the one hand we know that possession of wealth was a necessary requirement for office-holding. Census criteria apply, and office-holding involves sometimes considerable expenditure. But on the other hand membership of the political elite affords further possibilities for enrichment.[2]

Assessing the relative strength of these forces in opposite directions is not possible from the present data. For that purpose one could profitably use information about the time sequence of changes in the values of the two variables, but unfortunately both the data on wealth, and those on office-holding depend mainly on the same electoral propaganda.

But the historian may speculate and introduce variables outside the model, especially in that crucial area of change over time, in other words, social mobility. In this process we can see the mechanisms at work that determine a person's status.

In order to understand the importance of wealth we have to come to terms with the apparent contradiction between two observations. The first of these is that the Roman political elite was very wealthy, and the second is the ideological primacy of 'old fashioned' values of simplicity and political honour which find perhaps their most extreme expression in the story of Cincinnatus summoned from the plough to become dictator. Garnsey is of course right that the story is a myth, but what we can learn from the story is that it stresses the importance of political honour to the false extreme of denying any relevance to the possession of wealth.[3]

In his 1965 Past and Present article on elite mobility in the Roman empire, Hopkins proposes that 'social mobility may

[1]For independent freedmen: Garnsey (1981). Cf. Garnsey (1982).

[2]See below, p. 263 ff.

[3]For elite wealth, see e.g. Duncan-Jones (1982) 343 f. For the Cincinnatus story, see Livy 3, 26. Comments on the story e.g. Garnsey (1980b) 36-37. For the meaning of untrue stories: Hopkins (1978a) 198 ff.

usefully be seen as a process of status dissonance - especially in a society with a strong ideology of hereditary status.'[1]

This means that a person might rank high on one criterion of social status, but low on another, which is what we observe in our data. Hopkins uses this concept of status dissonance to analyse mobility into the very top, the senatorial order. The mechanisms at work at that level, such as imperial patronage, would have been different from those granting entry into the *ordo decurionum*, although they might show similarity. On this local level the characteristic form of the mobility problem is that of the wealthy freedman.

Some freedmen were well placed to obtain considerable fortunes. This made it possible for them to obtain a modest amount of political status by acting as *augustales*. This allowed them to show off their wealth to the community with benefactions, an integral part of the 'real' political life.[2] This is a nice example of what Merton calls anticipatory socialization.[3]

In the context of a discussion of reference group theory, Merton uses the term anticipatory socialization to describe the process by which people 'take the values of the non membership group to which they aspire, find readier acceptance by that group and make an easier adjustment to it.'[4] He remarks that whether anticipatory socialization is functional for the individual depends on the social structure. It is functional if the social structure is relatively open, in other words, if there are rewards. If social mobility is limited, an individual could find himself not accepted by the group he aspires to join, and disliked by the group he tries to leave. Interesting is Merton's observation that anticipatory socialization is apparently dysfunctional for the solidarity of the group or stratum to which

[1]Hopkins (1965). Now also: Hopkins (1983a) ch. II, III. For a general overview Pleket (1971).

[2]Perhaps some importance should be given to the possibility of a parallel between the importance for social mobility of the conflict between emperor and aristocracy - see Hopkins (1965) in Finley (1974) 111 ff. - and the predominance of the link between imperial cult and non-'ordo' offices - usually held by freedmen - on the local level. Cf. Finley (1980) 116.

[3]Merton (1957) 265 ff.

[4]Merton (1957) 265.

someone belongs. In this respect Merton asks about the connections between rates of mobility and the acceptance of the legitimacy of the stratification, because low mobility seems to go hand in hand with wide acceptance of the existing social divisions.

For an historical analysis of these phenomena we cannot heed his advice to pay attention to the social position and personality types of those mainly involved. The relevant group for us is that of the freedmen, and the problem is that of the ambivalence of social mobility. Many slaves were manumitted, and after manumission freedmen could become rich, or even: richer, and they were free citizens.[1] But at the same time an unsurmountable barrier remains: they can never become free*born*. Is this high or low social mobility? It is low in respect of the institution of slavery (and therefore a general acceptance of the legitimacy of the institution need perhaps not surprise us) in the sense that although some slaves can be manumitted, they cannot, however, escape their connection with slavery.[2] They are put so to speak in a waiting room, which may prevent them from being identified in the eyes of the slaves with the freeborn elite. On the other hand, the remaining barrier is automatically removed for future generations.

But free birth is not enough for them to become members of the elite. They have to be wealthy and share the ethos of office-holding. The link between these two is the expense involved in office-holding. And in the waiting room of the freedmen, ample opportunity is offered for anticipatory socialization. It is a stage where the foundations for family wealth can be laid. Many manumitted slaves would originate from the group of those slaves who had administrative or business experience, and the backing of a *patronus* could have its value as well. It is in this waiting room of libertine status that Hopkins' status dissonance is most visible. A rich freedman ranks high on wealth, but free birth is impossible to obtain. On

[1] See Pavis D'Escurac (1981) for the necessary qualifications.

[2] See e.g. Finley (1980) esp. ch. III.

the other hand it is automatically available for his son.[1] Proper political office is also unattainable because membership of the *ordo decurionum* requires free birth, but opportunity for anticipatory socialization is afforded by allowing *augustales* to act generously as benefactors. Because political success of future generations depends in part on the ability to show a family tradition of benefactions, this allows rich freedmen to show that they have adopted the elite values with regard to wealth.

An interesting example comes from Pompeii. In an inscription on the temple of Isis (CIL X 846, ILS 6367) we read:

> N.POPIDIUS N.F. CELSINUS/
> AEDEM ISIDIS TERRAE MOTU CONLAPSAM A FUNDAMENTO P.S. RESTITUIT. HUNC DECURIONES OB LIBERALITATEM/
> CUM ESSET ANNORUM SEXS ORDINI SUO GRATIS ADLEGERUNT.//

In other words, the young Celsinus is supposed to have acted as a generous benefactor at the advanced age of six years and was rewarded by adlection into the *ordo*, even though he was still a child.[2] All very well, but it disguises a more interesting truth, a truth about the limits to the upward social mobility of his father N. Popidius Ampliatus.[3] The latter was in all probability a freedman. A status suggested by his *cognomen*, but also by his presence in a list of *ministri*.[4] Ampliatus obviously belonged to the group of wealthy freedmen. He could of course not become a member of the *ordo decurionum*, but acting as benefactor he could obtain entry for his son.

One aspect has been left aside so far, and that is the type of wealth. This is important because not every type of wealth was equally acceptable as a means for inclusion into the

[1]Ignoring for the moment the possibility of the birth of a son before manumission, strictly speaking of the mother. Weaver (1972) 162 ff; Crook (1967) 40 f, 98 ff; Pavis D'Escurac (1981); Buckland (1908) 398 ff.

[2]For minimum age: Liebenam (1900) 233 ff, 268 ff.

[3]CIL X 847, X 848.

[4]CIL X 921. Cf. Castrén (1975) 207.

political elite. Cicero acknowledges the social benefits of commerce, but adds that 'it even seems to deserve the highest respect if those who are engaged in it, satiated, or rather, I should say, content with their profits, make their way from the harbour to a landed estate, as they have often made it from the sea to a harbour. But of all things from which one may acquire, none is better than agriculture, none more fruitful, none sweeter, none more fitting for a free man.'[1] One may wonder why this transformation of wealth was necessary to gain acceptance: is it just a matter of 'good taste' not to be known trading, a perseverance of an antiquated value system, or does it make sense in some calculus of maximization?[2]

In order to gain full acceptance within the elite, the availability of wealth would be necessary over a number of generations. A family tradition of spending wealth to the benefit of the community had to be built up. In other words, the long term security of the investments had to be high, a characteristic of investment in agricultural land.[3] In the *De Officiis* passage quoted above this judgement is evident. The harbour offers safety after the dangers of the sea, and similarly a landed estate offers financial security after the dangers of trading. Let us take Trimalchio as our guide again, that paragon of freedman success. After making a killing in trade - risky, as is shown by his initial disasters - he retreats to the land.[4]

An analogy from *ancien régime* Europe may be revealing. Pierre Goubert has made a study of the fortunes of two families, who both assembled their original wealth in trade. One family continues with this strategy, the other invests in land. After a few generations the traders have lost their wealth

[1] Cic. 'De Officiis' 1.150 - 1. Cf. Finley (1985a) 41 ff. Brunt (1973) prefers to read the 'haec fere accepimus' as a reference to literary borrowing, without much real social significance for the Ciceronian age. True enough, this would deny Cicero literary or philosophical originality, but that does not bother me. The real problems in my view are: is this often quoted passage representative of the views of the Roman elite, if so is this ideology also shared by other groups, or even everyone?

[2] For a discussion of utility maximization, see above, p. 41 ff.

[3] The literature on retreat to the safety of the land abounds for early modern Europe. Just one example: Soly (1975).

[4] But see now D'Arms (1981) 97 ff.

again, whereas the landowning family continues to prosper, and gains acceptance by the political elite.[1]

Apart from the investment security problem, we can add another angle, management effort. Although capital is important in trade, entrepreneurial skill and attention are perhaps more important. And elite social and political life could be time-consuming. 'Land ownership on a sufficient scale marks the "absence of any occupation",' with time available for socio-political life.[2]

The preceding and necessarily too general exposition may have made it clear once again that wealth was of vital importance for the social riser. But at the same time it must also be evident that a correlation between the possession of wealth and political office cannot have been very strong. Though a necessary condition for political office, the possession of wealth as such was not sufficient. Wealth could only have political consequence if it was spent, and over several generations as well, to perpetuate the fabric of society. And only a freeborn citizen could personally reap the benefits of political office. The available measures of correlation show this through the absence of a direct influence of the variable 'wealth' on 'prestige'. Wealth only gave status if it was transformed into a political role in the community. A transformation that carried the condition that the person concerned would be of free birth. Which is reflected in the correlation between legal status and prestige.

We have left open the possibility of obtaining wealth through political office. The previous discussion implies that this might take the form of further additions to family wealth. The initial wealth would have to be there already. The stories of the rapacity of provincial governors are too well known to need repeating. On the local level in Italian towns opportunities were probably considerably more limited because of the absence of opportunities to exploit Rome's imperial power. Here they would have to take the form of better chances to secure income

[1]Goubert (1959).

[2]Finley (1985a) 44. Finley (1983) also stresses the other side of the coin, politics as a means of defending or increasing inequality of wealth.

from the artisan and agricultural population. An important area could have been that of disputed rights on landed property, and the ability to make debtors pay up. Councillors would also be in a good position to rent city land.[1]

The model employed so far seemed able to elucidate a number of important social relations, although it is also clear that some aspects could not find a place in it, largely as a result of lack of data. Hopes should not be pitched too high because the quality of the data always leaves something to be desired. As a measure of the success of the whole operation we could employ the technique of multiple correlation. This involves answering the question how much of the variation of the variable 'prestige' has been explained by more than one variable. Unfortunately the development of measures of multiple correlation on an ordinal level is still in an early stage.[2] We can be certain that a multiple correlation should be stronger than a single correlation.[3] It is mathematically possible to derive the percentage of the variation of the dependent variable (prestige rating) that is explained by the independent variable (such as 'political office'). The tau = 0.7 for 'prestige rating' with 'political office' implies that 49% of the variation of the variable 'prestige rating' is explained by the variable 'political office'.[4]

The position of our data within Pompeian society

Until now we have left aside all problems about the representativeness of our data. The sampling was done for us in the past by the accident of record survival, following rules we do not know. It is up to us to make an educated guess to decide

[1] See e.g. Andreau (1980) 195.

[2] Blalock (1979) 468. At present, a value obtained for the multiple correlation would probably inform us more about the suitability of that specific measure of multiple correlation, than about the correlation itself.

[3] If two variables show a strong intercorrelation - e.g. legal status and political office - then their multiple correlation with a third variable - prestige rating e.g. - will be only slightly stronger than the strongest of the two single correlations with the third variable. If legal status and political office are almost two sides of the same coin in the Roman world, then knowledge about the one does not add a great deal to the knowledge about the other.

[4] Using those individuals who occur more than once. Similarly, but using r_s, the model explains at least 67%, which is not a bad result at all.

from which population the sample was drawn, and to investigate possible deviations from the randomness criterion. Is it true, as has been suggested in the literature, that the witnesses in Iucundus' wax tablets can in some way be considered an identifiably separate social group within Pompeian society?[1]

If this could be demonstrated we might still formulate two alternative hypotheses to explain their presence, and thereby define the character of their group. The first would be to assume that their presence represents a special interest in the content of these transactions. In that case one could think of the witnesses as a group with commercial interests.[2] A second hypothesis would revolve around the act of witnessing. Although these witnesses are not a small permanent group like the witnesses in the military *diplomata*, one could nevertheless conceive that they were chosen because of a special suitability for the role of witness. The strict ranking shows that social respectability was not unimportant.

But as a preliminary an effort should be made to establish the size of the population from which our witnesses originate. The two extremes of the range of possibilities would be on the one hand coincidence of the population of all known and unknown witnesses with the sample of actually known witnesses, and on the other an infinitely large group from which the known witnesses were recruited, or, more realistically, all free adult male Pompeians. The problem can be reformulated as a question about our sources. Does the actual number of known witnesses resemble the total number of witnesses, known and unknown, or would this number increase dramatically if we were to possess a full documentation? For this purpose a special statistical technique was employed in order to estimate the size of this statistical population of all witnesses - known and unknown - employing characteristics of the available sample of known witnesses (Appendix IV).

The underlying principle is an analysis of the marginal returns in information to be gained from employing more data.

[1] Frank (1918) 233 n. 2; Lepore (1950) 147; Andreau (1974).

[2] Above, p. 220; 224 f.

The first document we look at contains by definition only witnesses not yet known. Later documents will also contain names we have already come across before: they yield less new information. This decrease in information yield per unit of extra data depends on the size of the group of 'all witnesses, known and unknown'. If that group is very small, the additional information from additional data will decrease rapidly, if on the other hand the group is infinitely large, returns of information per unit of data will remain constant (if all Romans could appear in Iucundus' tablets, we might expect to see only new names on each document we look at).

We can plot these decreasing returns in information yielded per unit of data and fit a line through these points. Extrapolating such a regression line, we can calculate the point where additional data do not yield any additional information. Delury gives two equations to estimate this point, resulting in a calculated size of the group of witnesses, known and unknown, of 574 and 616 respectively.[1]

An analysis of the results does not provide enough support to choose between the two equations. In addition, the method employed is not extremely accurate, because the residuals are necessarily largest in the last part of the line before extrapolation. Therefore, we should be satisfied with the knowledge that the group of witnesses, known and unknown, has a probable size between 500 and 700 persons.

This is not a very small group. Eschebach's estimate of the size of the urban population of Pompeii is a figure somewhere between 8000 and 12,000 persons.[2] But of these, the slaves should be left aside for our purpose. Let us do so with some speculative guesses from the literature as to the proportion of slaves. In a by his own admission very uncertain estimate, Hopkins guesses that slaves represented about half the urban population of Italian cities around 28 B.C.[3] Other authors present somewhat lower estimates, but if Hopkins' estimate may

[1]Delury (1947), and my Appendix IV.

[2]For extensive discussion, above p. 108 ff.

[3]Hopkins (1978a) 68 f. esp. note h.

be too high for the average town around 28 B.C., it is perhaps correct for relatively prosperous Pompeii, little less than a century later.[1] If one half of 8000-12,000 Pompeians were slaves, this leaves us 4000-6000 free Pompeians.

Of these 4000-6000 free citizens of Pompeii, the majority were of course women and children, and thus unsuitable as witnesses. The ancient evidence does not tell us the proportion of Pompeian women and children, but we need not despair, because the range of possibilities is limited. I shall follow the methodology pioneered by Hopkins to put more trust in well documented comparative evidence (model life-tables) than in patchy, and in our case even nonexistent, ancient evidence.[2]

Adulthood needs definition of course, a definition that is especially critical in a society with many children, few adults and very few old people. Here, we need to define adulthood as the age from which men were allowed to act as witnesses. The problem is that we do not know this.[3] If necessary, the testimony of youngsters who had reached the age of puberty, would be valid in the courts.[4] Yet, I do not think that this gives a realistic idea of the minimum age of the witnesses in Iucundus' documents. The reason for this is that the law acknowledges that youngsters under the age of twenty-five might easily be cheated and fooled in the case of their own fortunes. Therefore it allowed - with restrictions - that transactions could be declared null and void.[5] As this would make them unattractive

[1]Lower estimates: Brunt (1971) 124 ff, 702 f; and esp. Duncan-Jones (1982) 273. A serious complication is that the age distribution of slaves is likely to have been quite different from that of the free. Many urban slaves would have been freed, provided that they survived to the right age. Some provisional demographic simulations gave fascinating results, but a lot more work remains to be done. If correct, they imply that fewer adult Pompeians were slaves, and more were freedmen. This refinement could, however, be counterbalanced for the purposes of my argument by a further reduction in the estimate for the total population of the town, such as given in Russell (1977).

[2]First employed in Hopkins (1966) and most recently in Hopkins (1983a) esp. 69 ff. I have used the 'south' tables from Coale and Demeny (1966). Below, 317 ff.

[3]I am grateful to Professor John Crook for pointing out to me that this matter is more complicated than I at first hoped, but do not want to implicate him with my 'solution'.

[4]Greenidge (1901) 483.

[5]Crook (1967) 116 f.

to enter into transactions with, a new 'caretaker' institution developed, the *curatio*, or *cura*. Thus, the legal position appears somewhat blurred. On the one hand - in our eyes - very young people could be called upon to testify in court, if necessary. On the other hand it was accepted that such people could not be trusted to always manage their own affairs without blundering. With this legal ambiguity, I propose to take twenty-five years as the minimum age for Iucundus' witnesses. Even if the law would perhaps allow for younger witnesses, I still think that they would not be preferred. Unlike some other witnesses, these were after all invited.

Next, we need to make an assumption about life expectancy. Below a life expectancy at birth of twenty years (e_0 = 20), it will be difficult for populations to reproduce themselves, whereas e_0 = 30 represents a level that was typically only reached by the aristocracies of early modern Europe.[1] Therefore, e_0 = 25 probably represents our best bet. These two assumptions made, we can estimate the number of adult (25+) free male Pompeians at between 925 and 1390. Therefore we can say that about half of the adult free male Pompeians acted as witnesses in Iucundus' tablets.

Knowing the differences - if there are any - between the one half that signed and the other half that did not, is of no mean importance. Unfortunately the answer will have to remain less unequivocal than one would wish. One undeniable selection criterion has been the walking distance from a person's home to the house of Iucundus. This is shown pretty clearly by the distribution pattern in Figure XI (above, p. 221). The intuitive interpretation of these dots on the map is that of a decreasing 'witness density', the further one moves away from Iucundus house. I have plotted this in Figure XVII.

This confirms the intuitive findings, but it equally shows that the number of observations is on the small side. But even so, if we were to draw a circle around Iucundus' house that would

[1]Hopkins (1983a) 71, with references. Hopkins (1978a) 68 f. On p. 68 we note that he defines adulthood as 17^+, justified for his purposes, but not for ours. We also need to make an assumption for the female Gross Reproduction Rate. Let us take GRR = 3.0.

include 20 hectares we would find that already fourteen of our twenty-two witnesses had their houses within this circular area (radius 252 m). This area does not include an unduly high proportion of excavated surface. As the total surface of Pompeii within its walls amounts to 66 hectares, the observed distribution pattern is probably enough to explain the difference between the two figures of 574-616 for all witnesses, and of 900-1400 for all adult (=25^+) free male Pompeians. Probably no further social characteristics of the witnesses need to be invoked to explain their presence.

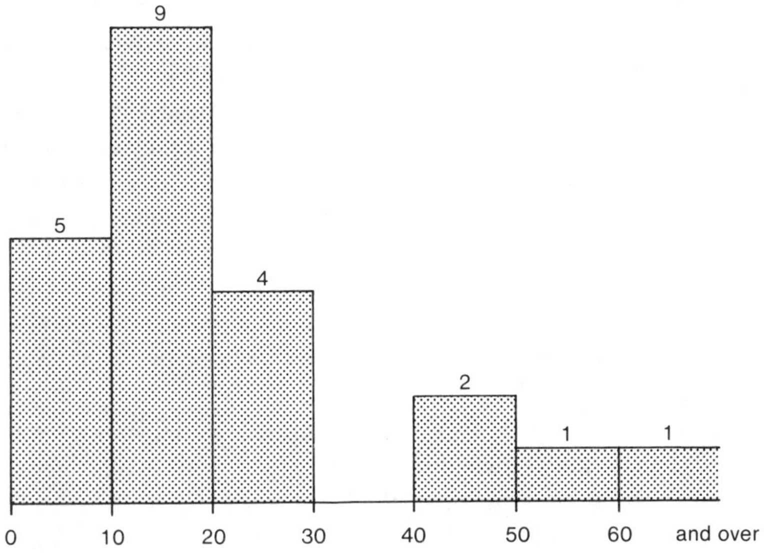

Figure XVII:
Witness density and the distance from Iucundus' home[1]

It has been an implicit assumption so far that the habitation pattern of the town does not show significant concentrations of certain social groups in specific areas. If that were the case the distribution pattern of the witnesses might be related to

[1]The figure plots the witness density for successive concentric rings of 10 hectare each. The centre for each of these circles is Iucundus' home (V 1, 26).

such concentrations of for example wealthy inhabitants, instead of being related to the distance from Iucundus' house. Various authors do indeed claim that for example Regio VI, near Iucundus' house, was such a residential area.[1] That may be true, but other regions - e.g. Regions I and VIII - also contain considerable quantities of residential property without producing significant numbers of witnesses.

It is very unfortunate that little systematic study of land use and habitation patterns has been made for Pompeii. The only exception is the work of Raper.[2] Though his interpretation is flawed by the use of questionable theories about commercialization and democratization, some of the empirical observations are valuable enough, just as the methodology is.[3] There can be no doubt that the distribution of commercial property follows a non-random pattern. Shops and workshops are largest in number along traffic arteries. But this does not mean that such parts of the town did not have any residential property. It is probably wise to think in terms of an omnipresence of residential usage of space, supplanted by commercial and manufacturing usage in certain parts. In other words, although Regio VI may be fairly residential, the property along the Via Dell' Abbondanza equally included splendid *atrium* houses, in that case with shop front façades (Plate XXIX).[4]

It is of course conceivable that although habitation was more or less evenly distributed within the city walls, more luxurious habitation was nevertheless concentrated in certain parts. Although some research has been done on 'lower class housing in Pompeii' the number of such independent houses remains very small.[5] In addition, research in Ostia has shown

[1]Latest is Raper (1977), though with a considerably more nuanced position.

[2]Raper (1977).

[3]For arguments against the 'rise of the bourgeoisie theory', see the present work, esp. chapter IV.

[4]In addition, Raper (1977), 204 ff. shows the varied use of space in the 'residential' Regio VI.

[5]Packer (1975) 133-146.

that the well known type of apartment from the Ostian *insulae* was not so lower class after all.[1]

In any case, it is remarkable how prominent and space absorbing the large *atrium* houses of Pompeii are. They can be found in all parts of the town, and are almost the only form of proper houses. Yet it would of course be perverse to suggest that such luxury was the prerogative of almost all Pompeians. Many inhabitants would indeed have lived in such splendour, but as domestic slaves. Many others, such as freedmen and the freeborn poor, must have slept in their shops. They may have cooked their meals there as well, but the prominence of inns of various kinds suggests that they may often have eaten out.[2] As workshops are very often adjacent to or part of a luxurious *atrium* house, an image emerges of a large number of wealthy households each with an *atrium* house and living-in slaves, surrounded by satellite shops run by freedmen, slaves and presumably also dependent freeborn.[3]

Although the 'walking distance' explanation for the selection of witnesses from the universe of all Pompeians may seem attractive, we cannot afford to ignore other potential (perhaps socially more significant) selection criteria. The proportion of candidates and magistrates among the witnesses - approximately 7% - does not suggest any over-representation of the *ordo* among the witnesses. The proportion of freedmen may seem high (77%), but we do not possess an external norm that is above suspicion.[4] It is hard to conceive how freedmen could still be under-represented in the data. If there is a bias, it is that of over-representation of freedmen. The data on prestige rating can only be checked in one way. It could be that frequency of occurrence in documents is correlated to prestige

[1]Frier (1977) and Frier (1980).

[2]Cf. Meiggs (1973) 428 ff; Kleberg (1957); Casson (1974) 197 ff.

[3]See e.g. Ling (1983); cf. above, p. 178 f.

[4]It has sometimes been argued that the high incidence of freedmen in urban epigraphy does not reflect their real proportion of the population, but their 'epigraphic mentality'. Cf. Solin (1971) 136, Taylor (1961) 127 ff. But the 'epigraphic mentality' argument cannot seriously be used for Iucundus' tablets, even though they are epigraphic, because they were not intended for public display. For freedmen prominence in libertine epigraphy, above p. 177 f.

rating (the higher the rating, the more documents a person signs in). But neither here, nor elsewhere was there a correlation between a variable in the model, and frequency of occurrence.

The last variable to look into is that of wealth/house size. Here we are not without problems. Almost all houses are of the large, comfortable and respectable *atrium* type. Depending somewhat on definitions and on estimates for the unexcavated parts of the town, the maximum number of these houses cannot very much have exceeded 600. The most likely conclusion to be drawn from this is that inhabitants of large houses are over-represented in our data.

So what can we say about the social place of our witnesses? How representative for Pompeian society as a whole are our observations about the various dimensions of social inequality? As noted earlier, women, slaves and children remain outside the picture, but this is not particularly serious for the debate in which our observations may figure. But what about the other Pompeians, the adult free males? We observed that the group of all witnesses, known and unknown, does not coincide with that of all adult free male Pompeians. An important selection criterion would appear to be proximity to Iucundus' home, and perhaps this could account for most of the selection. A remaining worry is of course that in the small number of cases where we can establish the size of the house someone lived in, such houses were mostly large and splendid.

We therefore have a bias indeed. Only, what is the nature of the bias? Are the witnesses overwhelmingly drawn from the main occupants of those 600 or so large and respectable houses, and is our sample 'witnesses known and unknown' therefore not representative in this respect for all adult free males? Or can the group of witnesses, known and unknown, indeed be treated as a representative sample of all adult free male Pompeians? In this latter case with one proviso: data on wealth are not available for a random cross section of the witnesses, but only for the rich among them. The truth probably lies somewhere in the middle, but one is tempted to give some preference to the second possibility as a result of the data on the spatial distribution of witnesses.

But perhaps all this does not matter too much for the points that we were trying to make, perhaps even reinforces them. That lack of wealth excludes from real respectability does not need much argument. The core of the problem is the extent to which wealth is enough to give respectability. The witnesses with known houses are of course not representative of all adult free male Pompeians with regard to their wealth. But we cannot say that they are also unrepresentative with respect to their rank as witnesses. The mean prestige rating of these 22 persons is 142, whereas the mean rating of all individuals in the documents is 163.5. Their prestige rating is therefore slightly above average, but not to a worrying extent.

We witness status dissonance under a magnifying glass. We see the wealthy inhabitants, the poor do not crop up in our data on wealth. But although we do know that wealth is a necessary requirement for high ranking, we can also see that it is not sufficient. Libertine status excludes from real respectability.

CHAPTER SEVEN

POWER AND OBLIGATION

'Politics'

Among the determinants of social status analysed in the previous chapter, the variable indicating whether someone had held office was of great importance. The political and social meaning of office-holding was not limited to the period of office-holding itself, but remained with the ex-office-holder for the rest of his life: office-holding gave entry to a social group, the group of ex-office-holders. This situation finds its formal expression in the *ordo decurionum*. It is a social group with very clear criteria as to who belongs to it, unlike many modern social groups. Membership is defined by law, doubts about membership are impossible - apart from the doubts of the poor historian who struggles with insufficient documentation. Ignoring for the moment complications that we shall turn to in time, we can say that election to the lowest office - in Pompeii that of aedile - secured membership of the *ordo decurionum*, the body of the political elite, probably numbering one hundred men.[1] The analogy with the Roman senate of the Republic as a body of former magistrates is obvious.[2] Just as the Roman citizen body

[1] See below, p. 311 ff.

[2] We shall also see that the analogy can be extended to the Roman senate of the early Empire. Co-optation and a measure of status inheritance will be shown in operation (below, p. 311 ff). For a recent survey on the early imperial senate: Ferrill (1985). To a certain degree, however, I find the debate on the 'ordo

as a whole is indicated by the phrase *senatus populusque romanus*, we find the phrase *ordo populusque* on the local level. In this sense the city-state model of politics applies to the Roman empire as a whole, and to its constituent parts. In this chapter I shall investigate the nature of this politically powerful group (the *ordo*), and in particular its relation to other groups in society. We have seen in the previous chapter that membership of the *ordo* gave prestige, but social precedence when witnessing a legal document would be a frivolous and empty game if there was nothing more to it. We should not forget that the star performers of such social ritual were rich, even if not all rich were, as yet, respectable enough to be seen in the spot-light. Roman inequality of wealth and income was staggering, and the modern observer is surprised by the seemingly unquestioned right of the rich to rule and be wealthy.

In this chapter I propose to study two aspects in particular. The first is the relationship between the rich office-holding elite and its electorate. That the elite was elected by all adult male citizens may seem all the more puzzling in the face of our knowledge of vast social inequality: how did the elite persuade its electorate? Did it at times yield sufficiently to pressure from below to (usually) avoid outright confrontation? In this sense Finley allows for a measure of popular participation in the late Republic.[1] Fear of food riots undoubtedly kept emperors and magistrates on their toes.[2] Fewer concessions might be necessary if relations of patronage could counter any feelings of unity among the lower classes, and bind its members to high placed individuals. But not only lower class solidarity (and therefore power) is threatened by the free rider who sacrifices the good of the group to his own advancement. Disintegration among the elite may persuade some of its members to forget their group solidarity, and employ lower class power to obtain leverage in a struggle for power within the elite.

senatorius' somewhat sterile without the conclusions of Hopkins (1983a) ch. 3 that the rate of social reproduction in the actual senate was low.

[1] Finley (1983), esp. ch. 4.

[2] Jongman and Dekker (1988).

This leads to the second aspect that I want to discuss: the process of entry into the political elite, and the resulting nature of the group. The *ordines* of Rome were not parliamentary bodies that consisted of 'expert representatives' of groups with specific interests or convictions. The members of these orders are themselves the social top of society *because they belong to their order*. But few elites are self-perpetuating. This has been brought home forcefully in Hopkins' work on the Roman senate: 'the senatorial aristocracy achieved a surprisingly low rate of social reproduction; surprising, that is, relative to Roman ideals of hereditary succession and modern scholarly views; and low, relative to aristocracies in other societies.'[1] Lack of documentation does not permit us to repeat Hopkins' work in the case of a Roman city. But we may accept there was some such social mobility in Roman cities, perhaps characteristically of sons of freedmen.[2] Yet, as Finley has rightly pointed out, Rome was a stable society, able 'to maintain without petrification [its] strong sense of continuity through change.'[3] So how did the social risers get in? Did they obtain entry as representatives of a new social group and thereby change the nature of the political elite? Or did they enter as individuals, changing their status position, and - perhaps - removing their origins from view? Pleket writes: 'The social ascent of successful sons of successful freedmen will not ordinarily change the mentality of the group that they join. Social mobility implies, and requires, an *imitatio domini*.'[4] Or to quote Veyne: 'La mobilité sociale s'accompagnait d'un "transformisme" des individus; ainsi le renouvellement de leur composition n'empêchait pas la stabilité des classes comme telles.'[5]

[1]Hopkins (1983a) ix; Runciman (1986) 261 ff adds a critical comparative perspective.

[2]Garnsey (1975) is a judicious and largely qualitative assessment of such possibilities. His efforts, and those in Gordon (1931) 71 and Pleket (1971) 243 f, at quantification leave me unconvinced. Available samples are small and of dubious quality. The more distant the descent is, the more likely it is to be libertine, but equally the more uncertain and irrelevant: what counts as social mobility?

[3]Finley (1983) 25.

[4]Pleket (1971) 245. His neologism 'imitatio domini' is taken from Wigboldus (1971) 190. Cf. above, p. 258 ff.

[5]Veyne (1961) 231.

Because membership of the *ordo decurionum* is the result of successfully meeting the entry criteria, in our case (apart from the wealth criterion) mainly winning an election, we are fortunate that the Pompeian evidence includes about 2800 election posters (*programmata*) informing us about the conduct of these elections (Plate XXXI).[1] The sight of Pompeian streets with the façades of the houses covered with these posters, usually painted in big red letters on a background of white plaster, has fascinated visitors - archaeologists, historians and tourists alike. But the link between past and present is tenuous. Elections and election posters do not by themselves imply anything similar to our modern political systems. Here again, many historians have felt that the relevance of the past is in its identity or similarity with the present, and have claimed attention for Pompeii on these grounds. Yet, I shall argue that similarity is only skin-deep, and extends no further than the identity of a few tangible pieces of the puzzle.

In earlier chapters I have rejected a number of such modernizing views on economic and social structure. Time and again discussion has focussed, sometimes explicitly, sometimes implicitly, on a comparison with later European history. A very important place in the historical debate of the last century has been given to the bourgeoisie. Its economic activities in the spheres of trading and manufacturing have been seen as prime dynamic factors in the economic and social development of late medieval and early modern Europe. These activities created a new road to personal wealth, separate from the agricultural wealth of the aristocracy. By its nature this was a way of getting rich quickly, or poor as the case might also be. Equally, they were an urban economic activity, and towns developed into an institutional harbour for those engaged in trade and crafts. Cities made themselves independent from aristocratic authority, and although certainly not correct in all cases, the ideal type of such a city still remains that of the town segregated from its surrounding countryside: the city ends at the city walls. This independence made possible the political ascendance

[1]Below, p. 311 ff. for 'adlectio' instead of election.

of the bourgeoisie, and included sometimes relatively quick entry into the new elite for social risers or a measure of popular participation.[1]

No doubt this picture leaves much to be desired as a description of the state of the art on late medieval and early modern history, and for a proper comparative analysis it would certainly have to be brought up to date.[2] But for our present purpose that would not seem to be so necessary. For us it is enough to have some idea of what the 'modernizers' among the ancient historians had in mind when they tried to fit the ancient world into this mould. The analysis of economic and social structure as developed in previous chapters clearly does not fit such a modernizing mould, and it is now time to extend my argument into the realm of politics, abstaining for the moment from any clear definition of that word.[3]

We shall have to deal with a number of different issues and we shall have to define our questions more precisely as we go along, but the two questions that I have just outlined (the *ordo*'s relation with the lower classes and its potential for renewal without change) are crucial to understanding the nature of this political elite. Although I shall not again pay much attention to the elite's wealth and its sources, we should not allow ourselves to forget its importance. Mere wealth was - as I hope to have shown in the previous chapter - an unsatisfactory indicator of social hierarchy. It was always necessary, but not invariably sufficient. It would be wrong to believe that it played no role.[4] Without wealth one could not lead a proper life. It was good to be wealthy, and the wealthy were good. When Cicero wrote about his class and his political friends as the *boni*, it is this coincidence of meaning that is often the key to a good understanding, even though it may irritate many

[1]For a comparative analysis of such matters, see e.g. Burke (1974).

[2]Cf. above, p. 48 ff.

[3]Finley (1983) has undeniably influenced this chapter, but using his restrictive definition would largely remove the object of our analysis. In these stages a vague word is appropriate.

[4]Finley (1983) ch.1.

a modern reader.[1] So far I have - almost implicitly - taken for granted a bipolar class structure: the wealthy and the poor. I do not want to suggest that there was a statistical concentration on two distinct levels of wealth, and that there were therefore only few (if any) people who were neither very rich nor very poor.

It is rare for data on social inequality (such as figures on income distribution) to show the sort of clustering that exonerates us from personally imposing the borderlines that divide classes. Normally we find a whole spectrum and no clustering at all: a smooth curve. Distribution data cannot suggest where we should draw divisions between classes, and how many classes we should distinguish. However many classes we create, we shall always be able to point to people who are mid-way. If we take that to mean that we should differentiate further, we can only end up with as many classes as there are people: all people are different. This is not a very illuminating truth. A practical consequence is that criticism of a two-class model on the grounds that there are people who are neither rich, nor very poor, is unjustified.[2] We gain in clarity by minimizing the number of classes, although we admittedly lose in precision.

In order to decide whether a two-class model actually distorts reality, it is not therefore enough to look at the size of the group of people who are neither rich nor poor. What should concern us instead is the extent to which there is enough to bind together such middling people into a social class. In the previous chapter I have argued that social inequality may have more than one dimension, and that those dimensions need not provide identical scalings ('status dissonance').[3] The prominence of freedmen at the middling level made me argue that they should be seen as in a phase of their personal social ascent, rather than as a permanent social group with a long term identity.[4] And we should remember that 'intergenera-

[1] For a recent discussion: Lotito (1981).

[2] I therefore disagree with e.g. Christ (1980) 218 ff.

[3] Above, p. 207 ff, esp. 258 ff.

[4] Above, p. 258 ff; cf. above, p. 177 f.

tional flexibility can coexist with rigid statuses into which each generation may be frozen.'[1] Or to quote Orlando Patterson: 'freedman status was not an end .... but merely the end of the beginning.'[2] It is for this reason that I propose to study the incorporation of social risers into the elite. Did they provide an economic and ideological alternative to the existing elite, or were they just part of a process of changeless change?

In order to argue my case, I shall - by way of introduction- commence with brief expositions of received opinion on 'Pompeian politics'. Subsequently I shall argue that the language of political mediation between the elite and its electorate (as expressed in the electoral propaganda) squares badly with received opinion, and suggests relations of patronage rather than opposition between social groups. The existence of elections in which all citizens could vote for their magistrates obviously puts severe constraints on any reconstruction of the elite's control over the mass of the population. I shall therefore analyse electoral procedure in detail, and argue that actual voting behaviour is governed by localized patronage networks. The elite's ability to control is strong, and the electorate obliges. The last part of my analysis will concern the relationship between the *ordo* and its aspiring new members. I shall argue that not all members of the *ordo* (or those who want to join) are created equal, and that this is likely to have served as a powerful incentive to conform: socialize or be damned. It is unlikely that the structure of power and obligation in Pompeii allowed those who had earned their wealth in trade and manufacturing to challenge the landowning elite as a group. Individuals made the transition, of course, but only by socializing to the norms and modes of conduct of the elite that they were to join. No bourgeoisie emerged. Popular participation was probably well past its prime: organizations of electoral procedure show signs of a transformation into organs of elite control.

[1]Kopytoff and Miers (1977) 20.

[2]Patterson (1982) 249; cf. 262 ff.

Pompeian democracy?

Although the Pompeian material has a unique wealth of information for at least parts of a political analysis, it is remarkable how little explicit discussion one finds in the literature about most of the issues raised above. It seems as if the fascination with the unique evidence has been strong enough to remove potential methodological doubts about the possibility of accepting the evidence at face value and lulled scholars into a false sense of *Verstehen.* In a recent and skilful monograph on Pompeian elections that I shall use to argue against an anachronistic conception of politics in Pompeii, we read in the conclusion, however, that 'there is every indication that these were genuine campaigns.'[1]

Ignoring for the moment the lack of a proper definition of the *genuine article*, this is the latest expression of a long tradition about Pompeian politics. Characteristic of this view is the assumption of fairly open access to the *ordo* and of elections in which different social groups fought for their share in government (in order to have programmes implemented which would be beneficial to their own socio-economic position). Often emphasis is placed on a bourgeoisie securing its position. Obviously not all authors would accept all these propositions, but it would seem a fair representation of received opinion. In recent years extreme examples of this view have been given by Moeller.[2]

In Mary Gordon's classic and often quoted article *The Ordo of Pompeii* the emphasis is different.[3] She believes that 'the governing class at Pompeii was aristocratic rather than bourgeois.'[4] Many families of the *ordo* would have had a long line of ancestors, and the settlement of Sullan veterans had made little difference. At the same time she believes that many of

[1]Franklin (1980) 124. Surprisingly enough this conclusion comes more or less out of the blue, and is hardly substantiated by the author's own text. This is all the more unfortunate since his own text provides many perceptive instances of implicit criticism of traditional views.

[2]Moeller (1970b); Moeller (1973b); Moeller (1976). These should have been criticized by Franklin (1980), but he refrains from doing so.

[3]Gordon (1927).

[4]Gordon (1927) 165.

these families were heavily involved in large scale trade, and that wealth gained in trade was an important means to enter the *ordo*. This confusion is further increased by her worries about the degeneration of the quality of the blood of the *ordo* through the entry of persons with slave ancestry. It is crowned by the statement that Pompeii was 'a sociable and even democratic little community', proven by the fact that decurion and small shopkeeper unite in their support of the same candidate for office.[1]

Étienne's description is less unsatisfying, though more anecdotal than analytical.[2] He gives his chapter the heading *fièvre électorale* and concludes with a remark that Cicero made, according to Macrobius (*Saturn.* 2,3,11.), to the effect that it was easier to make someone a senator in Rome than to make him *decurio* in Pompeii.[3] The point of the joke is not a comment on Pompeii, however, but on the facility with which Caesar obtained adlections to the senate in Rome. And if it was difficult to become a *decurio* in Pompeii, it remains to be seen for whom this was so. Was it difficult for those outside the elite of office-holding families, or was it difficult for all, due to a very wide recruitment?[4] Important, though, is Étienne's emphasis on the relevance of *clientela* and of localized support in the various quarters of the town.[5] Like many others he maintains that the *ordo* was composed of members of the landed aristocracy, well-to-do industrialists, and large merchants.[6] His discussion of the role of *collegia* of craftsmen is vague: he insists that their frequent participation in recommendations is an expression of their self-consciousness and pride.[7] The basis for these feelings is not made explicit, but seems to rest in their behaviour as responsible citizens. On the other hand

[1]Gordon (1927) 182.

[2]Étienne (1977) 110-136.

[3]Étienne (1977) 136.

[4]In addition, Macrobius is not exactly contemporaneous with Cicero, which adds to the problems in assessing the meaning of such anecdotes. Cf. Saller (1980a).

[5]Étienne (1977) 123 f, 129.

[6]Étienne (1977) 136.

[7]Étienne (1977) 129 f.

Étienne commences this paragraph with the words 'selon les occupations des candidats, leur position sociale, tous les groupements économiques prennent parti.'[1] This would suggest a professional link between candidates and *collegia* supporting them. This interest of *collegia* of craftsmen in the elections has been analysed separately by Schulz-Falkenthal.[2] He insists correctly that the craftsmen (such as the bakers and apple sellers) should be seen as *collegiati* when they are supporting candidates. That he believes that they felt they were doing something in their own interest is fair enough. Whether this also warrants his view that the lower classes in the town used zealously and with clear political views a 'politisches Mitbestimmungsrecht' remains to be seen.[3] In his view the local authorities contributed to the success of crafts and trade and the political activities of the *collegia* are motivated by this.

The language of obligation

If our problem is the extent to which politics in Roman cities such as Pompeii allowed a measure of popular participation (real politics in Finley's restrictive definition[4]) it becomes obviously of great interest to analyse elections in detail. Apart from the constitutional evidence we can, in the case of Pompeii, employ an entirely different type of data: the electoral propaganda painted on the walls of houses. Fascinating to the visitor, conjuring up all kinds of equations of politics past and present, they give a unique opportunity to analyse the practice of what was virtually the only constitutional form in which ordinary citizens could express political preferences (the popular assembly's functions outside the electoral were minimal[5]). To find out what these elections were about, we shall begin with an

[1] Étienne (1977) 129.

[2] Schulz-Falkenthal (1971).

[3] Schulz-Falkenthal (1971) 27.

[4] Finley (1983) 51-53.

[5] For a recent, still too optimistic account of political participation: Jacques (1984) 379 ff. His account is marred by his construction of a conceptual opposition between 'imperial intervention' and 'freedom'. Lack of imperial interference does not necessarily imply popular participation.

analysis of the language used by Pompeians to express support for a particular candidate. I shall argue that it suggest that personal relations between supporter and candidate are more important than dissent about the nature of political merit. In a subsequent section we shall investigate the nature of a candidate's relations with lower status groups as expressed in more formal and informal means of mobilizing the support of the bulk of the electorate. In the last section we shall pay attention to candidates' relations with members of the group that they aspire to join.

So how do Pompeians express the particular qualities of the candidate that they prefer? Is the candidate said to favour lower taxes, a redistribution of land, abolition or imposition of price controls or issues of a similar kind? Taxation could not have become an issue, because the citizen-poor were largely free from it; this is in clear contrast to its prominent role in medieval and modern social conflict.[1] A contrast that may be reflected in the fact that most supporters in Pompeian electoral recommendations mention nothing more than themselves, the name of the candidate that they favour, and the office for which he is standing. The man himself (and the voter's relation to him) may have been more important than anything else.

Such silence may be revealing, but only if its interpretation is not refuted by the electoral posters which explicitly tell us about the qualities of candidates. Is there merit beyond the personal relations with supporters, and are there different kinds of merit, enabling a choice between candidates? The nearest thing to a reference to the actual activities of magistrates is a poster for C. Iulius Polybius with the line '*panem bonum fert*'.[2] The man is standing as aedile candidate, and quality and price of the staple food are of course not without importance; they were the responsibility of the *aediles*.[3] The praise for Q. Brittius Balbus ('*hic aerarium conservabit*') is

[1] Finley (1983) 32 f. Notably absent are excise duties, which invariably hurt the poor most of all.

[2] CIL IV 429.

[3] Jongman and Dekker (1988) for a discussion of intervention in the urban food supply of pre-industrial Europe.

unlikely to refer to conservative financial policy, but probably means that he would meet many expenses out of his own pocket, as befits a respectable magistrate.[1] C. Gavius Rufus is *utilis rei publicae*, useful to the community.[2] In the language of political virtue, *utilitas* is usually combined with *communis*, and gives rise to *dignitas*.[3] We do not find an indication that the essence of politics would be potential disagreement on what constitutes such utility, and the link with *communis* (or here with the *res publica*) serves to remove any doubts. The more *utilitas* the better, and that is all there is to it.[4]

Dignitas is apparently the most important quality for Pompeian magistrates. The phrase *dignum rei publicae* returns in a fair number of commendations. Of the 41 electoral recommendations in Dessau's *Inscriptiones Latinae Selectae* which specify qualities of the candidate, 26 include the word *dignus*.[5] What are the merits of a *dignus vir*; is it possible that any voter would rather not have a *dignus vir* as magistrate (and prefer a *vir bonus*)? The prevalence of the word *dignus* in recommendations suggests that every candidate needs to be *dignus*.

Dignitas is a word that, significantly, can be used in a wide range of contexts, denoting *inter alia* suitability, beauty, impressiveness or duty.[6] Hellegouarc'h, in his study of political vocabulary, distinguishes two principal political meanings of *dignitas*: 'mérites d'un homme politique et plus particulièrement d'un candidat aux élections' and 'position d'un homme politique dans le *cursus honorum*.'[7] Such *dignitas* is a merit that would appear to originate in political position, but political positions require it. 'La *dignitas* est la qualité de celui qui est digne de

[1] CIL IV 3702 and perhaps similarly 3773.

[2] ILS 6401/CIL IV 3471.

[3] Hellegouarc'h (1963) 270, 273, 368, 382, 397, 537, 556.

[4] What was said in conversation is of course anybody's guess. The surviving evidence only relates to conscious representation, and vindicates my statement.

[5] ILS 6398a - 6438d. There is no reason to suppose that this is not a random sample, apart from an obvious under representation of recommendations where the supporter finds it apparently unnecessary to mention a candidate's qualities at all: Dessau was less interested in those.

[6] Hellegouarc'h (1963) 389 ff. discusses some of the possibilities.

[7] Hellegouarc'h (1963) 389.

remplir une fonction.'[1] It implies an obligation towards that position, as is amply attested in Pompeian election propaganda with the phrase *'dignus rei publicae'*. It justifies the right to wield power, and includes the concomitant obligations.[2] We shall follow Hellegouarc'h once again: 'à celui qui possède la *dignitas*, certains devoirs à l'égard des autres s'imposent, mais les autres ont aussi des obligations envers lui. Ces devoirs, ces obligations, ce sont les *officia*.'[3]

Cuspius Pansa is a *iuvenem probum dignum rei publicae*: 'a good chap, worthy of the community.'[4] *Probitas* returns in other inscriptions, e.g. Popidius Secundus is *d[ignum] r[ei] p[ublicae]* and a *probissimum iuvenem*.[5] And to give one more-lengthy - example (CIL IV 768/ILS 6438d):

M. EPIDIUM SABINUM D[uovirum].I[ure].DIC[undo].

O[ro].V[os].F[aciatis]./

DIG[nus]. EST/

DEFENSOREM COLONIAE EX SENTENTIA SUEDI

CLEMENTIS SANCTI IUDICIS/

CONSENSU ORDINIS OB MERITA EIUS ET

PROBITATEM DIGNUM REIPUBLICAE FACIAT[IS]/

SABINUS DISSIGNATOR CUM PLAUSU FACIT.//[6]

[1] Hellegouarc'h (1963) 397.

[2] Hellegouarc'h (1963) 408.

[3] Hellegouarc'h (1963) 393.

[4] CIL IV 702/ILS 6419a.

[5] CIL IV 3409/ILS 6424b.

[6] 'I ask you to make M. Epidius Sabinus the highest magistrate - he is worthy. Vote for the defender of the town by virtue of the decision of Suedius Clemens the sacred judge and the consent of the town council because of his merits, his 'probitas' and that he is worthy to the community. Sabinus the theatre official does so with applause.' The tribune T. Suedius Clemens was Vespasian's agent and had adjudicated in a conflict about property between the town and some private persons (CIL X 1018; cf. Castrén (1975) 117 and Duncan-Jones (1977) 197). He obviously also interferes with the elections; this is further corroborated by CIL IV 791 and 1059. The 'sententia', therefore, refers to the duoviral elections. 'Defensor coloniae' may refer to a role by Epidius in the property conflict, but may also recommend him: 'as "duovir" he will defend ...' I cannot escape the

Probitas is a quality closely connected to patronage: 'c'est la qualité de celui qui, respectant la *fides*, remplit ainsi les devoirs de l'*officium*.'[1] Of course, *probitas* is also used outside the context of patronage. It expresses positive qualities, but the wide range in which it is used serves to emphasize the vagueness. The context alone provides the specification of the word's meaning.

It is not very useful to employ these alleged qualities of candidates - and others not discussed here, such as *bonus*, *optimus*, or *benificus* - to differentiate between the candidates. The various words used to express the qualities of the candidates all refer to the traditional aristocratic ideal of office-holding, and in that sense the electoral propaganda reminds us of the language of personal patronage relations as analysed by Saller: 'the Romans continued to think of the ideal qualities of the good official as those of the aristocratic gentleman.'[2]

Perhaps the most striking feature of the posters is the prominence of the personal relationship between supporter/voter and candidate. Most posters are phrased as 'I ask you (the readers) to make so and so a magistrate *(oro vos faciatis)*.' In a number of instances this relationship between supporter and candidate is specified further. L. Popidius L.f. Ampliatus is recommended for the aedileship by *Montanus cliens*, and a number of other examples could be given.[3] The fuller Dionysius calls himself the freedman of L. Popidius Secundus, his favoured candidate for the aedileship.[4]

An intimate link between voting and patronage can be traced very neatly in the shift in the meaning of the Latin word for

curious possibility of a parallel between Sabinus' function as 'dissignator' in the theatre (umpire or, perhaps even more interesting, as official charged with showing people the places they were given as fitting to their social standing) and his role in this special controlled election. It is as if here, too, he shows the magistrate his - political - place. For places in the theatre: Kolendo (1981). Hopkins (1983a) ch. 1 for games as political theatre. Cf. above, p. 226 ff.

[1]Hellegouarc'h (1963) 286.

[2]The fundamental study is Saller (1982) 7-39 (for language), 94-111 (for the nature of merit); quotation on p. 96. For language and merit also: Saller (1980b).

[3]Franklin (1980) 103-118.

[4]Above p. 168 ; 171; 176. CIL IV 1041, 2966.

vote (*suffragium*), away from its original meaning and to that of 'influence, interest, patronage'.[1] Candidates for office would need influential supporters to deliver votes: *suffragatores*. Gradually such modes of support impinge on the original meaning of the word *suffragium*, and the word begins to denote patronage and support from above, rather than below. The disappearance of popular elections in Rome obviously helped to bring this about. It would appear that the patronage meaning of *suffragium* was well established by the early second century A.D.[2] That the Romans developed yet another word for patronage is not so important - that this word is the same word as the old word for vote is not without significance. It suggests that even if we still find local elections, they may be decidedly shaped by relations of personal patronage. In the following pages we shall test this hypothesis and add further specifications.

Support from the many

Few modern observers of Pompeii have failed to be impressed by the bulk of the electoral propaganda. The modern liberal likes elections and views them as the core of an open political system. That the ancients did not share our identification of elections with democracy is perhaps something we need not emphasize too much, even though it might serve as a warning. More damning is that a Roman election was an irrevocable mandate. Of course, the term of office was only one year, but it was followed by the ex-office-holder's incorporation into a powerful body politic: the senate in Rome or the *ordo decurionum* in the cities of the empire.[3] Censure of a magistrate could not consist of popular refusal to reelect, but only of elite

[1] de Sainte Croix (1954).

[2] de Sainte Croix (1954) 38 f.

[3] This concerns periods when there were still elections. This did not last. First in the case of the senate, but later also in the case of the 'ordo decurionum', membership was obtained by inheritance and co-optation or imperial appointment. For the senate: above, p. 275, for the 'ordo decurionum': below, p. 311.

refusal of incorporation into the appropriate *ordo*.[1] Not only was it impossible for the mass of the population to remove its leaders from power, it could not choose them from its own members either: the census criteria for office-holding ensured that all political leaders would be very rich. And yet magistrates were elected by all adult male citizens.[2] So how did the elite persuade its electorate?

An aspect of electoral procedure may give us our first clue. This is the fact that elections were conducted through a division of the town in electoral districts.[3] The candidate elected was the candidate who secured a majority of the districts. Each candidate would therefore have to ensure to win in at least his own district. Of course, he would need more than that, and I shall argue later that combinations with other candidates and powerful men in different parts of the town were an important means to obtain support outside one's own district. But such extension obviously depended on a candidate's ability to win in his own district and deliver support for his running mate. I shall therefore begin with an analysis of the ways in which local loyalties are articulated in the political behaviour of the bulk of the electorate. This involves primarily an analysis of specific institutional forms of ideological and 'practical' political mediation between the office-holding elite and its electorate. For the moment we shall concern ourselves with relations *within* the divisions of the town.

If the electoral districts are the primary units where obligation has to be ensured, we should expect to find the clearest

[1]Making the most junior faculty member its dean (and giving the most senior members the right to decide on tenure after this probation period) would no doubt ensure that little would shake the consensus in such an institution.

[2]With some practical restrictions however: the voting procedure required a measure of literacy (Lex Malacitana LII, LV; Nicolet (1976) 373), and on official occasions such as these, citizens were required to wear the 'toga', an inconvenient and expensive garment.

[3]Castrén (1975) 78 f. provides a brief survey. The basic evidence is the Lex Malacitana LII - LVII. Translation in Hardy (1912). I must admit that I do not understand from the text how Castrén can infer that the procedure could result in candidates with fewer votes still being elected, apart from the normal iniquities of any system with districts. The text is certainly obscure. Roman parallels are discussed in: Taylor (1966) 78-83. The Irnitana text (González (1986)) is missing for this part of municipal legislation.

indications of control on this level. Castrén recognizes that something is indeed the matter when he writes: 'I should interpret the notices, in which the voting districts canvass for certain candidates for municipal offices, as a semi-official election propaganda...'[1] In its brevity this sentence is both correct and confusing. I shall argue that we are indeed presented with documentation which seems to suggest that all inhabitants of a district unanimously favour particular candidates. Of course, unaided unanimity is suspicious, and would obviate the need for propaganda. Castrén's words 'semi-official election propaganda' provide the clue. I shall argue that within the electoral wards there were cult organizations - the *collegia vici et compiti* - which performed a crucial role in ensuring that 'the right candidates' were elected. When it suited them, these *collegia* could pose as 'representatives' of the entire ward.

In order to argue my case I shall first discuss the evidence from other towns for the existence of such *collegia* within the territorial divisions of towns. I shall conclude that such collegiate organizations are quite frequently attested - even though under different guises. Whereas in the late Republic the *collegia vici et compiti* of the city of Rome had been powerful foci of popular unrest, I shall suggest (even though proof will remain elusive) that in the cities of the Empire they were transformed into organs of elite control, and that this is an important- and neglected - part of the erosion of popular participation in Roman politics. Political participation was restricted from all citizens voting in their districts to small groups within these districts.

I shall secondly investigate the composition of these *collegia* and their cult activities. Their members were mostly freedmen, which is mirrored in their cult, which integrates lower status groups into the social fabric. That the imperial cult became incorporated in the cult activities of these *collegia* is a clear sign that they were becoming instruments of ideological control,

[1] Castrén (1975) 82.

and were losing their role as instruments of political participation.

Thirdly I shall investigate where Pompeii fits into the picture, and what it can add to our knowledge about the erosion of popular participation. I shall argue that Pompeii gives us a view of a staging post in the process of the erosion of participation. Of course this will be a somewhat confusing view: the beginning and the end of the process are inevitably clearer. The advantage is, however, that we can trace how the change came about. I shall argue that Pompeian electoral districts were called *vici*. There were still elections in which all citizens could vote. Yet we can also distinguish that the cult organizations of the wards are actively involved in ensuring that the 'right' candidates were elected. The restriction of the electorate to just the members of these *collegia* had not yet come about, but it is foreshadowed in their endorsement of particular candidates.

Our knowledge of territorial divisions and neighbourhood organizations in Roman towns is far less extensive than we would like. No individual city provides us with all the answers for even that city, and differences in practice and terminology between cities make it hazardous to extrapolate from one city to another. Equally, things change over time, even while the words denoting institutions may remain the same. Discussing all such problems here would be inappropriate, and would remove us too far from Pompeii.

The core of the debate has until now been the vexed question whether the membership of the various neighbourhood organizations such as *curiae* or *vici* extended to all adult free males, or whether it only comprised part of these people.[1] If all free males are members of the *curiae*, popular participation in politics, it is argued, must still be substantial. If, on the other hand, *curiae* or *vici* are *collegia* that together comprise only a proportion of the adult free males, then political participation cannot be widespread. Disagreement over these altern-

[1] Duncan-Jones (1982) 277 ff. is the best account, and supplies ample bibliography.

atives is of course important, and does not lack ideological overtones. Yet, it is unfortunate that the problem has been defined in terms of a choice between these two possibilities, because, as I hope to show, that has precluded an understanding of how to control the many through the few, and has ignored social change. The problem with our evidence is that it strongly resists a clear cut choice for one of these supposed alternatives. On the one hand one could point to a number of cases where the terms *curiales* and *vicani* undoubtedly refer to members of *collegia*, and do not comprise the entire citizen body of a ward.[1] Even Kotula, the strongest believer in continuing popular participation, has now retracted his earlier views and conceded that these are *collegia* of restricted membership.[2] And yet there is no denying that electoral districts comprising all free male citizens do indeed exist, and that one attested term for them is precisely the word *curia*.[3]

The way out of this apparent contradiction is not by forcing the evidence into one of two moulds, but by an appreciation that this seeming contradiction has its roots in the ambiguity of political participation. The dichotomy is false in the sense that towns could have electoral districts that were called *curiae*, and within these electoral wards there might be collegiate organizations that were equally called *curiae*. Of course, the electoral districts could comprise all free males; whether that implies real popular participation depends on the conduct and nature of such elections. Yet, as said before, within such territorial divisions *collegia* did indeed exist. They could be called *curiae* or *vici* as a *pars pro toto*. But it might be the *melior pars*; that remains to be investigated. In the late Republic these *collegia* had been an important organ of popular political participation, but in imperial times they seem to become more

[1]E.g. ILS 6824 and 6664. Perhaps it is unnecessary, but a reminder may be in order that the 'curia' we are discussing here is neither the same as the latin synonym for 'ordo decurionum', nor is it the same 'curia' as the building where the town council met.

[2]Kotula (1980).

[3]Lex Malacitana LII; Lex Irnitana L (González (1986) 187.

dependent upon elite patronage.[1] With the diminishing importance of elections, the wider definition (in the sense of comprising all citizens) lost much of its meaning. It is not particularly interesting to speculate when popular elections stopped being held. More relevant is to trace the decline of their importance as instruments of popular political expression. This decline seems to take place along two lines. The first of these is a restriction of choice, the second is a reduction - at least *de facto* - of the electorate to the collegiati. Such a process inevitably takes time, and produces confusing sources. Yet, the confusion may have been functional: the continuing use (in a fundamentally different political sense) of the word that was once used to denote real electoral districts may have served to dissimulate the break with the past. The analogy with the shift in the meaning of *suffragium* away from that of 'vote', and to that of 'patronage' is striking.[2] For Pompeii I propose to investigate how far political participation had in fact been restricted to an inner core of *collegiati*, and to what extent these *collegiati* were dependent upon elite patronage. In a later section ('support from the few') I shall investigate restrictions of choice.

In the later - mostly north African - evidence these organizations within the city wards are mostly called *curiae*, and that is also the term used for electoral districts in the *Lex Malacitana*. In the - mostly earlier - Italian evidence *vici* is the most prominent term, and I shall later argue that the Pompeian electoral districts were indeed called *vici*. The Italian *vici* have a long history, and we are fortunate that the cult activities of their *collegia* are fairly well known. The best evidence comes from the *vici* of the city of Rome.[3]

[1]Flambard (1977) and Flambard (1981) are excellent discussions of the Republican evidence for Rome.

[2]Above, p. 288 f.

[3]For a justification of the assumption that the 'vici' of Rome and those of the Italian towns are similar: Niebling (1956). Palmer (1974) 114-120 provides ample bibliography and references to the sources.

The main cult of the *collegia vicorum* was that for the *lares compitales*, the protecting spirits of the crossroads. The *collegia vicorum* could therefore also be called *collegium vici et compiti*. As *collegia* they had their officials: the *magistri*, who were usually freedmen, and the *ministri*, who were usually slaves.[1] Both the status of their officials, and the nature of their activities suggests that a central element of their existence was the integration into society of persons of lesser status.

The symbolic meaning of the crossroads (and in particular the link with manumission) has been emphasized by Patterson: 'another symbol of transition and a common location for ritual events the world over. Nor should we neglect the more obvious symbolic meaning of the crossroads as a sign of free choice.'[2] Dionysius of Halicarnussus (IV, 14) connects the institution of the *compitalia* to the Servian division of the city:

> ... The levies of troops, the collection of taxes for military purposes, and the other services which every citizen was bound to offer to the commonwealth, ... [he based upon] the four local divisions established by himself.[3]

He then continues to say that it was decreed that there should be chapels in each neighbourhood to the *lares compitales* and that a law should be made 'that sacrifices should be performed to them every year, each family contributing a honey cake.'[4] In similar fashion the rural territory was divided into districts

[1]Niebling (1956) is excellent for the status of the officials after the Augustan reform. In the previous period things had not always been so neat: Flambard (1983). Also Bömer (1957-61) vol. I 38, and Castrén (1975) 72.

[2]Patterson (1982) 215.

[3]In the last line I deviate from the Loeb translation ('... upon the four local tribes established by himself.'). The Greek text carefully distinguishes between three 'genikai phylai' and the four 'topikai phylai' that replace them. The Servian division is thus represented as a transition from an arrangement according to 'genos' to one according to locality. The 'national tribes' and the 'local tribes' of the Loeb translation obscure this.

[4]'Lares compitales' is what we apparently have to understand from his 'hêrôsi pronôpiois': Flambard (1981) 155; also the comment in the Loeb edition.

called *pagi*, which had their own festivals, the *paganalia*.[1] About the *paganalia* Dionysius of Halicarnussus (IV 15,4) writes:

> Towards the expense of this sacrifice and of this assemblage he ordered all those of the same district to contribute each of them a certain piece of money, the men paying one kind, the women another and the children a third kind. When these pieces of money were counted by those who presided over the sacrifices, the number of people, distinguished by their sex and age, became known.

Enumeration is equally apparent in Festus' description how woollen balls and woollen dolls of men and women would be suspended for the *lares compitales* as a replacement for human sacrifices: one ball would be hung up for each slave, and one doll for each free person.[2] This explicit reference to slaves invites scrutiny of their role in the cult. Dionysius of Halicarnassus (XIV, 14, 3-4) relates how slaves should assist in the cult, 'the ministry of servants being looked upon as pleasing to the heroes (i.e. the *lares*).'

> And they still observe the ancient custom in connection with those sacrifices, propitiating the heroes by the ministry of their servants, and during these days removing every badge of their servitude, in order that the slaves, being softened by this instance of *philanthrôpia*[3] which has something great and solemn about it, may make themselves more agreeable to their masters (i.e. owners) and be less sensible of the severity of their condition.

The similarity to the temporary removal of status distinctions during the *Saturnalia* is unmistakable. And it is a removal that

[1] D.H. IV 14 & 15,1-2 for treating 'compitalia' and 'paganalia' as parallel institutions. Cf. Flambard (1981) 149 - 151.

[2] Festus s.v. 'pilae et effigies' ed. Lindsay^2 p.343 f. Macrobius, 'Saturnalia' I 7,34,35 offers a variant, with heads of garlic and poppies, or 'maniae'. Cf. Flambard (1981) 156 n. 89 and Radke (1983).

[3] 'Philanthrôpia' in preference to the misleading 'humanity' of the Loeb translation.

not only concerns slaves, but also freedmen. During the *Compitalia* the *magistri*, who were freedmen, were allowed to wear the *toga praetexta*, a garb that was normally the privilege of magistrates and, therefore, something which they could never have in 'real' life.[1] To be *magister* of a *vicus* was, however, not the only 'pseudo' office that up and coming freedmen could aspire to. The most prestigious - and best documented - of these surrogates was of course the institution of the *augustales*.[2] Characteristically both the position of the *magistri vici* (or *vici et compiti*) and that of *augustales* was modelled on the proper magistracies. In this way a freedman might have a remarkable pseudo *cursus honorum*. It was indeed perceived in direct imitation of a proper *cursus*, as is evident from the funerary epigraphy. And it was a *cursus honorum* that could even begin before manumission: the *ministri vicorum* were usually slaves.[3] Of course this could only happen with the permission of their masters; in fact, one would presume that it occurred at the instigation of these masters. It demonstrates that freedmen's public careers were not a break with their past in slavery, but a continuation. Obligation to the master had been necessary to become *minister* and to be manumitted, the further career would owe much to the patron's support, and demanded continued obligation. Each stage is both an incentive and a test for socialization.[4]

Like magistrates, the *magistri vicorum* were assisted by attendants during the *Compitalia*: as if proper magistrates they would preside over the banquet.[5] After the Augustan reform of

[1] '... ludos facere et praetextatum volitare passus es ...' Asconius p. 7 ed. Clark. The 'toga praetexta' was also worn by boys (and girls). Originally by boys of noble birth, to mark their predestination for office; later especially by sons of 'liberti', to mark their aspirations of social ascent. The parallel with 'magistri' wearing the 'praetexta' is obvious. For more extended discussion, below, p. 318.

[2] Duthoy (1974) and Duthoy (1978) for 'augustales'. Hopkins (1978a) 211, in an otherwise very perceptive discussion, seems to confuse 'augustales' and 'vicomagistri'.

[3] See e.g. Niebling (1956); Flambard (1983); Bömer (1957-61) vol. I 38, and Castrén (1975) 72. Also below, p. 305.

[4] Above, p. 258 ff.

[5] 'Solebant autem magistri collegiorum ludos facere, sicut magistri vicorum faciebant Compitalicios praetextati, qui ludi sublatis collegiis discussi sunt.'

7 B.C. they were provided with one, or perhaps two, *lictores*.[1] In his discussion of republican *collegia compitalicia* Flambard assigns two functions to these *collegia*: integration and substitution.[2] The integrative function creates a training ground for civic vocabulary and behaviour. The predominance of freedmen means that these *collegia* perform a temporary function: the sons can do without them. By substitution he means what I have earlier called 'pseudo careers'. Even though these are in many respects not for real, they still provide a measure of satisfaction.

Yet, such ritual could easily backfire. It assumes that the temporary removal of status inferiority serves to reinforce the acceptance of inferiority at other times. But it might become a mode of expression for a desire to extend the status positions from the ritual into every day life. And indeed, in the political struggles of the late Republic the *collegia vicorum* play an important part, forming nothing other than private armies.[3] When Cicero describes Clodius' supporters in 58 B.C, he will miss no opportunity to describe them as slaves and rabble. But it is not an amorphous group, and his indignation is expressed in an account that stresses the importance of *vici* for seditious politicians, and which is couched in military terms.[4]

> ... a levy of slaves was held on the front of the Tribunal of Aurelius on the pretext of forming clubs: men were enlisted *vicus* by *vicus*, formed into squads, and incited to force, deeds of violence, murder and robbery. (Cic. *Pro Sestio* 34)

Asconius (ed. Clark p. 7). Cf. Flambard (1981) 152. For slave participation in festivities: Cic. 'Att.' 2.3.4; 7.7.3. Cato gave extra wine rations ('Agr.' 57).

[1]Flambard (1981) 160; Dio LV 8, 7. Purcell (1983) for 'apparitores'.

[2]Flambard (1981) 165 f.

[3]Flambard (1977) and Flambard (1981) are the best discussions. C.f. Nippel (1981).

[4]Cicero, Pro Sestio 34: '... servorum dilectus habebatur pro tribunali Aurelio nomine collegiorum, cum vicatim homines conscriberentur, decuriarentur, ad vim, ad manus, ad caedem, ad direptionem incitarentur.' Cicero, 'post red. in sen.' 33: 'simulatione collegiorum nominatim .... conscriptos.' Cicero, 'de domo' 54: 'ex omnibus vicis concitatos.' Also: Flambard (1977) 123.

Cicero's insistence that these were all slaves should presumably be taken as a slanderous way of saying that they were mostly freedmen.[1] The *collegia vicorum* were the backbone of the political revolt of the time. Cicero's concern about the 'Gestalt' change that they had undergone is evident in his words: '*...simulatione collegiorum...*' and '*...nomine collegiorum...*' This was not what they were meant to be![2] Legislation in the years 65-55 B.C. closely reflects the vicissitudes of political supremacy, and identifies the *sodalicia* or *collegia* not only with street violence, but also with electoral bribes and pressurizing of the electorate.[3] Clodius' supporters had not only agitated in a desire for petty bribes: once in office in 58 B.C. Clodius secured the passing of the *Lex Clodia Annonaria*, which abolished payment for the distributions of grain, and attempted to make the *collegia* responsible for the distribution.[4]

The subversive potential of the *collegia* of the *vici* had become plainly visible, and legislation followed.[5] It was Augustus, however, who also recognized their potential for integration and social stability.[6] The character and location of competition within the elite had changed through the concentration of power in the emperor's hands: the court had become its focus, rather than the senate.[7] *Collegia* could no longer serve as instruments in factional strife. Augustus had become the *primus inter pares*, and therefore these *collegia* were potentially his. In 7 B.C. the *collegia vicorum* of Rome (and subsequently also those of Italian cities) were reconstituted.[8] The cult of the *lares genii Augusti* is added to the existing cult of the *lares compitales*. In this manner Augustus brings about a fusion

[1]Flambard (1977) 123 n30.

[2]Cicero, 'post red. in sen.' 33 and 'Pro Sestio' 34.

[3]Flambard (1977) esp. 123 f; Nicolet (1976a) 415 ff; Taylor (1949) 210 n. 101 and n. 102.

[4]The 'recensio' was probably executed 'vicatim'. Flambard (1977) 145 ff. Nicolet (1976b) 29 - 51

[5]Flambard (1981) 164 ff.

[6]Best discussion in Hopkins (1978a) 211 ff.

[7]Hopkins (1983a) 122.

[8]Niebling (1956).

between local loyalty and loyalty towards himself as symbol of the existing social and political order. The similarity to that other organization for the imperial cult, the *augustales*, is striking. In both cases it is precisely freedmen who are charged with the cult: it is an incentive and reward for socialization. The minor officials (*ministri*) in the *collegia vicorum* were still slaves; after manumission they might expect to become *magistri*. Socialization of freedmen started before their manumission- and would be rewarded by this manumission. Their involvement in the imperial cult is also a feature of the later North African *curiae*, and is amply attested.[1]

How much of all this can we find back in Pompeii, and can we perhaps trace these matters in closer detail in the electoral propaganda in the town? The first instance where we find *collegia* in what has undoubtedly a flavour of late republican agitation is in the riot of A.D. 59 which was the subject of a well known wall painting (Plate XXXII), and is related by Tacitus (*Annales* XIV xvii) in the following words:

> About the same date, a trivial incident led to a serious affray between the inhabitants of the colonies of Nuceria and Pompeii, at a gladiatorial show presented by Livineius Regulus, whose removal from the senate has been noticed. During an exchange of raillery, typical of the petulance of country towns, they resorted to abuse, then to stones, and finally to steel; the superiority lying with the populace of Pompeii, where the show was being exhibited. As a result, many of the Nucerians were carried maimed and wounded to the capital, while a very large number mourned the deaths of children or of parents. The trial of the affair was delegated by the emperor to the senate; by the senate to the consuls. On the case being again laid before the members, the Pompeians as a community were debarred from holding any similar assembly for ten years, and the associations which they had formed illegally were

[1] Kotula (1968) 77 ff. Besides the imperial cult we hear of other deities, though here we may find divergence between the Italian and the North African evidence.

> dissolved.[1] Livineius and the other fomenters of the outbreak were punished with exile.

In its brevity, this text leaves a lot unsolved, and speculation has been rife. At the very least, however, it once again demonstrates the importance of gladiatorial shows as political theatre. A political theatre that might take to the streets.[2] In the present context the central question no doubt concerns the *collegia* mentioned in the text. The relative clause '...*quae contra leges instituerant*...' is indeed probably restrictive.[3] Yet, this does not bring us much closer to an identification of the *collegia* involved. Moeller and Richardson have suggested the involvement of *collegia iuvenum*, but cannot deliver any evidence.[4] To quote a skeptical Castrén: 'I find, however, that the very existence of this *collegium iuvenum* is questionable, and that the doubtful evidence does not allow it to be given too much value.'[5] But even if such a *collegium* did indeed exist, the Moeller and Richardson argument is still no more than that such riots are occasions in which *collegia iuvenum* would be involved. Galsterer's elaborations on these flights of fancy are no less circumstantial.[6] The only piece of further evidence that we have is a graffito that implicates *Campani* in the riot (CIL IV 1293):

CAMPANI VICTORIA UNA CUM NUCERINIS PERISTIS

There is some controversy over the construction of the sentence, which leaves in doubt whether the Campani had been

[1]'... collegiaque quae contra leges instituerant dissoluta ...'

[2]Hopkins (1983a) ch. 1 for murderous games and political theatre.

[3]Moeller (1970b) 86.

[4]Richardson (1955) 88 - 93; Moeller (1970b); followed by Galsterer (1980). Typical of the sloppy logic is the list in Richardson (1955) 91 that is supposed to support the notion of a 'collegium iuvenum Campanorum', but which only contains inscriptions mentioning Campani 'tout court'. They might refer to a 'collegium iuvenum', but only on the condition that we already have independent and unequivocal evidence for such 'collegium'.

[5]Castrén (1975) 33.

[6]Galsterer (1980).

on the side of the Nucerians, or on the Pompeian side.[1] But the important question of course concerns the identity of these '*Campani*'. They could be Capuans, but that would probably have been important enough for Tacitus to mention it.[2] Richardson and Moeller have connected them to a *collegium iuvenum*, but evidence to support this is lacking. Earlier, Mau had equated the *Campani* to the well known *Campanienses* as the inhabitants of a *vicus Campanus*.[3] This may indeed be true, and if so, the *vici* were indeed implicated in the riot, and showed that some of their riotous potential still existed, notwithstanding the Augustan reorganization.[4]

Unless further information becomes available we cannot, however, be certain that the *collegia* involved in the riot were the *collegia vicorum*. And a riot such as this is by no means a good example of elite control and successful curbs on popular participation. For that we must turn to the primary battle ground: the elections.

I shall attempt to argue two related points about the elections. Taken together these points provide the framework for an understanding of how these elections could be an instrument of elite control. The first point is that Pompeian electoral propaganda provides ample documentation of an active role for *collegia vicorum*. Candidates had their strongholds in their own ward, and the collegiate organization of the ward's cult was a powerful instrument in the mobilization of support. Libertine aspirations for integration are the other side of this same coin. The second point is that probably these *collegia vicorum* existed inside the town's electoral districts, and could pose as 'representatives' of all inhabitants of the ward. If this is indeed true, it means that right at the core of official electoral organization

[1]The first possibility: Campanians, in a single victory you perished with the Nucerians. Or alternatively: Campanians, in victory you perished together with the Nucerians. Richardson (1955) 89.

[2]Contra: Sgobbo (1942) 37.

[3]Mau (1889) 299 f. Unfortunately he translates 'vicus' here as village. Below, 304.

[4]Cf. Cicero's words of disapproval: '... simulatione collegiorum ...' ('post red. in sen.' 33) and '... nomine collegiorum ...' ('Pro Sestio' 34). Above, p. 299)

we have groups of officials actively ensuring the election of specific candidates; officials who are of lowly origin, with ambitions of social ascent and integration, and dependent of elite patronage. The argument that I want to present runs as follows:

The normal words for electoral districts (*curiae* or *tribus*) do not occur in the Pompeian evidence. On the other hand, *vicini* and *vicus* are well attested. These *vici* resemble what we know about *curiae*. Pompeii's electoral districts were therefore probably called *vici*, and as electoral districts they encompassed all free citizens of the town.

However, within these *vici* there were *collegia* (of restricted membership) responsible for the cult of the *lares compitales* and the imperial cult. In them, a prominent role was given to the slaves and freedmen of important families. When *vicini* actively campaign for specific candidates it is, therefore, likely that they should be understood as members of the *collegium vici*, a restricted group of - fairly dependent - persons within the ward, and not as the entire electorate of a district.

If this is correct, the implication is that even though there were undoubtedly still elections in Pompeii (and presumably all citizens could still vote in them) these were to some extent controlled, or dominated, by a small group within the electorate. A small group that was dependent upon elite patronage for their personal social mobility. Their cult activities are revealing in this respect. Both because they mimic magisterial activity, and because they stress integration of social risers to elite norms and values. Here we may have the solution to our paradox of the coexistence of elections and a social structure which gives enormous power to an elite.

As I said, Pompeii provides no instances of the terms *curia* or *tribus* for electoral districts or collegiate organizations in wards. Future finds are unlikely to alter this, because - I shall argue - Pompeii had *vici* (and - at least - one *pagus*). *Vicini* are supporters of candidates in numerous Pompeian *programmata*.[1] Traditionally this has been taken to refer to a

[1]Franklin (1980) 92 ff.

candidate's immediate neighbours, and has therefore been used as one of the means to identify the occupant of a house.[1] Even though the word could undoubtedly have this meaning, it is mistaken in our case. The first reason is that *vicini* (or *vicani*[2]) in the sense of members of a *collegium vici et compiti* are well attested in the epigraphy of other towns and in the literary sources concerning late republican Rome.[3] The second reason is that the programmata not only provide instances of the general term *vicini*. Instead, in a number of cases we hear particular names: *Forenses*, *Urbulanenses*, *Campanienses* and *Salinienses*.[4] Are these the names of *vicini* of a particular *vicus*? It was Willems who first ventured the idea that these named groups referred to electoral districts.[5] This met with fierce criticism from Mommsen, who commented that one could just as easily, and unjustifiably, link the *vicini* to the electoral districts.[6] Little could he know that a subsequent epigraphical find would demonstrate that - at least - the *Urbulanenses* were indeed *vicini*: in an - admittedly mutilated - inscription (CIL IV 7807, my Figure XVIII) we have what must be an *album* of *magistri* and *ministri* of what is explicitly called a *vicus*, and we can read the letters VRBVL in the third line. Therefore, they must be the *magistri* and *ministri vici et compiti Urbulani*.

Even though a large part of the inscription has been lost, we can still recognize the familiar traits of a collegiate *album*.[7]

[1]Della Corte (1965) p. 3 - 25 outlines the principle. Cf. above, p. 173 for at least one hard nut to crack.

[2]Flambard (1981) 144 ff. makes no bones about the identity of 'vicini' and 'vicani'. The latin thesaurus has unfortunately not yet reached as far as 'vicinus', but its director Dr. Flury kindly allowed me to consult the card files, where a scholar from an older age left a note scribbled on a card: 'vicinus = vicanus?'. Cf. also ILS 7010, where a 'vicina optima' is honoured by 'vicani'.

[3]CIL XI 377, 379, 417, 418, 419, 421; 'AE' 1954, n. 168; CIL X 415; Duncan-Jones (1982) 229, 232, 277-287. In CIL XI 4815 the 'magistri vicorum' are similar, but not identical, to the 'compitales Larum Augustorum'. Flambard (1981) 147 f.

[4]'Forenses': CIL IV 783; for CIL IV 60: below, p. 305. 'Urbulanenses': CIL IV 7807 (see below, p.000), 7706, 7747, 7676. 'Campanienses': CIL IV 371, 470, 480. 'Salinienses': CIL IV 128, also 1611, 4106, 5181.

[5]Willems (1887) 134 ff.

[6]Mommsen (1871-1888) vol. III, 350.

[7]For such albums: Waltzing (1895-1900) Vol. I 362 ff.

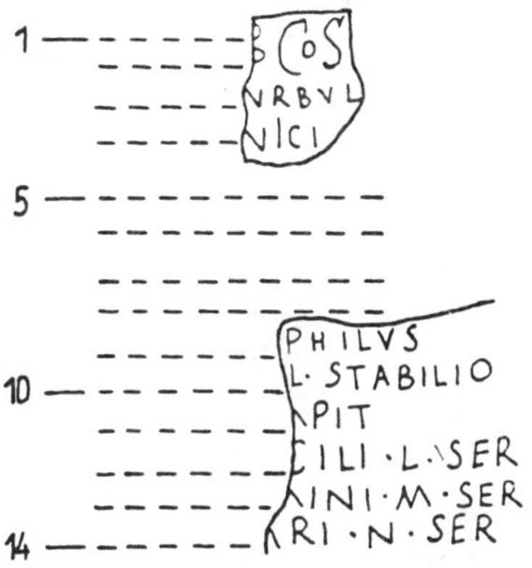

Figure XVIII: CIL IV 7807

In the first two lines we read a date, followed by the name of the *collegium* in the third line. Lines 4 and 11 must be captions for lists of officials (one would presume *magistri* and *ministri*). In the first group there is room for six names; the last two names have survived in part (lines 9 & 10) and indicate freedmen.[1] In the second group we have three slaves (lines 12, 13, 14).[2] With this inscription we have established the probable existence of a *vicus Urbulanus* (or *Urbulanensis*) in Pompeii, and it is not far fetched to argue from analogy for the

[1]The reading in Sgobbo (1942) 36, allowing for only three 'magistri', should now, with the availability of a proper CIL text, be discarded.

[2]A total of nine officials can also be found in an earlier (47 - 46 B.C.) inscription (CIL IV 60); there, all are 'magistri'. Because the text of CIL IV 7807 contains two groups, it is perhaps the case that after Augustus reform of 7 B.C. slaves would be made 'ministri'. Cf. the four 'ministri pagi Aug. Felicis suburbani primi' in 7 B.C, among whom 'Dama pupi Agrippae [servus]' (CIL X 924). In both CIL IV 60 and CIL IV 7807 the total number of officials is nine, which may serve as a serious argument against the tortuous efforts in Mommsen (1843) 75 f. to construct the 'compiti' as an organizational level above the 'vici'. Excellent discussion in Flambard (1981) 151 ff. Uncharacteristically, Castrén (1975) 73 passes speculation for fact when he says that CIL IV 60 refers to officials of the 'vicus Forensis'. He may be right, but the text does not substantiate his claim, only based on the location of the find. The text of the inscription is mutilated, but allows a speculative reconstruction with first six free men, followed by three slave 'magistri'. At this time some 'magistri' were still freeborn: a Blattius M. f. and a C. Ermatorius P. f. head the list for 46.

existence of a *vicus Forensis*[1], a *vicus Campaniensis* and a *vicus Saliniensis* (*vel sim.*). Equally, it would be too skeptical to assume that only the *vicus Urbulanus* had its *collegium*. The *vicini* of these *vici* cannot be 'neighbours', and these *vici* are regional divisions of the town.[2] But are the *vici* the electoral districts?

The presence of *collegia vicorum* does not, after all, preclude the existence of electoral wards of the same name, nor does it exclude the possibility that all Pompeian citizens could still vote in the elections. The ubiquity of the electoral propaganda, and the regulations in the municipal charters are sufficient testimony that elections were still being held. Can we find these electoral wards, and can we also find evidence for *vici* in a wider sense of the word, such as that for *curiae* or *tribus* as electoral districts of towns, comprising all citizens? Some authors believe that this is indeed the case and that the *vici* (of the *Forenses*, *Campanienses*, *Urbulanenses*, and *Salinienses*[3]) were the voting districts of the town.[4] Their most important argument is that Pompeii would have to have such voting districts, and that the substantial Pompeian evidence shows no traces of *curiae*, *tribus*, or *regiones*, the other possible candidates. If *vici* are not voting districts we would have to face the existence of two separate systems of territorial division of the town, or alternatively a two-tier system.[5] Everything is possible in principle (and the city of Rome provides ample documentation of the range of possibilities) but such complication seems overdone in a small city such as Pompeii.[6] But can we go beyond this 'it has to be the case' argument? The similarity between *vici* and some of the other divisions elsewhere is

[1]But see p. 304 f.

[2]Castrén (1975) 79 ff, relying on Spano (1937), Accame (1942) and Sgobbo (1942). See also below, p. 308.

[3]And perhaps the 'Pagus Augustus Felix Suburbanus' I might add, with much hesitation, because evidence is completely lacking.

[4]Castrén (1975) 79 ff, with references to older literature.

[5]With perhaps 'vici' as subdivisions of electoral districts.

[6]Rome's complexity is of course home grown, unlike the imposed arrangements of the 'leges municipales'.

notable. Collegiate presence is also part of the story of the *curiae*, including meals and other festivities. And so is the combination of the imperial cult and some more local deities.[1] A strong argument is that all these bodies are sometimes related to city gates. In Pompeii at least three of the four *vici* were named after city gates.[2]

The find-spots of the posters with these *Forenses*, *Urbulanenses*, *Campanienses* and *Salinienses* coincide with the presumed location of these *vici*, indicating that the wards were indeed relevant units for canvassing.[3] The *dipinti* with just *'vicini'* as supporters should therefore be taken as referring to *vicini* of a *vicus* whose identity would be obvious even without the mention of a name. In principle these *vicini* could of course belong to any of the (at least) four *vici* of the town. But they are notably concentrated near the houses of the candidates that they favour.[4] Those were occasions where a name would be unnecessary. Clustering can sometimes also be demonstrated with other *programmata*.[5] The problem is that if a candidate's support extends over a large part of the town, this still does not exclude the possibility that it consists of an accumulation of localized support in many parts of the town. Sometimes we can demonstrate that this is indeed the way in which the absence of clustering around one point should be interpreted. We should not be surprised: a candidate needed support in more than one district in order to be elected.[6] Because *programmata* have survived in such large numbers, the campaigns of M. Casellius Marcellus and L. Albucius Celsus for the aedileship (in A.D. 78) provide interesting documentation. They had joined forces in this campaign, and for each of them the *programmata* are

[1]Kotula (1968) 75 ff.

[2]Spano (1937) for Pompeii. See also Sgobbo (1942), Accame (1942) and Camodeca (1977). Kotula (1968) 26 ff. reviews the north African evidence. CIL VIII 26517: 'omnium portarum sententiis'.

[3]Castrén (1975) 81 f.

[4]Franklin (1980) 87. The argument has an element of circularity, but I still accept it, if only because there is so little evidence against it.

[5]Franklin (1980) 92 discusses the evidence. Franklin (1981) provides lists and maps.

[6]Above, p. 290.

concentrated around their own house and that of their running mate.[1] For other candidates such patterns of support can also be discerned, but never so clearly. Domination of a ward by one family can be surmised from the fact that several Puteolian *regiones* and *vici* carry the names of distinguished families.[2]

The Pompeian evidence resists the choice between *vici* as either electoral districts (grouping all citizens) or as *collegia* of limited size. There must have been electoral districts in Pompeii, and they were probably called *vici*. However, within these *vici* there are unmistakable signs of *collegia* of limited size. We only need to think of the *magistri*, *ministri*, the *alba* and the meetings.[3] *Vicini* are prominently present in the electoral propaganda. Are they the *collegiati* of their *vicus*, or do they refer to all voters, who would - in that case unanimously- support one particular candidate?

Unaided unanimity is, as I have said, suspicious. And if it were real there would hardly be any reason for so much propaganda in their own district. *Vicini* in the sense of *collegiati* are quite well attested from other Italian towns.[4] Pompeii is not so generous with unequivocal information on this score. I have earlier pointed to the similarity between *pagi* and *vici*, so perhaps it is justified to quote some Pompeian evidence on *pagani* here.[5]

In a number of Pompeian funerary inscriptions the qualification *paganus* is applied to the deceased.[6] Because the title is

[1]Franklin (1980) 93. For pairing of candidates: below, p. 312 ff.

[2]Camodeca (1977) 70 ('regio Hortensiana'), 73 ('regio vici Vestoriani et Calpurniani'), 75 ff. for several extramural 'vici'. Also: D'Arms (1974) 113, 118.

[3]One inscription refers to the latter (CIL IV 5181): 'VII K Dec. Salinis in conventu, multa HSS XX.'

[4]Above, p. 292 ff.

[5]Above, p. 295 f.

[6]The Pompeian 'Pagus Augustus Felix Suburbanus' remains enigmatic, even after all the ink that has been spilled over it. Castrén (1975) 72 f, 81, 122, 274 f. provides a skeptical account, concentrating on what we know (the officials) rather than on what we do not know (what and where it was) but might still like to know. For the argument for analogy: above, p. 295 f. 'Paganus' in funerary epigraphy: CIL X 1027-1028, 'Notizie degli Scavi di Antichità' 1894, p.15, CIL X 1030, plus an unpublished one from Porta Nocera, E 9a-d on Eschebach's map (see Castrén (1975) 193).

presented as if it were part of a *cursus 'honorum'* it must refer to some sort of distinction, and is, therefore, unlikely to just mean 'inhabitant of the *pagus*': that would not be a distinction. And in a recently found inscription the deceased *duovir* M. Obellius Firmus is honoured separately by the *pagani* (they give thirty pounds of frankincense and a *clipeus*) and by their *ministri* (who give H.S. 1000 for unspecified perfumes and another *clipeus*).[1] Such expenditure by *pagani* is perhaps easier to imagine if they are members of the *plebs* of a *collegium* than if they are just inhabitants of a - possibly rural - district.[2] If *pagani* are *collegiati*, then by analogy *vicini*, *Urbulanenses* and the like must refer to members of the *plebs collegii vici et compiti*.

Even if I am wrong and the territorial divisions for organizing support (the *collegia vicorum*) were not identical to those for the expression of support (the electoral districts), it would still remain true that local loyalties and patron-client relationships played an important part in political behaviour. What we have gained in knowledge is that these elections may have existed in a context where political support for candidates was at least in part organized by semi-official *collegia* that were both the focus of local loyalties and a means of binding these loyalties and the ambitions of lower groups in society (such as freedmen) to the highest authority in the state. Elections were not (or no longer) an instrument to bring about social change.

That neighbourhood loyalties were so prominent, both as expressions of solidarity between the poorer members of society, and as instruments of elite control, is perhaps not so surprising in a face-to-face society. In very general terms this is nothing unique or peculiarly Roman. Of course, comparative material should be used with much caution, but the temptation is too seductive to resist. Jacques Heers' *Le clan familial au moyen age* clearly demonstrates that neighbourhoods and neighbourhood

[1] Jongman (1978-79). See now also De Caro (1979a) 65-71. Note that the 'ministri', who must have been slaves, had quite considerable financial means.

[2] CIL X 415 provides a parallel with 'vicani' rather than 'pagani'. Cf. Jacques (1984) 419.

organizations (*vicinie*, *sestiers*, *fanti portes* etc.) were important means of mutual support and control, and of resistance to the urban nobility.[1] Often named after city gates, they organized games, had officials and held meetings.

> Ces Sociétés populaires des Portes, puissantes et, en bien des villes, parfaitement organisées, s'opposaient au XIIIe siècle aux grandes familles nobles qui, très souvent, gardaient, elles, une des tours de l'enciente. Plus tard, elles perdent, certes, leur caractère proprement militaire et politique mais se maintiennent parfois sous la forme d'associations de voisins, de natures fort diverses.[2]

The other side of the coin, local dependence and patronage, can equally be documented from the medieval record.[3] The great families tend to live in the same areas for many generations. Members of the same clan prefer to live close together. And next to the great *domus* would be living many of their dependents: 'C'est derrière l'hôtel principal, au-delà de la cour ou du jardin, que se trouvent les dépendances, les magasins, les *dominiculae*, maisonnettes, loges ou cabanes.'[4] The resemblance to a Pompeian *domus* surrounded by satellite workshops and habitation is too striking to be ignored.

It would obviously be foolish to make too much out of such resemblance. It would be even more foolish to suggest that because much - including terminology - appears similar, the explanation must be direct continuity.[5] On closer inspection, much may turn out to be different. But it also shows that such closer inspection may be interesting, both to the ancient historian, and to the medievalist.

[1] Heers (1974) 146 ff.

[2] Heers (1974) 149.

[3] Heers (1974) 151 ff.

[4] Heers (1974) 156.

[5] Mickwitz (1936) for the comparable case of the professional 'collegia'.

Support from the few

The mobilization of support in one's own electoral district was obviously necessary; without it political ambitions would be illusory. I have argued that organizations of local cults played an important role in this mobilization. The prominence of freedmen in these cults not only indicates the means by which the lower classes and their aspirations are integrated into the fabric of society, but also presupposes cooperation between elite residents of the ward: not all members of such a *collegium* would have the same patron. Candidates would need the support of patrons to make the *collegia* an instrument for their ambition. It is this dependence of candidates on the political establishment that we shall now turn to. In order to understand why we do this, we must remind ourselves of the question that has been the continuing thread in much that has gone before: to what extent was it possible for social risers with a background in commerce and manufacturing to penetrate the elite without completely reneging on the values and behaviour of their past. In other words, could social mobility seriously alter the values and behaviour of the elite to the effect that the elite might be more amenable to the sort of economically innovative behaviour characteristic of the later *bourgeoisie*? The alternative is that even though many may have risen into the elite, they did so as individuals, and by adapting to elite values and modes of behaviour. Was mobility a challenge or a renewal?

I shall argue that even if - perhaps - quite a few entrants to the *ordo* might be social risers, their entrance and further ascent was not unconditional, but depended on the approval of the sitting members of the *ordo*. Internally the *ordo* itself was highly stratified, and I shall try to demonstrate that each successive step on the ladder required the support of those in higher positions. I shall also argue that barriers to further advancement were real, and would in many cases not be removed by the advance of age. The need to conform was strong and social mobility could, therefore, not be a route to give effect to social dissent.

In order to develop my point I shall follow two lines of argument. The first is to investigate the remaining Pompeian evidence for traces of elite control upon entry to its body. Contested elections will be shown to have only existed in the case of the lower magistracies, the aedileship, and not in case of the higher and more powerful posts of *duovir* and *quinquennalis*.[1] In addition I shall argue that the *ordo* made (probably quite successful) efforts to control which candidates were elected as aediles. My second line of argument departs from Pompeian evidence in order to investigate the origin of those who aspired to become decurions. Employing demographic simulation techniques I shall argue that the town must have had a sizeable number of decurions who had entered without having been magistrate and who could either not hope to become aedile at all, or would have to wait a fairly long period before they could stand. And precisely this bottom group in the *ordo* would be coopted by its existing members, rather than elected.

We shall begin with the elections. The favoured means to increase one's support in elections would seem to have been for candidates to stand as a pair, a practice much maligned in the Republic, and at periods illegal.[2] The Pompeian electoral epigraphy supplies many examples of such pairs.[3] This pairing does not originate in the preferences of individual supporters: with only one possible exception a candidate is always only teamed up with the same other candidate.[4] The best documented pair is that of L. Albucius Celsus and M. Casellius Marcellus, candidates for the aedileship in A.D. 78. They are supported as a pair in twenty six programmata. Only two of the twenty four known

[1]The elections for the aedileship may have been contested, but a ceiling on the number of candidates seems to have been in operation: in no year do we know of more than four candidates for two posts. Franklin (1980) table 6 lists the evidence.

[2]Nicolet (1976a) 415 ff; Taylor (1949) 36, 64, 68, 210 n.102. The term is 'coitio': Gelzer (1912) 102.

[3]Franklin (1980) 36-44 lists all the evidence.

[4]The exception is A. Vettius Firmus, if the Vettius Firmus from CIL IV 380 should be read as A. Vettius Firmus, and not as C. Vettius Firmus (known from CIL IV 6851-6852). Franklin (1980) 40 chooses the praenomen A. Another - and not unlikely - solution to the problem is that Vettius Firmus stood twice, with different partners. Franklin (1980) 68 anticipates this solution, and his Table 6 shows that the link with Vettius Firmus is the only chronological peg for C. Sallustius Capito.

aedilician candidates from the last nine years of Pompeii's existence cannot be demonstrated as a pair: L. Ceius Secundus and M. Holconius Priscus, aedilician candidates in A.D. 76.[1] Of course, we do not know the names of all candidates, and paired candidates have a higher chance to be dated because more points of reference become available. However, even if we assume that none of the unknown candidates of these years were paired, the paired candidates still form at least 61% of all candidates.[2] Probably aediles usually stood as pairs.

In the case of the duovirate, the situation is somewhat different. In no year do we know the names of more than two candidates, suggesting to Franklin that elections for the duovirate went uncontested.[3] Proving absence is a hard task indeed, but we know two candidates, no more and no less, in each and every of the last seven years of the city's existence. And these fourteen candidates are each supported in on average 32.3 programmata: documentation is good, so we need not fear that the result is due to the chance survival of only a few documents. A possible falsification of this view of uncontested elections for the duovirate could be the presence in our documentation of a well attested (and therefore recent) but undated candidate for the duovirate, but no such person exists.[4]

We need perhaps not be so surprised that these were uncontested elections. If - apart from a few exceptions - *duoviri* were recruited from former aediles, the number of potential candidates might be fairly small: each year would only produce two new ex aediles. And some of these would die before they had a chance to stand for the duovirate.[5] Only considerable inequality within the *ordo* (with thus, for some, much reiteration in the duovirate) could substantially diminish the chances of all surviving former aediles to become *duovir*. We do not know to what extent this was the case. If it was common, the lack of

[1] Franklin (1980) compare his tables 1, 3 and 9.

[2] This assumes four candidates for the aedileship each year, not unreasonable given Franklin (1980) table 9. At least 22 candidates stood as a pair.

[3] Franklin (1980) 69, 100.

[4] For lists of candidates: Castrén (1975) 270 ff.

[5] The risk of dying would depend on age and length of time, below p. 321 ff.

opportunity (for some) to become *duovir* would probably, however, not have increased the number of candidates standing for the duovirate. Exclusion (for some) from the duovirate is precisely the expression of inequality within the elite, and is therefore unlikely to have been challenged effectively.

Candidates for the duovirate also seem to normally stand as a pair: in five of the last seven years they are supported as a pair in one or more programmata. Yet, the meaning of pairing for the duovirate must be something other than mutual support if there were never more than two candidates (they would be elected in any case). Notification was, however, still necessary, and persons supporting one candidate might wish to express support for the other as well.[1]

Mutual support by candidates obviously locked them into a web of future obligations towards one another, and presumably also towards the powerful among each other's supporters. The potential inequality of such relations was perhaps strongest where we find pairing between future *duoviri* and candidates for the aedileship. A very unequal team is that of L. Veranius Hypsaeus (three times *duovir* and *quinquennalis* candidate) and Casellius Marcellus, aedilician candidate: *optimos collegas*.[2] Mutual obligation is beautifully expressed in CIL IV 635:

SABINVM.AED.
PROCVLE.FAC.ET.ILLE
TE.FACIET

Proculus is exhorted to support Sabinus for the aedileship and

[1]We may surmise from the Lex Municipalis Malacitana LI that elections would in fact be held even if the results were known beforehand.

[2]CIL IV 187. This inscription should raise some doubts as to the accuracy of Franklin's reconstruction. M. Casellius Marcellus would be candidate for the aedileship in A.D. 78 - Franklin (1980) 62 f. - which is no quinquennial year. Two arguments to save his chronology would seem possible. The first is that one could postulate an earlier - failed - attempt. This is conceivable, but in that case the support of the 'quinquennalis' Hypsaeus would have been ineffectual, which is difficult to believe. Alternatively, one may believe that the Casellius Marcellus of CIL IV 187 is a different person from the aedilician candidate of A.D. 78. Or, Franklin's chronology could be wrong.

is told: he will also vote for you![1] The number of programmata showing pairing between duoviral and aedilician candidates is small, and yet we know of such pairings for four out of the last seven years.[2] This leads us to the presumption that such pairing would occur in (almost) every year. An interesting example of ties between important members of the *ordo* and prospective magistrates is afforded by the campaign of A.D. 77. One of the two candidates for the duovirate is A. Suettius Certus, probably the father of A. Suettius Verus, who is one of the four candidates for the aedileship in that same year.[3] But the support that young aspiring aediles could give to future *duoviri* or *quinquennales* would obviously be different from that offered by these powerful men, who were after all certain of election. So we may say that young aediles became magistrates on credit. Whether such credit was available to everyone on equally easy terms is of course a different matter: it could only be given to one pair of aspiring aediles each year.

It is worth investigating possible differences between those aedilician candidates who receive support from the future *duoviri*, and those who do not. Franklin has observed that it seems as if precisely the candidates from the least prominent families were supported in the largest number of election posters.[4] Prominence (or rather, the lack of it) is hard to establish, because much depends on the survival of documentation from earlier (and therefore less well known) periods. But Franklin is probably right. If we define prominent candidates as those who receive the support of the future *duoviri*, the correlation is impressive: aedilician candidates who had to do without duoviral support appear in twice as many programmata as those who are the future duovirs' favorites.[5] The

[1] Most likely Proculus is P. Paquius Proculus, 'duovir' candidate in A.D. 74, and Sabinus is M. Epidius Sabinus, aedilician candidate in that same year. They are known (CIL IV 222, 660) to form a pair.

[2] Franklin (1980) tables 3 and 9.

[3] Franklin (1980) esp. 42, 65 f; Castrén (1975) 'ad nom'.

[4] Franklin (1980) 94-100.

[5] With support from candidate 'duoviri': mean = 34; without: mean = 70. This uses the data from Franklin (1980) tables 3, 8 and 9, but only for the last seven

documentation is good enough to make it highly unlikely that this a chance result.

This is an important result for two reasons. The first is that it invalidates the use of electoral posters as a measure of a candidate's popularity[1]; they probably reflect campaigning effort. The second is that it underlines the hold of the existing political elite on entry into its body. If the elections for the duovirate went indeed uncontested, this means that the candidates for that office were in fact the *ordo*'s more or less official candidates. Chosen from among its members, they would require the formal seal of approval of the older of the two current *duoviri* before they could stand.[2] And now we see that they in turn - and presumably on behalf of the *ordo* - lend their prestige to some of the candidates for the aedileship.[3] A support that seems worth quite a lot: those lacking it need at least twice as many *programmata* to have a fighting chance. We are unable to see whether the support from the future *duoviri*, and by implication that of the *ordo*, was of decisive importance. But one would presume that it counted for much, or else these favoured candidates would have made sure that they were supported in more *programmata*.

If anything, this analysis of support between candidates has served to underline the inequalities within the elite, and the dependent position of aspiring members. The existence of voting districts gave an advantage to pairs of candidates who would pool their supporters. And who could presumably also count on the support of the powerful amongst each other's friends (and their clients). Tactical alliances and *quid pro quo* arrangements must have been an important part of political reality, obscuring from view any potential disagreement on what to do once in power. Even more revealing was that the elections for the

years. Although it makes little practical difference, I have assumed that L. Popidius Ampliatus was supported by M. Satrius Valens, like his running mate P. Vedius Nummianus.

[1]Franklin (1980) 25 contradicts his own result (94-100) that prominence correlates negatively with frequency of support when he writes: 'It is likely that most 'programmata' found their origins in individual choices and enthusiasms...'

[2]Lex Malacitana LI, LII, LIV. Cf. Nicolet (1976a) 326 ff.

[3]Cf. Jacques (1984) 444 ff. for possible parallels from a later period.

duovirate were not proper elections in any meaningful sense. On top of this we noted the 'official' support for one particular pair of aedile candidates each year. Respectable outsiders might still get in, but it would probably be difficult. Usually the winners would be those marked out in advance by the *ordo*, and they would often be sons of decurions. If not, they would still have to court favour with members of the *ordo* and socialize to their values. A requirement that would be repeated in case of aspirations for the duovirate.

A wider perspective on such links between the *ordo* and its new entrants can be provided by Garnsey's analysis of the presence of *pedani* and *praetextati* in the Canusian *album.*[1] This document (dating to A.D. 223) is a list of all decurions of this Italian city, and was drawn up by the *quinquennales* of the year. The order is hierarchical: the *album* is headed by lists of senatorial and equestrian patrons. Follow lists of former magistrates, in descending order according to the importance of the magistracy that had been held, and in order of seniority within each category.[2] Below that we read the names of 32 *pedani* (members who had not been magistrates) and of 25 *praetextati* (young men below the required age, but allowed to attend meetings as observers). If we count down from the *quinquennalicii* to the *pedani* inclusive (but excluding the *praetextati*) the number is exactly 100, suggesting that that is

[1]CIL IX 338. Garnsey (1974) 248 ff. No doubt the temporal and geographical distance from Pompeii means that conditions may have differed somewhat, but the various municipal charters also give an impression of strong constitutional similarity - at least for the western half of the empire. For municipal charters: Hardy (1912). The recent and stunning find of the Lex Municipalis Irnitana-González (1986) - is welcome corroboration.

[2]The headings are: 'patroni clarissimi viri', 'patroni equites romani', 'quinquennalicii', 'allecti inter quinquennalicios', 'IIviralicii', 'aedilicii', 'quaestoricii', 'pedani', 'praetextati'. An 'allectus inter quinquennalicios' was not quite the same as a proper 'quinquennalicius'. Note that this is the only rank for which there is 'adlectio'. Perhaps the reason is that it would be a much coveted and hard to obtain rank, only available once every five years. The argument that will be developed below also applies here: either it is a privilege for an inner core within the elite, or else it is the privilege of old age. The latter seems less the case because there are seven surviving 'quinquennalicii', thus going back at least fifteen years. It was therefore probably a rank reserved for the social top of the municipal elite, and from which most decurions would remain excluded. 'Adlectio' may have served to let off some steam, and perhaps mark some 'duoviri' for future election as 'quinquennales'.

the *ordo* proper. This means that a sizeable number of men had become members of the *ordo* without first fulfilling a magistracy. That Pompeii did not have quaestors only increases the problem that Garnsey has pointed to: due to high prevailing mortality the number of recent former magistrates would not be enough to fill all the places left vacant by deceased members of the *ordo*, if this was to stay at the level of 100 members. And indeed, the *ordo* of Canusium consisted of only 68 former magistrates and 32 *pedani*. Who are these *pedani*: youngsters, or decurions without a future of further social ascent? If the lower magistracies were filled by *novi homines* or *praetextati* there would hardly be any chance for the *pedani* to rise in the *ordo*, which is unlikely in Garnsey's view. He notes with regard to their *cognomina*, that the Canusian *pedani* do not appear to be any more plebeian in origin than the former magistrates.[1] Their social proximity to the former magistrates leads him to expect that they would be magistrates at some later time: 'local office was open only to those who had already been enrolled in the council.'[2] The later compulsory hereditary membership of the ordo was preceded by a voluntary trend towards restrictive membership.

The *praetextati* (in Canusium there were precisely 25 of them) were sons of prestigious families, and were allowed to attend the meetings as observers.[3] Presumably they gained some

[1]Garnsey (1974) 249. The problem is that one page earlier he himself has argued that the 'cognomen' is not a good test for 'novitas' in Canusium. Also below, p. 326 f.

[2]Garnsey (1974) 249; cf. Dig. 50,2,7,2.

[3]The 'toga praetexta' was worn by magistrates, but also by boys (and girls). Gabelmann (1985) 540 draws attention to a discrepancy between the age from which they would no longer wear the 'toga praetexta' but the 'toga virilis', i.e. 16-17 years, and the minimum age for membership of the 'ordo'. So perhaps not all 'praetextati' would actually be wearing the 'toga praetexta'.

It remains puzzling, however, that precisely the magisterial garb was also the garment for the young. Older explanations concentrate on special characteristics of the young (their infirmity and purity). Daremberg and Saglio (1877-1919) s.v. 'toga', claim that it indicates that the person of children should be no less respected than that of the highest magistrates of the Republic. That may be true, but it remains conjecture. The passages quoted are largely irrelevant. Hor. 'Epod.' 5,7 and Pers. 'Sat.' 5,30 only refer to the vulnerability and innocence of youth, not to parallels with magistrates. Quintil. 'Declam.' 340,13 (and not 311 as quoted) contains the remark that the 'toga praetexta', garb of priests and magis-

experience this way, but equally it implied that they were marked for future membership of the *ordo* proper.[1] The position of *praetextatus* would give them a seal of approval when they were of the right age to become *pedanus* or stand for office.

Because our knowledge of members of the Pompeian *ordo* largely derives from electoral propaganda, it need not surprise us that we do not know of any *pedani* or *praetextati* in Pompeii. Neither do we have any document (such as the Canusian *album*) in which we should expect to find them. What we can say, however, is that the demographic logic of Garnsey's argument applies even more strongly to Pompeii: unlike Canusium it did not have the office of *quaestor*. In Canusium aedileship and quaestorship might have been alternatives as first office.[2] What is a problem in Canusium, is therefore an even bigger problem in Pompeii. On the other hand, the absence of an,

trates, also serves to make helpless children sacred. Note that the text does not quite support the claim. If it would, the question still remains as to the status of such contemporary rhetorical explanations of social practice, and why precisely this comparison, which includes an extreme contrast of power versus infirmity.

Fowler (1920) 42 ff. stresses that 'it was a holy garment, worn by priests during the time of sacrifice, by the priests of Jupiter at all times, and by magistrates who had the right to sacrifice on behalf of the State. As worn by children too it must originally have been a holy garment, for the children of "ingenui", both boys and girls, were regularly employed in the household as ministrants attending on daily sacrifice ...'

A problem with such explanation is that it fails to differentiate socially. It was an expensive garment (this was so for any 'toga', but all the more so for one with a purple hem, even if made of imitation purple, and also true for the accompanying golden 'bulla') that was undoubtedly beyond the financial means of most parents: it was, therefore, not worn by all boys. Besides, purple was a mark of status superiority, rather than of infirmity or purity - Reinhold (1970) e.g. 51. The status distinction has recently been analysed in Gabelmann (1985). He shows - p. 511 ff. - that, originally, it had only been worn by the sons of patricians. 'Indem man den Knaben die Rangtracht der Väter anlegte, verband man damit die Erwartung, die Söhne würden dereinst die gleiche führende Stellung einnehmen' (p. 513). It was an 'Erwartungstracht'. Gradually, the privilege descended down the social ladder, to become the distinction of all 'pueri ingenui'. In sepulchral sculpture it is freedmen who come to represent their sons with 'bulla' and 'toga praetexta' (p. 527 ff.). For such 'imitatio domini', above, p. 276. The high cost of the garment would guarantee, however, that only sons of rich freedmen could be so pretentious (cf. Gabelmann (1985) 535 ff.). For social mobility and socialization also: above, p. 258 ff.

[1] Castrén (1975) 57, and more elaborately: Garnsey (1974) 248 ff. Horstkotte (1984) criticizes Garnsey, but his excessive legalism prevents him from understanding Garnsey's point that formal arrangements were preceded by a voluntary trend.

[2] Of course, in Canusium these might also have served as successive posts. The relative proportions of these two patterns are anybody's guess.

unquantifiable, alternative makes it easier to be more specific by employing the demographic simulation techniques as developed in recent years by Hopkins.[1] At prevailing levels of mortality, between three and four magistrates (who were not yet members of the *ordo*) would have to be elected to ensure that the *ordo* retained its size of one hundred members. We can demonstrate that only a demographic structure such as prevails in the modern industrialized world (i.e. e_0 = 73.6 in Figure XX) might almost allow two new entrants a year to be sufficient. Therefore, as long as we assume the availability of only two ex-magistrates per annum as new entrants for an *ordo* of one hundred members, it follows that a sizeable proportion of the *ordo* would consist of decurions who had not been magistrates. In the following pages I shall first demonstrate that the order of magnitude of the problem is considerable, and exceeds the range where it might be dismissed by an admission of our ignorance of ancient demography. Subsequently we shall investigate ways in which the issue might have been overcome. The first solution would be the simplest one: we drop the assumption of an *ordo* of one hundred members. Instances of town councils with fewer than one hundred members are indeed known, and then thirty members appears to be the norm.[2] But in Canusium as in the majority of other documented cases, we are unquestionably dealing with councils of one hundred about one hundred members.

Even if we cannot, therefore, be certain that the Pompeian *ordo* also counted one hundred members, this is still quite probable. If we retain the hypothesis of an *ordo* of about one hundred members, we can then investigate its consequences.[3] This means that the *ordo*'s size was maintained by inclusion of members who had not been magistrates: *pedani*. This could be effected in two different ways, which each have important

[1]Hopkins (1983a) ch. 2 & 3. I have used the model life tables from Coale and Demeny (1966), model south.

[2]Duncan-Jones (1982) 283 ff. collects and analyses the evidence. González (1986) should now be added, with 63 members in Irni. A puzzling figure, cf. my Figure XIX.

[3]And if Pompeii did not have an 'ordo' of one hundred members, my argument still applies to the cities that did.

consequences for the nature of this group of *pedani*. I shall not now pronounce on the likelihood of either of these possible solutions. Both have found supporters in the scholarly literature, but neither has been stated in a precise and rigorous form. My purpose here is to bring out into the open the implications of each alternative. The first way to bring the number of decurions up to 100 members is to include *pedani* as an inferior status group in the *ordo*. They are not expected to compete for office, because the number of available posts is not sufficient for all members to have a turn in office: the size of the entrance door to the group of decurions who are former office-holders is too small.

The second way in which the existence of *pedani* could ensure that the size of the *ordo* would remain around a figure of one hundred, is a variation of the previous solution: it employs the agency of death to reduce the number of people aspiring to become *aedilicii*. In its simplest form it means that every five years about fifteen to twenty young men between the ages of 25 and 30 are admitted into the *ordo* as *pedani*.[1] They then have to wait for a sufficiently long period for death to have reduced their number to go through the narrow election door at a rate of two per annum, thereby obviously pushing the normal age for holding the aedileship to well above the legal minimum age of 25 years. Garnsey is not entirely specific, but this is - by implication - the solution that he favours for Canusium.[2] *Pedani* would be the group of young members of the *ordo*.

The logic of all tentative reconstructions that are to follow rests on one simple equation: the size of the *ordo* (or groups within the *ordo*) equals the number of new entrants per year, multiplied by their average remaining life expectancy (if there are three entrants per year who have, say, another 25 years to live, then the group consists of 75 members, under stable conditions). Skeptics might argue that our knowledge of Roman

[1] I.e. five times the annual figures from table VIII.

[2] Garnsey (1974) 248 ff. The quantitative speculations in Horstkotte (1984) 222 are of no value. His choice of numbers is arbitrary, and he confuses stock and flow variables. See also below, p. 329.

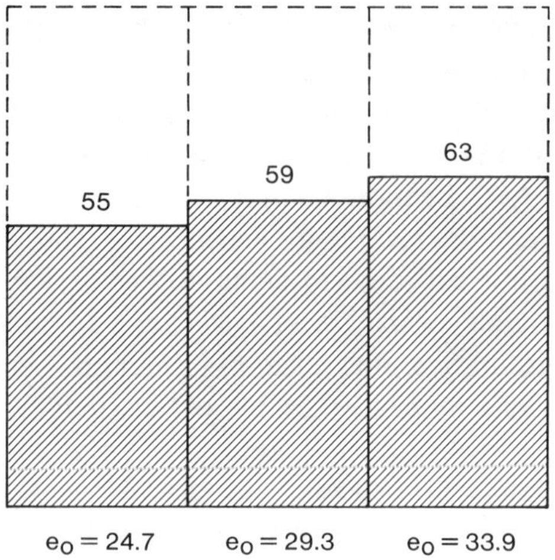

Figure XIX: Predicted ordo *size with only two aediles per annum as entrants*[1]

demography is insufficient to pronounce on Roman life expectancy. Indeed, the sources are of no help, and I shall therefore follow Hopkins in employing model life tables to replace defective ancient data.[2] These life tables predict the age specific

[1] I assume that they are elected at the earliest possible time, i.e. at 25 years. Incorporation into the 'ordo' proper would have to wait for - on average- another 3.5 years: one year because of office holding itself, plus on average 2.5 years waiting time until the next revision of the 'album' by the 'quinquennales'. A waiting time that is itself enough to account for a 4% reduction of numbers.

[2] Pioneered in Hopkins (1966) and used for purposes similar to mine in Hopkins (1983a) ch. 2 & 3; cf. above p. 267 f. Jacques (1984) 497 ff. surprisingly ignores Hopkins (1966). The best modern discussion of Ulpian's life table is Frier (1982). The methodological problem remains, however: if model life tables are our only yard-stick to evaluate the reliability of the ancient evidence, why bother with that evidence at all? If the ancient evidence does not accord with the model life tables, we ignore it. If it does indeed accord, we may decide to retain it. But then there is no harm in using model life tables. I must admit however that I derive comfort from the close match between the model life tables and Frier's impressive analysis of Ulpian's table. Jacques (1984) 478 ff. is unfortunately marred by a confusingly idiosyncratic use of terminology. His arguments can only be understood when one reads his term 'life expectancy' to mean the sum of 'age reached' and 'remaining life expectancy'. However, even if his analysis is technically not very elegant, I must concede that materially some of our observations run parallel.

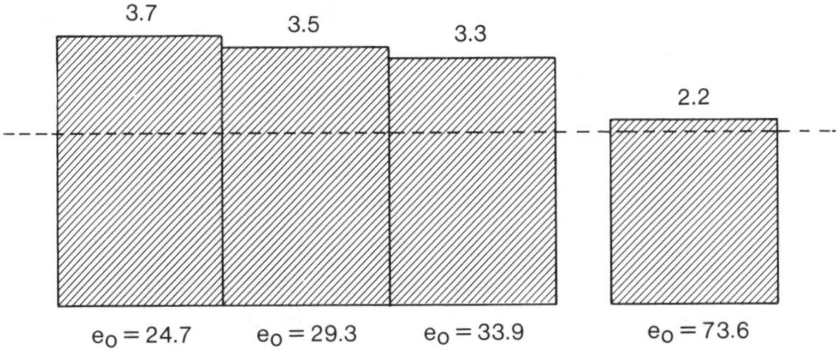

Figure XX:
How many aediles are necessary for an ordo *of 100?*[1]

incidence of death for various levels of life expectancy at birth. Thus, they allow a calculation of the remaining life expectancy at any other age: a 25 year old with a life expectancy at birth of 29.3 years (e_0 = 29.3) could expect to live, on average, for another 33 years (e_{25} = 33).[2] In order to demonstrate that our ignorance of Roman demography matters little for my argument, I shall present my calculations at different levels of life expectancy at birth (e_0), covering the entire range of what might be possible.[3]

The first calculation is that of the size of the *ordo* if there are only two aediles per annum as potential entrants (Figure XIX). It shows figures which are well below the target of 100, and, incidentally, also below the Canusian figure of 68 ex magistrates in the *ordo*.[4] We can also turn the argument around, and see how many aediles would be required if they are the only potential entrants for an *ordo* of one hundred (Figure XX).

[1]The assumptions are the same as in Figure XIX.

[2]This sum may be surprising to those who think e_{25} = 29.3 - 25 = 4.3 years. The explanation is simple: the survivors of a generation are not average. After the first year - with its high infant mortality - life expectancy increases!

[3]I employ the tables from Coale & Demeny (1966), model south. See above p. 268 for a discussion of plausible levels of life expectancy.

[4]Perhaps due to chance, but possibly because quaestorship and aedileship served as alternative routes for entry. Above p.318 f.

Note that even a very high modern life expectancy (e_0 = 73.6) does not quite suffice. The gap in numbers could of course be filled by inclusion of *pedani*, provided that they would not normally stand for office thereafter and compete for the insufficient number of available slots. They would have to be a socially inferior grade within the *ordo*. However, in Canusium Garnsey thought that he could find no evidence for such inferiority.[1] He therefore assumed that they would eventually stand as candidates. Here, his logic becomes problematic, because he ignores that once again aspiring aediles/quaestors would be competing for too few places. The only escape is to assume that *pedani* had to wait for quite a while before they could stand for office. In that period some of them would die, thus improving the chances for others to become aedile. But even at high levels of mortality this would have to be a long wait.

With the model life tables we can easily be more specific. After all, they predict the age-specific incidence of death. At what is perhaps the most probable level of life expectancy at birth for this social group (e_0 = 29.3, i.e level 5 in Coale & Demeny (1966)) they would - on average - have to wait until the age of 55.[2] This then creates a group of former office-holders of 28 men, with a remaining life expectancy of 14 years from the time of office-holding at the age of 55.[3] Table VIII tabulates the results for three different levels of life

[1]Garnsey (1974) 245 ff.

[2]I assume that they become 'pedani' at the lowest possible age, i.e. on average 27.5 years. If they are the only entrants into the 'ordo', the mean annual number of entrants (new 'pedani' per year) would have to be 3.18 to maintain a 100 member 'ordo'. To reduce this annual influx of 3.18 to the number of available aedile posts, i.e. 2, would take another 27.5 years. These figures differ slightly from those in Figure XIX because there death between election into office and incorporation into the 'ordo' had to be compensated. Equally, in that case the one year in office implied a minimum mean entrance age for the 'ordo' of 28.5 years.

[3]The figure of 28 is arrived at by multiplying the annual number of aediles with their remaining life expectancy: e_{55} = 14. My result is anticipated 'in nuce' in Jacques (1984) 480, even though his numerical work is not entirely correct: as a result he did not notice that the resulting reduction in the number of former magistrates - p. 480, n.169 - would have made this option incompatible with the Canusian proportions of 'pedani' and former magistrates. Below, p. 325 f.

expectancy, covering the whole range of potentially plausible levels.[1]

Table VIII:
What if every decurio *becomes a magistrate - if he survives?*

e_0	yearly entrants required	mean age at first office	percentage of pedani who become office holders[2]	sum of ex office holders
24.7	3.39	54	59	27
29.3	3.18	55	63	28
33.9	3.01	55	67	30

The mean age for first office-holding is remarkably insensitive to alternative assumptions about life expectancy: our ignorance does not matter. The question remains, however, whether this reconstruction of an *ordo* in which magistracy is the privilege of old age corresponds to reality.

I shall argue that it does not. The reason for this is that it is hard to think that a situation is realistic where the mean age at the time of first office-holding would be 55 years, and where the *duoviri* would - on average - be still older. It is a result that deviates too much from existing knowledge for it to be probable. The second reason is probably even more compelling. The idea that only between a quarter and a third of the

[1] I assume that they become 'pedani' at the lowest possible age, i.e. on average 27.5 years. If they are the only entrants into the 'ordo', the mean annual number of entrants (new 'pedani' per year) would have to be 3.18 to maintain a 100 member 'ordo'. To reduce this annual influx of 3.18 to the number of available aedile posts, i.e. 2, would take another 27.5 years. These figures differ slightly from those in Figure XIX because there death between election into office and incorporation into the 'ordo' had to be compensated. Equally, in that case the one year in office implied a minimum mean entrance age for the 'ordo' of 28.5 years.

[2] This represents the percentage that survives.

ordo would consist of former magistrates, of whom perhaps little more than half would be former *duoviri*, is well beyond what we may think possible. We only need to remind ourselves of the 68 former magistrates of the Canusian *album* to realize that magistracy cannot have been the privilege of old age.

The implications of this for our view of the nature of the group of *pedani* must be obvious. If they cannot really be an age group (with 63 - 70 members) patiently awaiting their chance in old age, they must largely be a socially inferior group within the *ordo*. Socially inferior because they would never have a chance to stand for office. Garnsey's view that *pedani* are a group of decurions who had not yet been magistrates, but would be the natural candidates in the future, has to be rejected. He does not realize that in this way these *pedani* would once again be competing for too few places. Postponing magistracy into old age is the only possibility to cope with this, but its implications make it improbable that this could be a predominant pattern.

This invites scrutiny of the internal social relations within the Canusian *ordo*. If *pedani* could never - or only rarely- become magistrates, one would expect them to be socially distinguishable from the group of former magistrates. In Garnsey's view there is no such difference.[1] If he is right, then it means that *pedani* are predominantly former *praetextati*, waiting to become magistrates. If on the other hand he is wrong, and *pedani* are an inferior status group within the *ordo*, with few chances of further advancement, they should be distinguishable, both from the former magistrates, and from the *praetextati*, who are - as we shall see - indubitably closely related to the former magistrates.

The first test is that of the proportion of Greek *cognomina* among the various groups within the *ordo*. It is a test that is not beyond criticism, especially in the case of Southern Italy.[2] Garnsey has his doubts, and quite rightly so. However, he still uses the test to claim that *pedani* are no different from the

[1]Garnsey (1974) 245 ff.

[2]Garnsey (1974) 247. For some comments on its usefulness, above, p. 241 ff.

former magistrates. This is methodologically problematic, since such observation could also be due to the failure of the test. We may only maintain the test if it shows marked differences between groups within the *ordo*. And indeed, this appears to be the case (Figure XXI).

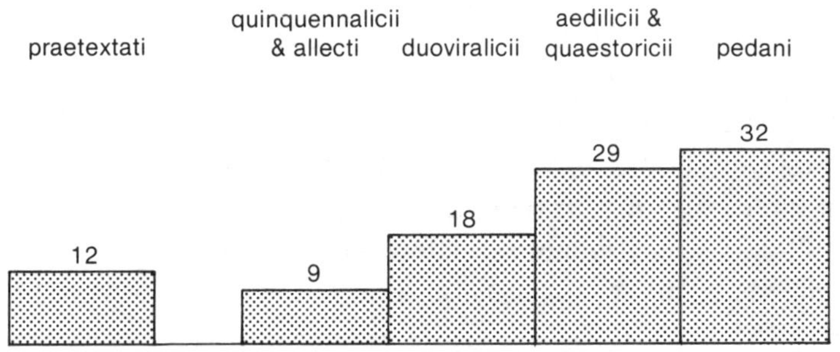

Figure XXI: The proportion of Greek cognomina *within the* ordo *of Canusium* (source: Jacques (1984) 525.[1])

The result is remarkable. It demonstrates the significance of Greek *cognomina* as a measure of respectability. The higher the grade within the *ordo*, the lower the proportion of Greek *cognomina*. For us, it is important to note the marked difference between *pedani* and *praetextati*. They appear to represent the two opposite ends of the scale of respectability within the elite. Garnsey is probably wrong in thinking that what distinguishes *pedani* from *praetextati* is only their age. If *praetextati* are onomastically close to the top of the *ordo*, this is not so for *pedani*.

A second test to decide what distinguishes *pedani* from *praetextati* and how both groups compare to former magistrates, is to trace possible family connections between *pedani* and *praetextati* on the one hand, and former magistrates on the other. Here too, *pedani* are quite different from *praetextati*.

[1]In order to avoid the dangers of working with too small numbers, 'quinquennalicii' and 'allecti inter q.q.' have been grouped together; for the same reason 'aedilicii' and 'quaestoricii' have been grouped together.

Real family connection remains elusive of course, but as a practical test we may consider identity of *praenomen* and *nomen gentilicium*. Three quarters of all *praetextati* share their *praenomen* and *nomen gentilicium* with former magistrates.[1] This is a very high proportion when we consider that about a quarter of the *praetextati* must have lost their fathers through death. The results for the *pedani* are different: only about 40% have *praenomen* en *gentilicium* in common with former magistrates.[2]

The difference between *pedani* and *praetextati* is also apparent when we look from the top down. No *quinquennalicius* (or *allectus inter q.q.*) is onomastically related to any *pedanus*. On the other hand, six out of these eleven *quinquennalicii* (including the *allecti*) are probably related to *praetextati*.[3] Whereas the *pedani* seem miles apart from the *ordo*'s top, *praetextati* are close to the top.

Each of these tests that I have employed has its own problems, but these problems become less worrying when we take all the results together. These results converge, and confirm the hypothesis that emerged from the demographic simulation: most *pedani* were men without much future of further political advancement and office-holding. The Canusian *ordo* is highly stratified internally, and office-holding is an important criterion within this hierarchy. Predestination of future magistrates was characteristic of the group of *praetextati* rather than of the

[1] 19 out of 25, i.e. 76%. Two 'praetextati' are only related to 'pedani', and four 'praetextati' cannot be related at all. But one of these latter, L. Eggius Maximus, is probably related to the consul L. Eggius Marullus (CIL IX 343). See: Kleijwegt (1987) 26.

[2] 12 out of 32, i.e. 37.5%, plus perhaps another 2 (M. Aurelius Maximus and Ti. Claudius Verus) where onomastic correspondence should perhaps be used with more caution. If we abandon this caution, the figure increases to 14 out of 32, i.e. 43.8%.

[3] In the case of two 'praetextati' possibly as e.g. uncles: T. Aelius Rufus and T. Aelius Flavianus both correspond with the 'praetextatus' T. Aelius Nectareus, and only one can be the father. The same is true for L. Abuccius Proculus and L. Abuccius Iulianus with respect to L. Abuccius Proculus Iunior, the 'praetextatus'. On the other hand, I have not assumed a relationship between the 'allectus' P. Aelius Victorinus and the 'praetextatus' T. Aelius Nectareus, possibly wrongly.

pedani.[1] In other words, family background appears to be an important criterion to determine where in the *ordo* someone will end up. *Novi homines* depend upon patronage from the existing inner core of the *ordo* to become *pedanus*, and perhaps also for election. A patronage that is of course only available to those who conform to this elite's norms and values.

This supposition of patronage links makes us return to Pompeii. There, we have seen that not all candidates needed to make an equally large propaganda effort. The evidence showed the existence of essentially two types of candidates for the aedileship. On the one hand those with the support of duoviral candidates - and presumably powerful members of the *ordo* behind them - and on the other hand candidates for the aedileship lacking such support. These latter had to compensate through much more active campaigning, and would probably still have considerably less chance of being elected. The Pompeian evidence irrefutably shows that popular election was still important, and - in the case of aediles - not yet an entirely foregone conclusion. But it also shows, most markedly of course in the case of the uncontested elections for the duovirate, that the *ordo*'s (and in particular the top of the *ordo*'s) hold over the outcome of these elections was considerable.

[1]To avoid confusion I should make it clear that my results should not be interpreted as a refutation of Garnsey's thesis that only existing members of the 'ordo', i.e. 'pedani', could stand for office. For that purpose, around 10 'pedani' would suffice, if they are subsequently elected at the earliest possible opportunity. The concentration among the most junior 'pedani' of 'pedani' who are onomastically related to former magistrates is noticeable (nrs. 20, 21, 22, 23, 26, 27, 28). It may therefore be true that even though most 'pedani' at any one time do not have a future of further advancement, yet all former magistrates have been predestined by a short spell as 'pedanus' (and by a period as 'praetextatus' of course).

APPENDICES

Appendix I: Contradictions in prestige ratings

As referred to in the text, p. 233 ff., a problem was encountered because a number of people were not always placed in the same ranking order in relation to each other. In one document person X would come before person Y, and in another document they would appear in reverse order. This lack of consistency could be the result of incorrect readings of the texts. Therefore, these contradictions were looked at in detail, and corrections were made where they seemed appropriate. This amended data input was then used for the subsequent construction of the ranking order of the persons in the tablets. As this might invite an accusation of data massaging, the original contradictions are listed and briefly argued below.

Contradictions in the original data input:

1 M. Cestilius Philodespotus and A. Messius Phronimus conflict in respective rank.

In text 34:

M. Cestilius Philodespotus ranks higher than A. Messius Phronimus;

In text 43:

A. Messius Phronimus ranks higher than M. Cestilius Philodespotus;

In text 101:

M. Cestilius Philodespotus ranks higher than A. Messius Phronimus.

In text 43, *pagina quarta* line 5, Zangemeister, the CIL editor, reads M. Cestilli Philode[m]i, and comments *'non videtur admitti posse Philodespot(i)'*. The latter reading was originally adopted following Castrén, but unjustifiably, as the drawing in CIL also shows.

2 M. Cestilius Philodespotus and N. Popidius Amarantus conflict in respective rank.

In text 43:

M. Cestilius Philodespotus ranks higher than N. Popidius Amarantus;

In text 101:

N. Popidius Amarantus ranks higher than M. Cestilius Philodespotus.

For M. Cestilius Philodespotus in text 43, see above, contradiction 1. In addition, in line 7, it might be asked whether we should not read N. Epidi Amaranti (cf. below, contradiction 8: A. Messius Phronimus vs. N. Popidius Amarantus).

3 M. Fabius Proculus and P. Terentius Primus conflict in respective rank.

In text 46:

M. Fabius Proculus ranks higher than P. Terentius Primus;

In text 93:

P. Terentius Primus ranks higher than M. Fabius Proculus.

Text 93 is very well readable, but 46 is rather insecure, especially for M. Fabius Proculus' *nomen gentilicium*. All that survives of the *gentilicium* in line 16, page four, of tablet 46 is the first F. He should therefore be treated as a new, otherwise unknown, person.

4 L. Laelius Trophimus and T. Sornius Eutychus conflict in respective rank.

In text 13:

T. Sornius Eutychus ranks higher than L. Laelius Trophimus;

in text 61:

L. Laelius Trophimus ranks higher than T. Sornius Eutychus;

in text 66:

L. Laelius Trophimus ranks higher than T. Sornius Eutychus.
This contradiction cannot easily be solved by adopting another reading. Possibly the Laelius Trophimus, without *praenomen*, in 61 and 66 is a different person from the L. Laelius Trophimus in 13, but it would be more honest to accept the contradiction as it stands.

5 A. Messius Phronimus and N. Nerius Hyginus conflict in respective rank.

In text 28:

N. Nerius Hyginus ranks higher than A. Messius Phronimus;

In text 57:

A. Messius Phronimus ranks higher than N. Nerius Hyginus.
In text 28, page four, line 16, we read N. [Ner]i Hygini, but the drawing shows clearly that the solution [Ner] is not based on any surviving traces. Therefore, one could read many other *gentilicia* with equal - lack of - justification. N. ...ius Hyginus was thus made into a new, otherwise unknown person.

6 A. Messius Phronimus and Sex. Numisius Iucundus conflict in respective rank.

In text 55:

Sex. Numisius Iucundus ranks higher than A. Messius Phronimus;

In text 111:

A. Messius Phronimus ranks higher than Sex. Numisius Iucundus.

The problem with tablet 111 is, that the fourth page consists of five separate pieces of wood, with badly legible text. No drawing or photograph is provided in the CIL edition, and it is therefore difficult to judge whether the pieces have been fitted together in the proper order. In line 3 we read ....SI PHRONIMI, and in l. 4. ....VMISI IVCVN.. So even if the jig saw puzzle has been solved correctly, we could e.g. still read Numisi Phronimi in line 3. Zangemeister's decision to reconstruct Messi Phronimi follows what Andreau describes in these words: 'En effet, si le prénom et le nom d'un témoin sont illisibles, mais que démeure son surnom, et si ce surnom n'est pas ailleurs, dans le reste des tablettes, porté que par un seul personnage, il a l'habitude d'assimiler le témoin au personnage en question.'[1] It was decided to remove tablet 111 from our database.

7 A. Messius Phronimus and A. Paccius Philodespotus conflict in respective rank.

In text 75:

A. Messius Phronimus ranks higher than A. Paccius Philodespotus;

In text 114:

A. Paccius Philodespotus ranks higher than A. Messius Phronimus.

In text 75 we read Paquius, and in text 114 Paccius. Zangemeister appears to consider this an inconsequential spelling variety, and for this case Castrén has followed him, although Castrén treats them also as two different families (297 and 301 in his list of families). Linguistically the two names are obviously closely related.[2] But such variation could have the conscious or unconscious meaning of distinguishing two families or branches of families. Castrén's ability to distinguish two families in the other evidence justifies a decision to treat the persons in these two tablets as two different persons. It may perhaps be added that all that remains of A. Messius Phronimus' name in tablet 114, page 4, line 7, are the letters .... SI PRONIMI. He has been treated as a new, otherwise unknown, person.

8 A. Messius Phronimus and N. Popidius Amarantus conflict in respective rank.

In text 43:

A. Messius Phronimus ranks higher than N. Popidius Amarantus;

[1] Andreau (1974) 17 n.1

[2] Schulze (1933) 204, 424, 476

In text 71:
N. Popidius Amarantus ranks higher than A. Messius Phronimus;
In text 101:
N. Popidius Amarantus ranks higher than A. Messius Phronimus.

In tablet 43, page 4, line 19, we may wonder whether we should not read Epidi instead of Popidi. The drawing only shows the letters ...IDI, and in the preceding line we read the name of M. Epidius Secundus. Cf. above, contradiction 2 (M. Cestilius Philodespotus vs. N. Popidius Amarantus).

9 A. Messius Phronimus and N. Popidius Sodalio conflict in respective rank.
In text 28:
A. Messius Phronimus ranks higher than N. Popidius Sodalio;
In text 102:
N. Popidius Sodalio ranks higher than A. Messius Phronimus.

This contradiction will have to be accepted as it stands.

10 A. Messius Phronimus and Cn. Vibrius Callistus conflict in respective rank.
In text 28:
Cn. Vibrius Callistus ranks higher than A. Messius Phronimus;
In text 68:
A. Messius Phronimus ranks higher than Cn. Vibrius Callistus;
In text 71:
A. Messius Phronimus ranks higher than Cn. Vibrius Callistus;
In text 75:
Cn. Vibrius Callistus ranks higher than A. Messius Phronimus;
In text 102:
A. Messius Phronimus ranks higher than Cn. Vibrius Callistus;
In text 114:
Cn. Vibrius Callistus ranks higher than A. Messius Phronimus.

Although in text 114 the presence of A. Messius Phronimus is insecure (above, contradiction 7), the number of contradictions is so large, that they will have to be accepted.

11 A. Messius Phronimus and L. Volusius Faustus conflict in respective rank.

In text 113:

A. Messius Phronimus ranks higher than L. Volusius Faustus;

In text 114:

L. Volusius Faustus ranks higher than A. Messius Phronimus.

A. Messius Phronimus in text 114 is very insecure (see contradiction 7, cf. contradiction 10).

12 N. Nerius Hyginus and Cn. Vibrius Callistus conflict in respective rank.

In text 28:

Cn. Vibrius Callistus ranks higher than N. Nerius Hyginus;

In text 74:

N. Nerius Hyginus ranks higher than Cn. Vibrius Callistus.

'Nerius' in text 74 is only a conjecture (see above, contradiction 5).

13 N. Popidius Amarantus and T. Sornius Eutychus conflict in respective rank.

In text 49:

T. Sornius Eutychus ranks higher than N. Popidius Amarantus;

In text 101:

N. Popidius Amarantus ranks higher than T. Sornius Eutychus.

In text 49, page 4, line 20, only the first two letters of N. Popidius' *cognomen* have survived. The alternative reading Ampliatus is preferred.

14 N. Popidius Sodalio and Cn. Vibrius Callistus conflict in respective rank.

In text 28:

Cn. Vibrius Callistus ranks higher than N. Popidius Sodalio;

In text 102:

N. Popidius Sodalio ranks higher than Cn. Vibrius Callistus.

This contradiction should be accepted.

15 C. Poppaeus Fortis and P. Terentius Primus conflict in respective rank.

In text 35:

P. Terentius Primus ranks higher than C. Poppaeus Fortis;

In text 38:

C. Poppaeus Fortis ranks higher than P. Terentius Primus.

In text 38, page 4, line 20, only the first F of the *cognomen* has been preserved, and it was therefore decided to treat C. Poppaeus in text 38 as a new, otherwise unknown person.

16 T. Sornius Eutychus and P. Terentius Primus conflict in respective rank.

In text 69:

T. Sornius Eutychus ranks higher than P. Terentius Primus;

In text 91:

P. Terentius Primus ranks higher than T. Sornius Eutychus;

In text 116:

T. Sornius Eutychus ranks higher than P. Terentius Primus.

Although the name of T. Sornius Eutychus in text 116 is not very clear, this is not enough to discard the contradiction.

Where contradictions could not be removed on epigraphical grounds, the program ignores the contradicting information, i.e. it does not choose between either of the two possible orders.

Appendix II: Iucundus' witnesses

This appendix contains the names of all witnesses in Iucundus' archive as they were used in chapter six. The list reflects all my manipulations of the original sources, and should, therefore, not be read as an index of the tablets, but as a documentation of my decisions. Problematic readings are discussed in appendix I, and many other decisions are argued in chapter six. The first column lists the names (in homogenized spelling) of the witnesses. Column two lists the sizes of the houses (where known). Column three lists the offices that were held by candidates (q: *quinquennalis*, d: *duovir*, ae: *aedilis*, au: *augustalis*, m: *minister* etc., v: various offices[1]). Column four lists the legal statusses which I decided to assign to witnesses (in: *ingenuus*, li: *libertus*). Column five lists the tablets in which the witnesses occur, and column six lists the relative position in that tablet.[2]

NAME	hou	off	sta	ta	ra
Aconius Primus, Sal.	0	?	li	95	7
Aefulanus Chrysanthus, P.	0	?	li	15	4
Aefulanus Chrysanthus, P.	0	?	li	89	5
Aefulanus Chrysanthus, P.	0	?	li	110	4
Aefulanus Chrysanthus, P.	0	?	li	85	3
Aefulanus Chrysanthus, P.	0	?	li	7	7
Aefulanus Chrysanthus, P.	0	?	li	12	8
Aefulanus Chrysanthus, P.	0	?	li	103	3
Aelius Pa..., L.	0	?	?	31	7
Aelius Turbo, L.	0	?	in	6	1
Aelius? Verna, L.	0	?	li	79	6
Aemilius Severus, C.	0	?	in	113	1

[1]This category only includes Cn. Alleius Logus, 'omnium collegiorum benemeritus'. The category was ignored in further calculations, since it is only a nominal and not an ordinal category.

[2]These numbers refer to the position relative to the other readable names. If, for example, the first two names are illegible, then I have listed the name in the third position as first (because usable) witness. After all, my procedure only uses relative positions. A consequence is that my rank numbers are not directly comparable to those listed in Castrén (1975).

Aemilius Celer, L.	0	?	?	27	2
Albucius Iustus, L.	0	d	in	70	4
Albucius Thesmus, L.	90	?	li	71	8
Alficius Vitalis	0	?	?	32	3
Alficius Vitalis	0	?	?	86	2
Alfius Abascantus, A.	0	?	li	19	8
Alfius Abascantus, A.	0	?	li	22	8
Alfius, Cn.	0	?	?	117	1
Alleius Logus, Cn.	0	v	li	83	1
Alleius Logus, Cn.	0	v	li	16	2
Alleius Nigidius Maius, Cn.	2290	q	in	77	1
Alleius Carpus, M.	0	?	?	74	8
Antistius Faustus, M.	0	?	li	88	4
Antistius Primigenius, M.	0	?	li	5	5
Antistius, P.	0	?	?	76	5
Antistius Secundio, P.	0	?	li	93	5
Antonius Tertius, M.	0	?	li	151	3
Antonius Optatus	0	?	li	82	8
Appuleius Severus, A.	0	?	in	49	2
Appuleius Severus, A.	0	?	in	106	2
Appuleius Severus, Q.	0	?	in	10	2
Appuleius Severus, Q.	0	?	in	12	2
Appuleius Severus, Q.	0	?	in	13	2
Appuleius Severus, Q.	0	?	in	14	1
Appuleius Severus, Q.	0	?	in	15	2
Appuleius Severus, Q.	0	?	in	17	1
Appuleius Severus, Q.	0	?	in	19	2
Appuleius Severus, Q.	0	?	in	25	1
Appuleius Severus, Q.	0	?	in	43	1
Appuleius Severus, Q.	0	?	in	67	1
Appuleius Severus, Q.	0	?	in	71	1
Appuleius Severus, Q.	0	?	in	73	1
Appuleius Severus, Q.	0	?	in	82	1
Appuleius Severus, Q.	0	?	in	88	1
Appuleius Severus, Q.	0	?	in	92	1
Appuleius Severus, Q.	0	?	in	99	2
Appuleius Severus, Q.	0	?	in	113	2
Arrius Auctus	0	?	li	59	3

Arrius Amaranthus, C.	0	?	li	100	3
Arrius, Q.	0	?	?	5	2
Arrius Philetus, Q.	0	?	li	75	8
Arrius Philetus, Q.	0	?	li	12	3
Arrius Philetus, Q.	0	?	li	17	2
Arrius Philetus, Q.	0	?	li	54	1
Arrius Proculus Q.	0	?	in	43	2
Artorius Liberalis	0	?	?	109	5
Artorius Primus	0	?	li	110	1
Atilius Firmus, M.	0	?	?	58	1
Attius Florus, Q.	0	?	?	93	2
Attius Amplus, Sex.	0	ae	in	74	2
Atullius Euander, C.	0	?	li	10	4
Atullius Euander, C.	0	?	li	19	4
Atullius Euander, C.	0	?	li	59	1
Atullius Euander, C.	0	?	li	60	1
Atullius Euander, C.	0	?	li	68	1
Atullius Euander, C.	0	?	li	112	3
Aurelius Saturninus, L.	0	?	?	75	3
Aurelius Felicio, M.	0	?	li	5	6
Aurelius Felicio, M.	0	?	li	34	8
Aurelius Larcus, M.	0	?	in	65	1
Aurelius Vitalis	0	?	?	49	4
Aurelius Vitalis	0	?	?	99	4
Avianus Vet..., L.	0	?	?	91	6
Badius Hermes, M.	0	?	li	7	4
Barbatius Cattus?	0	?	?	32	5
Betutius Iustus, L.	0	?	in	95	2
Blaesius Fructio, N.	0	?	li	86	3
Brittius Eros. L.	0	?	li	96	5
Brittius Balbus, Q.	285	d	in	56	2
Brittius Balbus, Q.	285	d	in	74	1
Caecilius Philologus, A.	0	?	li	40	2
Caecilius Communis	0	?	li	82	9
Caecilius Hermes, L.	0	?	li	18	6
Caecilius Hermes, L.	0	?	li	69	6
Caecilius Attalus, Q.	0	?	li	7	3
Caecilius Attalus, Q.	0	?	li	48	6

Caecilius Attalus, Q.	0	?	li	93	9
Caecilius Saturninus, Q.	0	?	?	73	4
Caelius Primogenes, P.	0	?	li	94	4
Caelius Primogenes, P.	0	?	li	104	2
Caelius Primogenes, P.	0	?	li	113	3
Caelius Primogenes, P.	0	?	li	79	4
Calavius Secundus, M.	0	?	?	31	4
Caltilius Iustus, L.	0	?	?	19	1
Calventius Quietus, Q.	0	au	li	51	1
Calventius Quietus, Q.	0	au	li	87	2
Calventius Quietus, Q.	0	au	li	50	3
Calventius? Tertius, L.	0	?	?	39	4
Caprasius Athictus, D.	0	?	li	106	4
Caprasius Eros, D.	0	?	li	71	2
Caprasius Eros, D.	0	?	li	84	1
Caprasius Eros, D.	0	?	li	90	1
Caprasius Felix, D.	531	?	li	59	2
Caprasius Felix, D.	531	?	li	61	1
Caprasius Gobio, D.	0	?	li	22	4
Caprasius Gobio, D.	0	?	li	82	5
Caprasius Th...nus, D.	0	?	li	80	9
Cassius Secundus, C.	0	?	?	115	3
Ceius Decidianus, L.	0	?	in	46	3
Ceius Decidianus, L.	0	?	in	67	4
Ceius Felicio, L.	0	?	li	22	9
Ceius Felicio, L.	0	?	li	82	6
Ceius Nymph..., L.	0	?	li	91	7
Ceius, Quartio, L.	0	?	?	14	9
Cerrinius Restitutus, M.	0	au	li	70	6
Cerrinius Restitutus, M.	0	au	li	76	2
Cerrinius Proculus	0	?	in	132	1
Cestilius Philodemus, M.	0	?	li	43	5
Cestilius Philodespotus, M.	0	?	li	22	6
Cestilius Philodespotus, M.	0	?	li	34	5
Cestilius Philodespotus, M.	0	?	li	101	5
Claudius Isthmus	0	?	li	77	2
Claudius M...nis	0	?	?	87	7
Claudius Ampliatus, Ti.	0	?	li	112	8

Claudius Ampliatus, Ti.	0	?	li	129	1
Claudius Ampliatus, Ti.	0	?	li	130	2
Claudius Nedymus, Ti.	0	?	li	99	1
Claudius Secundus, Ti.	0	?	li	35	7
Clodius Iustus, A.	0	?	in	143	4
Clodius Ampliatus, M.	0	?	li	97	4
Clodius Ampliatus, M.	0	?	li	66	5
Coelius Caltilius Iustus, Q.	0	d	in	79	1
Cornelius Adiutor	0	?	?	67	5
Cornelius Tages, P.	1125	?	li	67	7
Cornelius Tages, P.	1125	?	li	76	8
Cornelius Tages, P.	1125	?	li	101	7
Cornelius Tages, P.	1125	?	li	113	8
Cornelius Tages, P.	1125	?	li	115	5
Cornelius Amandus, L.	0	?	li	19	3
Cornelius Dexter, L.	0	?	in	103	6
Cornelius Maximus, L.	0	?	?	38	2
Cornelius Maximus, L.	0	?	?	133	2
Cornelius Primogenes, L.	1173	?	li	37	5
Cornelius Qu..., L.	0	?	?	68	5
Cornelius Erastus, P.	0	?	li	57	6
Crassius Firmus, T.	0	ae	in	31	1
Cuspius Secundus, C.	0	?	?	12	1
Deccius Hilario L.	0	?	li	93	4
Deccius Hilario L.	0	?	li	98	3
Decidius Pauper, M.	0	?	?	107	1
Dentatius? Panthera	0	?	in	101	8
Dentatius Faustus, A.	0	?	li	76	4
Didius Hyginus, Q.	0	?	li	128	1
Domitius Polydespotus?	0	?	li	84	3
Epidius, M.	0	?	?	85	7
Epidius ...andus, M.	0	?	?	106	5
Epidius? Amarantus, N.	0	?	li	43	7
Epidius Bucolus, M.	0	?	li	84	4
Epidius Bucolus, M.	0	?	li	89	6
Epidius Fortunatus, M.	0	?	?	108	3
Epidius Hymenaeus, M.	78	?	li	25	6
Epidius Hymenaeus, M.	78	?	li	77	4

Epidius Pagurus, M.	0	?	?	37	7
Epidius Secundus, M.	0	?	?	34	7
Epidius Secundus, M.	0	?	?	43	6
Epidius Stephanus, M.	0	?	li	18	4
Epidius Urbanus, M.	0	?	?	47	3
Epidius Urbanus, M.	0	?	?	112	6
Epidius P...	0	?	?	11	1
Fabius, M.	0	?	?	35	2
Fabius Agathinus, M.	0	?	li	91	3
Fabius Chryseros, M.	0	?	li	131	2
Fabius Diadumenos, M.	0	?	li	14	4
Fabius Diadumenos, M.	0	?	li	28	2
Fabius Eupor, M.	500	au	li	37	3
Fabius Eupor, M.	500	au	li	71	7
Fabius Eupor, M.	500	au	li	92	2
Fabius Eupor, M.	500	au	li	97	3
Fabius Nymphodotus, M.	0	?	li	34	3
Fabius Philocalus, M.	0	?	li	80	3
Fabius Proculus, M.	0	?	in	24	3
Fabius Proculus, M.	0	?	in	93	1
Fabius Secundus, M.	280	?	?	83	8
Fabius Secundus, M.	280	?	?	90	4
Fabius Terminalis, M.	0	?	li	27	3
Fabius Thelus, M.	0	?	li	34	1
Fabius Thelus, M.	0	?	li	77	3
Fabius Thelus, M.	0	?	li	97	2
Fabius Tyrannus	384	?	li	34	4
Fadius Nept..., L.	0	?	li	26	1
Flaminius Strobilus, L.	0	?	li	88	7
Fonteius Ha...	0	?	?	54	9
Fuficius Certus, A.	0	?	in	112	2
Fuficius Fuscus, M.	0	?	in	112	1
Fufidius? Agath...	0	?	li	132	4
Fufidius Faustus, C?	0	?	li	78	4
Fufidius Primus, N.	0	?	li	57	2
Fufidius Primus, N.	0	?	li	95	5
Fundilius Primio, C.	0	?	li	92	7
Furius Fortunatus, P.	0	?	li	2	1

Furius Fortunatus, P.	0	?	li	18	9
Furius Fortunatus, P.	0	?	li	69	7
Gavius Firmus, C.	0	?	in	89	2
Gavius Firmus, C.	0	?	in	81	2
Gavius Firmus, C.	0	?	in	95	3
Gavius Rufus, C.	0	d	in	89	3
Gavius Bu...a, M.	0	?	?	14	8
Granius Abinnaeus	0	?	in	76	7
Granius Constans?	0	?	?	54	6
Granius Lesbius, Q.	0	?	li	25	7
Granius? Coniunctus	0	?	?	15	5
Helvius Auctus	0	m	li	54	5
Helvius Apollonius, Cn.	0	?	li	32	4
Helvius Apollonius, Cn.	0	?	li	40	3
Helvius Apollonius, Cn.	0	?	li	43	8
Helvius Apollonius, Cn.	0	?	li	48	9
Helvius Apollonius, Cn.	0	?	li	69	3
Helvius Apollonius, Cn.	0	?	li	116	4
Helvius Apollonius, Cn.	0	?	li	59	4
Helvius Aprilis, Cn.	0	?	?	112	4
Helvius Proculus, L.	0	?	in	96	2
Helvius Rufus, L.	0	?	in	70	3
Helvius Adeptus, M.	0	?	li	61	5
Helvius Apriculus?, M.	0	?	?	57	3
Helvius Catullus, M.	0	?	in	39	3
Helvius Phoebus, M.	0	?	li	18	5
Helvius Phoebus, M.	0	?	li	105	1
Helvius Princeps, M.	0	?	li	83	5
Helvius Saturninus, M.	0	?	?	18	7
Helvius Scamander, Sex.	0	?	li	92	3
Helvius?, C.	0	?	?	51	2
Herennius, N.	0	?	?	5	4
Herennius Anthus, N.	0	?	li	12	7
Herennius Anthus, N.	0	?	li	91	4
Herennius Castus, N.	165	?	li	12	5
Herennius Ianuarius, N.	0	?	?	37	6
Herennius Ianuarius, N.	0	?	?	68	2
Herennius Primus	0	?	li	60	3

Herennuleius Communis, A.	710	?	li	94	7
Herennuleius Communis, A.	710	?	li	77	6
Herennuleius Communis, A.	710	?	li	113	4
Herennuleius Florius?	0	?	?	85	1
Holconius Iucundus, M.	0	?	li	73	3
Holconius Iucundus, M.	0	?	li	93	6
Holconius Proculus, M.	0	?	in	79	2
Holconius Rufus, M.	0	ae	in	70	5
Hordionius Philostorgus, M.	0	?	li	114	5
Istacidius Eutychus, L.	0	?	li	75	5
Istacidius Orion, N.	0	?	li	85	6
Iulius Agathocles, C.	0	?	li	31	6
Iulius Eutactus, C.	0	?	li	61	6
Iulius Memor, C.	0	?	?	89	4
Iulius Crescens, M.	0	?	?	25	4
Iulius Polybius	1000	d	li	88	2
Iulius Abascantus, Ti.	0	?	li	25	3
Iulius Gennaeus, Ti.	0	?	li	130	1
Iulius Gennaeus, Ti.	0	?	li	74	6
Iunius Corinthus, L.	0	?	li	12	6
Iunius Corinthus, L.	0	?	li	13	5
Iunius Corinthus, L.	0	?	li	87	5
Iunius Corinthus, L.	0	?	li	89	8
Laelius Fuscus, L.	0	d	in	10	1
Laelius Fuscus, L.	0	d	in	13	1
Laelius Fuscus, L.	0	d	in	15	1
Laelius Fuscus, L.	0	d	in	35	1
Laelius Fuscus, L.	0	d	in	103	1
Laelius Trophimus, L.	682	?	li	108	1
Laelius Trophimus, L.	682	?	li	13	4
Laelius Trophimus, L.	682	?	li	76	1
Laelius Trophimus, L.	682	?	li	61	2
Laelius Trophimus, L.	682	?	li	66	2
Laelius Prin...	0	?	?	10	5
Licinius Romanus I, M.	0	?	in	87	3
Licinius Romanus I, M.	0	?	in	153	1
Livineius Eutactus, L.	0	?	li	5	7
Livineius Eutactus, L.	0	?	li	38	4

Livineius Eutactus, L.	0	?	li	66	6
Lollius Saturninus, Q.	0	?	?	108	4
Loreius, M.	0	?	?	27	1
Lucceius, Th..., M.	0	?	li	94	8
Lucilius Fuscus, L.	0	?	in	67	6
Lucilius Philargyros, L.	0	?	li	82	3
Lucretius Satrius Valens, D.	0	d	in	101	1
Lucretius Satrius Valens, D.	0	d	in	52	1
Lucretius Epicalus?, M.	0	?	li	83	7
Lucretius Epicalus?, M.	0	?	li	110	5
Lucretius Lerus, M.	410	?	?	54	2
Lucretius Lerus, M.	410	?	?	60	2
Lucretius Lerus, M.	410	?	?	70	8
Lucretius Lerus, M.	410	?	?	90	2
Lucretius Lerus, M.	410	?	?	114	1
Lucretius Stephanicus	0	?	li	107	3
Lupattius Saturninus, M.	0	?	?	78	1
Maelissaeus? Crescens, Cn.	0	?	?	57	1
Maetennius Daphnus	0	?	li	88	8
Maetennius Daphnus	0	?	li	98	6
Magius Secundus, M.	0	?	?	104	1
Magulnius Donatus, L.	0	?	?	79	3
Magulnius Donatus, L.	0	?	?	94	3
Magulnius Donatus, L.	0	?	?	77	5
Manlius Secundus, A.	0	?	?	101	2
Melissaeus Fuscus	0	?	in	66	1
Melissaeus Fuscus	0	?	in	8	2
Melissaeus Fuscus	0	?	in	24	2
Melissaeus Atimetus, L.	0	?	li	37	8
Melissaeus Atimetus, L.	0	?	li	38	3
Melissaeus Coerasus, L.	0	?	?	103	5
Messius, A.	0	?	?	5	1
Messius Ba..., M.	0	?	?	32	1
Messius Faustus, A.	0	?	li	75	1
Messius Faustus, A.	0	?	li	98	4
Messius Inventus, A.	0	m	li	31	3
Messius Phronimus, A.	0	?	li	57	5
Messius Phronimus, A.	0	?	li	14	5

Messius Phronimus, A.	0	?	li	28	5
Messius Phronimus, A.	0	?	li	43	4
Messius Phronimus, A.	0	?	li	50	2
Messius Phronimus, A.	0	?	li	55	3
Messius Phronimus, A.	0	?	li	68	3
Messius Phronimus, A.	0	?	li	71	5
Messius Phronimus, A.	0	?	li	75	4
Messius Phronimus, A.	0	?	li	83	3
Messius Phronimus, A.	0	?	li	101	6
Messius Phronimus, A.	0	?	li	102	2
Messius Phronimus, A.	0	?	li	113	6
Messius Phronimus, A.	0	?	li	141	3
Messius Phronimus, A.	0	?	li	153	3
Messius Phronimus, A.	0	?	li	32	2
Messius Phronimus, A.	0	?	li	34	6
Mincullius Faustus, C.	0	?	li	93	7
Minicius Atticus	0	?	li	81	8
Minisius Fructus, Q.	0	?	li	95	4
Mulvius Fronto, P.	0	?	in	79	5
Naevoleius Nymphius, L.	0	?	li	103	7
Nasennius Nympheros, N.	0	?	li	81	6
Nerius Hyginus?, L.	0	?	li	7	2
Nerius Hyginus, N.	0	?	li	54	3
Nerius Hyginus, N.	0	?	li	57	7
Nerius Hyginus, N.	0	?	li	66	3
Nerius Hyginus, N.	0	?	li	74	4
Nerius Hyginus, N.	0	?	li	78	2
Nerius Hyginus, N.	0	?	li	81	5
Nevoleius Felix, C.	0	?	li	132	2
Ninnius Optatus, L.	0	?	li	19	7
Ninnius Calvus, N.	0	?	in	70	1
Ninnius Iustus, N.	0	?	in	70	2
Nonius Scamander, Sex.	0	?	li	17	4
Nonius Scamander, Sex.	0	?	li	103	2
Novellius Fortunatus, C.	0	?	li	22	7
Numisius Rarus, L.	0	ae	in	22	2
Numisius Iucundus, Sex.	175	?	li	7	1
Numisius Iucundus, Sex.	175	?	li	55	1

Numisius Iucundus, Sex.	175	?	li	62	2
Numistreius Saturninus	0	?	in	128	2
Numitorius Anthus?, C.	0	?	li	80	5
Numitorius Audius Bassus, C.	0	d	in	151	2
Numitorius Audius Bassus, C.	0	d	in	22	1
Numitorius Iason, C.	0	?	li	80	6
Nunnidius Syn..., C.	0	?	li	7	8
Obellius Firmus, M.	1780	d	in	8	1
Obellius Firmus p., M.	1780	?	in	81	3
Oppius Felicio, N.	0	?	li	26	2
Oppius Felicio, N.	0	?	li	65	2
Oppius Felicio, N.	0	?	li	76	6
Paccius Philodespotus, A.	0	?	li	114	6
Paquius Philodespotes, A.	0	?	li	75	7
Paccius Cerinthus, P.	0	?	li	7	5
Paccius Cerinthus, P.	0	?	li	18	3
Pacuvius Vitalis	0	?	?	109	4
Pompeius Grosphus Gavianus, Cn.	0	d	in	145	3
Pompeius Axsiochus, Sex.	434	?	li	47	2
Pompeius Axsiochus, Sex.	434	?	li	73	5
Pompeius Epaphus, Sex.	0	?	li	100	2
Pomponius Marcellus, P.	0	?	in	29	1
Pomponius Marcellus, P.	0	?	in	80	2
Popidius Donatus	0	?	?	98	5
Popidius Ampliatus I, L.	0	?	li	47	4
Popidius Ampliatus I, L.	0	?	li	82	2
Popidius Ampliatus I, L.	0	?	li	94	2
Popidius Ampliatus I, L.	0	?	li	98	2
Popidius Ampliatus I, L.	0	?	li	71	3
Popidius Amarantus, N.	0	?	li	48	4
Popidius Amarantus, N.	0	?	li	12	4
Popidius Amarantus, N.	0	?	li	71	4
Popidius Amarantus, N.	0	?	li	76	3
Popidius Amarantus, N.	0	?	li	96	6
Popidius Amarantus, N.	0	?	li	101	3
Popidius Amarantus, N.	0	?	li	109	6
Popidius Ampliatus, N.	0	m	li	49	7
Popidius Ampliatus, N.	0	m	li	83	2

Popidius Felicio, N.	0	?	li	80	8
Popidius Narcissus, N.	0	?	li	34	2
Popidius Narcissus, N.	0	?	li	37	2
Popidius Narcissus, N.	0	?	li	70	7
Popidius Narcissus, N.	0	?	li	110	2
Popidius Nymphius?, N.	0	?	li	57	4
Popidius Olynthus, N.	0	?	li	80	7
Popidius Sodalio, N.	0	?	?	28	6
Popidius Sodalio, N.	0	?	?	48	7
Popidius Sodalio, N.	0	?	?	99	5
Popidius Sodalio, N.	0	?	?	100	4
Popidius Sodalio, N.	0	?	?	102	1
Poppaeus Ephebus, C.	0	?	li	82	4
Poppaeus F..., C.	0	?	?	38	5
Poppaeus Felix, Q.	0	?	li	18	1
Poppaeus Felix, Q.	0	?	li	94	1
Poppaeus Fortis, C.	0	?	?	35	6
Poppaeus Narcissus, P.	0	?	li	69	4
Poppaeus Sorex, Q.	0	?	li	29	2
Poppaeus Sorex, Q.	0	?	li	94	6
Postumius, N.	0	?	?	56	3
Postumius Modestus, Q.	0	q	in	96	1
Postumius Primus, Q.	0	?	li	74	3
Postumius Primus, T?	0	?	li	49	1
Proculeius, C.	0	?	?	39	2
Proculeius Deutericus?, C.	0	?	li	132	3
Pupius Rufus, M.	0	d	in	109	1
Quintius Primus	0	?	li	12	9
Rufellius Horus, M.	0	?	li	48	5
Rufellius Horus, M.	0	?	li	74	7
Rufellius Horus, M.	0	?	li	116	3
Rufellius Horus, M.	0	?	li	133	1
Ruleius Horus, C.	0	?	li	19	6
Saenius Aper, A.	0	?	?	56	1
Salvius Eut..., A?	0	?	li	110	6
Sandelius A?	0	?	?	107	2
Seius Herma, Cn.	0	?	li	87	6
Seius Herma, Cn.	0	?	li	95	8

Septumius Phlegon?, L.	0	?	li	92	6
Sestius Cytissus, L.	0	?	li	13	7
Sestius Trophimus?, L.	0	?	li	108	2
Sestius Maximus	0	?	li	10	6
Sestius Maximus	0	?	li	84	2
Sevius Rufus, L.	0	?	in	81	1
Sevius Rufus, L.	0	?	in	89	1
Sextilius Abascantus, L.	0	?	li	92	5
Sextilius Faustus, L.	0	?	li	71	9
Sextius Primus, P.	0	?	li	40	7
Sittius Speratus, P.	0	?	li	14	7
Sittius Zosimus, P.	0	?	li	43	3
Sittius Zosimus, P.	0	?	li	99	6
Sornius Eutychus, T.	0	?	li	66	4
Sornius Eutychus, T.	0	?	li	110	3
Sornius Eutychus, T.	0	?	li	69	1
Sornius Eutychus, T.	0	?	li	73	2
Sornius Eutychus, T.	0	?	li	5	3
Sornius Eutychus, T.	0	?	li	13	3
Sornius Eutychus, T.	0	?	li	14	3
Sornius Eutychus, T.	0	?	li	17	3
Sornius Eutychus, T.	0	?	li	49	5
Sornius Eutychus, T.	0	?	li	61	3
Sornius Eutychus, T.	0	?	li	90	3
Sornius Eutychus, T.	0	?	li	91	2
Sornius Eutychus, T.	0	?	li	101	4
Sornius Eutychus, T.	0	?	li	106	3
Sornius Eutychus, T.	0	?	li	113	5
Sornius Eutychus, T.	0	?	li	116	1
Sornius Eutychus, T.	0	?	li	85	2
Stabius Chryseros, M.	0	?	li	40	4
Stabius Valens, M.	0	?	?	55	4
Staius Ph...	0	?	li	47	5
Statius Stasimus	0	?	li	54	4
Stlaborius Nymphodotus, M.	0	?	li	94	5
Stlaborius Nymphodotus, M.	0	?	li	114	2
Stronnius Fau..., M.	0	?	?	76	9
Stronnius Secundus, M.	0	?	?	18	2

Stronnius Secundus, M.	0	?	?	139	2
Stronnius Secundus, M.	0	?	?	142	3
Stronnius Secundus, M.	0	?	?	153	2
Sulpicius Phosphorus, C?	0	?	li	98	1
Sulpicius Phosphorus, Q.	0	?	li	93	3
Sulpicius Soter, Q.	0	?	li	91	5
Terentius Apollonius, P.	0	?	li	95	6
Terentius Eros, P.	0	?	li	18	8
Terentius Eros, P.	0	?	li	85	4
Terentius Primus, P.	0	?	li	25	5
Terentius Primus, P.	0	?	li	35	4
Terentius Primus, P.	0	?	li	38	6
Terentius Primus, P.	0	?	li	39	1
Terentius Primus, P.	0	?	li	46	2
Terentius Primus, P.	0	?	li	48	3
Terentius Primus, P.	0	?	li	55	2
Terentius Primus, P.	0	?	li	67	3
Terentius Primus, P.	0	?	li	69	2
Terentius Primus, P.	0	?	li	81	4
Terentius Primus, P.	0	?	li	86	1
Terentius Primus, P.	0	?	li	91	1
Terentius Primus, P.	0	?	li	93	8
Terentius Primus, P.	0	?	li	109	3
Terentius Primus, P.	0	?	li	112	5
Terentius Primus, P.	0	?	li	116	2
Terentius Primus, P.	0	?	li	145	4
Terentius Prosodos, P.	0	?	li	100	5
Terentius Q.	0	?	?	52	2
Terentius Felix, T.	0	ae	in	80	1
Terentius Maximus, T.	0	?	?	31	8
Terentius Maximus, T.	0	?	?	80	4
Tetteius Festus, A.	0	?	?	83	6
Tetteius Festus, L.	0	?	?	69	5
Tettienus Priscus, N?	0	?	?	47	1
Tettius Rufus, M.	0	?	in	100	1
Thermius Secundus?, L.	0	?	?	92	8
Thoranius Secundus, P.	0	?	?	109	2
Thoranius H..., Q.	0	?	?	131	1

Tussidius Verus, L.	0	?	in	95	1
Ubonius Cogitatus, M.	0	?	li	37	9
Ubonius Cogitatus, M.	0	?	li	115	2
Umbricius Modestus, A.	0	?	?	104	3
Umbricius Modestus, A.	0	?	?	113	9
Urbanius H..., M.	0	?	?	112	7
Valerius Peregrinus, L.	0	?	?	22	5
Valerius Peregrinus, L.	0	?	?	70	9
Valerius Peregrinus, L.	0	?	?	115	4
Valerius Dec..., M.	0	?	?	51	3
Valerius Bassus, Q.	0	?	?	48	1
Vedius Ceratus, L.	0	?	li	40	1
Vedius Primus, P.	0	?	li	6	2
Veius Atticus, A.	0	au	li	22	3
Veius Atticus, A.	0	au	li	35	3
Veius Atticus, A.	0	au	li	49	3
Veius Atticus, A.	0	au	li	67	2
Veius Atticus, A.	0	au	li	99	3
Veius Atticus, A.	0	au	li	115	1
Veius Nymphius, A.	0	?	li	81	7
Veius Nymphius, A.	0	?	li	103	4
Veius Felix, M.	0	?	li	88	5
Veius Martialis, N.	0	?	?	28	3
Veius Martialis, N.	0	?	?	108	5
Velasius Terminalis, A.	0	?	li	14	6
Venerius Secundus, M.	0	?	li	139	3
Vera... Phile..., L.	0	?	li	142	4
Veratius Hermes, M.	0	?	li	28	8
Veratius Atticus, N.	0	?	li	26	4
Vesonius Hermes	0	?	li	66	7
Vesonius Marcellus, M.	0	q	in	143	3
Vesonius Primus	650	?	?	31	5
Vesonius Le..., T.	0	?	?	25	8
Vettius Conviva, A.	1048	au	li	96	4
Vettius Iliacus, A.	0	?	li	65	3
Vettius Iliacus, A.	0	?	li	78	3
Vettius Donatus	0	?	?	54	8
Vettius Donatus	0	?	?	7	6

Vettius Aethon, L.	0	?	li	38	1
Vettius Auctus, L.	0	?	li	88	6
Vettius Valens, L.	0	?	?	26	3
Vettius Valens, L.	0	?	?	35	5
Veturius Sennaeus?, C.	0	?	?	88	3
Vibius Alcimus, C.	0	?	?	40	8
Vibius Cresimus, C.	0	?	li	26	5
Vibius Palepatus, C.	0	?	li	92	4
Vibius Macer, T.	0	?	in	106	1
Vibrius Callistus, Cn.	0	?	li	28	1
Vibrius Callistus, Cn.	0	?	li	61	4
Vibrius Callistus, Cn.	0	?	li	68	4
Vibrius Callistus, Cn.	0	?	li	71	6
Vibrius Callistus, Cn.	0	?	li	74	5
Vibrius Callistus, Cn.	0	?	li	75	2
Vibrius Callistus, Cn.	0	?	li	87	4
Vibrius Callistus, Cn.	0	?	li	102	3
Vibrius Callistus, Cn.	0	?	li	114	4
Vibullius Felicio	0	?	li	13	6
Volcius Thallus, D.	0	?	li	40	5
Volusius Faustus, L.	210	?	li	87	1
Volusius Faustus, L.	210	?	li	113	7
Volusius Faustus, L.	210	?	li	114	3
Volusius Faustus, L.	210	?	li	130	3
Volusius Faustus, L.	210	?	li	37	4
F... Proculus, M.	0	?	in	46	4
...ius Hyginus, N.	0	?	li	28	4
...sius Pronimus	0	?	li	114	7

Appendix III: The houses of some witnesses

L. Albucius Thesmus IX, 1, 28

L. Albucius Thesmus was probably the occupant of the *stabulum* IX 1, 28. To the right of the entrance we read L. Albucium AED/Thesmus LIBERT ROG.[1] He seems a humble freedman, but with at least regular means of support.[2]

Cn. Alleius Nigidius Maius VI, 6, 1

With Cn. Alleius Nigidus Maius we are dealing with a major figure from Pompeian social and political life. He was e.g. *quinquennalis* in 55/56, *flamen Caesaris Augusti* and *princeps coloniae*. On the house VI 6,1 we find CIL IV 138, in which we read that shops and other property which is are part of the *'Insula Arriana Polliana Cn. Alleii Nigidi Maï'* are for rent. He does not seem to live in the house at this late date, however. Restorations were not yet entirely finished. Cn. Alleius Nigidius is seller in t. 16, from the year that he was *quinquennalis*. He signs first there. He is first witness in t. 77.[3] A lot more could be said about him, but nothing that is specifically relevant for our purpose.[4]

Q. Brittius Balbus IX, 2, 16

He can be identified with the occupant of the rather modest house IX 2, 16. The identification seems quite acceptable. The *dipinti* where we find him as candidate are very concentrated around the house.[5] On or opposite the house we find him as a supporter.[6] In some of these inscriptions we find only the *cognomen*, but I feel justified that we can use them, because we have such a concentration of them (and sometimes together with *praenomina* and *gentilicia*). Also found in Balbus' house

[1]CIL IV 2983.

[2]For a short description of the building, see: Della Corte (1965) p. 212.

[3]This is an interesting tablet because we possibly find so[ci] in this tablet.

[4]Cf. van Buren (1947).

[5]CIL IV 935 c (?), 935 g, 3159, 3607, 3702, 3773.

[6]CIL IV 935b, 935d, 935h, 2958 (?).

was the seal with the name of T. Dentatius Panthera, and not in the shop 15, as Andreau says, or in 26 as CIL X suggests.[1] Possibly he was a later occupant.

We know Balbus obtained the position of *aedilis* - in CIL X 826 he is used as a dating. Della Corte thinks that we have the father in this inscription, but does not produce an argument. Castrén dates Balbus' aedileship in A.D. 56/57. We also find Balbus as *duovir* candidate, where it is said of him *'hic aerarium conservabit'*.[2]

One more thing that we know about him, although Castrén does unfortunately not give a reference to it, is that his full name occurs in the dative/ablative on an amphora (Schoene X) found in the house V 2, e, which may indicate that he was either a producer or more likely an intermediary for the product, probably wine, or a wine based product.[3]

Balbus seems to have been a political ally of A. Vettius Caprasius Felix, whose candidature is dated as Flavian by Castrén.[4] In t. 56 Balbus is second witness and in t. 74 first witness.

D. Caprasius Felix IX 7, 20

The identification of the house IX 7, 20 as the house of Caprasius Felix is not very certain, but I am prepared to accept it. In the house an *amphora* was found with the text *'D. Caprasio Felici'*. [5] As it was not found in a shop it was probably bought for private consumption.[6] We find a graffito in the house that reads *'Suc(ces)sus Fel[i]ci salutem et*

[1] 'Giornale degli Scavi di Pompei.' N.S. I (1868-1869) p. 246.

[2] CIL IV 3702, and perhaps similarly 3773. I do not think that the phrase should be read to mean that he will follow a conservative financial policy. I rather think that it suggests that he will pay much out his own pocket, as befits a proper magistrate and benefactor. Cf. my discussion of the content of 'political' discourse, above, p. 284 ff.

[3] CIL IV 5783. Cf. Andreau (1974) 244.

[4] CIL IV 935b, 935h, 935i, cf. also 935 g.

[5] CIL IV 5650, form VII.

[6] Andreau (1974) 243 f.

For(tu)natae'.[1] But Felix is of course a rather common name. The third element in the identification is that in the small street opposite the house a Caprasius supports A. Vettius Syrticus and Q. Brittius Balbus.[2] In CIL IV 3687, on the house, '*vicini*' want A. Vettius Caprasius Felix as aedile.[3] This suggests a relationship between him and D. Caprasius Felix. Perhaps D. Caprasius Felix was his father.[4]

Maiuri remarks that the restoration of the house was almost finished in A.D. 79.[5] Moeller argues that spinning and/or weaving were done in this house, because a graffito records 19 pounds or weights of wool.[6] I do not know whether this is enough evidence to make it into a spinning and/or weaving establishment.[7]

L. Cornelius Primogenes VI, 9, 2

The identification of the house of L. Cornelius Primogenes is not very secure. In the house VI 9, 2 a seal was recovered reading PHOEBUS/L.C. PRIMOG.[8] It was not found in a shop-like environment, when one could deduce nothing about the position of the master. The main problem is that the C. could of course also be read differently, but L. Cornelius Primogenes is the only name in Castrén that fits.[9]

There are two *amphorae* with initials that fit his name.[10] It is very hazardous to deduce anything about economic activity from the wallpaintings of the house. Perhaps the paintings in

[1]CIL IV 5378.

[2]CIL IV 935g.

[3]For 'vicini': above, p. 173; 304.

[4]Andreau (1974) 201.

[5]Maiuri (1942) 127.

[6]Moeller (1976) 40.

[7]See above, p. 164.

[8]CIL X 8058, 66.

[9]L. Caecilius Primogenes would be such a possibility. Cf. Andreau (1974) 35 and also CIL X 849.

[10]CIL IV 9495 and 5756.

an entrance hall may have some significance.[1] They depict Bacchus, Mercury and Neptune, while Bacchic scenes recur elsewhere in the house. But it would be improper to derive too much from this.

P. Cornelius Tages *I, 7, 10-12.18.19*

The house I 7, 10-12.18.19 (Plate XXVIII) has been identified as the house of P. Cornelius Tages. Two *amphorae* were found with his name. In the *atrium* of I 7, 11 one was found with the insciption: *Oliva alba/Publo TegETI* (CIL IV 9437), and in the peristyle of I 7, 19 one that reads after some numbers: *P COR*.[2] The latter *amphora* is of form VIII, about which Andreau remarks that the products transported in these *amphorae* had more to do with an intermediary than the wines in the amphorae of form XII.[3]

Additional support for the identification of the 'ownership' of the house is provided by two programmata on I 8, 18, i.e. opposite the house.[4] Here we see parts of his name as supporter. I do not see the force of Della Corte's argument that the '*...vs rog*' in CIL IV 7258 must refer to Cornelius Tages.

His ranking as witness is consistently rather low. But the house is certainly fairly large and richly decorated. Structurally, however, it is not a very grand affair. In fact it consists of several smaller houses, joined together.

Everything points to someone who has amassed a large fortune in a short time. It also shows that it was not always possible for such a person to obtain a grand house on the market.[5] The owner obviously had to improvise and make do with lavish decoration instead of another house. It is not improbable that P. Cornelius Tages was in fact a wine

[1] Andreau (1974) 240. Cf. Petronius, 'Satir.' 29.

[2] CIL IV 9493.

[3] Andreau (1974) 250.

[4] CIL IV 7314 and 7315.

[5] The ideology for rich and prestigeous families to cling their ancestral property is of course not only Roman. In 1536 Stafano di Antonio Bernardi - of Lucca- writes in his will: 'Ipsa domus magna semper postea teneatur, habitetur et usufructetur per maiores natu de domo et familia illorum de Bernardis de Luca in perpetuum.' Heers (1974) 113.

merchant.[1] In Andreau's view this is suggested by the occurrence of Tages' name on an amphora with numbers.[2]

M. Epidius Hymenaeus III, 4, 3

With him we seem to reach the lower strata of Pompeian society. The building is rather modest, although it is difficult to decide whether the entrance 3 should be taken as the only part in which Hymenaeus has an interest, or whether he was the only occupant.[3] It seems to be a wine store or shop. Inside, six *amphorae* were found with either his name in the dative or his initials.[4] We find him as supporter in a poster on the house with his *nomen* and *cognomen*.[5] It seems he was a wine trader, but not of great wealth.

M. Fabius Eupor VI, ins. occ, 39

M. Fabius Eupor styles himself *'princeps libertinorum'*. I take *'libertini'* here as freedmen, and not as a sect of Jews, as has been argued.[6] This inscription (CIL IV 117), and another where he is supporter (CIL IV 120) was found on VI *ins. occ.* 39. Only the façade has so far been excavated. But given the width of it I would not be surprised if it would be a fairly large house. And with a nice view of the sea. On an *amphora* we read *'M. Fabi Eupori/Cnidium'*, below another name.[7] So maybe M. Fabius Eupor was a wine merchant. On two other *amphorae* we find his initials.[8]

All this gives a picture of M. Fabius Eupor as a rather wealthy man of freedman status. M. Fabius Thelus seems to have been more prestigious than Eupor, and may have been his patron. We find Thelus in t. 97, where he signs above Eupor.

[1]Andreau (1974) 268.

[2]Andreau (1974) 246 ff. The inscription on the amphora is CIL IV 9493.

[3]Cf. Andreau (1974) 245 n. 2.

[4]CIL IV 9517 and 9518.

[5]CIL IV 7692. There are a few more programmata of secondary interest: CIL IV 7691, 7708, 7709. To complicate things we also find 7509 on II 4,4.

[6]Ginsburg (1934) for the correct interpretation.

[7]CIL IV 5535. Found in VI, 15, 8.

[8]CIL IV 9444 and 9445.

M. Fabius Secundus V, 4, 13

The basis for the identification of the house of M. Fabius Secundus as V, 4, 13 is a seal with his full name.[1] Additional support for the identification is provided by CIL IV 6755: *'Optata Secundo suo salutem'*. The house seems to have been inhabited in the latest period.[2]

M. Fabius Secundus erects a sculpture with inscription in the temple of Venus, for the Tellus Dea, it seems after A.D. 62.[3] It is possible that M. Fabius Secundus was a trader. In the entrance hall to the house we find paintings of Mercury and maritime scenes. The ship concerned is a merchant ship.[4] Andreau considers him one of the most prestigious traders.[5]

Fabius Tyrannus VI, 7, 19

Between VI 7, 18 and 19 we find two posters, one in which a Fabius supports the candidature of a Samellius (CIL IV 217), the other in which a Tyrannus supports a Cerrinius (CIL IV 224). Between 19 and 20 we see how Tyrannus supports, *'cupiens cum sodalibus'*, M. Cerrinius Vatia.[6]

It is clear that this is not much to support the view that Fabius Tyrannus has something to do with the house VI 7, 19. On the other hand, Fabius Tyranus is the only Tyrannus in Pompeii with a *nomen*. I have no idea who the *'sodales'* are.

N. Herennius Castus V, 2, f

In house V 2, f., a seal was found with the text:[7]

N. Herenni/ Casti Musaes/ (HAVE)//

[1]Della Corte (1965) sign. 42. 'Notizie degli Scavi di Antichità.' 1905 p. 97. For a description of the house see 'idem' p. 85 ff. The seal was found in room S on the map on p. 87.

[2]Recent coins were found, including two asses of Domitian.

[3]CIL X 801.

[4]For a picture see: Warscher (1925) 130 fig. 29.

[5]Andreau (1974) 306.

[6]CIL IV 221.

[7]Della Corte (1965) sign. 49. 'Notizie degi Scavi di Antichtà.' 1891 p. 133.

So he must have been the freedman of some Musa. To the right of the entrance to V 2, f. we find CIL IV 4268, 'Musa'. This looks like a rather modest and utilitarian building.

A. Herennuleius Communis VI, 7, 23
In VI 7, 23 a seal was found with virtually his complete name.[1]

C. Iulius Polybius IX 13, 1-3
C. Iulius Polybius figures in so far close to sixty inscriptions. But that was before the start of the excavation of what is allegedly his house. This house is clearly a grand affair and my guess from what I have seen is that it is over 1000 sq. m. Because this excavation is still going on I do not want to come forward with too outspoken conclusions. But for the time being I accept the identification of the house. On the house we find CIL IV 7945 and 7954 with *'Polybius rogat'*. Opposite the house, on I, 9, 1 we find CIL 7316 referring to the *'collega'* of C. Iulius Polybius, A. Rustius Verus, with the line, *'et ille Polybium faciet'*.[2] Nearby, on IX, 12, 17, we find in CIL IV 7925 the *'vicini'* asking for Polybius.[3] Further, in 7958, on the house, he is supported as candidate.

An interesting poster is CIL IV 429, where it is said of him *'panem bonum fert'*. I do not suppose that he was a baker, I think the phrase must be read in the context of euergetism, or more likely as referring to an activity of the *aediles*. Polybius is *aedilis* candidate in this inscription. But he seems to have had some contacts with the bakers, because in two insciptions he is supported by bakers.[4] Elsewhere he is supported by *'muliones'*.[5]

His candidature is probably from the last period before the eruption. This should explain the very large number of election

[1]CIL X 8058, 39.

[2]Cf. CIL IV 7942, on IX, 13, 1.

[3]For 'vicini': above, p. 173; 304.

[4]CIL IV 875 and 886.

[5]CIL IV 134.

posters with his name.[1] His name suggests that he was the son of an imperial freedman. Hopefully the excavations in his house will yield a lot more information about him. His initials occur on three *amphorae*, although it is unclear to me what the meaning of this is.[2]

L. Laelius Trophimus VI 7, 20-21

A seal with the letters L. LAE.TRO was found in the house VI 7, 20-21.[3] It seems pretty certain that this must be L. Laelius Trophimus. No other person from Castrén's prosopography can be fitted to these letters. Yet it is not so easy to be precise about Trophimus' relations with the house. Another seal with the name of P. Antistius Maximus was also found in the house.[4] It is possible, but by no means certain, that a L. Laelius Erastus also lived in the house. L. Laelius Trophimus was probably the freedman of L. Laelius Fuscus, who signs as first witness in t. 13, where Trophimus signs as fourth witness.[5]

Eschebach says about the house that it is a combination of two previously private houses, formed into one house with a workshop.[6]

M. Lucretius Lerus V, 4, 11.a

In house V 4, 11. a we find in the *peristylium*, on fourth style wallpaintings, two graffiti, *'M. Lucretius Lirus'* and *'Lirus'*.[7] So it is not unreasonable to assume a relationship between him and the house. The more so since there are a number of election posters for and by M. Lucretius Fronto on and near the

[1]But cf. above, p. 315 f.

[2]CIL IV 9365 and 5997. Cf. Andreau (1974) 238.

[3]CIL X 8058, 44. Della Corte (1965) sign. 55.

[4]Della Corte (1965) sign. 3.

[5]Andreau (1974) 172.

[6]Eschebach (1970) 131.

[7]CIL IV 6797 and 6799.

house.[1] Fronto was a *quinquennalis* candidate of the Flavian period.[2]

Bastet, who has done a recent campaign in the house, believes that the house was not yet inhabited in A.D. 79.[3] It would be tempting to see in M. Lucretius Lirus a freedman representative of Fronto, while the latter was away. But this depends somewhat on the dating of the graffiti with Lirus' name. Although we normally take fourth style decorations as post-earthquake, this need not be the case. Another element is that in t. 10, Lirus receives HS 38079 from a sale, and signs as third witness, while Fronto is not one of the known witnesses. This tablet is dated 22 January A.D. 55. Altoghether he seems to be a not unimportant man, who could command some financial resources, but who clearly does not belong to the *ordo*.

Sex. Numisius Iucundus VII 4, 24-25

On VII 4, 24-25 *'Numisius Iucundus cum Secundo et Victore'* supports A. Vettius Firmus. The building is an *officina olearia*, with shop, workshop and a house.

M. Obellius Firmus, father and son IX, (14), 2.4.b

Elsewhere I have discussed M. Obellius Firmus at greater length than is required for our purpose here.[4] In recent years a tomb has been excavated and produced a funerary inscription.[5] The most important conclusion that could be drawn from this inscription was of course that we now know for certain that M. Obellius Firmus was *aedilis* and *duovir*, and dead by A.D. 79. He receives a public funeral and substantial honours. The main problem is that there are a father and a son with the same name. I think it is the son who reached the highest social status, and consequently it seems to be his tomb that has been excavated. My main argument is CIL IV 3828, where *'Obelli cum*

[1]CIL IV 6796, 6795, 6693, 6626, 6625.

[2]Castrén (1975) 'ad nom'.

[3]Bastet (1975).

[4]Jongman (1978-79).

[5]See now also: De Caro (1979a) 65-71.

patre' is encouraged to favour a candidate. But we cannot be certain.

In t. 8, Obellius Firmus signs first, while in t. 81 a p, for *pater*, is added to the name. There the Obellius Firmus signs third. The house identification is primarily on the basis of three graffiti in the house, *'M. Obellius'*, *'Firmus'*, and *'Obellius'*.[1] We find an election poster *'M. Obelium'* on the house itself, and a few others nearby.[2]

The restoration of the house was still in progress at the time of the eruption, and since I assume that M. Obellius Firmus, the son, was dead at that time, we must ask ourselves the question who was responsible for this. Perhaps it was a freedman of the family, since we don't know a grandson. This might be suggested by the fact that it was the *lararium* that was first restored. M. Obellius Firmus seems to have been *duovir* in the post earthquake period, so perhaps he lived on a country estate in that period.[3]

Sex. Pompeius Axsiochus VI, 13, 19

In the house VI, 13, 19 a seal was recovered with the text Pompei/Axiochi.[4] The house is beautiful and old, with traces of all styles of wallpainting.[5]

M. Pupius Rufus VI, 15, 5.24.25

About his social status we can be clear. He is candidate *aedilis* and *duovir*.[6] The identification of the house VI 15,5 seems reasonably certain. A graffito *'M. Pupius Ruphus'* comes from the house.[7] CIL IV 3537 (*'....Pupius Ruphus facit/ IDEM probat'*) is on the house. We find an election poster with the name in the accusative on the house (CIL IV 3534), and others on houses

[1] CIL IV 8970, 8971b, 8996.

[2] CIL IV 7806. CIL IV 3829, 6621, 3828.

[3] Cf. Andreau (1973) 369 ff.

[4] CIL X 8058, 68. Fiorelli in: 'Notizie degli Scavi di Antichtà.' 1876, p. 59.

[5] Giornale degli Scavi di Pompei. n.s.III, p. 50 ff. 'Bullettino dell' Instit. di Corr. archeol. di Roma' (1875) 188 ff.

[6] CIL IV 142, 302, 3527, 3529, 3534, 3562 (?).

[7] CIL IV 4615.

nearby.[1] Two more are found on other houses in Regio VI.[2] CIL IV 5013 (*'Pupius'*, on IX 2, 26) seems irrelevant. In the house three seals were found with names of otherwise unknown people.[3] According to Andreau, the candidature of M. Pupius Rufus possibly dates from after A.D. 62.[4] The house is clearly a rather large one.

A. Vettius Conviva VI, 15,1.27

And now we come to the house of the Vettii (Plates IX and X). This identification is quite secure, it seems. In the house we find two seals with *'A. Vetti Convivaes'* and *'A. V. Co.'*.[5] However, we also find a seal for A. Vettius Restitutus.[6] On the house we find a poster exhorting Vettius Conviva, *augustalis*.[7]

It is quite interesting that he was an *augustalis*. The house has many fourth style wallpaintings. The mural decorations in the house indicate perhaps wine production and trade, but not necessarily by the last occupant.

L. Volusius Faustus I 2,10

The basis of the identification with the house I 2,10 is a seal reading L. Vol. Fau., which seems to refer to L. Volusius Faustus.[8] The inscription on the *garum* jar that was found in the house and that carries his name, has probably been read incorrectly.[9]

[1]CIL IV 3527 and 3529 on VI 15, 1 and 3562 between VI, 15, 5 and VI 15, 6.

[2]CIL IV 142 on VI 2, 15.22 and CIL IV 302 on VI 13, 21.

[3]Della Corte (1965) sign. 81 (L. Seponius Amphion), sign. 88 (C. Stlaccius Epitynchanus) and sign. 92 (Titinia Saturnina?).

[4]Andreau (1974) 201.

[5]Della Corte (1965) sign. 98 and sign. 99 ('Notizie degli Scavi di Antichità.' 1895 p. 32).

[6]Della Corte (1965) sign. 100.

[7]CIL IV 3509.

[8]CIL X 8058, 96.

[9]CIL IV 10281a. Cf. Andreau (1974) 295. See Mau on CIL IV 5713.

Appendix IV: How many witnesses?[1]

In this appendix a more extensive discussion will be given of the technique that was employed to estimate the number of witnesses, including those not known from the documentation. This is an important problem that many historians have to face in their research, and for which they often employ - in an intuitive fashion - the same principle as that which will be used here in more formal fashion. Historians are used to incomplete documentation, and have for many questions adapted to that problem by treating their documentation as a random sample. Much argument centers around the problem whether such documentation can indeed be treated as a random sample, even though we may surmise that it has not been drawn according to the rules which govern random sampling. My own chapter six provides many of such arguments.

Yet, the problem is that a sample can never be representative of a population in one respect: its size. Therefore, whenever a question concerns the size of a population, ordinary techniques of statistical inference from samples to populations are of no use.[2] The technique employed here tries to overcome this problem. Its core consists of the notion that there is a relationship between the quantity of documentation and the amount of information gained from this documentation. The relationship takes the form of decreasing marginal information returns per marginal unit of documentation. The first document will only provide previously unknown information, but with each additional document the proportion of information that was already known from previous documents increases. Therefore, more documentation provides less and less new and previously unknown information.

The crucial element of the methodology is the notion that

[1]This analysis was performed and written in cooperation with my brother Pieter Jan Jongman. I should like to express my appreciation to Adam Lomnicki for encouraging me to search in the biological literature.

[2]One of the advantages of estimating population size from properties in a documentation that has been 'sampled' by the hazards of record survival, is that it provides an additional means to evaluate the representativeness of that documentation. We can better answer the question: 'representative for what?' Knowing the size of a population we may compare it to the size of the group with which it is supposed to coincide.

this decrease in information yield per unit of documentation is a function of the total amount of information. If the latter is small, only a small number of documents will provide us with all possible information: the information yield per document declines rapidly. If the total amount of information is large, then each new document is - for a long time - likely to produce largely previously unknown information. The rate at which the information yield per unit of documentation decreases therefore allows us to estimate the total quantity of information. Intuitively, this is what we often do. If an - incomplete - set of documents keeps informing us about the same small number of persons, we conclude that more documentation will probably not bring many more persons to light, and that consequently we are dealing with a small social group.

Presented in this fashion, the problem is similar to what biologists have to face when they have to estimate the size of biological populations. By diligently catching fish, they gradually deplete the number of fish in a lake, and the rate at which the catch per unit of fishing effort decreases, allows them to estimate the total population of fish that were originally in the lake. Delury (1947) provides the following equation to estimate population from the decreasing returns to units of effort:

$$C(t) = kN(0) - kK(t)$$

where $C(t)$ equals the catch per unit effort for the time interval t, $K(t)$ equals the total catch up to interval t, and k is called the catchability, i.e. the proportion of the population captured during interval t by one unit of effort. $N(t)$ equals the number of individuals in the population at time t, so $N(0)$ is the total population before any fishing has occurred.[1] In our case one unit of effort may be equated to randomly drawing 10 documents from the 153 available documents, and $C(t)$ equals the number of persons that were not yet known from previously drawn documents, but only became known because these last ten documents were drawn.

[1]The assumptions, in this case a closed population and constant catchability, are largely and entirely fulfilled respectively.

Actual catching procedure requires some more explanation. In order to avoid too much random scatter, drawing the documents was repeated one hundred times. We employ our advantage that for us catching need not be a one-off thing; besides, repeating the sampling also copes with the varying numbers of witnesses per document. The mean result of these 100 samples was used as input in the regression analysis. The regression results were:

$$C(t) = 31.134 - 0.05426\ K(t)$$

(Estimated coefficients differ significantly from 0 at five percent level, adjusted $R^2 = 0.89$)

This implies that $k = 0.05426$ and $kN(0) = 31.134$. Therefore, $N(0) = 574$.

A different way of estimating the same would be by means of the following equation.[1]:

$$\ln C(t) = \ln (kN(0)) - kE(t)$$

$E(t)$ represents the total effort up to t. The regression results were:

$$\ln C(t) = 3.463 - 0.05178\ E(t)$$

(Estimated coefficients differ significantly from 0 at five percent level, adjusted $R^2 = 0.86$) Hence, $k = 0.05178$; $\ln (kN(0)) = 3.463$. Therefore, $N(0) = 616$.

The two equations (the linear and the logarithmic) describe the same process, and can be mathematically derived from each other. Yet the statistical results differ somewhat, though not to a large extent. We can therefore avoid choosing between the two equations.

[1]We employ the natural logarithm (ln) even though Delury's text quotes the common logarithm (log). His calculations show that he means ln: he ascribes the properties of ln to what he writes as log. This is apparent on page 159 in the derivation of equation 1.

BIBLIOGRAPHY

Abrams, Ph. (1978) Towns and economic growth: some theories and problems. in: Abrams and Wrigley (1978) 9-33.

Abrams, Ph. and Wrigley, E.A. (eds.) (1978) *Towns in societies. Essays in economic history and historical sociology.* Cambridge.

Accame, S. (1942) La legislazione Romana intorno ai collegi nel I secolo A.C. in: *Bullettino del Museo dell' Impero Romano.* XIII (= suppl. to *Bullettino della commissione archeologica del governatore di Roma.* (1942) LXX).

Alonso, W. (1960) A theory of the urban land market. in: *Papers and Proceedings, Regional Science Association.* VI 149-157.

Andreae, B. (1975) Rekonstruktion des grossen Oecus der Villa des P. Fannius Synistor in Boscoreale. in: Andreae and Kyrieleis (1975) 71-92.

Andreae, B. and Kyrieleis, H. (eds.) (1975) *Neue Forschungen in Pompeji und den anderen vom Vesuvausbruch 79 n. Chr. verschütteten Städten.* Recklinghausen.

Andreau, J. (1973) Histoire des séismes et histoire économique: le tremblement de terre de Pompéi (62 ap. J.-C.). in: *Annales E.S.C.* XXVIII 369-395.

Andreau, J. (1974) *Les affaires de monsieur Iucundus.* (collection de l'école française de Rome 19) Rome.

Andreau, J. (1976) Pompéi. Enchères, foires et marchés. in: *Bulletin de la Société nationale des Antiquaires de France.* 104-127.

Andreau, J. (1977a) Fondations privéés et rapports sociaux en Italie romaine (Ier-IIIe S. ap. J.C.). in: *KTEMA.* II 157-209.

Andreau, J. (1977b) M.I. Finley, la banque antique et l'économie moderne. in: *Annali della Scuola Normale Superiore di Pisa. Classe di lettere e filosofia.* 3rd. ser. VII, 3. 1129-1152.

Andreau, J. (1979) Les banquiers romains. in: *L'Histoire*, no. 18. 15-21.

Andreau, J. (1980) Pompéi: mais où sont les vétérans de Sylla? in: *Revue des Études Anciennes.* LXXXII 183-199.

Ausbüttel, F. (1982) *Untersuchungen zu den Vereinen im Westen des römischen Reiches.* (Franfurter Althistorische Studien. XI) Kallmünz.

Austin, M. and Vidal-Naquet, P. (1973) *Economies et sociétés en Grèce ancienne.* Paris.

Aymard, M. (1973) Mesures et interprétations de la croissance. Rendements et productivité dans l'Italie moderne. in *Annales E.S.C.* XXVIII 475-98.

Baehrel, R. (1961) *Une croissance: la Basse-Provence rurale (fin du XVIe siècle, 1789).* Paris.

Bairoch, P. (1973) Agriculture and the industrial revolution. in: Cipolla (1972-6) III 452-506.

Baldacci, P. a.o. (1972) *Recherches sur les amphores Romaines.* (Collection de l'École Française de Rome. vol. 10) Rome.

Barendregt, J. (1984) Simulatie: geschiedenis zonder bronnen? in: *Concept. Tijdschrift voor maatschappijgeschiedenis.* I 34-48.

Barker, G. (1981) *Landscape and Society. Prehistoric central Italy.* London.

Barker, G., Lloyd, J. and Webley, D. (1978) A classical landscape in Molise. in: *Papers of the British School at Rome.* XLVI 35-51.

Barnabei, F. (1901) *La villa Pompeiana di P. Fannio Sinistore.* Roma.

Bastet. F.L. (1975) Forschungen im Hause des M. Lucretius Fronto. in: Andreae and Kyrieleis (1975) 193-97.

Bastet, F.L. (1976) Villa rustica in contrada Pisanella. in: *Cronache Pompeiane.* II 112-43.

Beloch, [K.]J. (1886) *Die Bevölkerung der griechisch-römischen Welt.* (Historische Beiträge zur Bevölkerungslehre I) Leipzig.

Beloch, [K.]J. (1899) Die Grossindustrie im Altertum. in: *Zeitschrift für Sozialwissenschaft.* II 18-26. reprinted in Finley (1979).

Beloch, [K.]J. (1890) *Campanien. Geschichte und Topographie des antiken Neapel und seine Umgebung.* 2nd. rev. ed. Breslau.

Beloch, [K.]J. (1898) Le città dell'Italia antica. in: *Atene e Roma.* I 257-78.

Beloch, [K.]J. (1902) Zur griechischen Wirtschaftsgeschichte. in: *Zeitschrift für Sozialwissenschaft.* V 95-103, 169-179.

Beloch, [K.]J. (1903) Die Bevölkerung Italiens im Altertum. *Klio.* III 471-90.

Beloch, K.J. (1937-1961) *Bevölkerungsgeschichte Italiens.* 3 vols. Berlin/Leipzig.

Bender, B. (1975) *Farming in prehistory. From hunter-gatherer to food-producer.* London.

Blalock, H.M. Jr. (1968) The measurement problem: a gap between the languages of theory and research. in: Blalock and Blalock (1968) 5-27.

Blalock, H.M. Jr. and Blalock, A.B. (eds.) (1968) *Methodology in social research.* New York.

Blalock, H.M. (1979) *Social statistics.* 2nd. ed. New York.

Blaug, M. (1985) *Economic theory in retrospect.* 4th. ed. Cambridge.

Bloch (1931) *Les caractères originaux de l'histoire rurale française.* Oslo.

Blümner, H. (1912) *Technologie und Terminologie der Gewerbe und Künste bei Griechen und Römern.* 2nd. rev. ed. of vol. I (4 vols. in 1st. ed. 1874-87) Leipzig.

Bömer, F. (1957-61) *Untersuchungen über die Religion der Sklaven in Griechenland und Rom.* (4 vols. in: *Abhandlungen Akademie Mainz* 1957,7 1960,1 1961,4 1963,10.)

Boersma, J., Yntema, D. and van der Werff, J. (1986) Excavations in the house of the porch (V. ii. 4-5) at Ostia. in: *Bulletin Antieke Beschaving.* LXI. 77-137.

Bohannan, P. and Dalton, G. (eds.) (1962) *Markets in Africa.* Evanston, Ill.

Boserup, E. (1965) *The conditions of agricultural growth.* London.
Boserup, E. (1970) *Woman's role in economic development.* London.
Boserup, E. (1981) *Population and technology.* Oxford.
Bottomore, T. and Nisbet, R. (eds.) (1978) *A history of sociological analysis.* London.
Braudel, F. (1966) *La Méditerranée et le monde méditerranéen à l'époque de Philippe II.* 2nd. ed. 2 vols. Paris.
Braudel, F. (1979) *Civilisation matérielle, économie et capitalisme, XV*e*-XVIII*e *siècle.* 3 vols. Paris.
Breglia, L. (1950) Circolazione monetale ed aspetti di vita economica a Pompei. in: Maiuri (1950) 41-59.
Brenner, R. (1976) Agrarian class structure and economic development in pre-industrial Europe. in: *Past and Present.* LXX 30-75.
Breton, E. (1869) *Pompeia décrite et dessinée.* Paris.
Bruhns, H. (1985) De Werner Sombart à Max Weber et Moses I. Finley: la typologie de la ville antique et la question de la ville de consommation. in: Leveau (ed.) (1985) 255-273.
Brunt, P.A. (1971) *Italian Manpower. 225 B.C.-A.D. 14.* Oxford.
Brunt, P.A. (1972) review of: White (1970a) in: *Journal of Roman Studies.* LXII 153-8.
Brunt, P.A. (1973) Aspects of the social thought of Dio Chrysostom and of the Stoics. in: *Proceedings of the Cambridge Philological Society.* XIX 9-34.
Brunt, P.A. (1981) The revenue of Rome. in: *Journal of Roman Studies.* LXXI 161-72.
Bücher, K. (1919) *Die Entstehung der Volkswirtschaft.* Vol. I 11th. ed. Tübingen.
Bücher, K. (1922a) *Beiträge zur Wirtschaftsgeschichte.* Tübingen.
Bücher, K. (1922b) Zur griechischen Wirtschaftsgeschichte. in: Bücher (1922a) 1-97, reprinted in: Finley (1979).
Buckland, W.W. (1908) *The Roman law of slavery. The condition of the slave in private law from Augustus to Justinian.* Cambridge.
Buren, A.W. van (1947) Gnaeus Alleius Nigidius Maius of Pompeii. in: *American Journal of Philology.* LXVIII 382-93.

Burke, P. (1974) *Venice and Amsterdam. A study of seventeenth-century élites*. London.

Camodeca, G. (1977) L' ordinamento in *regiones* e i *vici* di Puteoli. in: *Puteoli* I 62-98.

Carandini, A. (1979) *L'anatomia della scimia. La formazione economica della società prima del capitale*. Torino.

Carrié, J.-M. (1986) L'esercito: trasformazioni funzionali ed economie locali. in: Giardina (1986) I 449-488.

Carrington, R.C. (1931) Studies in the campanian 'villae rusticae'. in: *Journal of Roman Studies*. XXI 110-130.

Carter, H.B. and Charlet, P. (1956) Modern problems in the improvement of wool production. in: *VIIth International Congress of Animal Husbandry*. Madrid. section 4.

Cartledge, P.A. (1983) 'Trade and politics' revisited: archaic Greece. in: Garnsey a.o. (1983) 1-15.

Cartledge, P.A. and Harvey, F.D. (eds.) (1985) *Crux. Essays presented to G.E.M. de Ste. Croix on his 75th birthday*. Exeter.

Carus-Wilson, E. (1952) The woollen industry. in: *Cambridge economic history of Europe*. Cambridge. II 355-428.

Casale, A. and Bianco, A. (1979) Primo contributo alla topografia del suburbio pompeiano. in: *Pompei 79*. (Suppl. to *Antiqua*. IV no. 15) 27-56.

Casella, D. (1950) La frutta nelle pitture Pompeiane. in: Maiuri (1950) 355-86.

Casson, L. (1974) *Travel in the ancient world*. London.

Castrén, P. (1975) *Ordo populusque Pompeianus. Polity and society in Roman Pompeii*. Rome.

Caves, R.E. and Jones, R.W. (1981) *World trade and payments: an introduction*. 3rd. ed. Boston.

Cébeillac-Gervasoni, M. a.o. (1983) *Les 'bourgeoisies' municipales Italiennes aux IIe et Ier siècles av. J.-C.* (Colloques internationaux du Centre National de la Recherche Scientifique, n. 609, sciences humaines / Bibliothèque de l'Institut Français de Naples, deuxième série - vol. VI) Paris/ Naples.

Chayanov, A.V. (1966) *On the theory of peasant economy*. (ed. D. Thorner, B. Kerblay and R.E.F. Smith) Homewood.

Cherry, J.F. (1983) Frogs around the pond: perspectives on current archaeological survey projects in the Mediterranean region. in: Keller and Rupp (1983) 375-416.

Chisholm, M. (1979) *Rural settlement and land use. An essay in location.* 3rd. ed. London.

Christ, K. (1980) Grundfragen der römischen Sozialstruktur. in: Eck a.o. (1980) 197-228.

Cipolla, C.M. (ed.) (1972-6) *The Fontana economic history of Europe.* 6 vols. London.

Cipolla, C.M. (1981) *Before the industrial revolution. European society and economy, 1000-1700.* 2nd. ed. London

Clammer, J. (ed.) (1978) *The new economic anthropology.* New York.

Clark, C. and Haswell, M. (1967) *The economics of subsistence agriculture.* 3rd. ed. London.

Clarke, D.L. (1973) Archaeology: the loss of innocence. in: *Antiquity.* XLVII 6-18.

Clarke, D.L. (ed.) (1977) *Spatial archaeology.* London.

Clemente, G. (1972) Il patronato nei collegia dell' impero Romano. in: *Studi Classici e Orientali.* XXI 142-229.

Coale, A.J. and Demeny, P. (1966) *Regional model life tables and stable populations.* Princeton.

Congdon, L. (1976) Karl Polanyi in Hungary, 1900-19. in: Journal of Contemporary History. XI,1 167-83.

Cook, S. (1966) The obsolete 'anti-market' mentality: a critique of the substantivist approach to economic anthropology. in: *American Anthropologist* LXVIII 323-345, reprinted in: Leclair and Schneider (1968) 208-228.

Corbier, M. (1985a) Idéologie et pratique de l'héritage (Ier s. av. J.-C. - IIe s. ap. J.-C.) in: *Index.* XIII.

Corbier, M. (1985b) Fiscalité et dépenses locales. in: Leveau (ed.) (1985) 219-232.

Corbier, M. (1986) Svalutazioni, inflazione e circolazione menetaria nel III secolo. in: Giardina (1986) 489-533 (notes: 772-779).

Corvisier, A. (1976) *Armées et sociétés en Europe, de 1494 à 1789.* Paris.

Craeybeckx, J. a.o. (1975) *Album Charles Verlinden.* Gent.

Crawford, M.H. (1970) Money and exchange in the Roman world. in: *Journal of Roman Studies*. LX 40-48.

Crawford, M.H. (1977) Rome and the Greek world: economic relationships. in: *Economic History Review*. XXX 42-52.

Crook, J.A. (1967) *Law and life of Rome*. London.

D'Arms, J.H. (1970) *Romans on the bay of Naples. A social and cultural study of the villas and their owners from 150 B.C. to A.D. 400*. Cambridge (Mass.).

D'Arms, J.H. (1974) Puteoli in the Second Century of the Roman Empire: a Social and Economic Study. in: *Journal of Roman Studies* LXIV 104-124.

D'Arms, J.H. (1977) M.I. Rostovtzeff and M.I. Finley: the status of traders in the Roman world. in: D'Arms and Eadie (1977) 159-80.

D'Arms, J.H. (1980) Republican senators' involvement in commerce in the late Republic: some Ciceronian evidence. in: D'Arms and Kopff (1980) 77-89.

D'Arms, J.H. (1981) *Commerce and social standing in ancient Rome*. Cambridge (Mass.).

D'Arms, J.H. and Eadie, J.W. (eds.) (1977) *Ancient and modern: essays in honor of Gerald F. Else*. Ann Arbor.

D'Arms, J.H. and Kopff, E.C. (1980) *The seaborne commerce of ancient Rome: studies in archaeology and history*. (Memoirs of the American academy in Rome vol. XXXVI). Rome.

Dalton, G. (1971) *Economic anthropology and development*. New York.

Daremberg, Ch. and Saglio, Edm. (1877-1919) *Dictionaire des antiquités grecques et romaines*. Paris. 9 vols.

Dawson, Chr. M. (1944) Romano-Campanian mythological landscape painting. in: *Yale Classical Studies*. IX.

Day, J. (1932) Agriculture in the life of Pompeii. in: *Yale Classical Studies*. III 165-208.

De Caro, S. (1976) Sculture dalla villa di Poppea in Oplontis. in: *Cronache Pompeiane*. II 184-225.

De Caro, S. (1977) Pagus Augustus Felix Suburbanus. in: *Cronache Pompeiane*. III 217-8.

De Caro, S. (1978) Boscoreale. in: *Cronache Pompeiane*. IV 234.

De Caro, S. (1979a) Scavi nell' area fuori Porta Nola a Pompei. in: *Cronache Pompeiane.* V 61-101.

De Caro, S. (1979b) Boscoreale. in: *Cronache Pompeiane.* V 192-3.

De Franciscis, A. (1975) La villa Romana di Oplontis. in: Andreae and Kyrieleis (1975) 9-38.

Delano Smith, C. (1979) *Western Mediterranean Europe. A historical geography of Italy, Spain and southern France since the neolithic.* London.

Delille, G. (1973) *Croissance d'une société rurale. Montesarchio et la vallée Caudine aux XVII*e *et XVIII*e *siècles.* Naples.

Delille, G. (1977a) *Agricoltura e demografia nel regno di Napoli nei secoli XVIII e XIX.* Naples.

Delille (1977b) Crises et productivité agricole: l'exemple du Royaume de Naples. in: *Cahiers de la Méditerranée.* (Typologie des crises dans les pays méditerranéens, XVIe-XXe siècles. Actes des journées d'études Bendor, 13, 14 et 15 Mai 1976). Nice.

Delille, G. (1985) *Famille et propriété dans le royaume de Naples (XV*e*-XIX*e *siècle).* (bibliothèque des écoles françaises d'Athènes et de Rome. vol. 259). Rome.

Della Corte, M. (1965) *Case ed abitanti di Pompei.* 3rd ed. Naples.

Delumeau, J. (1957-59) *Vie économique et sociale de Rome dans la seconde moitié du XVI*e *siècle.* 2 vols. Paris.

Delury, D.B. (1947) On the estimation of biological populations. in: *Biometrics.* III 145-167.

Dexter, C.E. (1975) *The casa di L. Cecilio Giocondo in Pompeii.* (Ph.D. dissertation Duke University, University microfilms 75-10,696.)

Di Capua, F. (1938-39) Contributi all'epigrafia e alla storia della antica Stabia. in: *Rendiconti dell' Accademia di Archeologia, Lettere e Belle Arti di Napoli.* XIX 83-124.

Drinkwater, J.F. (1983) *Roman Gaul. The three provinces, 58 B.C.-A.D. 260.* London.

Duby, G. (1973) *Guerriers et paysans, VII*e*-XII*e *siècle. Premier essor de l'économie européenne.* Paris.

Duby, G. (ed.) (1980 -) *Histoire de la France urbaine*. 5 vols. Paris.

Duff, A.M. (1928) *Freedmen in the early Roman empire*. Oxford.

Duncan-Jones, R.P. (1976) The size of the modius castrensis. in: *Zeitschrift für Papyrologie und Epigraphik*. Band 21, 53-62.

Duncan-Jones, R.P. (1977) review of Castrén (1975) in: *Journal of Roman Studies*. LXVII 195-198.

Duncan-Jones, R.P. (1978) Pay and numbers in Diocletian's army. in: *Chiron*. VIII 541-560.

Duncan-Jones, R.P. (1982) *The economy of the Roman empire. Quantitative studies*. 2nd ed. Cambridge.

Duncan-Jones, R.P. (1985) Who paid for public buildings in Roman cities? in: Grew and Hobley (1985) 28-33.

Duthoy, R. (1974) La fonction sociale de l'augustalité. in: *Epigraphica*. XXXVI 134-54.

Duthoy, R. (1978) Les *Augustales. in: Temporini (1972 -) II 16.2 1254-1309.

Eadie, J.W. and Ober, J. (eds.) (1985) *The craft of the ancient historian. Essays in honour of Chester G. Starr*. Lanham.

Eck W, Galsterer H, and Wolff H. (eds.) (1980) *Studien zur antiken Sozialgeschichte. Festschrift Friedrich Vittinghoff*. Köln/Wien.

Eisermann, G. (1956) *Die Grundlagen des Historismus in der deutschen Nationalöconomie*. Stuttgart.

Eschebach, H. (1970) *Die städtebauliche Entwicklung des antiken Pompeji*. (Römische Mitteilungen, siebzehntes Erganzungsheft) Heidelberg/Rome.

Eschebach, H. (1975) Erläuterungen zum Plan von Pompeji. in: Andreae and Kyrieleis (1975) 331-38.

Étienne, R. (1977) *La vie quotidienne à Pompéi*. 2e éd. Paris.

Étienne, R. (1982) Villas du Vésuve et structure agraire. in: Schefold (1982) 183-91.

Ferrill, A. (1985) The senatorial aristocracy in the early empire. in: Eadie and Ober (1985) 353-371.

Finley, M.I. (1955) Mariage, sale and gift in the Homeric world. in: *Revue Internationale des Droits de l'Antiquité*. 3e sér. II 167-94, reprinted in Finley (1981) 233-245.

Finley, M.I. (1957) Homer and Mycenae: property and tenure. in: *Historia.* VI 133-59, reprinted in Finley (1981) 213-232.
Finley, M.I. (1957-8) Mycenaean palace archives and economic history. in: *Economic History Review.* 2nd. ser. X 128-41, reprinted in Finley (1981) 199-212.
Finley, M.I. (1965b) Classical Greece. in: Finley (1965a) 11-35.
Finley, M.I. (1968a) *Aspects of antiquity: discoveries and controversies.* London.
Finley, M.I. (1968b) Manpower and the fall of Rome. in: Finley (1968a) 146-153.
Finley, M.I. (1970) Aristotle and economic analysis. in: *Past and Present.* XLVII 3-25, reprinted in Finley (1974) 26-52.
Finley, M.I. (1977) The ancient city: from Fustel de Coulanges to Max Weber and beyond. in: *Comparative Studies in Society and History.* XIX 305-27. Reprinted in: Finley (1981) 3-23.
Finley, M.I. (1978a) Empire in the Greco-Roman world. in: *Greece & Rome.* XXV 1-15.
Finley, M.I. (1978b) *The world of Odysseus.* 4th. rev. ed. London.
Finley, M.I. (1980) *Ancient slavery and modern ideology.* London.
Finley, M.I. (1981) *Economy and society in ancient Greece.* (ed. B.D. Shaw and R.P. Saller) London.
Finley, M.I. (1983) *Politics in the ancient world.* Cambridge.
Finley, M.I. (1985a) *The ancient economy.* 2nd. ed. London.
Finley, M.I. (1985b) *Ancient history: evidence and models.* London.
Finley, M.I. (ed.) (1965a) *Trade and politics in the ancient world.* (second international conference of economic history. Aix-en-Provence, 1962. Vol. I) Paris/The Hague. Reprinted: New York, 1979.
Finley, M.I. (ed.) (1974) *Studies in ancient society.* London.
Finley, M.I. (ed.) (1976) *Studies in Roman property.* Cambridge.
Finley, M.I. (ed.) (1979) *The Bücher-Meyer controversy.* New York.
Fiorelli, G. (1875) *Descrizione di Pompei.* Naples.
Firth, R. (ed.) (1967) *Themes in economic anthropology.* London.

Fischer, H. (1986) Zur Entwicklung Ostias und Puteolis vom 1. Jh. v. u. Z. bis zum 3. Jahrhundert. in: *Münstersche Beiträge zur Antiken Handelsgeschichte.* V 3-16.
Fisher, I. (1906) *The nature of capital and income.* New York.
Flach, F. (1878) La table de bronze d'Aljustrel. in: *Revue Historique de Droit Français et Etranger.* II 269-82 and 645-94.
Flambard, J.-M. (1977) Clodius, les collèges, la plèbe et les esclaves. Recherches sur la politique populaire au milieu du Ier siècle. in: *Mélanges d' Archeologie et d' Histoire de l'École Française de Rome* LXXXIX 115-156.
Flambard, J.-M. (1981) Collegia compitalicia: phénomène associatif, cadres territoriaux et cadres civiques dans le monde romain à l'époque républicaine. in: *Ktèma* VI 143-166.
Flambard, J.-M. (1983) Les collèges et les élites locales à l'époque républicaine d'après l'exemple de Capoue. in: Cébeillac-Gervasoni (1983) 75-89.
Fogel, R.W. and Engerman, S.L. (1974) *Time on the cross. The economics of American negro slavery.* 2 vols. London.
Fowler, W.W. (1920) *Roman essays and interpretations.* Oxford.
Foxhall, L. and Forbes, H.A. (1982) *Sitometreia*: the role of grain as a staple food in classical antiquity. in: *Chiron.* XII 41-90.
Frank, T. (1918) The economic life of an ancient city. in: *Classical Philology.* XIII 225-240.
Frank, T. (1933-40) *An economic survey of ancient Rome.* 5 vols + index. Baltimore.
Frank, T. (1962) *An economic history of Rome.* 2nd. rev. ed. New York.
Franklin, J.L. Jr. (1980) *Pompeii: the electoral programmata, campaigns and politics, A.D. 71-79.* Rome.
Franklin, J.L. Jr. (1981) *Materials for research in the Pompeian electoral programmata.* Unpublished, deposited for consultation in the library of the American Academy in Rome.
Frayn, J.M. (1979) *Subsistence farming in Roman Italy.* London.
Frayn, J.M. (1984) *Sheep-rearing and the wool trade in Italy during the Roman period.* Liverpool.

Frederiksen (1966) Caesar, Cicero and the problem of debt. in: *Journal of Roman Studies*. LVI 128-141.

Frederiksen, M.W. (1975) Theory, evidence and the ancient economy. (review of the first edition (1973) of Finley (1985a), in: *Journal of Roman Studies*. LXV 164-171.

Frederiksen, M.W. (1980-81) Puteoli e il commercio del grano in epoca Romana. in: *Puteoli*. IV-V 5-27.

Frederiksen, M. W. (1981) I cambiamenti delle strutture agrarie nella tarda republica: la Campania. in: Giardina and Schiavone (1981) I 265-287.

Friedländer, L. (1919-22) *Darstellungen aus der Sittengeschichte Roms*. 9th. ed. 4 vols. Leipzig.

Frier, B.W. (1977) The rental market in early imperial Rome. in: *Journal of Roman Studies*. LXVII 27-37.

Frier, B.W. (1980) *Landlords and tenants in imperial Rome*. Princeton.

Frier, B. (1982) Roman Life Expectancy: Ulpian's Evidence. in: *Harvard Studies in Classical Philology*. LXXXVI 213-251.

Gabba, E. (1976) *Republican Rome, the army and the allies*. Oxford.

Gabba, E. and Pasquinucci, M. (1979) *Strutture agrarie e allevamento transumante nell'Italia romana (III-I sec. a.C.)*. Pisa.

Gabelmann, H. (1985) Römische Kinder in *toga praetexta*. in: *Jahrbuch des Deutschen Archäologischen Instituts*. C. Berlin. 497-541.

Gallant, T.W. (1985) *A fisherman's tale*. (Miscellanea Graeca, fasc. 7) Gent.

Galsterer, H. (1980) Politik in Römischen Städten: Die 'Seditio' des Jahres 59 n. Chr. in Pompeii. in: Eck a.o. (1980) 323-338.

Garnsey, P.D.A. (1971) Honorarium decurionatus. in: *Historia*. XX 309-325.

Garnsey, P.D.A. (1974) Aspects of the decline of the urban aristocracy in the empire. in: Temporini (1972 -) II,1 229-252.

Garnsey, P.D.A. (1975) Descendants of freedmen in local politics: some criteria. in: Levick (ed.) (1975) 167-180.

Garnsey, P.D.A. (1979a) Where did Italian peasants live? in: *Proceedings of the Cambridge Philological Society*. CCV (n.s. XXV) 1-25.
Garnsey, P.D.A. (1979b) review of Patlagean (1977) in: *Journal of Roman Studies*. LXIX 198-9.
Garnsey, P.D.A. (ed.) (1980a) *Non-Slave Labour in the Greco-Roman World*. (Cambridge Philological Society. Supplementary Volume no. 6). Cambridge.
Garnsey, P.D.A. (1980b) Non-slave labour in the Roman world. in: Garnsey (1980a) 34-47.
Garnsey, P.D.A. (1981) Independent freedmen and the economy of Roman Italy under the principate. in: *Klio*. LXIII 359-371.
Garnsey, P.D.A. (1982) Slaves in business. in: *Opus* I 105-108.
Garnsey, P.D.A. (1983a) Grain for Rome. in: Garnsey, Hopkins and Whittaker (1983) 118-130.
Garnsey, P.D.A. (1983b) Famine in Rome. in: Garnsey and Whittaker (1983) 56-65.
Garnsey, P.D.A. (1985) Grain for Athens. in: Cartledge and Harvey (1985) 62-75.
Garnsey, P.D.A, Hopkins, K. and Whittaker, C.R. (eds.) (1983) *Trade in the ancient economy*. London.
Garnsey, P.D.A. and Whittaker, C.R. (eds.) (1983) *Trade and famine in classical antiquity*. (Cambridge Philological Society, Suppl. vol. no. 8). Cambridge.
Geertz, Cl. (1963) *Agricultural involution: the process of ecological change in Indonesia*. (Association of Asian Studies monographs and papers; 11) Berkeley.
Geiger, Th. (1962) *Arbeiten zur Soziologie*. (ed. P. Trappe) Neuwied am Rhein.
Gelzer, M. (1912) *Die Nobilität der Römischen Republik*. Leipzig.
Giardina, A. (ed.) (1986) *Società romana e impero tardoantico. vol. I: Instituzioni, ceti, economie*. Roma/Bari.
Giardina, A. and Schiavone, A. (eds.) (1981) *Società romana e produzione schiavistica*. 3 vols. Roma/Bari.
Ginsburg, M.S. (1934) 'Princeps Libertinorum.' in: *Transactions and Proceedings of the American Philological Association*. LXV 198-206.

Godelier, M. (1971) *Rationalité et irrationalité en économie.* nouv. éd. 2 vols. Paris.
Gonzáles, J. (1986) The lex Irnitana: a new copy of the Flavian municipal law. in: *Journal of Roman Studies* LXXVI 147-243.
Gordon, M. L. (1927) The ordo of Pompeii. in: *Journal of Roman Studies.* XVII 165-183.
Gordon, M. L. (1931) The freedman's son in municipal life. in: *Journal of Roman Studies* XXI 65-77.
Gossen, H.H. (1889) *Entwicklung der Gesetze des menschlichen Verkehrs, und der daraus fliessenden Regeln für menschliches Handeln.* new ed. Berlin.
Goubert, P. (1959) *Familles marchandes sous l'ancien régime: les Danse et les Motte, de Beauvais.* Paris.
Goudineau, Chr. (1983) reply to Leveau (1983b). in: *Études Rurales.* 89-90-91 :283-289.
Graeber, A. (1983) *Untersuchungen zum spätrömischen Korporationswesen.* Frankfurt am Main.
Greenidge, A.H.J. (1901) *Legal Procedure of Cicero's Time.* Oxford.
Grew, F. and Hobley, B. (eds.) (1985) *Roman urban topography in Britain and the western empire.* (CBA Research Report 59).
Grigg, D. (1983) *The dynamics of agricultural change.* New York.
Gunderson, G. (1976) Economic change and the demise of the Roman empire. in: *Explorations in Economic History.* XIII 43-68.
Halstead, P. (1987) Traditional and ancient rural economy in mediterranean Europe: plus ça change? in *Journal of Hellenic Studies.* CVII. 77-87.
Halstead, P. and O'Shea, J. (eds.) (1988) *Bad year economics: cultural responses to risk and uncertainty.* (New Directions in Archaeology) Cambridge.
Hardy, E.G. (1912) *Three Spanish Charters and Other Documents.* Oxford.
Harris, W.V. (1980) Roman terracotta lamps: the organisation of an industry. in: *Journal of Roman Studies.* LXX 126-145.
Heers, J. (1974) *Le clan familial au moyen age. Étude sur les structures politiques et sociales des milieux urbains.* Paris.

Hellegouarc'h, J. (1963) *Le vocabulaire latin des relations et des partis politiques sous la république.* Paris.
Hennipman, P. (1945) *Economisch motief en economisch principe.* Amsterdam.
Herlihy, D. (1958) The agrarian revolution in southern France and Italy, 801-1150. in: *Speculum.* XXXIII 23-41.
Herskovits, M.J. (1940) *The economic life of primitive peoples.* New York.
Herzog-Hauser, G. (1932) 'Milch.' in: *Paulys Real-Encyclopädie der Classischen Altertumswissenschaft.* Stuttgart. XV 1569-80
Hesnard, A. (1980) Un dépot Augustéen d'amphores à la Longarina, Ostie. in: D'Arms and Kopff (1980) 141-156.
Hicks, J.R. (1946) *Value and Capital. An inquiry into some fundamental principles of economic theory.* 2nd. rev. ed. Oxford.
Hicks, J.R. (1956) *A revision of demand theory.* Oxford.
Hicks, J.R. (1969) *A theory of economic history.* Oxford.
Hicks, J.R. and Allen, R.G.D. (1934) A reconsideration of the theory of value. in: *Economica.* n.s. I 52-76 & 196-219.
Hilton, R. (1976) Capitalism - what's in a name? in: Hilton (ed.) (1976) 145-158.
Hilton, R. (ed.) (1976) *The transition from feudalism to capitalism.* London.
Hodges, R. and Whitehouse, D. (1983) *Mohammed, Charlemagne & the origins of Europe. Archaeology and the Pirenne thesis.* London.
Hoffmann, M. (1964) *The warp-weighted loom.* Oslo.
Hopkins, K. (1965) Élite mobility in the Roman empire. in: *Past and Present.* XXXII 12-26, reprinted in: Finley (1974) 103-120.
Hopkins, K. (1966) On the probable age structure of the Roman population. in: *Population Studies.* XX 245-64.
Hopkins, K. (1978a) *Conquerors and slaves. Sociological studies in Roman history I.* Cambridge.
Hopkins, K. (1978b) Economic growth and towns in classical antiquity. in: Abrams and Wrigley (1978) 35-77.
Hopkins, K. (1980) Taxes and trade in the Roman empire (200 B.C. - A.D. 400). in: *Journal of Roman Studies.* LXX 101-25.

Hopkins, K. (1982) The transport of staples in the Roman empire. in: *Eighth International Economic History Congress. Budapest. (B 12 theme: Trade in staples in antiquity, Greece and Rome)*. 80-87. Budapest.

Hopkins, K. (1983a) *Death and renewal. Sociological studies in Roman history II*. Cambridge.

Hopkins, K. (1983b) Models, ships and stapels. in: Garnsey and Whittaker (1983) 84-109.

Hopkins, K. (1983c) Introduction. in: Garnsey a.o. (1983) ix-xxv.

Hopkins, K. (forthcoming) review of: Russell (1985).

Horstkotte, H. (1984) Magistratur und Dekurionat im Lichte des Albums von Canusium. in: *Zeitschrift für Papyrologie und Epigraphik*. Band 57. 211-224.

Houston, J.M. (1964) *The western Mediterranean world. An introduction to its regional landscapes*. London.

Howard, M. (1976) *War in European history*. Oxford.

Hug (1925) 'Lactarius Mons.' in: *Paulys Real-Encyclopädie der Classischen Altertumswissenschaft*. Stuttgart. XII 361.

Humphreys, S.C. (1969) History, economics and anthropology: the work of Karl Polanyi. in: *History and Theory*. VIII 165-212, reprinted in: Humphreys (1978) 31-75.

Humphreys, S.C. (1978) *Anthropology and the Greeks*. London.

Hymer, S. and Resnick, S. (1969) A model of an agrarian economy with nonagricultural activities. in: *American Economic Review*. LIX 493-506.

Iggers, G.G. (1968) *The German conception of history. The national tradition of historical thought from Herder to the present*. Middletown.

Jackson, E.F. and Curtis, R.F. (1968) Conceptualization and measurement in the study of social stratification. in: Blalock and Blalock (1968) 112-149.

Jacques, F. (1984) *Le privilège de liberté. Politique impériale et autonomie municipale dans les cités de l'occident romain (161-244)*. Rome.

Jashemski, W.F. (1979) *The gardens of Pompeii, Herculaneum and the villas destroyed by Vesuvius*. New Rochelle/New York

Jones (1974a) *The Roman economy. Studies in ancient economic and administrative history*. (ed. P.A. Brunt) Oxford.

Jones (1974b) The economic life of the towns of the Roman empire. in: Jones (1974a) 35-60.

Jones (1974c) The cloth industry under the Roman empire. in: Jones (1974a) 350-364.

Jongman, W.M. (1978-79) M. Obellius M. f. Firmus, Pompeian duovir. in: *TALANTA* X-XI 62-65.

Jongman, W.M. (1988) Adding it up. in: Whittaker (1988).

Jongman, W.M and Dekker, R.M. (1988) Public intervention in the food supply in pre-industrial Europe. in: Halstead and O'Shea (1988).

Kajanto, I. (1965) *The Latin cognomina.* (Societas Scientarum Fennica. Commentationes Humanarum Litterarum. XXXVI, 2). Helsinki.

Kajanto, I. (1968) The significance of non-Latin cognomina. in: *Latomus.* XXVII 517-534.

Keller, D.R. and Rupp, D.W. (eds.) (1983) *Archaeological survey in the Mediterranean area.* (British Archaeological Reports. Int. Ser. 155) Oxford.

Kindleberger, Ch.P. and Lindert, P.H. (1978) *International Economics.* Homewood.

Kleberg, T. (1957) *Hôtels, restaurants et cabarets dans l'antiquité romaine. Études historiques et philologiques.* Uppsala.

Kleijwegt, M. (1987) Erfelijkheid van het decurionaat en sociale mobiliteit. in: *Leidschrift.* III, 9 14-39.

Kolb, F. (1984) *Die Stadt im Altertum.* München.

Kolendo, J. (1981) La répartition des places aux spectacles et la stratification sociale dans l'Empire Romain. A propos des inscriptions sur les gradins des amphithéâtres et théâtres. in: *KTEMA.* VI 301-315.

Kopytoff, I. I. and Miers, S. (1977) African slavery as an institution of marginality. in: Miers and Kopytoff (1977) 18-29.

Kotula, T. (1968) *Les curies municipales en Afrique romaine.* Warsaw.

Kotula, T. (1980) Les curies africaines, origine et composition. *Retractatio.* in: *Eos.* LXVIII 133-146.

Krause, W. (ed.) (1977) *Application of vegetation science to grassland husbandry*. (part XIII of *Handbook of vegetation science*). The Hague.

Kriedte, P. (1980) *Spätfeudalismus und Handelskapital. Grundlinien der europäischen Wirtschaftsgeschichte vom 16. bis zum Ausgang des 18. Jahrhunderts*. Göttingen.

Kriedte, P., Medick, H. and Schlumbohm, J. (1977) *Industrialisierung vor der Industrialisierung. Gewerbliche Warenproduktion auf dem Land in der Formationsperiode des Kapitalismus*. Göttingen.

Kuznets, S. (1966a) *Economic growth and structure. Selected essays*. London.

Kuznets, S. (1966b) Toward a theory of economic growth. in: Kuznets (1966a) 1-81.

Lamprecht, K. (1878) Beiträge zur Geschichte des französischen Wirtschaftsleben im elften Jahrhundert. in: *Staats- und Sozialwissenschafliche Forschungen ... von Gustav Schmoller*. I, 3. p. 1-38.

Le Houerou, H.N. (1977) Plant sociology and ecology applied to grazing lands research, survey and management in the Meditaerranean basin. in: Krause (1977) 211-74.

LeClair, E.E. and Schneider, H.K. (eds.) (1968) *Economic anthropology. Readings in theory and analysis*. New York.

Lee, R.B. and DeVore, I. (eds.) (1968) *Man the hunter*. New York.

Léon, P. (ed.) (1977-78) *Histoire économique et sociale du monde*. 6 vols. Paris.

Lepelley, Cl. (1979-81) *Les cités de l'Afrique Romaine au bas-empire*. 2 vols. Paris.

Lepore, E. (1950) Orientamenti per la storia sociale di Pompei. in: Maiuri (1950) 144-66.

Leveau, Ph. (1983a La ville antique et l'organisation de l'espace rural: *villa*, ville, village. in: *Annales E.S.C.* XXXVIII 920-942.

Leveau, Ph. (1983b) La ville antique, 'ville de consommation'? (parasitisme social et économie antique). in: *Études Rurales*. 89-90-91: 275-283.

Leveau, Ph. (1985) Richesses, investissements, dépenses: à la recherche des revenues des aristocraties municipales de l'antiquité. in: Leveau (ed.) (1985) 19-37.

Leveau, Ph. (ed.) (1985) *L'origine des richesses dépensés dans la ville antique. Actes du colloque organisé à Aix-en-Provence par l'U.E.R. d'histoire, les 11 et 12 Mai 1984.* Aix-en-Provence.

Levi, M.A. a.o. (1974) *Actes du colloque 1972 sur l'esclavage.* (Annales Littéraires de l'Université de Besançon, 163) Paris.

Levick, Barbara (ed.) (1975) *The ancient historian and his materials. Essays in honour of C.E. Stevens on his seventeeth birthday.* Farnborough.

Lewis, N. (1983) *Life in Egypt under Roman Rule.* Oxford.

Liebenam, W. (1900) *Städteverwaltung im Römischen Kaiserreiche.* Leipzig.

Ling, R. (1977) Studius and the beginnings of Roman landscape painting. in: *Journal of Roman Studies.* LXVII 1-16.

Ling, R. (1983) The insula of the Menander at Pompeii: interim report. *Antiquaries Journal.* LXIII 34-57.

Lipsey, R.G, Steiner, P.O. and Purvis, D.D. (1984) *Economics.* 7th. ed. New York.

Lis, C. and Soly, H. (1979) *Poverty and capitalism in pre-industrial Europe.* Hassocks.

Lloyd, P.E. and Dicken, P. (1977) *Location in space. A theoretical approach to economic geography.* 2nd. ed. London.

Lopez, R.S. (1971) *The commercial revolution of the middle ages, 950-1350.* Englewood Cliffs.

Lotito, G. (1981) Modelli etici e base economica nelle opere filosofiche di Cicerone. in: Giardina and Schiavone (1981) vol. III, 79-126.

Lucassen, J. and Trienekens, G. (1978) Om de plaats in de kerk. in: *Tijdschrift voor Sociale Geschiedenis.* XII 239-305.

MacMullen, R. (1970) Market-days in the Roman empire. in: *Phoenix.* XXIV 333-41.

MacMullen, R. (1974) *Roman social relations, 50 B.C. to A.D. 284.* New Haven.

MacMullen, R. (1980) How big was the Roman Imperial army? in: *Klio.* LXII 451-460.

Macve, R.H. (1985) Some glosses on 'Greek and Roman accounting'. in: Cartledge and Harvey (1985) 233-64.
Maggi, G. (1976a) Scavo della 'villa di Poppea'. in: *Cronache Pompeiane*. II 249.
Maggi, G. (1976b) Scavo della villa di L. Crasso Terzo. in: *Cronache Pompeiane*. II 249.
Maggi, G. (1978) Oplontis. in: *Cronache Pompeiane*. IV 234.
Maiuri, A. (1942) *L'ultima fase edilizia di Pompei*. Rome.
Maiuri, A. (ed.) (1950) *Pompeiana. Raccolta di studi per il secondo centenario degli scavi di Pompei*. (Bibliotheca della Parolo del Passato) Naples.
Malinowski, B. (1922) *Argonauts of the western Pacific*. London.
Malthus, Th.R. (1976) *An essay on the principle of population*. (ed. Appleman, Norton Critical Edition of the 1798 edition, with commentaries). New York.
Martin, R. (1974) 'Familia rustica': les esclaves chez les agronomes latins. in: Levi a.o. (1974) 267-97.
Mathias, P. (1987) The emergence of a world economy, 1500-1914. in: *Vierteljahrschrift für Sozial- und Wirtschaftsgeschichte*. LXXIV 1-17.
Mau, A. (1889) Bibliografia Pompeiana. in: *Mittheilungen des Kaiserlich Deutschen Archaeologischen Instituts. Roemische Abteilung*. IV 292-305.
Mau, A. (1892) Osservazioni sull' edificio di Eumachia in Pompeii. in: *Mittheilungen des Kaiserlich Deutschen Archaeologischen Instituts. Roemische Abteilung*. VII 113-143.
Mau, A. (1908) *Pompeji in Leben und Kunst*. 2nd. ed. Leipzig.
Mazzarino, S. (1951) *Aspetti sociali del IV secolo*. Roma.
Meiggs, R. (1973) *Roman Ostia*. 2nd. ed. Oxford.
Meiggs, R. (1982) *Trees and timber in the ancient Mediterranean world*. Oxford.
Melitz, J. (1970) The Polanyi school of anthropology on money. An economist's view. in: *American Anthropologist*. LXXII 1020-1040.
Merrington, J. (1976) Town and country in the transition from feudalism to capitalism. in: Hilton (ed.) (1976) 170-195.
Merton, R.K. (1957) *Social theory and social structure*. rev. ed. London.

Meyer, E. (1924a) *Kleine Schriften.* 2 Vols. 2nd. ed. Halle.
Meyer, E. (1924b) Die wirtschaftliche Entwicklung des Altertums. in: Meyer (1924a) I 79-168, reprinted in Finley (1979).
Mickwitz, G. (1936) *Die kartellfunktionen der Zünfte, und ihre Bedeutung bei der Erstehen des Zunftwesens. Eine Studie in spätantiken und mittelalterlicher Wirtschaftsgeschichte.* Helsingfors.
Miers, S. and Kopytoff, I.I. (eds.) (1977) *Slavery in Africa.* Wisconsin.
Millar, F. (1984) Condemnation to hard labour in the Roman Empire, from the Julio-Claudians to Constantine. in: *Papers of the British School at Rome.* LII 124-147.
Mitchell, S. (1983) The Balkans, Anatolia, and Roman armies across Asia Minor. in: Mitchell (ed.) (1983) 131-50.
Mitchell, S. (ed.) (1983) *Armies and frontiers in Roman and Byzantine Anatolia. Proceedings of a colloquium held at University College, Swansea, in April 1981.* (British Institute of Archaeology at Ankara Monograph No. 5/British Archaeological Reports. International Series 156) Oxford.
Moeller, W.O. (1966) The *lanifricarius* and the *officinae lanifricariae* at Pompeii. in: *Technology and Culture.* VII 493-6.
Moeller. W.O. (1970a) The felt shops of Pompeii: summary. in: *American Journal of Archaeology.* LXXIV 200.
Moeller, W.O. (1970b) The riot of A.D. 59 at Pompeii. in: *Historia* XIX 84-95.
Moeller, W.O. (1971) The felt shops of Pompeii. in: *American Journal of Archaeology.* LXXV 188-9.
Moeller, W.O. (1973a) *Infectores* and *offectores* at Pompeii. in: *Latomus.* XXXII 368-9.
Moeller, W.O. (1973b) Gnaeus Alleius Nigidius Maius, princeps coloniae. in: *Latomus* XXXII 515-520.
Moeller, W.O. (1976) *The wool trade of ancient Pompeii.* Leiden.
Mommsen, H. and Schulze, W. (1981) *Vom Elend der Handarbeit. Probleme historischer Unterschichtenforschung.* Stuttgart.
Mommsen, Th. (1843) *De collegiis et sodaliciis romanorum.* Kiel.
Mommsen, Th. (1871-1888) *Römisches Staatsrecht.* 3 vols. 2nd. ed. Leipzig.

Mommsen, Th. (1877) Die pompeianische Quittungstafeln des L. Caecilius Iucundus. in: *Hermes*. XII 88-141 (= Gesamm. Iuristische Schriften III 220-270).

Morel, J.P. (1978) La laine de Tarente (de l'usage des textes anciens en histoire économique). in: *KTEMA* III 93-110.

Mrozek, S. (1978) Le prix des céréales à Puteoli en 37 de n.è. in: *Eos*. LXVI 153-155.

Muir, E. (1981) *Civic ritual in renaissance Venice*. Princeton.

Nabers, N. (1968) The architectural variations of the macellum. Summary. in: *American Journal of Archaeology*. LXXII 169.

Neesen, L. (1980) *Intersuchungen zu den direkten Staatsabgaben der Romischen Kaiserzeit (27. v. Chr.-284 n. Chr.)*. Bonn.

Neeve, P.W. de (1984) *Peasants in peril: location and economy in Italy in the second century B.C.* (inaugural lecture). Amsterdam.

Nicolet, Cl. (1966-74) *L'ordre équestre à l'époque républicaine (312-43 av. J.-C.)*. 2 vols. Paris.

Nicolet, Cl. (1976a) *Le métier de citoyen dans la Rome républicaine*. Paris.

Nicolet, Cl. (1976b) Le temple des Nymphes et les distributions frumentaires à Rome à l'époque républicaine d' après des découvertes récentes. in: *Comptes Rendus de l'Académie des Inscriptions et Belles-Lettres*. 29-51.

Nie, N.H. a.o. (1975) *S.P.S.S. Statistical package for the social sciences*. 2nd. ed. New York.

Niebling, G. (1956) Laribus Augustis magistri primi. in: *Historia*. V 303-331.

Nippel, W. (1981) Die *plebs urbana* und die Rolle der Gewalt in der späten römischen Republik. in: Mommsen and Schulze (1981) 70-92.

Nissen, H. (1877) *Pompeianische Studien zur Städtekunde des Altertums*. Leipzig.

Nissen, H. (1883-1902) *Italische Landeskunde*. 2 vols. Berlin.

Noethlichs, K.L. (1985) Spätantike Wirtschaftspolitik und Adaeratio. in: *Historia*. XXXIV 102-116.

North, D.C. and Thomas, R.P. (1973) *The rise of the western world. A new economic history*. Cambridge.

O'Brien, P. (1982) European economic development: the contribution of the perifery. in: *Economic History Review*. 2nd. ser. XXXV 1-18.

Ohr, K. (1973) Die Basilika in Pompeji (doctoral dissertation, Technische Hochschule Darmstadt D17). Karlsruhe.

Ostrow, S.E. (1985) *Augustales* along the bay of Naples: a case for their early growth. in: *Historia*. XXXIV 64-101.

Overbeck, J. (1884) *Pompeji in seinen Gebäuden, Alterthümer und Kunstwerken*. 4th. ed. Leipzig.

Packer, J.E. (1975) Middle and lower class housing in Pompeii and Herculaneum: a preliminary survey. in: Andreae and Kyrieleis (1975) 133-46.

Palmer, R.E.A. (1974) *Roman Religion and the Roman Empire. Five Essays*. Philadelphia.

Panella, Cl. (1974-75) Per uno studio delle anfore di Pompei, le forme VIII e X della tipologia di R. Schoene. in: *Studi Miscellanei*. XXII 151-65.

Panella, Cl. (1981) La distribuzione e i mercati. in: Giardina and Schiavone (1981) vol. II 55-81.

Panella, Cl. and Fano, M. (1977) Le anfore con anse bifide conservate a Pompei: contributo ad uno loro classificazione. in: Vallet a.o. (1977) 133-77.

Parker, G. (1972) *The army of Flanders and the Spanish road. The logistics of Spanish victory and defeat in the Low Countries' wars*. Cambridge.

Parkin, F. (1978) Social stratification. in: Bottomore and Nisbet (1978) 599-632.

Pas, H.T. van der (1973) *Economic anthropology 1940-1972. An annotated bibliography*. Oosterhout.

Paterson, J. (1982) 'Salvation from the sea': amphorae and trade in the Roman west. in: *Journal of Roman Studies*. LXXII 146-157.

Patlagean, E. (1977) *Pauvreté économique et pauvreté sociale à Byzance. 4e-7e siècles*. Paris/The Hague.

Patterson, O. (1982) *Slavery and social death. A comparative study*. Cambridge (Mass.).

Pavis D'Escurac, H. (1981) Affranchis et citoyenneté: les effets

juridiques de l'affranchissement sous le Haut Empire. in: *KTEMA* VI 181-192.
Peters, W.J.T. (1963) *Landscape in Romano-Campanian mural painting*. Assen.
Pirenne, H. (1927) *Les villes du moyen age. Esay d'histoire économique et sociale*. Brussels.
Pleket, H.W. (1971) Sociale stratificatie en sociale mobiliteit in de romeinse keizertijd. in: *Tijdschrift voor Geschiedenis*. LXXXIV 215-251.
Pleket, H.W. (1984) Urban elites and the economy in the Greek cities of the Roman empire. in: *Münstersche Beiträge zur Antiken Handelsgeschichte*. III 3-37.
Pleket, H.W. (1985) review of Garnsey and Whittaker (1983), in: *Gnomon*. LVII 148-54.
Polanyi, K. (1944) *The great transformation. The political and economic origins of our time*. New York.
Polanyi, K. (1957) The economy as an instituted process. in: Polanyi a.o. (eds.) (1957) 243-270.
Polanyi, K, Arensberg, C.M. and Pearson, H.W. (eds.) (1957) *Trade and market in the early empires. Economies in history and theory*. Glencoe.
Popkin, S.L. (1979) *The rational peasant: the political economy of rural society in Vietnam*. Berkeley.
Postan, M.M. (1975) *The medieval economy and society*. Harmondsworth.
Pounds, N.J.G. (1973) *An historical geography of Europe, 450 B.C.-A.D. 1330*. Cambridge.
Pounds, N.J.G. (1974) *An economic history of medieval Europe*. London.
Prevenier, W. (1975) Bevolkingscijfers en professionele strukturen der bevolking van Gent en Brugge in de 14e eeuw. in: Craeybeckx a.o. (1975) 269-303.
Purcell, N. (1983) The *apparitores*: a study in social mobility. in: Papers of the British School at Rome. LI 125-173.
Purcell, N. (1985) Wine and wealth in ancient Italy. in: *Journal of Roman Studies*. LXXV 1-19.
Radke, G. (1983) Wollgebilde an den Compitalia. in: *Würzburger*

Jahrbücher für die Altertumswissenschaft. Neue Folge Bd. 9 173-178.

Raper, R.A. (1977) The analysis of the urban structure of Pompeii: a sociological examination of land use (semi-micro). in: Clarke (1977) 189-221.

Rathbone, D. (1981) The developement of agriculture in the 'ager Cosanus' during the Roman republic: problems of evidence and interpretation. in: *Journal of Roman Studies.* LXXI 10-23.

Rathbone, D. (1983) The grain trade and grain shortages in the Hellenistic east. in: Garnsey and Whittaker (1983) 45-55.

Rawson, E. (1976) The Ciceronian aristocracy and its properties. in: Finley (1976) 85-102.

Reinhold, M. (1970) *History of purple as a status symbol in antiquity.* (Collection Latomus, 116) Brussels.

Reynolds, J.M. and Fabricotti, E. (1972) A group of inscriptions from Stabiae. in: *Papers of the British School at Rome.* XL. 127-134.

Ricardo, D. (1951) *On the principles of political economy and taxation.* (ed. P. Sraffa) Cambridge.

Richardson, L. Jr. (1955) *Pompeii: the Casa dei Dioscuri and its Painters.* Rome.

Rickman, G.E. (1971) *Roman granaries and store buildings.* Cambridge.

Robbins, R. (1937) *An essay on the nature and significance of economic science.* 2nd. ed. London.

Roll, E. (1973) *A history of economic thought.* 4th. ed. London.

Rostowzew, M. (1904) Pompeianische Landschaften und Römische Villen. in: *Jahrbuch des Kaiserlich Deutschen Archäologischen Instituts.* XIX 103-126.

Rostowzew, M. (1911) Die Hellenistisch-Römische Architekturlandschaft. in: *Mitteilungen des Kaiserlich Deutschen Archäologischen Instituts. Römische Abt.* Bd. XXVI 1-185.

Rostovtzeff, M. (1957) *The social and economic history of the Roman empire.* 2nd. ed. (revised by P.M. Fraser) 2 vols. Oxford.

Roxan, M.E. (1978) *Roman military diplomas 1954-77.* (Univ. of London Inst. of Archaeol. Occass. Publ. II) London.

Roxan, M.E. and Morris, J. (1977) The witnesses to Roman military diplomata. in: *Acta Archaeologica*. Ljubljana, XXVIII 299-333.

Ruggiero, M. (1881) *Degli scavi di Stabia dal MDCCXLIX al MDCCLXXXII*. Naples.

Runciman, W.G. (1986) review of Hopkins (1983a) in: *Journal of Roman Studies*. LXXVI 259-65.

Russell, J.C. (1958) *Late ancient and medieval population*. (Transactions of the American Philosophical Society. n.s. XLVIII, n. 3). Philadelphia.

Russell, J.C. (1972) Population in Europe 500-1500. in: Cipolla (1972-6) I 25-70

Russell, J.C. (1977) The population and mortality at Pompeii. in: *Bulletin of the International Committee on Urgent Anthropological and Ethnological Research*. IXX 107-14.

Russell, J.C. (1985) *The control of late ancient and medieval population*. Philadelphia.

Ruyt, Cl. de (1983) *Macellum, Marché alimentaire des Romains*. Louvain-la-Neuve.

Ryle, G. (1949) *The concept of mind*. London.

Sahlins, M. (1968) Notes on the original affluent sociey. in: Lee and DeVore (1968) 85-89.

Sahlins, M. (1972) *Stone age economics*. Chicago.

Sainte Croix, G.E.M. de (1954) *Suffragium*, from vote to patronage. in: *British Journal of Sociology*. V 33-48.

Saller, R.P. (1980a) Anecdotes as historical evidence for the Principate. in: *Greece and Rome*. sec. ser. XXVII 69-83.

Saller, R.P. (1980b) Promotion and patronage in equestrian careers. in: *Journal of Roman Studies*. LXX 44-63.

Saller, R.P. (1982) *Personal patronage under the early Empire*. Cambridge.

Saller, R.P. (1984a) Roman dowry and the devolution of property in the principate. in: *Classical Quarterly*. XXXIV 195-205.

Saller, R.P. (1984b) Familia, domus, and the Roman conception of the family. in: *Phoenix*. XXXVIII 336-355.

Saller, R.P. and Shaw, B.D. (1984) Tombstones and Roman family relations in the Principate: civilians, soldiers and slaves. in: *Journal of Roman Studies*. LXXIV 124-156.

Schefold, K. a.o. (1982) *La regione sotterrata dal Vesuvio. Studi e prospettive. (Atti del convegno internazionale 11-15 novembre 1979).* Naples.

Schneider, H.K. (1974) *Economic man. The anthropology of economics.* New York.

Schulze, W. (1933) *Zur Geschichte lateinischer Eigennamen.* (Abhandlungen Göttingen, Neue Folge, Band V, 5) Berlin.

Schulz-Falkenthal, H. (1971) Die Magistratswahlen in Pompeji und die Kollegien. in: *Das Altertum* XVII 24-32.

Schumpeter, J.A. (1954) *History of economic analysis.* New York.

Schuring, J.M. (1984) Studies on Roman amphorae, I (A historical survey of methods of research). in: *Bulletin Antieke Beschaving.* LIX 137-47.

Sergejenko, M.J. (1953) *Pompeji.* Leipzig.

Sgobbo, I. (1942) Un complesso di edifici Sannitici e i quartieri di Pompei per la prima volta riconosciuti. in: *Memorie della R. Accademia di Archeologia, Lettere e Belle Arti, Napoli.* VI 17-49.

Shaw, B.D. (1984) Bandits in the Roman Empire. in: *Past and Present.* CV 3-52.

Sherwin-White, A.N. (1966) *The Letters of Pliny.* Oxford;

Siegel, P.M. and Hodge, R.W. (1968) A causal approach to the study of measurement error. in: Blalock and Blalock (1968) 28-59.

Sjoberg, G. (1960) *The preindustrial city. Past and present.* Glencoe.

Skydsgaard, J.E. (1961) *Den romerske villa rustica.* Kopenhagen.

Slicher van Bath, B.H. (1960) *De agrarische geschiedenis van west-Europa, 500-1850.* Utrecht.

Slicher van Bath, B.H. (1963a) De oogstopbrengsten van verschillende gewassen, voornamelijk granen, in verhouding tot het zaaizaad, ca. 810-1820. in: *A.A.G. Bijdragen.* IX 29-125.

Slicher van Bath, B.H. (1963b) *Yield ratios, 810-1820.* (A.A.G. Bijdragen X) Wageningen.

Smith, A. (1976) *An enquiry into the nature and causes of the wealth of nations*. (The 'Glasgow' edition, eds. R.H. Campbell, A.S. Skinner and W.B. Todd.) Oxford.

Snodgrass, A.M. (1982) La prospection archéologique en Grèce et dans le monde méditerranéen. in: *Annales E.S.C.* XXXVII 800-12.

Solin, H. (1971) *Beiträge zur Kenntnis der griechischen Personennamen in Rom*. (Societas Scientarum Fennica. Commentationes Humanarum Litterarum XLVIII, 1). Helsinki.

Soly, H. (1975) The 'betrayal' of the sixteenth-century bourgeoisie: a myth? Some considerations on the behaviour pattern of the merchants of Antwerp in the sixteenth century. in: *Acta Historiae Neerlandicae*. VIII 31-49.

Sombart, W. (1916-28) *Der moderne Kapitalismus*. 2nd. rev. ed. 3 vols. München.

Spano, G. (1937) Porte e regioni Pompeiane e vie Campane. in: *Rendiconti dell' Accademia di Archeologia, Lettere e Belle Arti di Napoli*. XVII 269-361.

Spano, G. (1961) L'edificio di Eumachia in Pompei. in: *Rendiconti dell' Accademia di Archeologia, Lettere e Belle Arti di Napoli*. XXXVI 3-35.

Spurr, M.S. (1983) The cultivation of millet in Roman Italy. in: *Papers of the British School at Rome*. LI 1-15.

Stonier, A.W. and Hague, D.C. (1972) *A textbook of economic theory*. 4th. ed. London.

Talbert, R.J.A. (1984) *The senate of imperial Rome*. Princeton.

Taylor, L.R. (1949) *Party Politics in the Age of Caesar*. Berkeley.

Taylor, L.R. (1961) Freedmen and freeborn in the epitaphs of imperial Rome. in: American Journal of Philology. LXXXII 113-132

Taylor, L.R. (1966) *Roman Voting Assemblies*. Ann Arbor.

Tchernia, A. (1971) Les amphores vinaires de Tarraconaise et leur exportation au début de l'Empire. *Archivo Español de Arqueología*. XLIV 38-85.

Tchernia, A. (1986) *Le vin de l'Italie Romaine. Essai d'histoire économique d'apres les amphores*. (École Française de Rome) Rome.

Tchernia, A. and Zevi, F. (1972) Amphores vinaires de Campanie et de Tarraconaise à Ostie. in: Baldacci a.o. (1972) 35-67.

Temporini, H. (ed.) (1972 -) *Aufstieg und Niedergang der Römischen Welt.* Berlin/ New York. many vols.

Thomsen, R. (1947) *The Italic regions from Augustus to the Lombard invasions.* Copenhagen.

Treggiari, S.M. (1980), Urban labour in Rome: *mercennarii* and *tabernarii.* in: Garnsey (1980a) 48-64.

Ultee, W.C. (1983) Het aanzien van beroepen, op andere plaatsen en vooral in andere tijden. Een analyse van een aantal recente historische studies. in: *Tijdschrift voor Sociale Geschiedenis.* IXXX 28-48.

Unger, L. (1953) Rural settlement in the Campania. in: *Geographical Review.* XLIII 506-24.

Vallet, G. a.o. (1977) *Méthodes classiques et méthodes formelles dans l'étude des amphores. (Actes du colloque de Rome, 27-29 mai 1974).* (Collection de l'école française de Rome, 32) Rome.

Veyne, P. (1961) Vie de Trimalcion. in: *Annales. E.S.C.* XVI 213-247.

Veyne, P. (1976) *Le pain et le cirque. Sociologie historique d'un pluralisme politique.* Paris.

Veyne, P. (1979) Mythe et réalité de l'autarcie à Rome. in: *Revue des Études Anciennes.* LXXXI 261-280.

Vita-Finzi, Cl. (1969) *The mediterranean valleys: geological changes in historical times.* Cambridge.

Vries, J. de (1974) *The Dutch rural economy in the golden age, 1500-1700.* New Haven.

Vries, J. de (1976) *The economy of Europe in an age of crisis, 1600-1750.* Cambridge.

Vries, J. de (1984) *European urbanization. 1500-1800.* London.

Wallerstein, I. (1974) *The modern world system. Vol. I: Capitalist agriculture and the origins of the European world economy in the sixteenth century.* New York.

Waltzing, J.P. (1895-1900) *Étude historique sur les corporations professionelles chez les romains depuis les origines jusque à la chute de l'Empire d'Occident.* Louvain. 4 vols.

Warscher, T. (1925) *Pompeji. Ein Führer durch die Ruinen.* Berlin.

Weaver, P.R.C. (1972) *Familia Caesaris: a social study of the emperor's freedmen and slaves*. Cambridge.

Weber, M. (1976) *Wirtschaft und Gesellschaft. Grundriss der Verstehende Soziologie*. 5th ed. 3 vols. Tübingen.

Werff, J.H. van der (1986) The amphora wall in the house of the porch, Ostia. in: Boersma, Yntema and van der Werff (1986) 96-133.

White, K.D. (1967) *Agricultural implements of the Roman world*. Cambridge.

White, K.D. (1970a) *Roman farming*. London.

White, K.D. (1970b) *A bibliography of Roman agriculture*. Reading.

Whittaker, C.R. (1983) Trade and frontiers of the Roman Empire. in: Garnsey and Whittaker (1983) 110-127.

Whittaker, C.R. (ed.) (1988) *Pastoral economies in classical antiquity*. (Cambridge Philological Society, supplementary volume) Cambridge.

Wigboldus, J.S. (1971) Ontwikkelingen in de stratificatietheorie in geschiedsociologisch perspectief. in: *Tijdschrift voor Geschiedenis*. LXXXIV 179-214.

Wild, J.P. (1970) *Textile manufacture in the northern Roman provinces*. Cambridge.

Will, E. (1954) Trois quarts de siècle de recherches sur l'économie grecque antique. in: *Annales. E.S.C.* IX 7-22.

Willems, P.G.H. (1887) *Les élections municipales à Pompéi*. Paris.

Wiseman, T.P. (1971) *New men in the Roman senate, 139 B.C. - A.D. 14*. Oxford.

Wrigley, E.A. (1978a) A simple model of London's importance in changing English society and economy 1650-1750. in: Abrams and Wrigley (1978) 215-243.

Wrigley, E.A. (1978b) Parasite or stimulus: the town in a pre-industrial economy. in: Abrams and Wrigley (1978) 295-309.

Zanden, J.L. van (1985) *De economische ontwikkeling van de Nederlandse landbouw in de negentiende eeuw, 1800-1914*. (A.A.G. Bijdragen 25) Wageningen.

INDEX

I View of Pompeii (from the west)

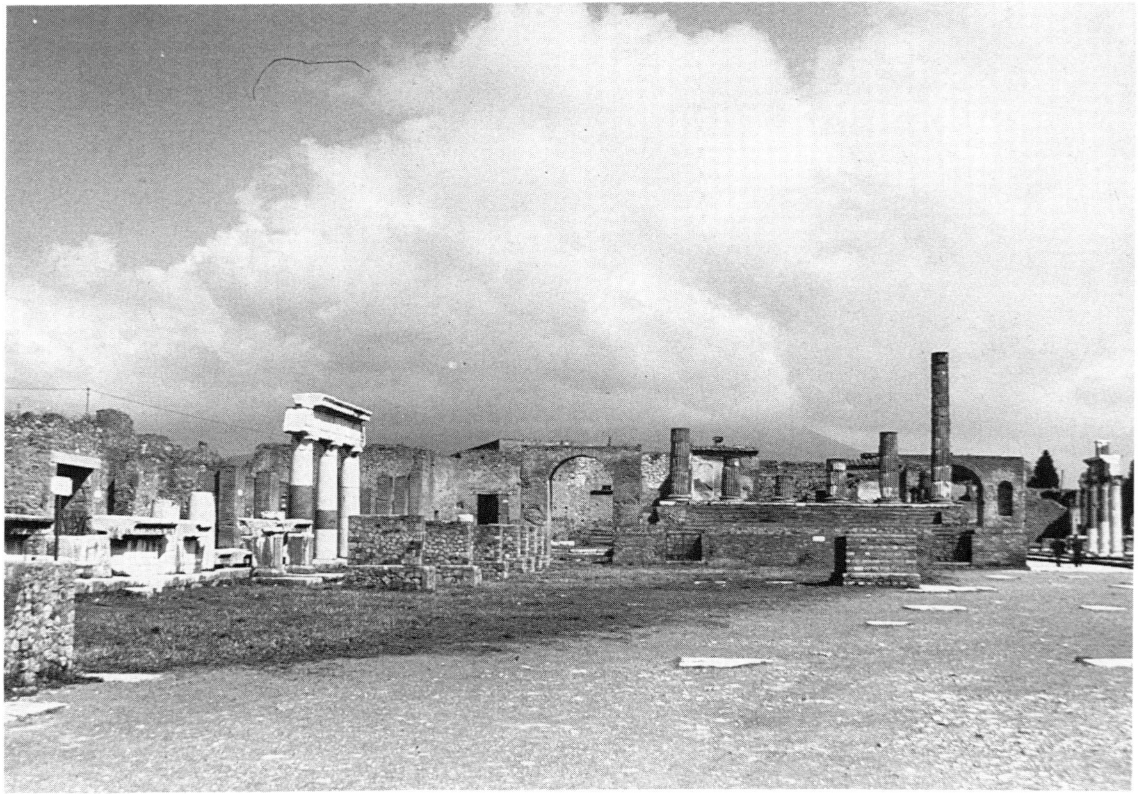

II The forum of Pompeii

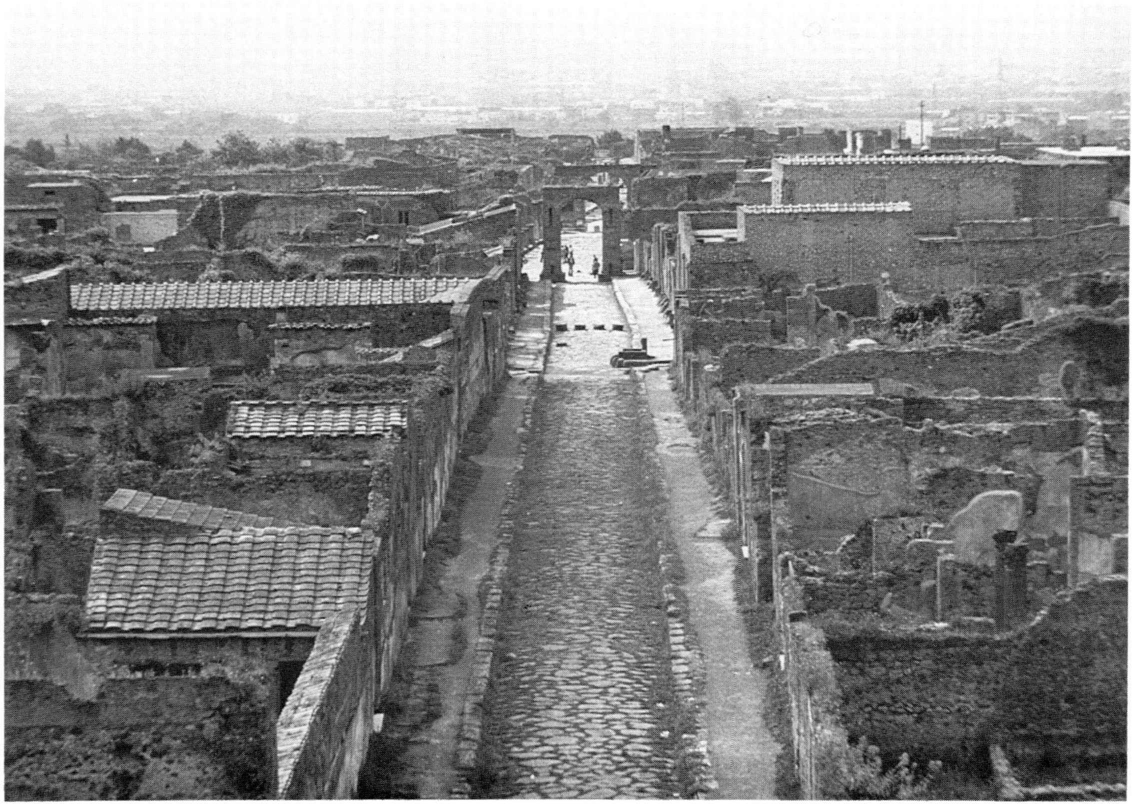

III View of Pompeii, from tower XI

IV The plain south of Pompeii, near villa 34

V The plain east of Pompeii, near villa 19

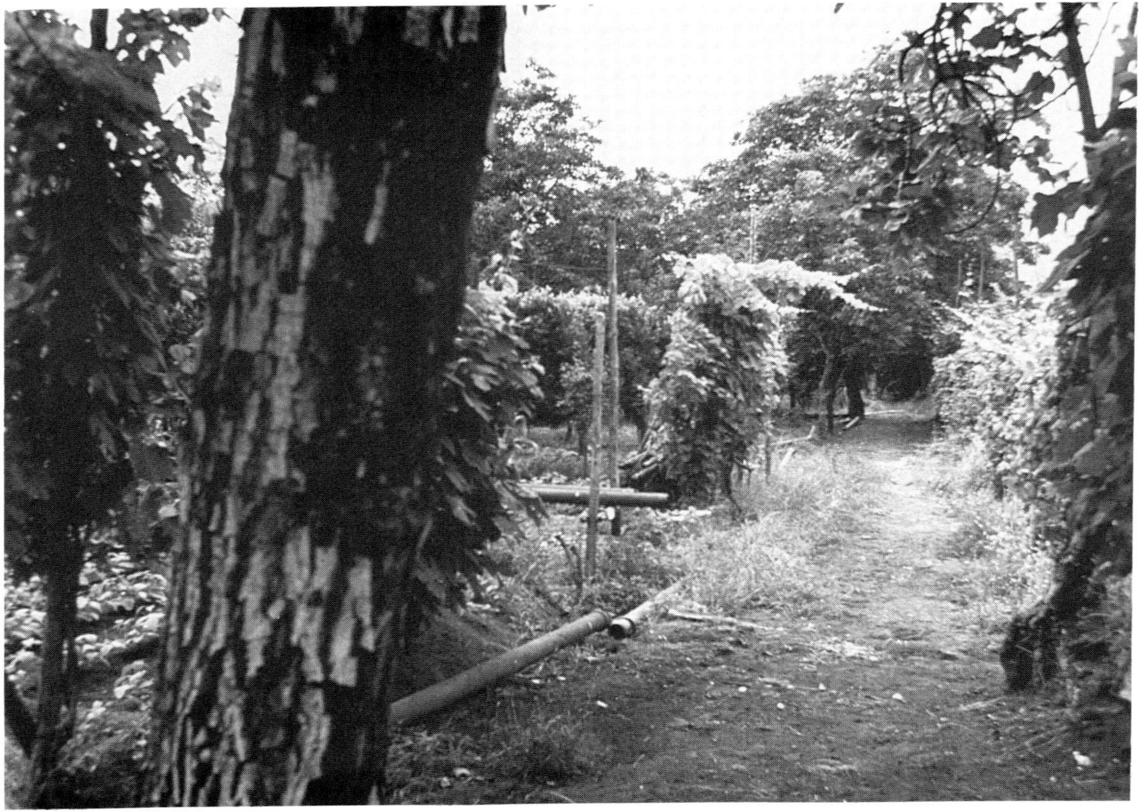

VI The landscape north of Pompeii, near villa 26

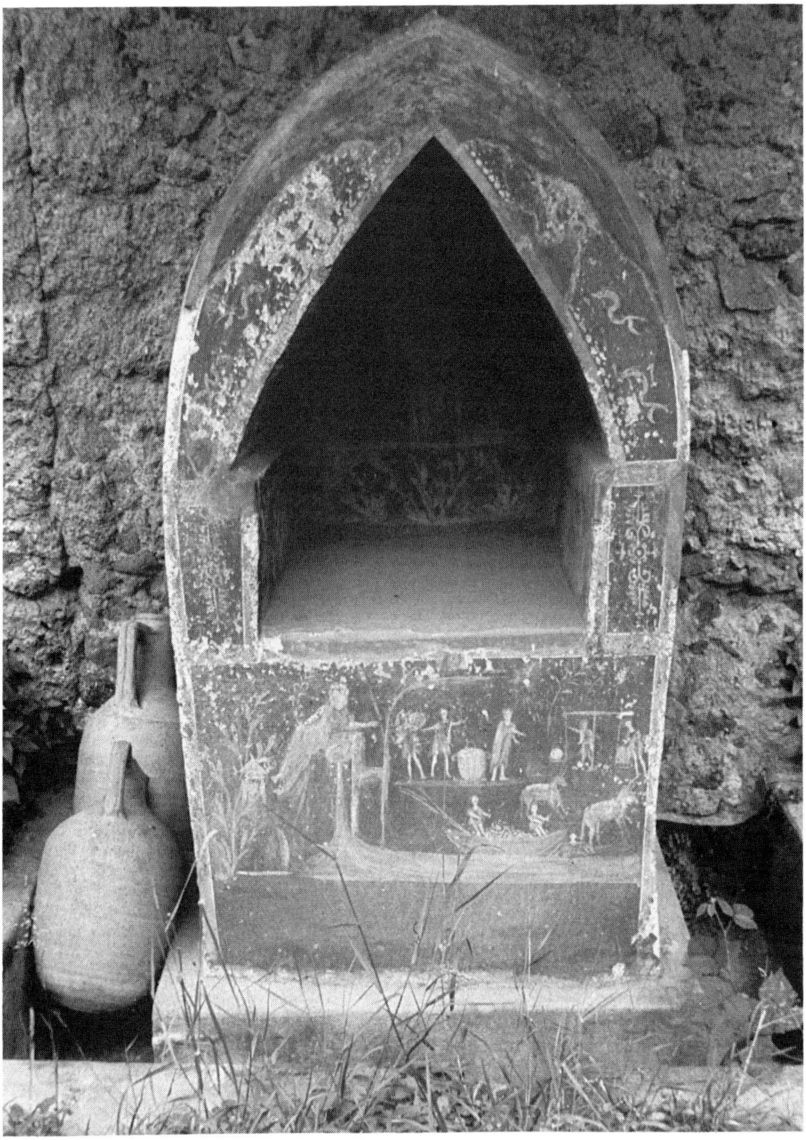

VII *Lararium* from I, xiv, 6, with scenes of river trade

VIII. Villa of the Mysteries: reconstructed *torcularium*

IX The house of the Vettii (VI, xv, 1.27)

XI An alleged *officina lanifricaria* (VII, xii, 17); south wall

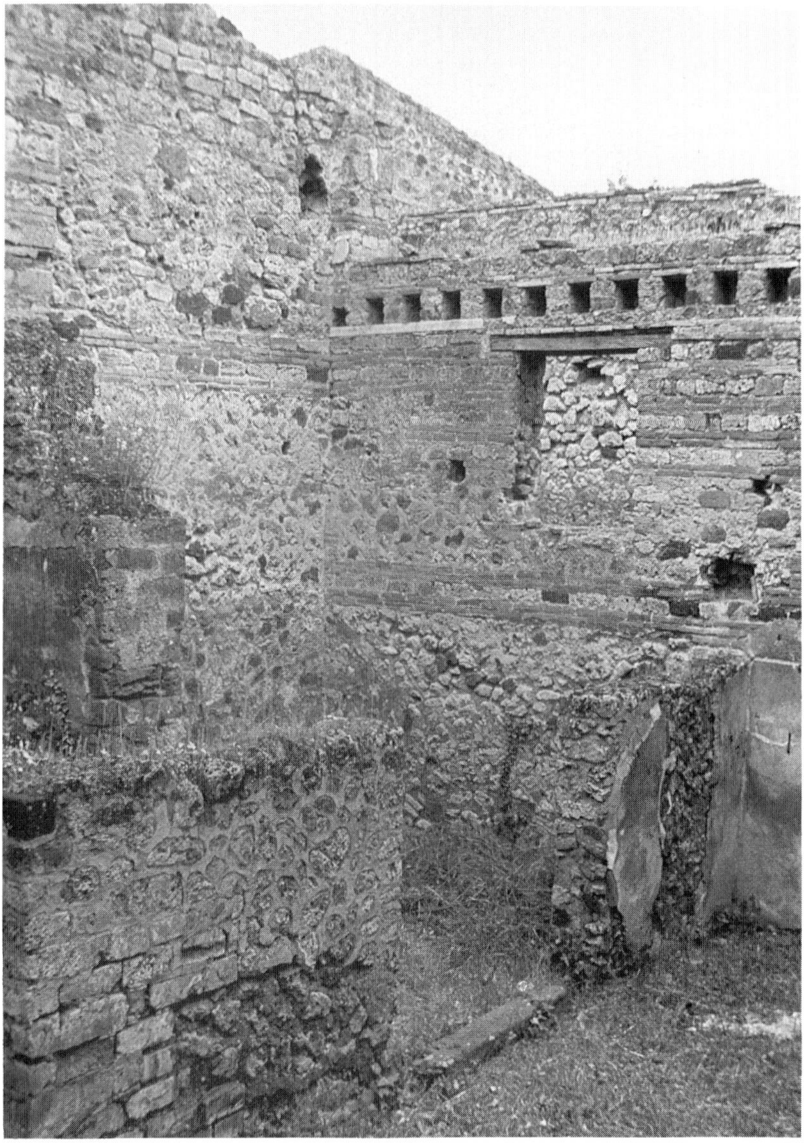

XII An alleged *officina lanifricaria* (VII, xii, 17); north wall

XIII Shop (bar?) similar to *'officinae lanifricariae'* (VII, xii, 21)

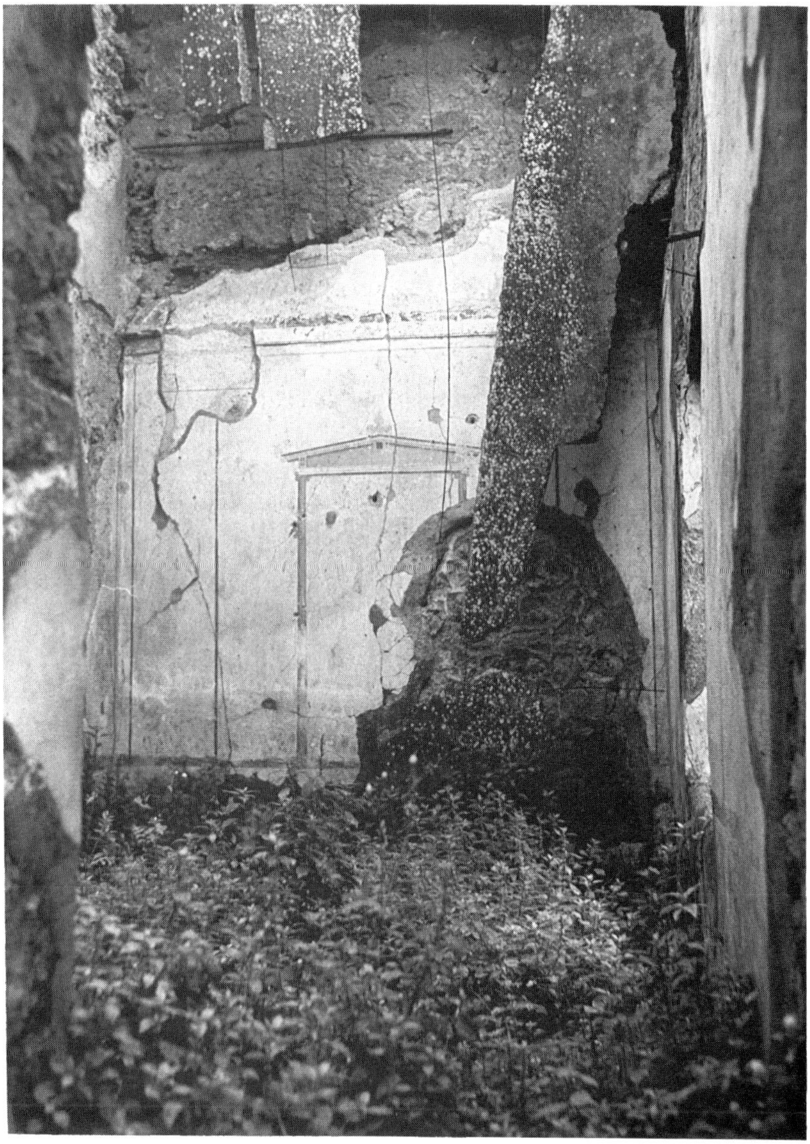

XV Alleged *textrina* (I, x, 8)

XVI Front of an *officina tinctoria* (IX, vii, 2)

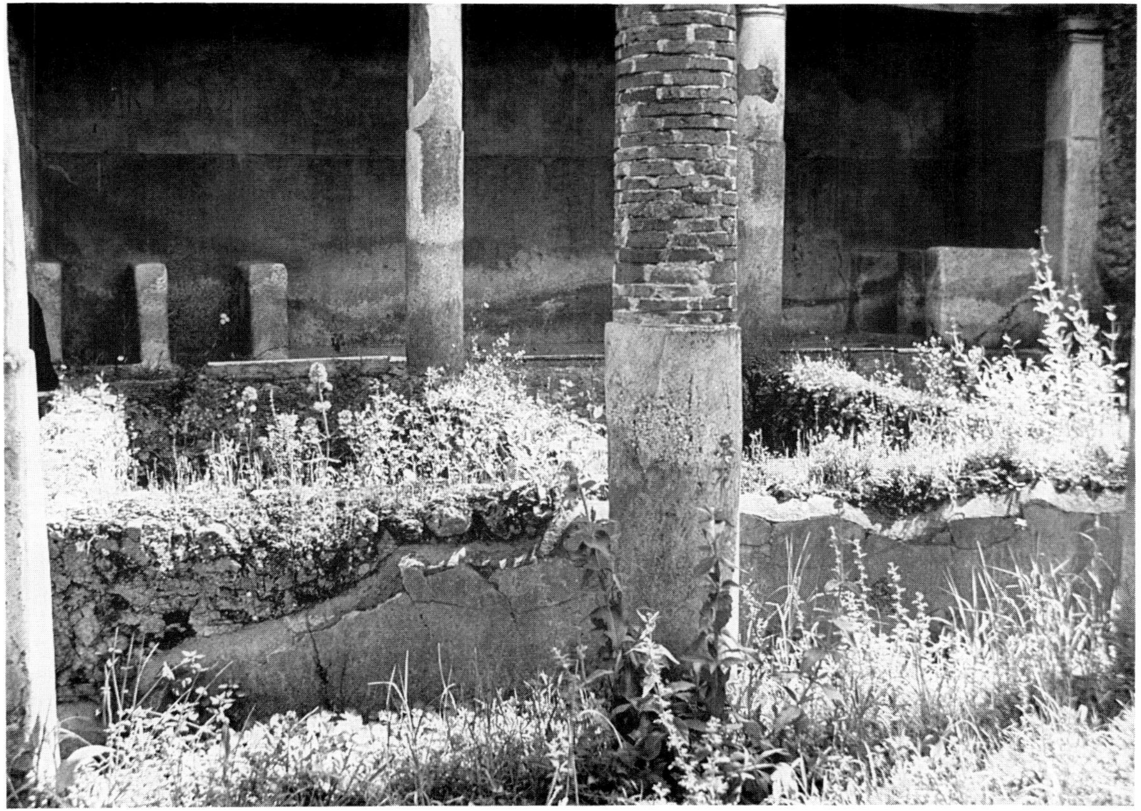

XVII The fullery of Vesonius Primus (VI, xiv, 21-22)

XVIII Scenes of fullers' collegiate life, from VI, xiv, 21-22

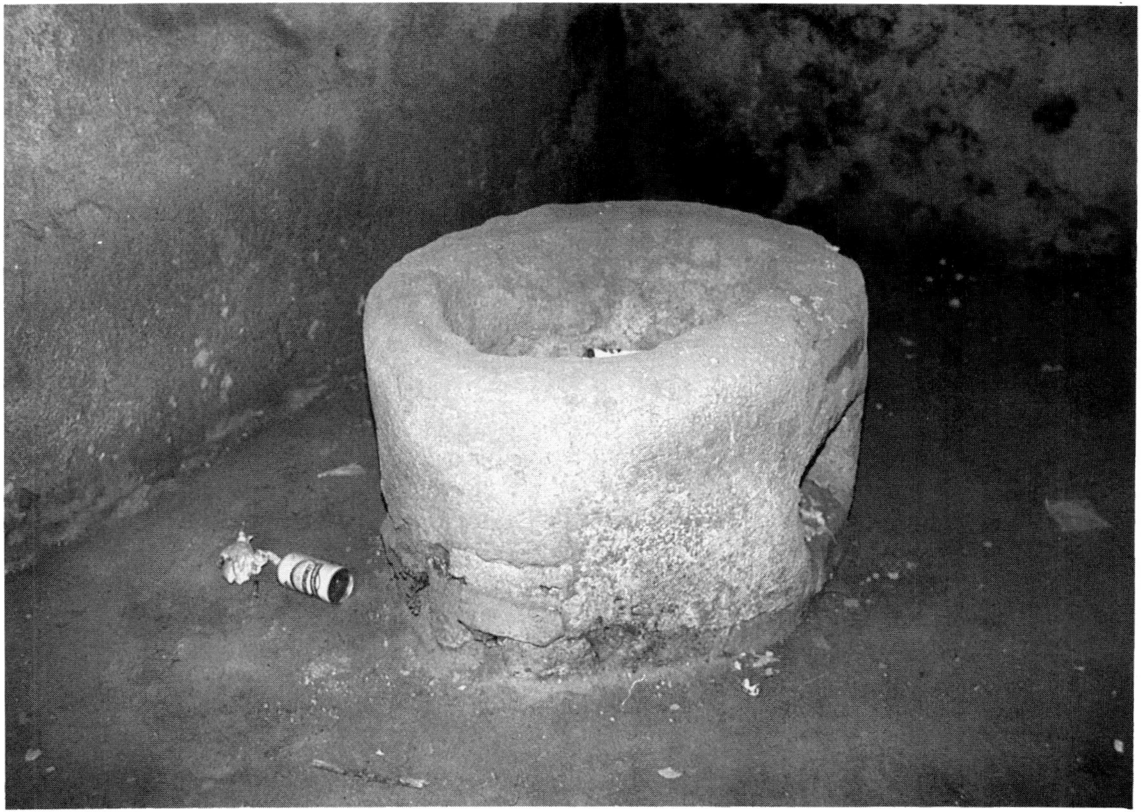

XIX Alleged felter's furnace from I, xii, 4 (restored)

XX Painting from the front of Verecundus' workshop (IX, vii, 5-7)

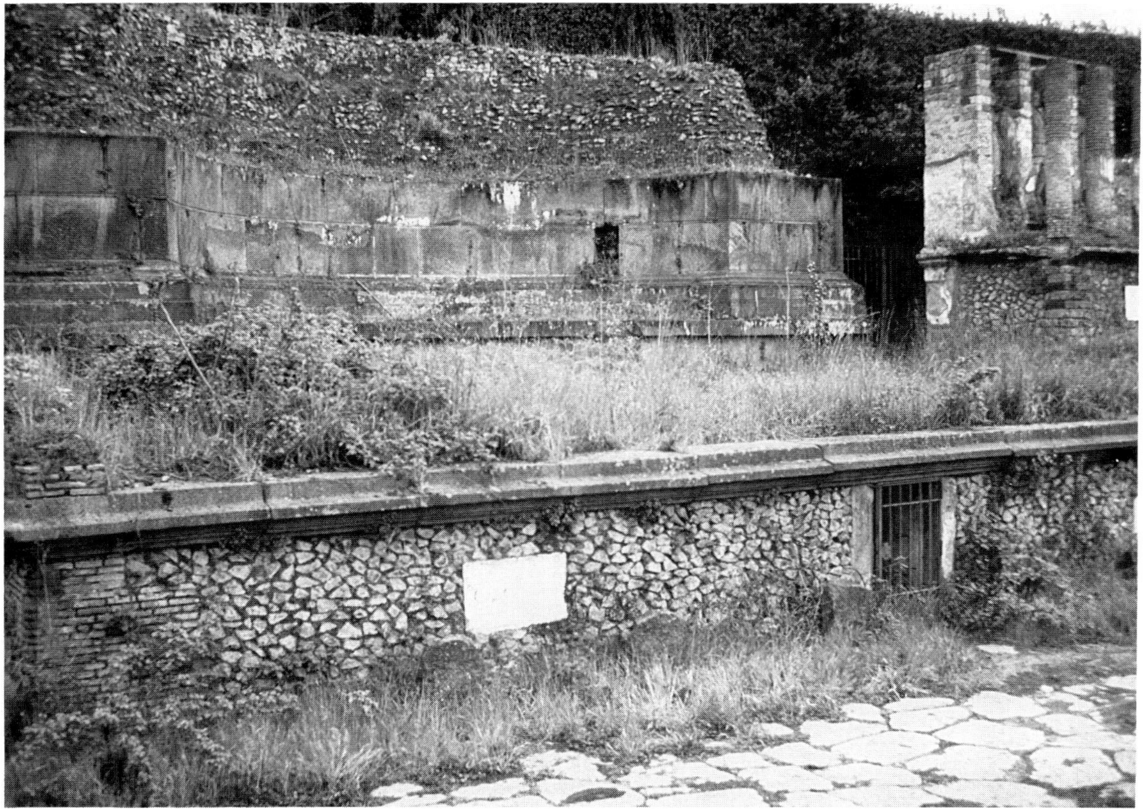

XXI The tomb of Eumachia, outside the porta Nocera

XXII The Building of Eumachia, as seen from the forum

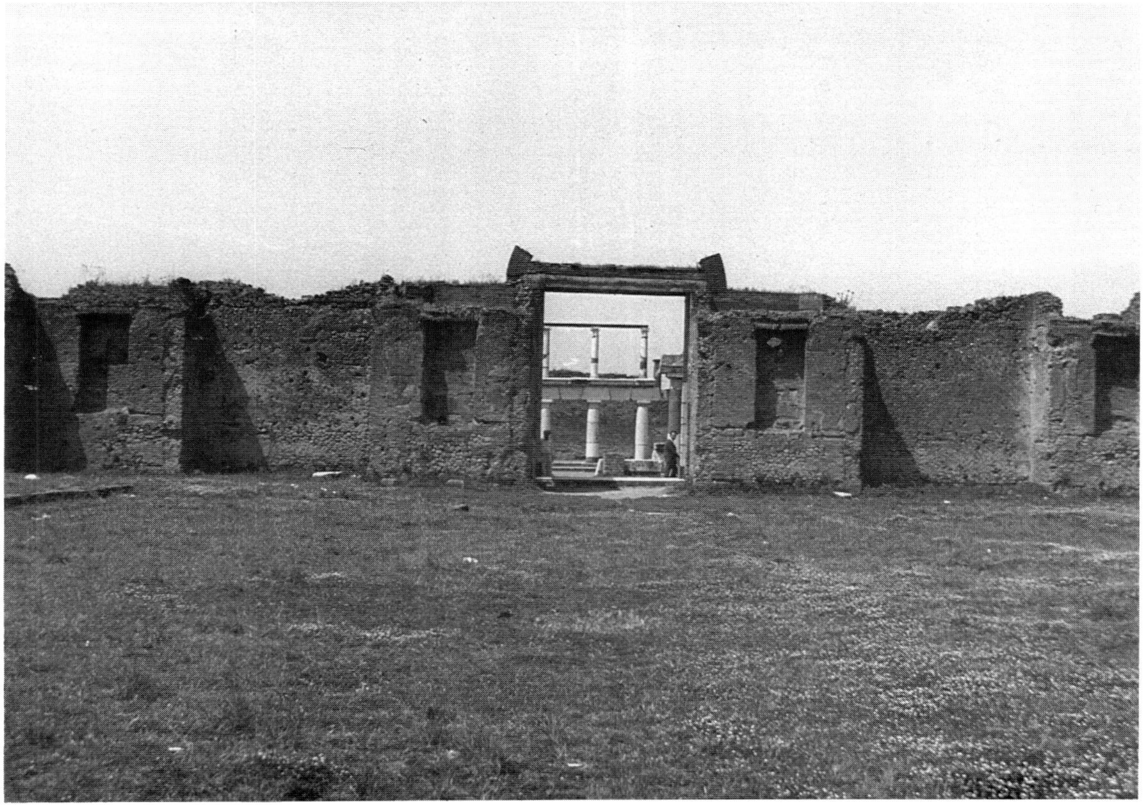

XXIII The Building of Eumachia, interior viewed from east

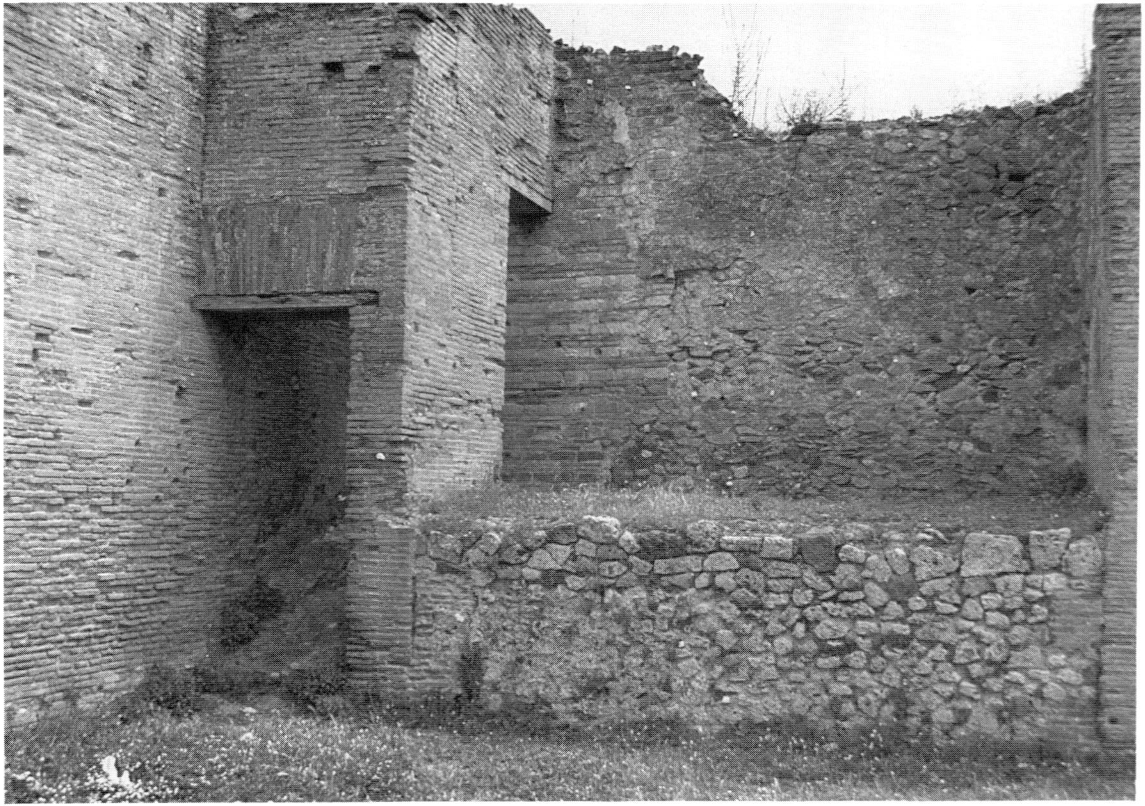

XXIV The Building of Eumachia: alleged auction block (left of entrance)

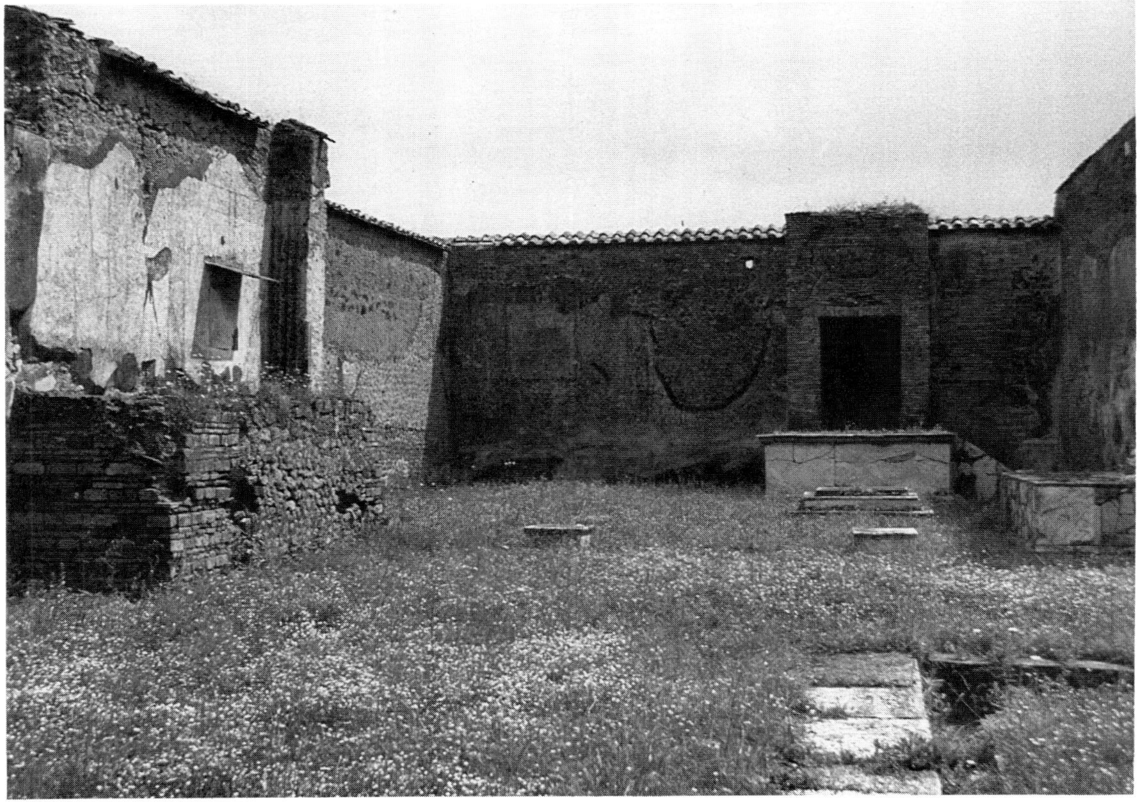

XXV Inside the Macellum

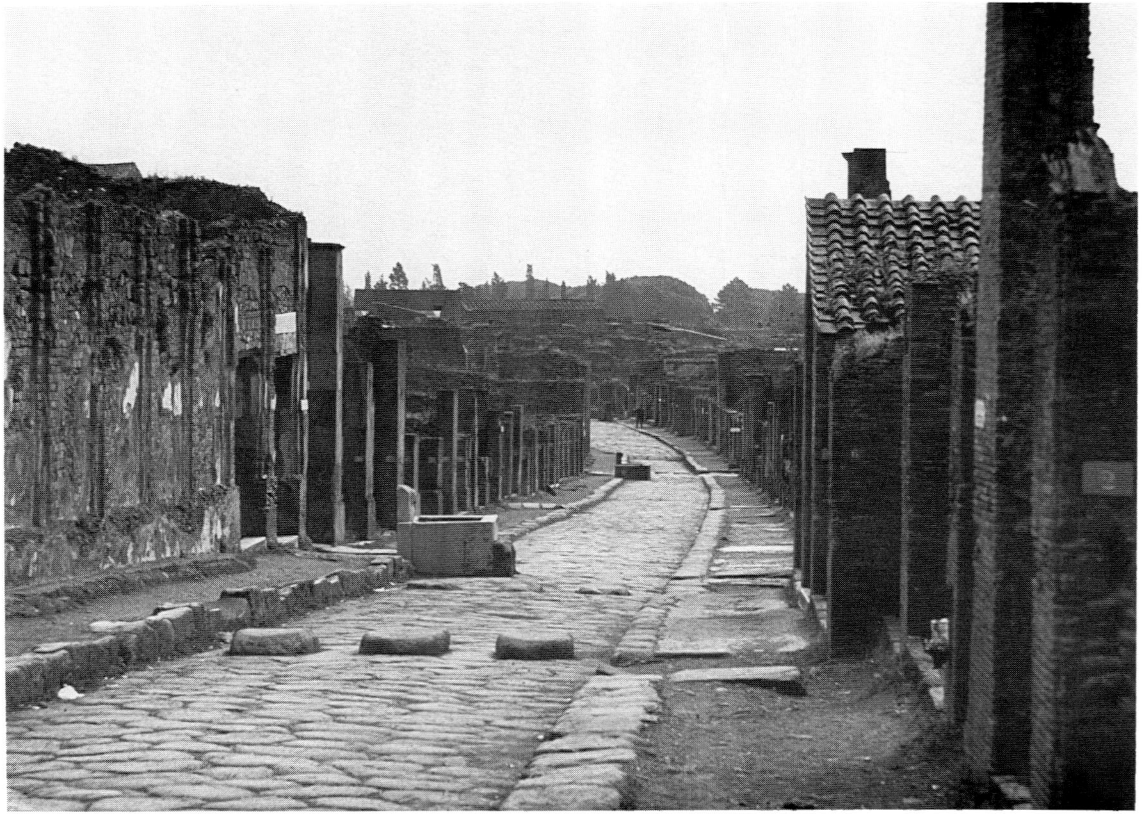

XXVI Via dell' Abbondanza (foreground left: south wall of the

XXVII The house of L. Caecilius Iucundus (V, i, 10.23-27)

XXVIII Garden triclinium in the house of P. Cornelius Tages (I.vii.10.12.18.19)

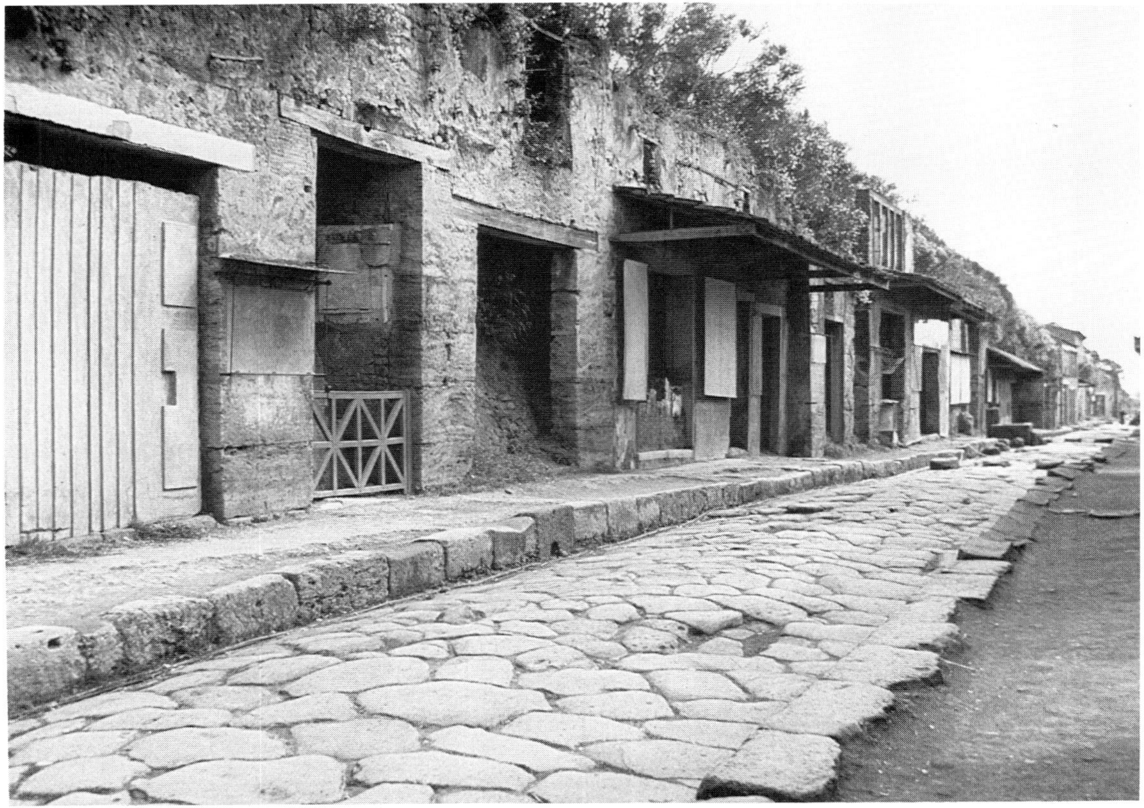

XXIX Shops along the Via dell' Abbondanza

XXX. Bar (I. viii. 8)

XXXI Electoral *programmata*

XXXII The riot of A.D. 59 (from I, iii, 23)

of

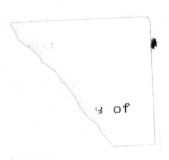